"No longer can physicians simply discharge a 'pree
tell the parents—as ours did two decades ago—'Take him home
like a normal baby!' Instead, these vulnerable infants need to come home with an information-packed instruction manual that weighs at least as much as they do. Amy Tracy and Dianne Maroney have performed an immensely valuable service in creating such a manual—a 'how-to' book that manages to combine the medical and practical facts of premature infant care with the warmth and support that can come only from parents who have 'been there' too."

—HELEN HARRISON,
AUTHOR OF *THE PREMATURE BABY BOOK*

"Despite progress in many aspects of obstetrical and newborn care, the percentage of births in the United States that are premature has been increasing for two decades. Many premature babies, often after long and heroic struggles, need exceptional care. Their families, in turn, require additional support and guidance on what to expect and how to respond to the challenges of caring for their babies. This book is full of practical advice based on the wisdom and actual broad experience of its authors, reassuring parents that they can provide their special children with the best possible care."

—RICHARD B. JOHNSTON, JR., M.D.,
MEDICAL DIRECTOR, MARCH OF DIMES BIRTH DEFECTS FOUNDATION

"*Your Premature Baby and Child* balances both informational and emotional needs of mothers and fathers of preterm children. I have no doubt this book is going to become an excellent resource. Parents will refer to it often during their preemie's childhood."

—JACINTO A. HERNÁNDEZ, M.D., PROFESSOR OF PEDIATRICS,
NEONATOLOGY SECTION, UNIVERSITY OF COLORADO SCHOOL OF MEDICINE

"As a comprehensive reference, this book is an invaluable tool for bridging the communication gap between the healthcare provider and parent."

—JAMES BOEHLKE, M.D., F.A.A.P.,
PEDIATRICIAN AND FATHER OF PRETERM TWIN DAUGHTERS

Your Premature Baby and Child

HELPFUL ANSWERS AND
ADVICE FOR PARENTS

Amy E. Tracy and Dianne I. Maroney, R.N.
with Judy C. Bernbaum, M.D.
and Jessie R. Groothuis, M.D.

BERKLEY BOOKS, NEW YORK

The reader may notice we have not used trademark symbols on the trademarked names throughout the text. This is done to facilitate readability, and is not intended to infringe on any trademark.

Your preterm baby's unique medical and developmental care requires the guidance of healthcare experts. The information in this book is intended to complement, but not substitute for, the care of your baby's healthcare providers.

This book is an original publication of The Berkley Publishing Group.

YOUR PREMATURE BABY AND CHILD

A Berkley Book / published by arrangement with the authors

PRINTING HISTORY
Berkley trade paperback edition / September 1999

Text design by Pauline Neuwirth, Neuwirth & Associates, Inc.
A list of illustrations and photo credits appears on page 329.

The Penguin Putnam Inc. World Wide Web site address is http://www.penguinputnam.com

ISBN: 0-425-16506-X

BERKLEY®
Berkley Books are published by The Berkley Publishing Group, a division of Penguin Putnam Inc., 375 Hudson Street, New York, New York 10014.
BERKLEY and the "B" design are trademarks belonging to Penguin Putnam Inc.

PRINTED IN THE UNITED STATES OF AMERICA

10 9 8 7 6 5 4 3

To my sons, Daniel and Steven, who are truly miracles; to my parents for always believing in me; and to George, my husband and best friend.

—A.E.T.

To Mackenzie—her love of life is forever inspiring. To my sons, Frankie and Michael—the compassion they've learned early in life shines from their hearts every day—and to my husband, Jimmy, for his patience and support. Finally, to Reagan, who will always be a part of our family.

—D.I.M.

Acknowledgments

Special thanks to Jane Chelius, our literary agent, who recognized the need for this book; to Hillary Cige and Grace Paik for their editorial expertise; to Mary Jo Broer for her wonderful illustrations; and to Preemie-l, the Internet support group who provided us with insight. Also, many heartfelt thanks to our families and friends, who supported us throughout this project.

A book like this could not have been written without the input of professionals and parents. We wish to thank the following people who unselfishly gave their time and expertise to help the families of premature children:

Reviewers and Contributors

Andrew T. Bauer, M.D.
Pediatrician
Englewood, Colorado

Paul S. Bernstein, M.D., Ph.D.
Assistant Professor of Ophthalmology
Moran Eye Center
University of Utah School of Medicine
Salt Lake City, Utah

Cynthia M. Bissell, R.N.
Preemie Parent

Susan L. Blumberg, Ph.D.
Clinical Psychologist
Children, Families and Couples
Denver, Colorado

Emily Boehlke, R.N.
Preemie Parent and Neonatal Nurse

Jacqueline Bolders Frazier, M.A., C.C.C.-S.L.P.
Speech-Language Pathologist
Children's Hospital of Denver
Denver, Colorado

Joy Browne, R.N., Ph.D.
Assistant Professor of Pediatrics
JFK Partners for Promoting Families' Health and Development
University of Colorado Health Sciences Center
Denver, Colorado

Susan M. Brugman, M.D.
Associate Professor of Pediatrics
University of Colorado Health Sciences Center
Denver, Colorado

Sheena L. Carter, Ph.D.
Applied Developmental Psychologist
Assistant Professor, Division of Neonatology
Emory School of Medicine
Atlanta, Georgia

Ann Cotton, M.A., P.T.
Pediatric Physical Therapist
Denver, Colorado

Diann Dreiling, O.T.R.
Pediatric Occupational Therapist
Douglas County, Colorado

Joyce Emde, C.N.S., Ph.D.
Family Therapist
Englewood, Colorado

Daniel J. Feiten, M.D.
Pediatrician
Englewood, Colorado

Cindy Gardner, P.T.R.
Physical Therapist
Memorial Hospital NICU
Colorado Springs, Colorado

Marsha Gerdes, Ph.D.
Codirector and Psychologist
The Neonatal Follow-up Program
Seashore House and Children's Hospital of Philadelphia
Philadelphia, Pennsylvania

Suzi D. Gillen, M.S.
Preemie Parent

Robin Gonzalez, M.A., C.C.C.
Speech Language Pathologist
Presbyterian/St. Lukes Hospital
Denver, Colorado

Pamela Haag Schachter, M.S.Ed.
Training and Technical Assistance Coordinator
Family Link Regional Early Intervention Collaborative
Union, New Jersey

Becky Hatfield
Parent Support Specialist
Parent to Parent
University of Utah Hospital
Salt Lake City, Utah

Andrea M. Herbert, R.N.
Parent Advocate

Michael T. Hynan, Ph.D.
Associate Professor of Clinical Psychology
University of Wisconsin at Milwaukee
Milwaukee, Wisconsin

Lori Johnston Ganz, O.T.R.
Occupational Therapist
Memorial Hospital NICU
Colorado Springs, Colorado

Martha Libster, R.N., B.S.N., B.S.
Healthcare Consultant
Denver, Colorado

David E. Lindeman, D.D.S., M.S.
Orthodontist
Englewood, Colorado

Kathy Lundberg
Preemie Parent

Amy Lutz, R.N., C.L.E., I.B.C.L.C.
Lactation Consultant
The Lactation Program
Denver, Colorado

Fran Mandell, R.N., M.S.
Clinical Nurse Specialist
Boulder County Mental Health
Boulder, Colorado

C. Shay Markle, O.T.R.
Pediatric Occupational Therapist
Denver, Colorado

Allison Martin
Preemie Parent

Donna Massine, Ed.S., C.C.C.
Audiologist/Speech-Language Pathologist
Douglas County, Colorado

Sally Maxey
Preemie Parent and Regional Coordinator of Family Voices
Denver, Colorado

Patricia Maxwell Malmstrom, M.A.
Director of Twin Services
Berkeley, California

William A. Mueller, D.M.D.
Chairman of Pediatric Dentistry
Children's Hospital of Denver
Denver, Colorado

Andrea O'Brien, M.S.
Preemie Parent and Consultant

Pam Parker-Martin, M.S.
School Psychologist
Douglas County, Colorado

Sandra Peters
Preemie Parent

Steven S. Rothenberg, M.D.
Chief of Pediatric Surgery
Director of the Minimally Invasive Surgery Center for Children
Presbyterian/St. Lukes Hospital of Denver
Denver, Colorado

Kelly Lynn Stahlman
Preemie Parent

Lyn Stevenson, R.D., C.S.P.
Clinical Dietician
Newborn High-Risk Follow-up Clinic
Children's Hospital of Denver
Denver, Colorado

Deb Stover
Parent Advocate and Author

Mara Tesler Stein, Psy.D.
Clinical Psychologist
Adjunct Faculty, Chicago School of Professional Psychology
Chicago, Illinois

Kay A. Toomey, Ph.D.
Pediatric Psychologist
Director, Pediatric Feeding Clinic
Rose Medical Center
Denver, Colorado

Denise C. Webster, R.N., Ph.D., C.S.
Professor, School of Nursing
University Health Science Center
Denver, Colorado

Aziz John Yazdi, M.D.
Pediatric Gastroenterologist
Rocky Mountain Pediatric Gastroenterology
Denver, Colorado

Contents

PART 4: YOUR GROWING PREEMIE

PART 5: YOUR SCHOOL-AGED PREEMIE

EPILOGUE: COPING, HEALING, AND FINDING MEANING

Appendices

Foreword

During the past decade, advances in neonatology have dramatically improved the survival rate among the more than 400,000 premature babies born each year in the United States. It is no longer unusual for babies born weighing less than a pound or delivered little more than halfway through a term pregnancy to survive and go home to their families. In addition, changes in healthcare have placed hospitals under increasing financial pressure to discharge babies—even babies with complex medical requirements—as quickly as possible. As a result, a brave new world of "preemie parenthood" has emerged in which parents must become not only mothers or fathers to their babies, but also nurses, doctors, therapists, and educators.

Bringing a tiny baby home from the hospital has always been a frightening and exhausting prospect, and new medical knowledge has created additional concerns and uncertainties. When should a premature baby receive immunizations? What are the latest recommendations for sleeping positions for a baby with lung or digestive problems? How do parents hook up with follow-up care, early intervention programs, and the multitude of other new services that they and their baby may need? Today's preemies require operating manuals weighing nearly as much as they do.

Now, at last, mothers and fathers have the manual they need to help navigate the previously uncharted waters of modern preemie parenthood. The authors honestly describe the practice and psychological challenges of parenting a preemie without minimizing the difficulties, yet they always manage to impart this information in a warm and reassuring manner that can come only from parents who have "been there" too.

I sincerely hope that NICU professionals, pediatricians, therapists, and educators will read this book for a fuller picture of the lives of the families they serve. In addition, I hope this excellent work will be read by policy-makers and that it will inspire legislation to give the families of high-risk infants the practical and financial aid they so desperately need. Most important, this book should be on the shelf, or beside the bed, or next to the apnea monitor in every preemie household.

—HELEN HARRISON, AUTHOR OF *THE PREMATURE BABY BOOK*

Introduction

During different times in our lives and in our own individual ways, we both imagined the joyful homecoming of our new babies. Amy anxiously waited for the birth of a son, and Dianne eagerly anticipated a daughter. Never did we imagine the arrival of babies who weighed less than two pounds, or that we would spend our first months of new motherhood in an intensive-care nursery. The homecoming days of our babies, Daniel and Mackenzie, were indeed joyful, but ones burdened with the fear and concern of parents about to embark on a difficult journey.

Once our babies were home, we began searching for a book to answer our parenting questions. Both Daniel and Mackenzie had many of the common medical and developmental problems of babies born early, and we needed help. At libraries and bookstores, the shelves seemed to overflow with parenting resources, but none addressed the special childhood issues of preemies and their parents. As our children grew, more questions arose, and we continued to feel alone in a world of full-term babies and their families.

This book evolved out of our need for information and our desire to help other preemie families. We initially planned to write a 250-page book, but when we began asking parents what questions they wanted answered, we quickly realized we had a lot more research to do. A year and a half later, we surprised our publisher with 650 typed pages.

Our hope is that this extensive information will give you the confidence to become "partners" with your child's healthcare providers and educators—that it will empower you to be your child's best advocate. Always remember that you are the expert on your child, and you *can* help your child reach his or her fullest potential.

Equally important, we wanted this book to be a source of comfort. Having experienced the prematurity crisis ourselves, we know about the complex emotions parents face after the birth of a critically ill infant. The quotes included throughout this book include a wide range of experiences: from parents of 23-weekers to those of 34-weekers, single parents,

parents of all races, first-time parents, and parents of multiples. We refer to babies and professionals as "he" and "she" by section and address readers by "you" to eliminate any gender bias. Although your family's situation is unique, we hope you find supportive friends within these pages.

Finally, we just had to share six photographs of some very special children. Although we wanted to include pictures of every child we met during this project, space wouldn't allow it. Instead, these faces must represent the courage, strength, hope, and love of all our children and of all our families. They are the small miracles who brighten our lives every day.

Visit our Web sites and write to us at *www.PreemieParents.com* and *www.Premature-Infants.com.*

Our best to your families,
Amy and Dianne

PART ONE

Homecoming

PART ONE

Introduction

You never thought it could happen—the once-strange world of the intensive-care nursery actually feels like "home." After all, you have spent many hours by your baby's bedside. You even know how to operate some of the medical equipment. A few of the doctors, nurses, and parents have become your friends. This is the only home your baby has known, the only home you have shared with him, and soon it will be time to leave. Along with your joy, you feel a little sad and frightened.

Part 1 will help you make the adjustment from hospital to home and relieve many of your worries. Preparing for your baby's discharge in advance is important. Finding helpful resources before and after discharge and surrounding yourself with supportive family and friends are also critical. The more help you have, the more time you can spend focusing on your new family.

CHAPTER ONE

Before Your Preemie Comes Home

WHEN YOUR BABY was born early, the doctors most likely told you not to expect him to come home until around his "due date," the day when he should have been born. Many preterm infants meet discharge requirements around this projected date, but some with more serious complications stay longer. To learn about your NICU's discharge requirements, ask your baby's primary nurse or neonatologist.

While waiting for your baby's release, you can learn and practice the skills you will need to care for him at home. Building confidence in your parenting abilities can ease some of your homecoming fears. Participate in your baby's routine care: take his temperature often, give him baths, and change his diapers. Learn his feeding schedule and let the staff know when you would like to feed your baby. Your hospital may encourage or require you to spend an entire night in a hospital room with your baby. With the nurses close by, "rooming-in" is a great way to learn more about your baby's needs.

Visiting and observing your hospitalized baby at different times during the day and night can also help. Keep notes (use the margins in this book, if you like) about your infant's likes, dislikes, reactions (also called cues or signals), favorite positions, and other unique characteristics. Your written observations will help when your baby is first home (and your anxiety is high!).

To learn more about your baby's unique cues—when he is ready for activity and when he is not—consult his primary nurse, neonatologist, or developmental specialist. Understanding your baby's behaviors can tell you when you can be active with him and when you should reduce activity. For instance, your baby may be ready to interact with you and the outside world if he:

- has regular breathing;
- has overall pink skin color;

- is not gagging, spitting up, coughing, grunting, yawning, or sighing;
- is able to maintain his position without squirming;
- grasps your finger, an object, or his hands together;

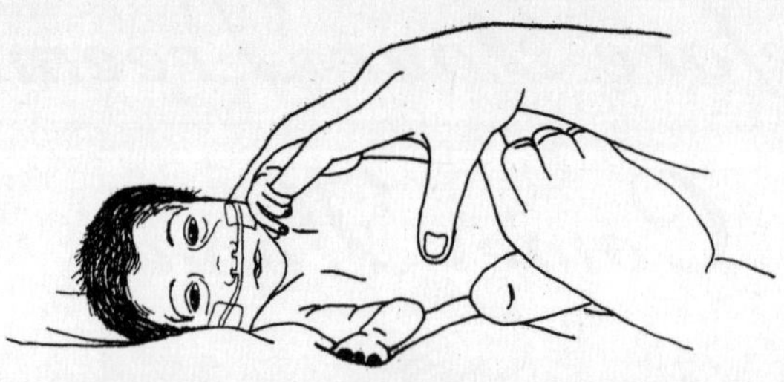

Just holding on to your finger can help your baby stay calm.

- holds one foot on top of the other, or one foot next to the other;
- is able to focus his eyes on you or an object;
- is actively sucking;

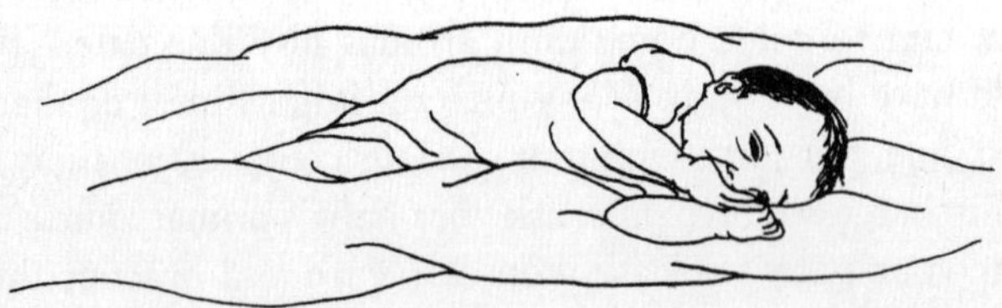

Your baby can calm himself by sucking on his hand or fingers.

- smiles or makes an "ooh" face; and/or
- stays calm while awake or asleep.

Swaddling your baby in a light blanket, dimming the lights, and keeping noise minimal can make social interactions less stressful for your baby.

When your baby shows signs of readiness to interact, you can slowly touch or hold him, softly speak to him, or simply look into his eyes. These are his earliest social skills.

On the other hand, your baby is not ready to interact if he:

- is fussy or cries;
- turns pale or mottled;
- shows a decreased heart rate on his heart monitor;
- has an increase in his rate of breathing and/or has long pauses in breathing;
- yawns, trembles, twitches, or holds his hands up as if to say "no" or "stop";

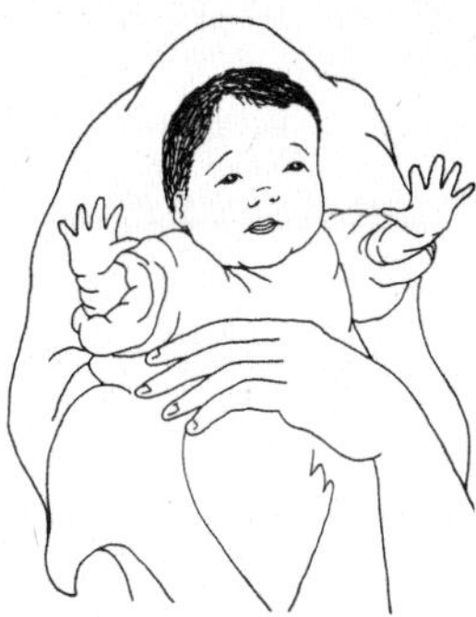

If your baby holds his hands up in the air, he may be saying "no" or "stop" to stimulation.

- appears as if his eyes are floating;
- exhibits a hyper-alert or panicked expression;

If your baby's eyes become wide and he appears scared or panicked, he needs comforting.

- gags, spits up, and/or hiccups;
- has a bowel movement; and/or
- exhibits weak or tired muscle tone.

TYPICAL DISCHARGE REQUIREMENTS

NICUs have different criteria for releasing premature infants, so it is important for you to consult your hospital. A baby typically needs to weigh between four and five pounds before discharge is allowed. He may also need to:

- take a bottle or nurse every feeding and gain weight daily (However, a baby may go home with a feeding tube passed through his nose or mouth to take some or all of his feedings);
- keep his body temperature normal in an open crib;
- be free of apnea (a pause in breathing lasting 20 seconds or more), bradycardia (a decreased heart rate), or change in color for five to ten days (Some nurseries discharge infants with equipment to monitor breathing and heart rate);
- be off oxygen or remain stable on a low flow of oxygen (Some babies are sent home on supplemental oxygen); and
- be free of any infection.

Many pediatricians also suggest that a plan be established for home and follow-up medical care before a preterm baby's discharge.

Because your baby's brain is immature, he will sometimes become "overstimulated" by the activities around him and exhibit some of these nonreadiness cues. When this happens, he needs comforting. Swaddle him in a blanket and hold him. Reduce noise, lights, and activity, and encourage him to suck on his hand (or yours) or on a pacifier.

Once home, your baby may become overwhelmed with all the sights and sounds of his new environment. Your baby will learn how to cope with sensory experiences as he grows. The comforting techniques you learn and practice now will help your baby adjust more easily.

I was thrilled when the doctors said James might be discharged by Christmas. For me, the best gift would be to hold and love our baby in the privacy of our home—without a medical staff buzzing around. I eagerly anticipated nursing my baby while listening to Christmas carols.

I was also terrified. Could I really take care of our fragile baby—on oxygen, an apnea monitor, and special medications—without a nurse's help? What if James stopped breathing? What if he wouldn't eat? As much as I wanted to take our baby home, part of me wanted to stay in the safety of the NICU.

—ELIZABETH, MOTHER OF 28-WEEKER JAMES

PARENT TIPS:

GETTING THE MOST OUT OF "ROOMING-IN"

Parents who have stayed overnight in the hospital with their babies offer these helpful suggestions:

- Choose a day that works best for your family's schedule, and do not sleep over the night before your baby comes home. You need a good night's rest before discharge day.
- If staying an entire night does not work for you, try spending a long stretch of time during the day and/or night instead.
- Both parents should experience nighttime care. Having Mom spend one night and Dad spend another may work better for your family, particularly if you have other children at home.
- Take a stuffed animal from your house to introduce your baby to the smells of home.
- If your baby is on timed feedings, an alarm clock can help wake you.
- Take a notebook and pen to the hospital and write down any questions that may arise during the night.
- Do not forget your favorite pillow to help you sleep!

MORE HOMECOMING PREPARATIONS

BECAUSE YOUR BABY arrived weeks or months before you expected, you probably did not have time to do the typical before-baby tasks. Those parenting books are probably still sitting on your nightstand and the nursery is bare. Nor have you had the time or energy to search for a pediatrician or buy a car seat.

Well, now is the time to catch up. The following sections can help.

FINDING A PEDIATRICIAN

If you do not have a pediatrician or family practitioner, begin searching for one at least a few weeks before discharge. Your NICU may offer a list of local physicians with preemie experience. Ask if a developmental pediatrician, specializing in issues involving developmental delays, is available in your community. The American Academy of Pediatrics will send you a list of physicians in your area if you send them a self-addressed stamped envelope (see "Pediatricians" in appendix C).

You will spend a lot of time with your child's doctor, so it is important that you interview him. Be sure he makes you feel comfortable and that you trust him. If your health insurance requires you to see a network of doctors and your child's care will be handled by several physicians, you really should interview them all. The following are some questions you may want to ask:

- "What experience have you had caring for premature infants?" Ask specifically about conditions your preemie has (feeding difficulties, bronchopulmonary dysplasia, or developmental delays). If a physician does not feel particularly comfortable with a certain problem, he should say so.
- "How are the preterm infants you have cared for doing today?" Hoist a warning flag if the physician answers, "They're all fine." All preemies have some difficulties during their first years. You want a doctor who will be open and honest.
- "What requirements do you have for referring patients to specialists or therapists?" If the doctor says he usually handles everything himself, be wary. A good physician realizes his limitations and will not be afraid to refer difficult cases to specialists.
- "Is the practice a one-person or group practice?" (If it is a group practice, make every attempt to have your child seen by one primary physician, ensuring as much continuity as possible.) Ask which days your preferred physician is in the office. Are there special days or times he sees children with special needs? Find out how coverage is handled when the physicians are out of town or on vacation. You will want a doctor familiar with your child available twenty-four hours a day.
- "How are fees handled? Will you accept direct insurance payments, or do you require payment at each visit?" Since you will be making frequent doctor visits, you need to know how to pay.
- "What are the office hours?" Are there office hours during the evening or on weekends? If not, ask the doctor how you can reach him if your baby needs immediate medical attention.
- "Does the office have designated times for well-child care?" If your germ-susceptible preemie is there for a well-baby checkup, you do not want to expose him to a room full of sick children.
- "What hospital do you use for hospitalization?" You will probably feel more comfortable returning to the hospital where your baby was born, or to one with a special emphasis on high-risk infants.

You should also ask a potential physician his opinions on issues that are important to you. How does he feel about breast-feeding and bottle-feeding? What is his opinion on circumcision? What are his suggestions for disciplining a child? By asking specific questions, you will get a good feel of how the doctor views parents' participation in health-related decisions. Is he a good listener? Does he feel your opinions are important?

Is There a Preemie Specialty Clinic near You?

Over sixty specialty clinics for premature infants exist across the United States. These are multidisciplinary clinics housing some or all of the following healthcare professionals:

a pediatrician versed in the special needs of preemies, a respiratory therapist, an occupational therapist, a physical therapist, a speech pathologist, a nutritionist, a developmental psychologist, and a social worker. Some clinics focus only on medical care; some focus only on developmental care; others focus on both medical and developmental care. There are also follow-up clinics for special health issues, such as hydrocephalus.

The benefit of a follow-up clinic is that a child sees all specialists in one visit. Some programs give parents the option to have their child seen at the clinic on a regular basis or on a consulting basis (one to six times a year) in conjunction with their own doctor. To find out if there is a preemie specialty clinic located near you, consult your neonatologist, developmental specialist, or social worker.

Choosing a Car Seat

Before your preemie's first ride home from the hospital, you must make sure you have a suitable car seat, and you need to know how to position your baby in it. While most infants can ride semireclined in a car seat, babies born more than three weeks early may have difficulty breathing when sitting in this position. Ask your doctor if your baby can ride sitting semireclined or if he needs to lie flat in a special bed made for use in the car until he gets older and bigger. Before purchasing a car seat or a special bed, consider these recommendations from the American Academy of Pediatrics (1996):

- To provide the best comfort, fit, and positioning for your premature baby, you should look for either an infant-only car seat with a three-point harness system or a convertible car seat with a five-point harness system.
- Your baby should *not* be placed in a car seat with a shield, abdominal pad, or arm rest that could come in contact with the face and neck during an impact. Similarly, a car seat designed only for use by a child weighing more than twenty pounds should not be used for your preterm infant.
- A car seat with a distance of less than five and a half inches from the crotch strap to the seat back should be selected to reduce the potential of slumping forward. The car seat should have a distance of less than ten inches from the lower harness strap to the seat bottom to reduce the potential of harness straps crossing your infant's ears (see figure A).
- In a rear-facing car seat, shoulder straps must be in the lowest slots until your infant's shoulders grow above the slots; the harness must be snug; and the car seat's retainer clip should be positioned at the midpoint of your preemie's chest, not on the abdomen or in the neck area (see figure C).

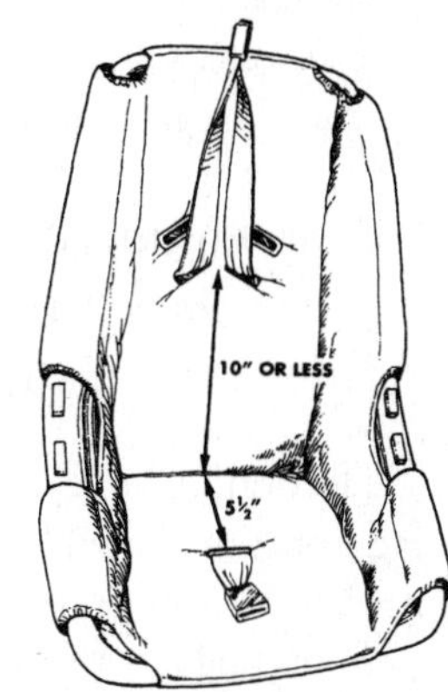

A. Car seat with maximum dimensions for correct fit of a premature infant

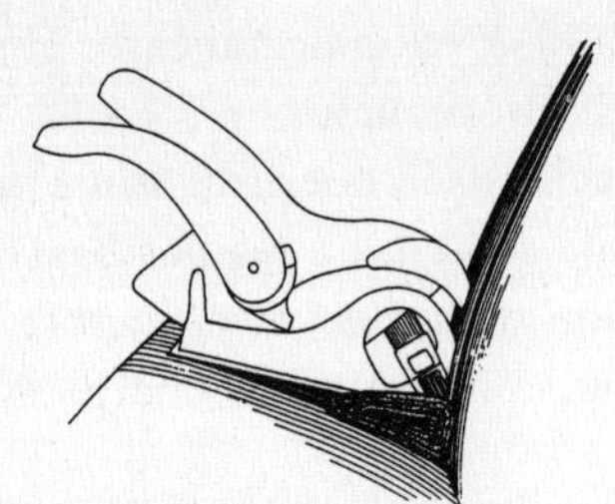

B. Car seat with wedge to recline halfway back at a 45-degree tilt

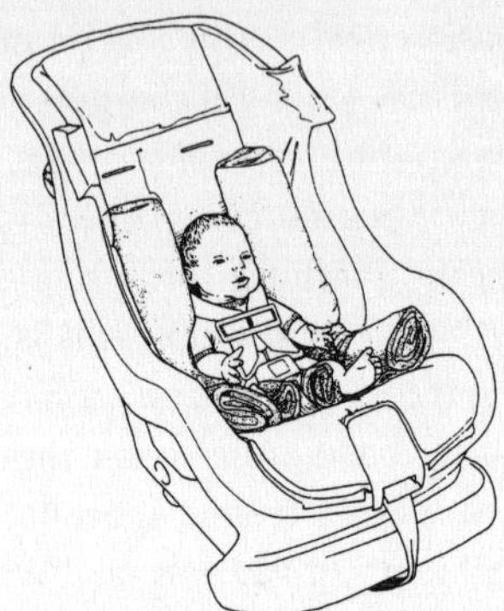

C. Premature baby properly placed in convertible car seat with padded sides and crotch and retainer clip positioned on infant's chest

- If the vehicle seat slopes, making your baby's head flop forward, the car seat should be reclined halfway back at a 45-degree tilt. To achieve this angle, wedge a firm roll of cloth or newspaper under the car seat below your child's feet (see figure B).
- A rear-facing car safety seat must *not* be placed in the front passenger seat of any vehicle equipped with a passenger-side front air bag because of risk of death or serious injury from the impact of the air bag.
- Your baby should be positioned with buttocks and back flat against the back of the car seat. Rolled-up blankets may be placed on both sides of your infant to provide support for the head and neck. A small rolled diaper or blanket between the crotch strap and your child may be added so he will not slouch forward in the car seat (see figure C).
- The rear seat is the safest position in which your child can ride in a vehicle. Whenever possible, arrange for an adult to sit in the rear seat adjacent to your baby to observe him closely.
- If heart and breathing monitors are prescribed, use this equipment during travel using portable, self-contained power. Power should be ample for at least twice the expected travel time. Equipment should be secured or wedged on the floor or under the seat.

Always remember that your infant should never be left unattended in a car seat.

Preparing the Nursery and Shopping

Decorating your baby's room can be fun but tiring, especially when you are still spending hours at the hospital. Do not push yourself so much that you become overtired. You need to be well rested to care for your baby.

Shopping *is* a good idea, however. The following are some items you may want to collect in advance:

Formula, bottles, and nipples. Buy enough formula to last at least one to two weeks. Powder is the least expensive; liquid is the most convenient. Your doctor may recommend a special formula designed for premature infants called Similac NeoSure (formerly known as Neocare) or Enfamil 22. With a prescription from your doctor, the company will send the formula to your doctor's office. WIC (a federally funded supplemental food program for women, infants, and children) and Medicaid will typically pay for NeoSure or Enfamil 22.

Cloth diapers or washcloths. You will use a lot of these for burping. Soft kitchen or hand towels can also work.

A breast pump and supplies for storing breastmilk (bags and labels). If you have been using the hospital's pump, you may want to have one at home for at least a few weeks. Keep a supply of bags and labels on hand.

Nasal bulb syringe. The hospital should provide you with a nasal bulb syringe for cleaning your baby's nose and mouth. You will want to have two in case one gets misplaced or needs cleaning, or for keeping an extra in your baby bag.

Thermometer. A standard glass thermometer is fine, but a digital thermometer is handy for late-night temperature-taking.

Medicine syringes. The hospital or your pharmacy should provide some free syringes for dispensing medicines. Ask for extras or purchase a few 1-cc, 3-cc, and 5-cc syringes.

Infant acetaminophen (such as Tylenol) or infant ibuprofen (such as Motrin). Keep a supply on hand. Check the dosage with your doctor: Infant drops are more concentrated than the children's liquid form. Always check the label and dosage on the bottle before giving medication. Overdoses of medicines, even over-the-counter ones, can damage the liver, kidneys, and other organs. *Never give aspirin to your child without consulting your doctor, as it is associated with a rare condition known as Reye's Syndrome.*

Surgical tape and leads. If your baby will come home on a home monitor and/or oxygen, the medical equipment provider should give you these. Be sure to get extra leads.

Cloth or disposable diapers. This is a personal preference. Some babies tolerate cloth better on their skin; others do well with disposable diapers. If your preemie gets frequent diaper rashes, you may need to change your diaper choice. Several diaper companies will mail disposable preemie-sized diapers. Diaper services are convenient and cost-effective, especially with multiple babies.

Special preemie clothes. Your preemie may fit into regular baby clothes, or he may still need preemie clothes. Some doll clothes can work, but make sure they are sewn well.

Blankets. Have plenty of blankets in varying thickness on hand, especially in the colder months. In the summer, your baby may need covering from air-conditioning.

Groceries. Once your baby is home, it will probably be difficult for you to get to the store, so stock up on groceries now.

Portable crib or bassinet. A portable crib or bassinet will allow you to keep your baby nearby.

A Baby Shower? Sure!

If someone offers to throw you a shower before homecoming—accept. It will be easier for you to attend and enjoy an outing now. Parents who wait and take their baby to the shower often are so anxious about germs and overhandling that they do not enjoy themselves.

Preparing Your Older Children for Baby's Homecoming

Adjusting to a new brother or sister is difficult, and introducing a sibling with special needs complicates matters. Children must cope with their own feelings of fear, anger, guilt, jealousy, resentment, and confusion. Sensing your stress and anxiety, they may act out and demand extra attention from you.

Children under age six are the most vulnerable and have the most difficult time accepting a new baby, but older children can have trouble coping, too. To make the transition easier, experts suggest these ways to prepare siblings:

- If the hospital allows, let your children care for their brother or sister by assisting with temperature-taking and diaper changes. This helps build a sibling relationship.
- While the baby is still hospitalized, ask your children how they feel. Encourage them to share their concerns about the baby's homecoming. Let them know that it is okay to be angry about the time you must spend with the baby, and reassure them that what has happened is not their fault (some children may feel they somehow caused the household stress).
- Younger children may wonder who will take care of them when their brother or sister comes home. Assure your children that you will still be there for them.
- Talk to siblings about ways they can make the new baby be a part of the family: "We can take him to the park with us"; "He can watch you when you play your favorite game or play an instrument"; "You can teach him how to be silly." Get your children excited about holding and caring for *their* new baby.
- Discuss with siblings the things they can do for themselves that a baby cannot, making them feel grown-up and special.
- The day before your premature infant's homecoming, give a small gift from the baby to his big brother or big sister.
- Explain to your children how their lives will be better when the baby comes home—no more hospital visits or baby-sitters!

■ ■ ■

HOMECOMING CHECKLISTS

IN ADDITION TO the previous suggestions, veteran preemie parents have shared other helpful homecoming preparations, which are included in the following checklists. At first glance, these lists may seem a bit overwhelming; however, they are only reminders of what you may need to do before that special day (not all of the lists and items will apply to you and your baby). If you cannot check off an item that pertains to you, consult a healthcare professional.

MY PREEMIE'S BASIC CARE

I know how to:

____ take my baby's temperature with a thermometer similar to the one I will use at home;

____ give my baby a bath, wash his hair, and cut his nails;

____ give all the medications my baby will need after he comes home (Obtain prescriptions for home medications and have them filled in advance);

____ feed my baby, and I know how much and how often to feed him;

____ mix my baby's formula;

____ contact a lactation consultant and local breast-feeding support group;

____ weigh my baby on an infant scale (Do not forget to record your baby's discharge weight for his baby book!);

____ give my baby any respiratory treatments he will need at home; and

____ read my baby's cues.

I also know:

____ my baby's favorite sleep positions;

____ my baby's schedule (when he typically sleeps, eats, and his alert times);

____ the signs of illness and when to call the doctor;

____ what to do in case of an emergency;

____ cardiopulmonary resuscitation (CPR);

____ when my baby's first doctor's appointment should be;

____ what follow-up doctors' appointments my baby needs; and

____ how to transport my baby home.

I have obtained:

____ an infant car seat;

____ a copy of my baby's medical history, including his discharge summary, so that I can share it with healthcare professionals after homecoming;

____ the results of my baby's screening tests (neonatal screen, head ultrasound, hearing test, and eye examination);

____ a written copy of my baby's immunizations with dates given;

____ the telephone numbers of all doctors, specialists, and emergency personnel, and I have placed them near telephones in my home; and

____ information on nearby specialized daycare programs (childcare centers familiar with special needs).

My Preemie's Oxygen

I know how to:

____ read oxygen levels on both the portable tank and the main supply tank at home;

____ change and retape my baby's nasal cannula;

____ contact the oxygen provider; and

____ contact the medical supply company to arrange for oxygen equipment delivery.

My Preemie's Cardiorespiratory Monitor

I know how to:

____ read the monitor and respond to alarms;

____ place the monitor's leads on my baby;

____ contact the monitoring equipment provider; and

____ contact the medical supply company and arrange for home monitor equipment delivery.

■ ■ ■

My Emotional Health

I have obtained:

____ the phone numbers of parent support groups from the hospital staff;

____ the phone numbers of respite care organizations (qualified individuals who will care for your baby while you take a break) from the hospital social worker; and

____ the phone numbers of counselors from a clergy member, social worker, or the NICU staff (Also ask other parents for referrals).

Financial Concerns

I have:

____ obtained the phone numbers for financial assistance programs from my hospital's social worker;

____ filled out appropriate health insurance forms;

____ filled out appropriate Medicaid and Social Security Insurance (SSI) forms (If your baby is on SSI, notify them of the pending discharge); and

____ obtained referral forms from my primary care physician for any specialists my baby needs to see after homecoming.

YOUR PREEMIE IS COMING HOME!

AMID ALL THE preparation for your baby's homecoming, try to enjoy the occasion—it is a day to celebrate! Decorate your home's door with a banner announcing your baby's homecoming. Tie some balloons to the mailbox. Make flyers announcing your preemie's discharge and send them to family, friends, and coworkers. Do not forget to videotape or photograph your baby leaving the hospital and arriving home—this is a special event you will want to remember.

■ ■ ■

IMPORTANT PHONE NUMBERS

Make several copies of this important list—carry one with you, post one on the refrigerator, and place one near your telephone.

In case of an emergency, call 9-1-1 or:________________________

Pediatrician or family practitioner:________________________

After-hours clinic:________________________

NICU:________________________

Neonatologist:________________________

Preemie parent support group:________________________

Lactation consultant:________________________

Local breast-feeding support group:________________________

Neighbor:________________________

Oxygen/cardiorespiratory monitor provider:________________________

Speech/feeding therapist:________________________

Occupational therapist:________________________

Physical therapist:________________________

Case worker/social worker:________________________

Social services:________________________

Health department:________________________

Insurance company:________________________

Other specialists:________________________

____

____

____

____

Poison control:________________________

CHAPTER TWO

Now That Your Preemie Is Home

YOUR PREEMIE IS finally home—congratulations! You probably feel relieved and happy, yet anxious and a little frightened. This anxiety is part of the transition process of leaving around-the-clock hospital care and becoming a twenty-four-hour parent to your tiny baby.

Adapting to a lifestyle change created by a newborn is always stressful, and your child's special needs and medical concerns add to the pressure. Your marriage or relationship may become strained because of the emotional and physical burden a sick baby places on both parents. If you are a single parent, you may feel emotionally and physically overwhelmed from facing this crisis alone. If there are other children, they will probably demand extra attention and energy that you just do not have.

Making the transition from hospital to home is a big adjustment for your baby, too. After all, he has been following the same routine in the same environment, for all of his short life—then suddenly everything is disrupted. This abrupt change can throw off your baby's internal clock, and he may have trouble conforming to a day-night schedule.

To help with this transition, some nurseries simulate a day-night schedule before homecoming. However, babies often need time to adjust themselves—to the feel, sounds, and smells of their new surroundings. It is similar to going on vacation and staying in an unfamiliar bed: Most people have some trouble adjusting and sleeping.

Your overtired preemie may take longer to eat, and he may require feedings every two to four hours. This can be time-consuming and frustrating for you. After eating, your baby may have difficulty settling down, especially during certain times of the day. Again, your baby needs time to adjust.

To lessen your stress during these first weeks, have a family member or a friend stay with you. Make sure it is someone who will be helpful and not burdensome. (Some family and friends may actually add to your anxiety.) Also, do not plan on doing much more than caring for your baby. Those household projects can wait. If you have not yet connected with a local or Internet preemie parent support group, now is a good time. A support group can be a great source of comfort and guidance.

Only time and practice will reduce your anxiety about caring for your baby, but educating yourself about your baby's needs can help. This chapter discusses the basic care of your preterm infant. Chapter 3 addresses special concerns of technology-dependent preemies.

> *I waited four months for this day. My baby was finally coming home! I wanted to be happy, but mostly I felt scared. I was worried about my baby getting enough oxygen so I kept checking the color of his lips. He seemed fussy and he wouldn't nurse. To top it off, friends stopped by while I was trying to nurse him and they wanted to hold him. I actually missed the hospital.*
>
> —MARIA, MOTHER OF 28-WEEKER JUSTIN

■

> *Bringing home our little boy was certainly a triumphant event. He made it! We made it! But when you have to deal with all the issues surrounding a high-risk baby—learning CPR, giving medications, watching for illness—some of the joy of bringing home your baby is lost.*
>
> —MELINDA, MOTHER OF 34-WEEKER KRISTEN

■

> *I don't think I slept at all that first night. I kept putting my fingers underneath my baby's nose to make sure he was breathing. The apnea monitor went off three times because of a loose lead. Every time I breast-fed him, he fell asleep. An hour later, he'd wake up hungry. It was the longest night of my life.*
>
> —MARY, MOTHER OF 30-WEEKER CARL

PARENT TIPS:

HELPING SIBLINGS ADJUST TO THE NEW BABY

Parents suggest these ways to help your other children during the homecoming months:

- If it is difficult for you to provide the attention your other children need, arrange for a close friend, relative, or favorite baby-sitter to spend some time with them.

- Young siblings may start behaving in less mature ways when the new baby comes home. For instance, they may have more "accidents" if recently potty-trained, or they may regress to thumb-sucking. Try not to scold, punish, or talk negatively about these behaviors since your children are merely trying to express their need for some attention and love. In time, your children will feel secure again and return to their former level of development.
- Remind siblings that you love them just as much as before the baby came home, and try to provide them with special one-on-one time (for instance, during breakfast or when the baby is sleeping).
- Talk to your children about how your family loves their new baby, but do not expect them to show love right away. Tell them it is okay to feel anger toward the new baby, but it is not okay to hurt the baby.
- Be careful about what you say in front of your children. They often hear more than you think they do, sometimes causing unnecessary anxiety. Encourage them to ask questions and express their feelings.
- Try to keep siblings on a familiar routine (naps, bedtime, meals, and other activities). Let their teachers know what is going on at home so they can provide understanding and attention.
- If siblings are having difficulty adjusting to a new brother or sister, encourage them to express their feelings by acting out with puppets or dolls. If you become concerned about a sibling's unusual behavior (hitting, not sleeping, frequent crying), you may want to talk to a family counselor.
- Let your children care for the baby as much as possible. Let them hold their brother or sister and help with "parenting" tasks, such as temperature-taking and diaper changes. Keeping your preemie's siblings involved requires a great deal of patience, but it will pay off.

TAKING CARE OF YOUR PREEMIE

THE HOSPITAL STAFF taught you care-giving basics—taking your baby's temperature, suctioning his nose and mouth, feeding him, and giving him a bath. When a nurse was standing by, these tasks seemed manageable. At home, alone, you may begin questioning your abilities.

Try to have confidence in yourself as a parent, and remember your preemie is not as fragile as you may sometimes think. The following sections will help you parent your baby. If you have concerns and questions, do not hesitate to consult your pediatrician.

Keeping Your Baby Warm

Maintaining your home at a comfortable temperature, usually in the low 70s (degrees Fahrenheit), should be adequate for your baby. Try to prevent any breezes from windows, fans, or air-conditioning from blowing directly on your baby. Follow this guide-

YOUR PREEMIE'S AGE

Your child born prematurely has two ages: his "actual age" (also called "chronological age") and his "corrected age" (also called "adjusted age"). His corrected age is the age he would be if he had been born at term. For example, if he was born two months early and is now ten months old, his corrected age is eight months.

10 months actual age minus
2 months born prematurely equals
8 months corrected age

In reading this book and dealing with healthcare professionals, you will also find and hear the term "gestational age." Gestational age is a baby's age in weeks while in the womb. Forty weeks gestational age is full term. Parents often refer to their preemies as "28-weekers" or "32-weekers," referring to the gestational age they were at birth.

line: If your baby's hands and feet feel cold and he looks pale, he is probably cold. If your baby is fussy, he feels hot to your touch, and his cheeks are flushed, he is probably too warm.

Try not to overdress or underdress your baby. Thinking a preterm infant must need extra warmth, some well-meaning family or friends will suggest adding an extra sweater or blanket on your baby. Politely ignore them. A good rule of thumb is to dress your baby as you would dress yourself, but remember to be conscious of your baby's physical signs of cold and heat. If you feel cold, add a layer of clothing or a blanket on your baby. If you feel warm, remove a layer.

GIVING BATHS

You need to give your baby a full bath only once or twice a week. Washing his face and neck daily and washing him after changing each diaper will be sufficient. Bathing too often can cause dry skin.

When bathing your preemie, be sure that you move slowly and do not do too many tasks at once, which may overwhelm him. Talk to your baby in a calm, soothing voice. To help him feel safe and comfortable, keep your baby's limbs tucked close to his body. Bathing can be stressful, and your baby may need to rest or sleep after his bath.

You can bathe your baby in an infant bathtub or in a large, clean sink. Be careful not to give the bath where there is a cool draft. Follow these steps for bathing your preemie:

1. Collect everything you need ahead of time and place in arm's reach: bathtub, washcloth, towel (laid flat with one corner folded down), baby soap, baby lotion, special shampoo, a clean diaper, and baby's clothes.
2. Fill the tub or sink with lukewarm water. *Always* test the water's temperature immediately before putting your baby in the water. It should feel neither hot nor cold, but rather a soothing warm temperature.
3. When the water is ready, undress your baby and place him slowly and gently in the water, holding one arm football-style under his neck, back, and bottom. (Some experts suggest keeping your baby wrapped in a blanket and unwrapping areas as needed. This technique may make your baby feel more secure.) While you place him in the water, bundle his arms and legs together with your other hand so he will feel safe. If he jumps when placed into the water, the water may be too hot or too cold.

4. Wash your baby's face first. Wipe his eyes, from the inside of the eye outward, with a soap-free washcloth. Gently wash the rest of his face using very little or no soap. Next, wash the creases of his neck, the rest of his body, and the perineum (around the genitals) last. For girls, always wipe from front to back.
5. Before washing your baby's hair, make sure the towel with a corner folded down is handy. Slowly remove your baby from the tub and place him on the towel with his neck along the folded corner. Wrap your baby snugly in the towel and hold him in a football hold. Turn on the water in the sink, check the temperature, and wet the top of your baby's head. If your water temperature changes quickly, use a basin of water. *Never run water over your baby's face.* Your baby may tolerate running water on his head, or you may need to use a washcloth or a small cup of water. After wetting your baby's head, using a dime-sized amount of shampoo, wash his hair, then rinse. Now, unfold the corner of the towel and dry your baby's head.
6. If your baby's skin is dry or you live in a dry climate, gently rub baby lotion on your baby's body.
7. If your baby has cradle cap (dry, flaky skin on his scalp), he has an imbalance in his skin's pH. Cradle cap is not necessarily a result of poor hygiene. Rub mineral oil in his hair *before* you wash it, moisturizing the scalp and making it easier to wash off the scaly skin. You can also use a fine-toothed comb to loosen the flakes. Cradle cap can last a few weeks. If your baby gets frequent cradle cap, try changing shampoos. Dandruff shampoos are another option, but avoid getting any shampoo into the eyes.
8. Finally, clean your baby's ears by gently wiping the upper ear area with a washcloth. *Never put an object like a Q-Tip in the ear canal*—you can damage your baby's ear or push wax into the ear canal.

Never leave your baby unattended in the bath for even a few seconds.

PUTTING YOUR PREEMIE TO BED

The American Academy of Pediatrics recommends that babies should *not* be placed on their stomachs for sleeping as it may increase the risk of Sudden Infant Death Syndrome (SIDS). However, because preterm infants sometimes have special considerations, you should discuss your baby's sleep position with your pediatrician.

An infant who struggles with frequent spitting and/or gastroesophageal reflux may sleep better if he is positioned with his head elevated about 30 degrees. You can raise the head of your baby's bed 30 degrees by putting the front legs of his crib on four- to six-inch blocks. Be sure the blocks are secure and cannot be knocked down. You can also place telephone books or towels under the head of the crib's mattress, but make sure the raised mattress is flush—elevated from edge to edge—to prevent your baby from rolling facedown into a corner and accidentally suffocating.

Whether in a crib or bassinet, your preemie will feel most comfortable with snug boundaries. Use rolled towels or blankets to keep his arms and legs close to his body and to prevent him from rolling into a corner. Your baby should not sleep on top of soft surfaces, such as pillows or quilts.

Even though you may find it easier to have your baby sleep in an infant carrier, sleeping in one for long periods of time is not recommended. A carrier prevents your baby from moving and exercising his muscles.

After your infant eats, lay him on his right side. He will digest his food more efficiently on this side. You can place a rolled towel or receiving blanket behind his back to keep him from rolling. Change your baby's sleep position each time you lay him down to encourage equal development of neck and shoulder muscles.

For at least the first few days at home, create a nighttime atmosphere similar to the hospital's. Your baby is accustomed to the noisy NICU. If music was played in the nursery throughout the night, play soft music. Many parents find that tapes with human heartbeats soothe their babies. A small fan blowing toward a wall—and not on your infant—can drown out unfamiliar noises of the house and sleep-disruptive siblings. A dim light may also help.

PARENT TIPS:

SURVIVING THE NIGHTS

The most common advice from parents for surviving nights is borrowed from the Boy Scouts: Be prepared. Here are some suggestions:

- Make several bottles in advance for nighttime and early morning feedings. When your baby is hungry, all you have to do is warm a pre-made bottle.
- If your baby needs medication during the night, measure the dosage before you go to bed. Reading labels and measuring when you are not fully awake can be challenging. Be sure to label syringes clearly if your baby has more than one medicine.
- Before bedtime, review what to do if your baby's monitor alarm sounds. If you have any questions, call the medical supply company or your pediatrician.
- If the monitor's alarm sounds during the night, try not to panic. Research shows that 95 percent of these alarms are false. If you panic, you might not think clearly or be able to properly handle a real emergency. Practice responding to alarms by following the steps in chapter 3.
- Check your baby's oxygen levels and settings before bedtime. Make sure the liter flow is set properly; that there is ample oxygen in the tank; and that all the connections are secure.
- Share parenting responsibilities throughout the night. By supporting each other, both parents will be less tired and overwhelmed than if one parent

assumes primary responsibility. You will also be better prepared to handle any future concerns if you are both involved in your baby's care from the start.

- If you are a single parent, try to arrange for some help from a family member or a friend for at least the first week your baby is home.

Coping with Crying

Crying is your baby's form of communication; he is asking for something, or he is telling you he is uncomfortable. Your baby has several different cries and soon you will know what each one means. When your preemie cries, he may be:

- hungry;
- uncomfortable because he is wet or soiled, too hot or too cold, because he is wearing something that does not feel good, or because he wants his position changed;
- overtired and struggling to fall asleep (Sometimes when babies are overtired, they have difficulty getting into a sleep pattern. This is why a schedule is important.;
- overstimulated from too much noise or too many people paying attention to him (If this happens, move your baby to a quiet room.);
- hurting from a stomachache and needs to burp or pass gas (Positioning your baby on his tummy with his legs curled up under him and patting him on the back may help.);
- upset and he needs to release some tension; or
- ill (Check for other signs of illness, such as a fever).

When Your Preemie Has the Hiccups

Preterm babies have frequent hiccups because the nerves in the muscles of their diaphragms are not fully developed. Hiccups cause a little discomfort for your baby (and for you watching), but you should not be concerned. Hiccups are often a sign of overstimulation, and you should evaluate your baby's environment and eliminate any stimulating factors. Giving your baby water in a bottle may help, too.

When Your Preemie Sneezes or Is Congested

Babies sneeze when they have tickles in their noses, just like adults do. Dry climates or air-conditioning can trigger sneezes. Frequent sneezing and/or a runny nose may mean you need to clean your baby's nostrils with a nasal bulb syringe.

To use a bulb syringe:

1. Hold the syringe between your fingers and push the bulb with your thumb to remove the air.

2. While continuing to squeeze the bulb, gently place the tip of the syringe into your baby's nostril or mouth, then release *slowly*. This causes a suction that removes mucus.
3. Remove the syringe and squeeze out its contents onto a tissue or washcloth.
4. Repeat suctioning in other nostril.
5. Wash the bulb syringe in soapy water, squeezing it several times. You can also put it in the dishwasher or boil it in hot water for 10 minutes.

Be careful not to overuse the bulb syringe—the suction can be hard on your baby's nostrils and overuse can cause bleeding. If secretions are dry, gently squeeze one to two drops of normal saline (commercially prepared saltwater) into your baby's nostrils and suction after he sneezes.

Suctioning can also be done with an electrically powered suction machine. With a doctor's prescription, your health insurance company may buy or rent you one, or you may rent or purchase a suction machine from a medical supply company. To use a suction machine:

1. Turn the suction machine on, then place a clean medical glove on the hand you will use to hold the suction catheter.
2. Place a few drops of normal saline into each nostril.
3. Keeping the hole that creates the suction uncovered, gently place the tip of the suction catheter into your baby's nose.
4. Quickly place your thumb over the suction hole for no more than three to five seconds, then gently pull the catheter out.
5. Repeat suctioning in other nostril.

After you suction once or twice in each nostril, give your child a rest. You should suction a total of only four to five times per nostril. If you need to suction using a machine more than every one to two hours, consult your doctor.

Taking Temperatures

A rectal temperature is the most accurate way to measure your baby's temperature, but if it is not done correctly it can be dangerous. Temperatures taken under the arm are the safest. Most doctors recommend using a glass or electronic thermometer. At around five years of age, children can have their temperatures taken by mouth.

If you are using a glass thermometer, quickly shake it until the mercury is under 97 degrees Fahrenheit (36.1 degrees Celsius). When taking your baby's rectal temperature, place a small amount of lubricant, such as Vaseline, on the end of the glass or electronic thermometer and gently place it about one-half inch into the rectum. Hold the glass thermometer in place for three to four minutes, then read the number at the end of the mercury. The electronic thermometer will beep when the temperature is assessed. For an axillary (armpit) reading, place the tip of the thermometer in the center of your baby's armpit. Make sure no clothing touches the thermometer. Hold the glass thermometer for three to four minutes. Hold the electronic thermometer until it beeps. A normal axillary temperature is 98° to 99°F (36.7° to 37.2°C), and a normal rectal temperature is 98° to 99.5°F (36.7° to 37.8°C). (See appendix B for a temperature conversion table.)

Remember that a fever under 99.5°F serves an important purpose: It is the body's way of naturally repairing itself. The height of your child's temperature does not necessarily indicate the seriousness of your child's illness. A better indicator of your child's health is how sick he acts.

A temperature over 101°F should be monitored closely. In rare instances, an extremely high temperature can cause a seizure. About 4 percent of all children experience a brief fever-induced seizure before the age of five.

To help relieve your child's fever, give him a bath or sponge him with tepid (slightly warm) water. If your child shivers, make the water a little warmer. Tepid water on the body keeps the blood moving into the skin and brings the heat from a fever to the surface. The heat leaves the body as the water evaporates. If the water is too cool, this process will not happen.

Many doctors recommend giving infant acetaminophen (such as Tylenol) or infant ibuprofen (such as Motrin). Check the dosage with your doctor, and never give your baby aspirin without consulting your doctor first.

KEEPING YOUR PREEMIE HEALTHY

DURING THE LAST trimester of pregnancy, a full-term healthy infant receives many antibodies that help fight infection. Your child born prematurely may not have received all of these protective antibodies and may be more susceptible to illness. In addition, if your preemie has chronic lung disease, the damaged lung tissue is easy prey for viruses and bacteria.

Keeping your preemie healthy can be challenging. Your doctor may want you to stay away from possible germs in crowded places, such as grocery stores and malls. Many doctors suggest avoiding daycare centers and indoor playgrounds, where ill children may spread infection.

You will also need to educate others about your preemie's health (sometimes repetitively!). Friends may not understand that a simple visit or trip to the mall could be life-threatening for your child, and they may even accuse you of being overprotective. Try not to let others who may not understand your child's special concerns make you feel bad.

While keeping your baby well can be isolating and lonely at times, remember that a proactive approach is the best way to prevent illness. Here are some other ways you can reduce your child's chances of catching a bug:

- Wash your hands often, especially before you touch your baby. Using an antibacterial soap and scrubbing vigorously for at least thirty seconds is the best way to prevent the spread of infection. Keep a nailbrush handy and scrub under your nails.

- When visiting your doctor, ask to wait in an isolated area away from sick children. Try to get the first appointment in the morning or after lunch to avoid extended waits and contact with other ill children. Do not hesitate to speak up if you do not see healthcare workers washing their hands.
- When relatives, friends, and strangers want to touch your baby, communicate your concerns. Explain that germs pose a serious threat to your child. People usually take you seriously when you tell them that your baby was born prematurely and spent many weeks or months in the hospital. One preemie parent tells strangers, "You can look, but you can't touch!" Some parents pass out notes explaining their baby's special concerns. One preemie mom writes this on her baby's bib: "Germs make me very sick. Please do not touch me."
- Anyone with a cold needs to stay six feet away from your baby.
- When cleaning your home, use a disinfectant cleanser to destroy germs.
- In the early fall, get your six-month (actual age) or older preemie a flu shot. All siblings and caregivers should get flu shots, too.
- Ask your doctor about RSV (respiratory syncytial virus) prevention.
- Do not allow anyone with cold symptoms in your home. Avoid letting young children who often carry germs near your baby. Post a sign near your door saying, "Please do not come in unless you know you are healthy!"
- Keep the rest of your family well. Take vitamins and eat healthy. Avoid putting your nose or mouth directly on public telephones or on drinking fountains, and wash your hands after touching doorknobs and mailboxes.
- If a family member becomes sick, treat symptoms quickly.
- Frequently wash clothes and bed linens in hot water.
- Dispose of tissues immediately and wash your hands after use.
- If you are ill, wear a surgical mask or bandanna over your mouth when caring for your baby.
- Do not smoke or let other people smoke anywhere in your home or near your baby (smoke travels). Post a "No Smoking" sign on your front door. Smoke can weaken your baby's lungs and make him more susceptible to respiratory illness.

Your Preemie's Doctor Visits

To monitor your baby's health, growth, and development, your doctor will want to see him routinely. If your child has any specific medical problems, is on a home monitor, or needs supplemental oxygen, you will visit the doctor more often. During your preemie's follow-up appointments, discuss any of your concerns. Some parents like to write down their questions, as well as the doctor's answers, for future reference.

■ ■ ■

Chart 2-1: Typical Well-preemie Doctor Visits

SCHEDULED VISIT	WHAT TO EXPECT	TESTS
3–7 days after discharge	Physical exam Measure growth Discuss feedings and routine care	
2–4 weeks after discharge	Physical exam Measure growth Discuss routine care	Hemoglobin
4 months actual age	Physical exam Measure growth Assess development	
6 months actual age	Physical exam Measure growth Assess development Discuss solid foods	
9 months actual age	Physical exam Measure growth Assess development Discuss safety	Urinalysis Hemoglobin
12–15 months actual age	Physical exam Measure growth Assess development Speech and hearing evaluation (optional) Ophthalmology	
15–18 months actual age	Physical exam Measure growth Assess development	
2 years actual age	Same as 18 months	Urinalysis Hemoglobin
3 and 4 years actual age	Same as 18 months Assess hearing and vision	Hemoglobin Assess blood pressure Urinalysis Tuberculosis screen
5 years actual age	Same as 18 months Discuss behavior, discipline, safety, emotional stability, and assess school readiness	
6, 8, and 10 years	Same as 18 months	Urinalysis Hemoglobin

(Adapted with permission from *The Owner's Manual,* copyright © 1994 by Daniel J. Feiten, M.D., and Andrew T. Bauer, M.D.)

Your Preemie's Immunizations

Your child needs to receive immunizations at certain ages to prevent some serious illnesses. Your doctor should give immunizations to your child at the same age a term child would receive them. For example, your baby receives the first DPT (Diphtheria, Tetanus, Pertussis) at two months actual age. Immunizations are not given if your child has a fever.

The philosophy behind actual-age vaccinations is that your preemie has been exposed to the world for the same amount of time as a term child. He is at the same risk (or greater risk because of his size and health problems) of catching a life-threatening infection. Therefore, your baby should be protected as early as possible. In a few cases, a physician will postpone some vaccinations until a child reaches a specific weight or age.

Your child needs these immunizations:

- Hepatitis B
- Diphtheria, Pertussis, Tetanus (DPT)
- Haemophilus Influenzae Type B (HIB)
- Polio
- Measles, Mumps, Rubella (MMR)
- Varicella (Chicken Pox)

The first Hepatitis B vaccine was most likely given in the NICU. The second Hepatitis B is usually given one month after the first and, depending on the length of your child's hospitalization, it may or may not have been given before discharge. The first DPT, HIB, and Polio are due at two months actual age and may have been given in the NICU if your baby was still hospitalized. Also ask your doctor about any new vaccines. Your doctor should have your child's immunization records from the hospital, and you should also keep a record. If you did not get a copy before discharge, ask your doctor for one.

Watching for Signs of Anemia

Anemia is caused by a lack of adequate red blood cells that carry oxygen throughout the body. Preterm infants often do not produce red blood cells quickly enough to keep up with their rapid growth. They also do not have adequate iron stored in their bodies to produce red blood cells (unlike term infants). In the NICU, preterm babies may have excessive blood drawn. All of these factors can contribute to the development of anemia.

Research shows that premature infants experience a normal drop in red blood cells beginning at around two to three months following birth that lasts for about three months. The timing of this "drop" can be affected by blood transfusions or the use of Epogen (a medication given in the NICU to help prevent the need for blood transfusions).

Because of this timing uncertainty, your baby needs to be monitored closely for anemia.

Your pediatrician will periodically screen your baby for anemia by measuring your child's hemoglobin and hematocrit (H & H) levels. *Hemoglobin* is a measure of the amount of red cell protein that carries oxygen in the blood. *Hematocrit* is the percentage of your child's blood that is composed of red blood cells. A screen is usually done with a quick finger-prick in the doctor's office and the results can be read immediately. If more information is needed in addition to an H & H, such as a look at the shape and color of the red blood cells or the number of new red blood cells being produced, your child may need blood drawn with a needle.

While most preemies compensate for a lower amount of red blood cells without any significant problems, some show symptoms. With mild anemia, your baby may have no symptoms at all or he may:

- sleep more;
- exhibit poor growth;
- act irritable; and/or
- eat less.

If anemia is significant, your baby's health can become compromised. You should consult your pediatrician if your baby:

- eats poorly;
- looks pale (especially around the lips or fingernails);
- has an increased heart rate or respiratory rate;
- acts listless;
- requires an increase in oxygen (if your baby is on supplemental oxygen);
- loses weight or has poor weight gain.

Iron is essential for making red blood cells; therefore, anemia is treated with iron supplements through iron-fortified formula, vitamins with iron, and/or iron drops. Babies who are bottle-fed should receive iron-fortified formula to help prevent anemia. Breastfed babies should be given vitamins with iron or iron drops.

In time and with enough iron, most preemies begin producing adequate red blood cells on their own. Rarely does a baby have anemia so severe that he requires a blood transfusion to replace lost red blood cells.

When to Call the Doctor

Preemie parents often worry about whether they will know when to call the doctor. Even typical baby actions, such as hiccups and spitting up, may alarm you. It is only natural that your baby's difficult beginning has caused you to be on the lookout for signs of health problems.

DO NOT WORRY ABOUT:

- hiccups;
- sneezes;
- yawns;
- occasional spitting up;
- straining with bowel movements (as long as the stool is soft);
- chin or lip quivering;
- passing gas;
- "jitteriness" of arms and legs when crying;
- startling to noises with brief body stiffening (called the Moro reflex); and
- mild congestion of the nostrils in dry climates.

(Adapted with permission from *The Owner's Manual,* copyright © 1994 by Daniel J. Feiten, M.D., and Andrew T. Bauer, M.D.)

In time, you will understand your baby's signs and know when something is not right. Until then, you should not hesitate to call your health-care provider about any concerns. As a general guide, your preemie may be getting sick if he:

- is sleeping more and is less active, or he is unable to sleep and is fussy;
- refuses to eat or eats very little;
- cries excessively;
- breathes faster and his chest rises and falls, indicating he is working harder to breathe;
- is frequently coughing;
- is vomiting or frequently spitting up; and/or
- has frequent and/or watery stools.

If you suspect your baby is sick, take his temperature before calling your doctor. In the early months, your doctor may want you to call him at the first sign of illness. As your preemie's health improves, you will be better able to manage colds and other illness on your own (but you should always call your doctor if you are uncomfortable with any aspect of your baby's care).

Coping with All Those Medications

If your baby was discharged on several medications, you may find it useful to post the times medications need to be given in an easy-to-see location, such as the refrigerator. Set the timer on your watch or stove as a reminder. For example:

8:30 A.M.—*Vitamins .5 cc*
NOON—*Iron .5 cc*
4:00 P.M.—*Caffeine .8 cc*
MIDNIGHT—*no medications*

If giving medications becomes too time-consuming and difficult, ask your doctor about ways to simplify the schedule. Medicines can sometimes be taken at the same time. For tips on giving your child medications, see box on page 79.

■ ■ ■

CALL THE DOCTOR IMMEDIATELY IF YOUR PREEMIE:

- has a fever over 99.5°F and is under six months corrected age;
- has a fever over 102°F without an obvious cause for illness;
- has had a fever for over three days (even if he looks well);
- is sleeping poorly for two nights in a row;
- shows signs of dehydration (decrease in urination, sunken eyes, listlessness, dark yellow or brownish urine, dry mouth);
- has a seizure;
- has a dramatic decrease in wet diapers (about half of normal amount);
- has not had a bowel movement for over three days;
- has purple spots on the skin that may look like blood blisters;
- has a fever with joint swelling (or does not move one or more limbs);
- is crying inconsolably for one hour;
- is unable to be awakened from sleep;
- has a change in his breathing (his nostrils flare when he breathes; he is primarily breathing through the mouth; his chest is retracting; he has secretions from his nose; and/or he is coughing frequently); and/or
- is acting unusual and you are concerned.

(Adapted with permission from *The Owner's Manual,* copyright © 1994 by Daniel J. Feiten, M.D., and Andrew T. Bauer, M.D.)

Preparing an Emergency Plan

Hopefully you will never have to face a medical emergency, but in case you do, you need to be prepared. Make sure you:

- have emergency telephone numbers posted clearly by each telephone in your home;
- know which hospital/emergency clinic to go to if there is an emergency. Find out if your health insurance covers the hospital/emergency clinic closest to you and if your doctor practices at that hospital;
- learn the fastest route, as well as an alternative route, to the hospital and/or emergency clinic closest to your home;
- make a folder of important information you need to take to the hospital: a list of your child's medications and dosages, a list of medications your child is allergic to, your baby's hospital discharge summary, and health insurance information;
- notify your telephone company, fire department, and electrical company that a child with special needs lives in your home. They will place you on a priority service list in case of a power outage;
- frequently review the CPR instructions listed in Appendix A;

MEDICATIONS, DOSAGES, AND SPECIAL INSTRUCTIONS

Make several copies of this list for future use and to give to caregivers.

Medication:
How much?
How often?
Possible side effects:

Medication:
How much?
How often?
Possible side effects:

Medication:
How much?
How often?
Possible side effects:

Note: 5 cc = 1 teaspoon; 30 cc = 1 ounce

Dosages less than 1 teaspoon should *always* be measured with a syringe. For 1 teaspoon and over, use a true measuring teaspoon. Never use a silverware teaspoon.

- place a CPR instruction poster in an easy-to-see location in your home (ask your pediatrician for one); and
- know your options if you need to leave siblings unexpectedly.

Write down important emergency information for your child's caregivers and review your emergency plan with anyone who watches your baby.

Accept the Help of Others

Once your baby is home, family and friends will undoubtedly ask how they can help. It is probably hard for you to think about anything other than caring for your baby and family. If you have difficulty accepting a helping hand, ask a friend or relative to act as a liaison and provide that person with ideas for helping you. When friends ask what they can do, refer them to your contact person. Here are some ways friends can help:

- Prepare a meal and deliver it. A meal for the freezer would be especially helpful.
- Organize a week's or month's worth of food preparation and delivery among friends, family, and organizations.
- Take your other children on a morning or afternoon outing.
- Organize a telephone tree for announcing baby's progress.
- Spend one morning cleaning, or doing laundry or lawn work.
- Do some grocery shopping or run some errands.

Do not try to "do it all" once your baby is home. By accepting the help of others, you will have more time and energy to spend with your new family.

CHAPTER THREE

Bringing the NICU Home with You

LEARNING THAT YOUR child is coming home attached to medical equipment can be disheartening and frightening, to say the least. You have looked forward to the day your child will become entirely yours, only to discover that the NICU is coming home, too. You have numerous questions and many worries.

The hospital and medical equipment professionals should thoroughly educate you about the technical aspects of your child's medical equipment. They should also teach you how to care for your technology-dependent child and what to do in case of an emergency. This chapter is a review of these basics.

I didn't just leave the hospital with a baby. I left the hospital with a monitor, a portable oxygen tank, and a heart full of fear. Full-term parents must learn how to change a diaper, but preemie parents have to become healthcare providers and technicians.

—ROBIN, MOTHER OF 30-WEEKER TREVOR

WHEN YOUR PREEMIE NEEDS A HOME MONITOR

A CARDIORESPIRATORY MONITOR, often referred to as a home monitor, monitors your baby's apnea and/or bradycardia episodes. These are two terms with which you are probably already familiar. *Apnea* is a pause in breathing that lasts twenty seconds or more and occurs most often during sleep. Apnea is sometimes accompanied by changes in skin color

APNEA VERSUS PERIODIC BREATHING

Apnea is not the same as periodic breathing. *Periodic breathing* is a pattern of breathing: An infant breathes normally for about five to ten seconds, then stops breathing for five to ten seconds. A "gasp" may be heard after each five- to ten-second pause. This repetitive breathing pattern is normal for many preterm and full-term infants as long as it occurs for a small percentage of time during sleep and is not accompanied by color or muscle tone changes.

APNEA VERSUS SHALLOW BREATHING

If your child has shallow breathing alone or within his periodic breathing pattern, the monitor alarm may sound. The monitor is not able to detect shallow breathing and it "thinks" your baby is not breathing. As your preemie grows, his breathing will get deeper and breathing patterns will become more regular.

and/or muscle tone. (Pauses in breathing lasting less than twenty seconds in duration can be accompanied by these changes as well.)

Apnea in a premature infant is typically caused by an immature nervous system, and it usually resolves once the baby reaches his full-term due date. Other problems, including infection, low blood sugar, seizures, change in body temperature, anemia, neurological problems, upper airway congestion, gastroesophageal reflux, and lack of oxygen, can also cause apnea.

Apnea is often treated with medications that stimulate the area of the brain that controls breathing. Side effects are rare, but can include mild restlessness, vomiting, and an increased heart rate.

Bradycardia occurs when a baby's heart rate slows down below what is normal for his age (see chart 3-1). Occasional bradycardia is most often due to apnea. Other causes of bradycardia include infection, anemia, seizures, gastroesophageal reflux, and upper airway congestion.

The monitor you take home records your baby's heart rate and respiratory rate. If his heart rate slows below a preset level during bradycardia, the alarm will sound. The alarm also sounds if your baby stops breathing for more than fifteen to twenty seconds (apnea).

Each NICU has its own criteria for discharging a baby on a home monitor. Make sure you understand why your baby is on a monitor. The most common reasons include:

- your baby's apnea did not resolve by the time of hospital discharge, but all serious causes of apnea and bradycardia have been ruled out;
- your baby experienced one or more life-threatening apnea episodes requiring vigorous stimulation or resuscitation during hospitalization;
- your baby exhibited skin color change within five to seven days before discharge;
- your baby has a tracheostomy (a surgical opening in the windpipe);
- your baby has bronchopulmonary dysplasia (chronic lung disease) and is on home oxygen (in selected instances only); and/or
- your baby has a sibling who died from Sudden Infant Death Syndrome (SIDS).

Your hospital may also discharge your baby on a monitor if you are unusually fearful of bringing your baby home because of extreme complications during his NICU stay.

Chart 3-1: Bradycardia in infancy

When your baby's heart rate slows down below what is normal for his age, it is called bradycardia. Your home monitor will be preset according to what is considered normal for your child. If your baby's heart rate falls below that level, the alarm will sound. The chart below shows normal heartbeats per minute by age; anything below that number indicates bradycardia.

Age	Bradycardia (beats/minute)
Birth	Less than 100
1–3 months corrected age	Less than 80
3–6 months corrected age	Less than 70
6–12 months corrected age	Less than 60
1–2 years corrected age	Less than 60

(Adapted with permission from *Primary Care for the Preterm Infant,* Judy C. Bernbaum, M.D., and Marsha Hoffman-Williamson, Ph.D., St. Louis, Mo.: Mosby-Year Book, Inc., 1991, p. 181.)

When my son P.J. was born during my twenty-sixth week of pregnancy, I never dreamed that I would be taking him home from the NICU seventy-six days later. His primary care nurse told me that because he had experienced apnea and bradycardia spells ("a's and b's") in the hospital, he would be going home on a monitor.

I felt relieved to hear this, probably because I was unsure about my ability to care for this four-pound baby. After my husband and I took the infant CPR course, we were given monitor instructions two hours before P.J.'s discharge. I felt fairly confident about its operation; that is, until I arrived home.

Frazzled by my new baby, I wondered how I would ever remember all the home monitor instructions. I prayed that I would never hear that horrible, obnoxious alarm that told me my son was in trouble.

Well, that alarm rang exactly four days after P.J.'s homecoming. I recall the panic I felt when I rushed to see which light was flashing while I counted the "beeps." Everything was okay that time. I soon became used to hearing the alarms and recording the a's and b's. I also learned to look at my baby during the alarms, instead of at the machine.

There were two occasions, both in the middle of the night, when P.J. became severely apneic and required vigorous physical stimulation to restart his breathing. The fear I felt was indescribable. I have no doubt that the apnea monitor saved his life both times.

As with most stressful events, keeping a sense of humor throughout this ordeal was vital for my sanity. One day I left P.J. home with his dad so I could do some grocery shopping. While in the store, the paging alarm sounded, a noise identical to that of the monitor's alarm. I raced to my shopping cart to "save" my baby, when I realized he was at home. I laughed at my conditioned response.

About a month after P.J.'s last apnea spell and with encouragement from our doctor, I started to wean myself off the machine. I gradually stopped using it during naptimes and eventually during the nights. Shortly thereafter, I returned the monitor and felt confident that my son had reached another milestone.

I know that surviving the monitor experience has made me a stronger person. When I look back, I remember the worry, fear, and stress I dealt with daily. But when I look at my active, adorable, and devilish two-year-old, I'm thankful that this machine was available. Without it, P.J. wouldn't be sharing his life with us today.

—KATHY, MOTHER OF 26-WEEKER P.J.

(Originally appeared in *Intensive Caring Unlimited,* Vol. 10, No. 4, Summer 1992.)

CHOOSING A HOME MONITOR AND SUPPLIER

Monitoring equipment varies in appearance and function. Some equipment only monitor the heart rate; others monitor both the heart rate and the respiratory rate. Most

IN RESPONSE TO AN APNEA ALARM

1. Observe and feel your baby for respiratory movement. If respiratory movement is noted, proceed to 2a. If no respiratory movement is detected, proceed to 2b.

2a. If respiratory movement is felt, this indicates that your baby is breathing, but breathing may be too shallow for the monitor to note the movement. Shallow breathing is okay if your baby looks normal otherwise (he has good color and muscle tone).

2b. If respiratory movement is *not* noted, or your baby has poor color (pale, gray, or blue), attempt to stimulate breathing by calling loudly and then touching your baby, starting with a gentle touch and proceeding to a vigorous touch if necessary. *Never shake your baby!* Your preemie does not have good head control, and vigorous shaking could cause head injury and even death. If there is no response, proceed with mouth-to-mouth resuscitation and CPR if necessary.

(Adapted with permission from *Home Care for the High-Risk Infant,* 2nd ed., by Elizabeth Ahmann, "Home Care of the Infant on a Cardiorespiratory Monitor," revised by Maggie Farrar-Simpson, R.N., M.S.N., C.P.N.P., p. 197. Copyright © 1996 Aspen Publishers, Inc.)

monitors record rates for the doctor to review later, but some do not. All monitors are equipped with alarm lights, an audible alarm, and a reset button. Alarm limits, telling the monitor when to sound, are prescribed by your physician and programmed by the leasing company.

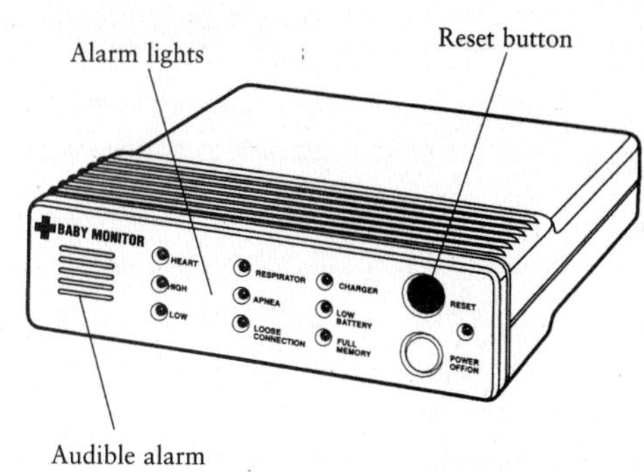

3-1: A standard home monitor

Some home monitors are similar to the type used in hospitals. Two or three sticky leads with wires running to the monitor are attached to the infant's chest. The sticky leads are changed about every three to seven days, or when they no longer adhere to the skin. Another type of monitor lead has a soft, sponge-like two- to three-inch strap that wraps around the infant's chest and back and is secured with Velcro. Two hard plastic leads under the strap monitor the heart and respirations. The leads do not need changing, but require daily washing; the strap needs occasional handwashing. Consult your physician regarding other types of monitoring equipment that may be available.

When choosing a medical supply company for your monitor, consult your health insurance company. If you have a choice of suppliers, look for one that is familiar with premature infants, is willing to take the time to educate you, and is available twenty-four hours a day.

When your home monitor is delivered, be sure to write down the following information, and make sure it coincides with your doctor's orders:

Apnea time delay:____________________________

Bradycardia setting:____________________________

Monitor type:____________________________

Model number:____________________________

Monitor company name:____________________________

Monitor company phone number:____________________________

Emergency number:____________________________

■ ■ ■

IN RESPONSE TO A BRADYCARDIA ALARM

If a bradycardia alarm sounds, stimulating your preemie is usually sufficient. However, if the alarm continues, or your baby has poor color, take the following steps:

1. Gently stimulate your infant by calling loudly and then touching your baby, starting with a gentle touch and proceeding to a vigorous touch if necessary. *Never shake your baby!* Your preemie does not have good head control, and vigorous shaking could cause head injury and even death.
2. Make sure your baby's airway is clear by sweeping his mouth for objects with your index finger and suctioning the airway.
3. Increase the oxygen flow to one to two liters per minute if your baby is on home oxygen.
4. Increase stimulation to vigorous if needed, but *do not shake your baby.*
5. If there is no response, proceed with mouth-to-mouth resuscitation and CPR if necessary.

(Adapted from *Home Care for the High-Risk Infant,* 2nd ed., by Elizabeth Ahmann, "Home Care of the Infant on a Cardiorespiratory Monitor," revised by Maggie Farrar-Simpson, R.N., M.S.N., C.P.N.P., p. 197. Copyright © 1996 by Aspen Publishers, Inc.)

RESPONDING TO ALARMS

Your baby may be on a monitor all the time (except during baths), or only when he is sleeping. When your baby is on a monitor, you need to respond to any alarms within ten seconds.

FALSE ALARMS

If your baby's monitor constantly alarms and you believe they are inaccurate reflections of what is happening with your baby, they are most likely false alarms. These may be caused by faulty equipment, or the heart rate alarm is set to go off at a higher rate than is necessary. First, check the placement of leads or straps and the connection of the wires. Make sure the electrical connection is secure. If you still cannot figure out the cause of the false alarms, consult your home monitor handbook or call the equipment company.

■ ■ ■

Chart 3-2: Event chart for infant monitoring

Fill out this chart after each event.

PARENT DIARY											COMMENTS
Date:											
Time A.M. or P.M.:											
Time it took to get to infant:											
ABOUT THE BABY											
Color (pink, pale, gray, dusky, blue):											
Muscle tone (limp, floppy, stiff, or seizure-like activity):											
Asleep:											
How long has baby been asleep?											
Awake:											
Feeding:											
Breathing:											
Not breathing:											
Could not tell:											
ALARM CONDITION											
Loose lead/loose connection:											
Apnea:											
Heart rate alarm high:											
Heart rate alarm low:											
Full memory:											
Battery low or power failure:											
WHAT ACTION WAS NECESSARY?											
Lead or electrode correction:											
Nothing, baby was O.K.:											
Gentle stimulation:											
Moderate stimulation:											
Vigorous stimulation:											
CPR:											
Observer's initials:											

Discontinuing the Monitor

If your child has apnea and/or bradycardia caused by prematurity and no other underlying causes, he will be on a home monitor until you and your doctor are confident that your baby has outgrown the apnea and/or bradycardia. This can take a few weeks or many months. As your baby grows, the respiratory centers in his brain will develop and mature to better regulate his breathing. If the cause of apnea is another problem, such as reflux or seizures, these problems need controlling or eliminating before the apnea and/or bradycardia will stop.

Each physician has his own criteria for removing a home monitor. Ask your doctor for his. Some believe an infant should not have an apnea and/or bradycardia episode for a designated number of weeks before the monitor is removed. Others wait until the parents feel comfortable taking the child off (within a reasonable period of time). Many physicians wait until a child no longer needs apnea and/or bradycardia medication, or has completed his first three baby shots.

PARENT TIPS:
Living with a Home Monitor

Parents who have survived the home-monitor experience suggest these ways to cope:

- Ask for a home healthcare nurse to visit soon after homecoming. The nurse will make sure you understand everything about your baby's monitor and what to do when the alarm sounds.
- Place the monitor in a location where the alarm light can be seen easily and the alarm sound cannot be muffled.
- Do not let your baby sleep in bed with you. This is an unsafe practice, and the monitor might interpret your movements as your baby's breathing.
- Place the monitor at least one foot away from other sources of interference, such as televisions, baby room monitors, air conditioners, and cordless telephones.
- At night, keep a lamp or flashlight near your baby's crib so you can quickly assess his color.
- Keep children and pets away from the monitor to avoid disconnecting by accident.
- Be sure your outdoor house or apartment number can be seen clearly by emergency personnel.
- Create a nighttime plan for responding to alarms (who will respond at what times).
- Order extra supplies, such as leads or straps, so they are readily available when you need them.
- If your child is going to be on a monitor for several months, ask your health

insurance company if it would be cheaper to buy the monitor, rather than renting.

- Rinse the monitor's strap in fabric softener after washing to decrease static electricity.
- Review CPR techniques and your emergency plan often, and keep emergeny telephone numbers near the monitor.

WHEN YOUR PREEMIE NEEDS SUPPLEMENTAL OXYGEN

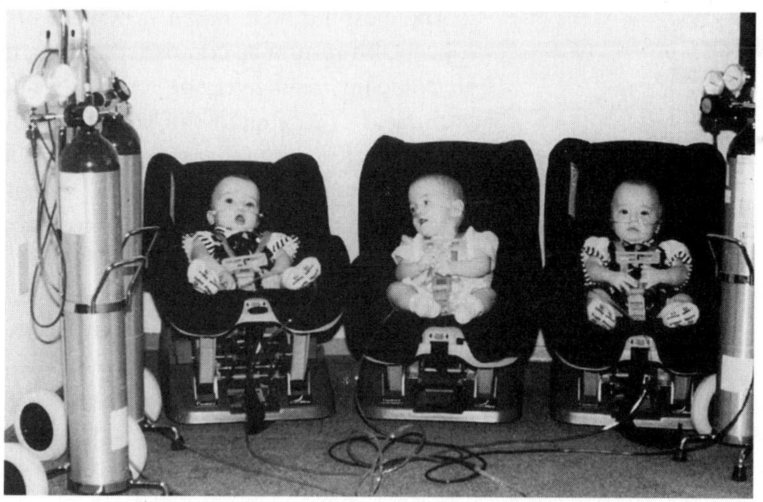

An outing with two brothers and a sister—all on oxygen!

AS PRETERM INFANTS are being saved earlier and earlier, it is not uncommon for some preemies to be discharged on oxygen. If your discharged baby's lungs are still healing and unable to transport an adequate amount of oxygen to his body, he will need supplemental oxygen. His lungs need to heal and develop new, healthy lung tissue before he can breathe on his own.

Estimating how long your child will need supplemental oxygen is difficult: It may be several weeks or many months. Some preemies, especially those who live at high altitudes and those with severe lung disease, may require extra oxygen for longer. Generally, the more severe the lung disease that was experienced in the NICU, the longer a child will need added oxygen.

It is possible that your child may start weaning from supplemental oxygen, then become sick and require oxygen for a longer time than anticipated. Your child will benefit from staying healthy and eating well. Babies on oxygen require more calories: Make sure his caloric intake is adequate for optimal growth, and give him lots of love and support.

As a NICU nurse, I sent many preemies home on supplemental oxygen. I had no idea what life with a child on oxygen was really like until I lived through it myself.

Going out was the hardest part. It was difficult trying to manage all the normal baby supplies along with the portable oxygen tank. I hated the stares from strangers. I just wanted my daughter to be "normal," and for people to stare at her because she was beautiful, not because of the tube on her face.

—DIANNE, MOTHER OF 26-WEEKER MACKENZIE

HOME OXYGEN EQUIPMENT

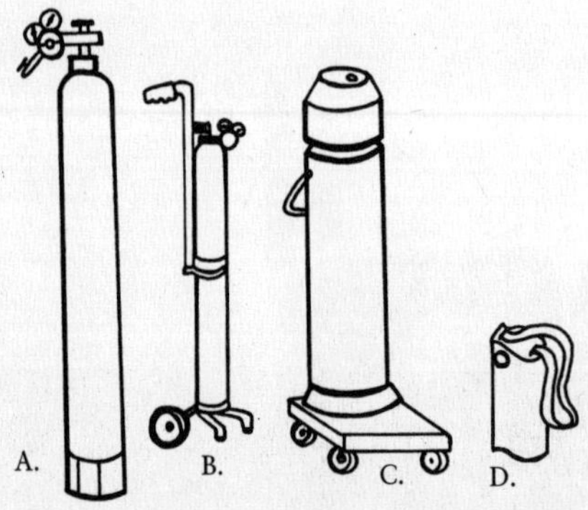

3-3: A. Large cylinder of compressed oxygen
B. Small portable compressed oxygen tank
C. Large liquid oxygen tank
D. Small portable liquid oxygen tank

The hospital will make arrangements with you, your health insurance company, and the medical supply company for delivery of your baby's home oxygen equipment. You should call your insurance company in advance to verify what they will and will not cover.

The oxygen should be delivered to your home one or two days prior to discharge. A medical supply company will provide a large tank (H- or K-tank) to be used at home and a few portable tanks (E- or D-tanks) for use outside the home. Do not forget to take a portable tank to the hospital on homecoming day!

If you know your baby will need oxygen for more than a few weeks, try to set up a regular (usually weekly) delivery date for a new supply of oxygen. If you do not have a set delivery date, give the supply company at least twenty-four hours' notice for refilling the tank. Have an extra portable tank available in case you accidentally run out of oxygen, or the oxygen cannot be delivered due to weather or an emergency. Always store the portable tanks on their sides—they can explode if they fall.

Place the large tank in a central area of your home, allowing for easy movement of the tubing. The delivery person may prefer putting the heavy tank on the main floor, but you can ask for it to be put upstairs if you wish. Do not be afraid to test the tubing's length while the delivery person waits. Ask for extensions and extra adapters that hook the tubing together and to the tank, and make sure you know how to read the gauge that shows the level of the oxygen. The tubing should not be longer than fifty feet or the oxygen flow will be diminished.

You will most likely be given concentrated oxygen. Older preemies who need a greater amount of oxygen often use liquefied oxygen. Although expensive, liquefied oxygen lasts longer. The portable liquid oxygen tank is filled from a main tank in the home.

■ ■ ■

Managing the Equipment

Oxygen tubing and humidifier

Changing the oxygen tubing and cleaning the humidifier bottles are essential for preventing bacteria and fungi from growing and causing illness to your child. The long oxygen tubing should be changed once a month. The shorter tubing with the cannula attached should be changed weekly. *Never wash and reuse the tubing.*

Most doctors order the oxygen to be humidified, especially in dry climates. Keep the amount of distilled water in the humidifier bottle close to the indicator line. You should have an extra humidifier bottle to use during cleaning and in case of breakage.

Ask your medical supply company how often you should clean the humidifier bottle. Cleaning is typically recommended every two days by washing the bottle in hot soapy water, then soaking it in a one-part vinegar and one-part water solution for thirty minutes. Your company may recommend running the bottle through the dishwasher. Always wash your hands before replacing the bottle.

The nasal cannula

Your baby's nasal cannula will need frequent retaping and weekly changing. If your baby has a cold and his cannula prongs get plugged with mucus, the cannula may need more frequent changing. Before discharge, a respiratory therapist or nurse will show you how to change and secure the cannula. He may recommend a brand of tape for securing. Some parents use paper tape or hospital tape; others prefer using Op-site or Tegaderm, two brands of special tape that are thin and durable.

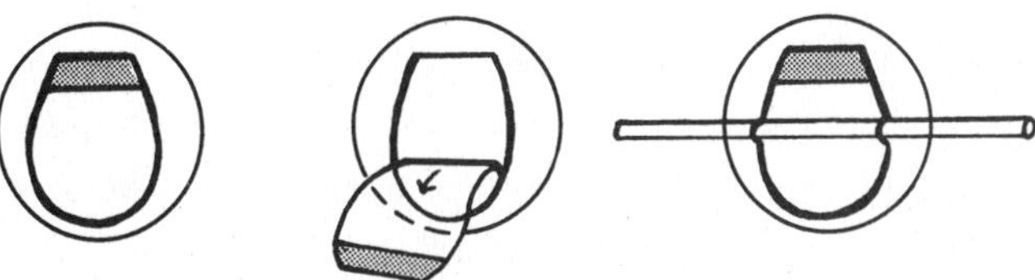

While changing the oxygen tubing and using Tendergrips, simply pull back the clear flap (leaving the facial tab intact) and replace the flap over the cannula.

An attachment called Tendergrips and a thick tape-like material called Duoderm can stay on your baby's cheeks, eliminating having to tape directly onto the skin. Any special equipment should be provided by your medical supply company.

To change your preemie's nasal cannula:

1. Wash your hands.
2. Snugly wrap your baby in a blanket, so he cannot grab the cannula or your hands.
3. Using tape remover liquid, such as Detachol (supplied by your oxygen provider or pharmacy), gently remove the old tape.

4. With the cannula still in your baby's nostrils, wash and dry your baby's face.
5. Now quickly remove the old cannula, replace it with the new one, and attach it to the long tubing.
6. Hook the cannula up and over your baby's ears. This will keep the tubing in place for taping.
7. If your baby has become upset during this process, try to calm him by using a pacifier or by softly singing to him. He needs to remain still for the tape placement. Place the tape or Op-site over the cannula as close to your baby's skin as possible. Any air that gets between the tube and your baby's skin will cause the tape to loosen. Remember to slightly shift the tape's placement each time you retape, allowing your baby's sensitive skin to heal.
8. Gently tighten the tubing so that it is snug around the back of your baby's head or neck.
9. Run the tubing down the back of your child's shirt or outfit and down the leg, if possible, to help prevent twisting or wrapping.
10. Now hold and snuggle your baby!

PARENT TIPS:

Coping with Supplemental Oxygen

The following are suggestions for handling supplemental oxygen and its equipment:

- Do not forget to ask the supply company how long each oxygen tank (the main one and any portable ones) should last—and write it down.
- When tanks are not used for long periods of time, they can leak oxygen. The level of oxygen may be much lower than you expected when you begin using it.
- Post "No Smoking" and "Oxygen in Use" signs in windows and on your door so visitors cannot miss them.
- Always keep the oxygen tank and tubing away from fire and heat.
- A hissing noise means the tank is leaking.
- There are several different sizes of cannulas: an infant size, a pediatric size, and an in-between size. Your child may outgrow a size if he requires oxygen for a long time.
- When traveling by air, airlines will insist you use their oxygen. Call the airlines in advance to alert them of your needs. They may require a doctor's prescription. You must leave the portable tank at the airport and have the supply company pick it up. Do not forget to arrange for oxygen at your destination; ask your oxygen supplier to recommend a company.
- If you plan to travel a long distance by car, find out where you can get oxygen along the way and at your final destination.
- Alert your local fire department that you have oxygen in your home.

WHEN YOUR PREEMIE NEEDS A GAVAGE TUBE

IN A FEW rare cases, a premature infant is sent home from the hospital on gavage feedings, also called tube feedings. There are two types of gavage feeding tubes: a tube through the nose called nasogastic (NG), and a tube through the mouth called orogastric (OG). If your infant is sent home on NG or OG feedings, you should receive written and verbal instructions for the management and care of a feeding tube, prior to discharge. You should also place the gavage tube yourself and do an actual feeding before homecoming. Make sure you know about how many weeks or months you should expect to give tube feedings, when you should decrease the number of tube feedings, and whether your pediatrician is comfortable overseeing your questions and concerns (you may need to find a specialist).

Even though your baby has a feeding tube, try to give "normal" feedings often. Your child should bottle- or breast-feed a few times each day. These feedings are important for developing and maintaining normal feeding skills, and they will help your milk supply if you are pumping. Giving your baby a pacifier during gavage feedings can help your baby relate sucking with the feeling of a full stomach.

MANAGING A GAVAGE TUBE

The following is a step-by-step refresher for inserting a gavage tube and giving intermittent and continuous tube feedings:

1. Collect all the supplies you will need: the tubing, syringe with a plunger, stethoscope, formula or breastmilk, any medications, and tape. The hospital should supply you with one or two sets of tubing and syringes. You can get more from a medical supply company.

   If your baby is on continuous feedings, you will need to use a special tubing that is soft and more pliable than the intermittent feeding tubing. Ask the hospital or your doctor to recommend a size and type of syringe and tubing. You may also need a special feeding pump for feedings longer than thirty minutes, which can be provided by a medical supply company.
2. Place your baby upright in an infant seat (raised at least 30 degrees). Wrap him snugly so that his arms are secured under a blanket and he cannot grab the tubing.
3. To measure how far to insert the tubing for a nasogastric (through the nose) feeding, hold the end of the tubing and stretch it from the tip of your baby's nose to the earlobe and back to the

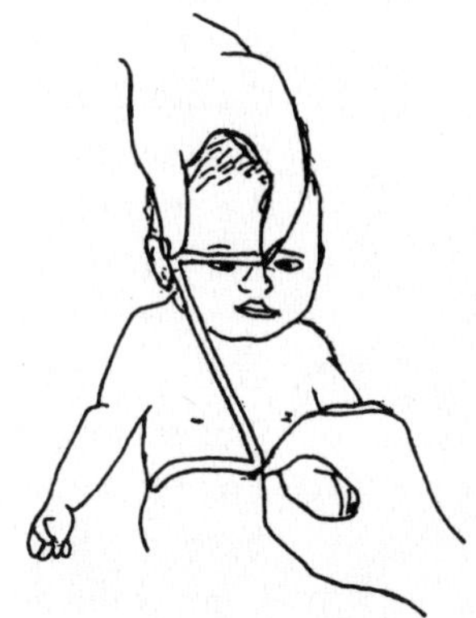

Measuring a nasogastric tubing

bottom of the sternum (the area between the ribs where the chest meets the abdomen). To measure for an orogastric (through the mouth) feeding, measure the same way as a nasogastric except start at the mouth. Mark the length of the tubing with a small piece of tape.

4. Prepare the tape that will hold the tubing in place.
5. If the tube is going through the nose, place a small amount of water-soluble lubricant (Surgilube) on the tip of the NG tubing. Gently insert the tubing into the nose or mouth to the premeasured point. If your baby gags, continue to pass the tubing while gently patting him on the chest to calm him. Use a small piece of tape to hold the tubing in place.

   For continuous feedings, place the tubing in the nose and tape it on the cheek with a sturdy tape. Change the tubing weekly (or as recommended by your doctor) and alternate nostrils to prevent skin breakdown.
6. Attach the syringe (with the plunger) to the tubing. Pull back on the syringe to see if anything is left in the stomach from the previous feeding. If your infant has a large amount of formula or breastmilk left in the stomach, record the amount to tell your doctor. Push the formula or breastmilk back into the stomach (unless your pediatrician has advised you otherwise).
7. Before removing the syringe, pinch the tubing together to prevent any leftover formula or breastmilk from flowing in or out. Now remove the syringe from the tubing. Pull the plunger back so that a few cc's of air enters the syringe, then put the syringe back onto the tubing.
8. With a stethoscope, listen to the left side of your baby's stomach as you push the air in the syringe into the stomach. If you hear air pushing into the stomach, your placement is correct. If you do not hear air, pull back slightly on the tubing and listen again. You may need to reinsert the tubing if you are unable to hear the air insertion a second time. If your baby is on continuous feedings via a pump, you should check every twelve hours to see if the tubing is still in its correct place.

   Some doctors recommend using the pH method to test for proper placement of a tube. After you have placed the tubing in the stomach, draw back some of the fluid into the syringe. Remove the syringe (while pinching the tubing together to prevent aspiration) and place a small amount of the contents from the syringe onto the pH paper. If the pH shows a measurement between zero and six, then you are in the stomach. If the pH is greater than six, you should reinsert the tubing.
9. Once you are sure the feeding tube is in the stomach, remove the syringe. Take the plunger out, then place the syringe back onto the tubing.
10. Pour formula or breastmilk into the syringe (along with any medications your baby needs). Let the formula or breastmilk flow in slowly by gravity. You can control the flow by raising or lowering the syringe. If your baby gags, lower the syringe and let the flow stop, or let it go back into the syringe until your baby

stops gagging. If your infant is given his feedings via a pump, connect the pump per your doctor's and the medical supply company's direction.

11. If you can manage it, give your baby a pacifier during the feeding.
12. When the feeding is finished, clear the tubing of the last few cc's of formula or breastmilk by gently pushing a few cc's of air into the syringe.
13. Before removing the tubing, pinch it together to prevent the formula or breastmilk from flowing in or out of the tubing as you remove it from the nose or mouth. Many parents like to leave the tubing in place from one feeding to another, rather than replacing it before each feeding. Although it may interfere somewhat with oral feedings, it avoids the added trauma of frequent insertions.
14. Now hold and snuggle your baby!

WHEN YOUR PREEMIE NEEDS A TRACHEOSTOMY

A TRACHEOSTOMY IS a surgical opening in the windpipe (trachea). Instead of through his mouth or nose, your child breathes through a small, pliable plastic tube. A tracheostomy (or "trach") may be temporary or permanent, depending on the reason for placement.

A trach is necessary in only a small percentage of children born prematurely. Those preemies who required extended mechanical ventilation that caused prolonged irritation from the ventilator tube are more at risk. The most common reasons for a trach include:

- an obstruction (blockage) in the upper airway prevents air from getting to the lungs. This often happens when a soft area of tissue in the larynx or trachea collapses and obstructs the movement of air during breathing (laryngomalacia or tracheomalacia), or when the upper trachea narrows (subglottic stenosis);
- to provide continued mechanical ventilation at home; and/or
- to allow for suctioning of excess secretions (mucus) that cannot be swallowed, thus preventing possible aspiration into the lungs.

When your child comes home on a trach, you will need to rent or purchase a suction machine to keep your child's trach clear of secretions. Your child may or may not need supplemental oxygen.

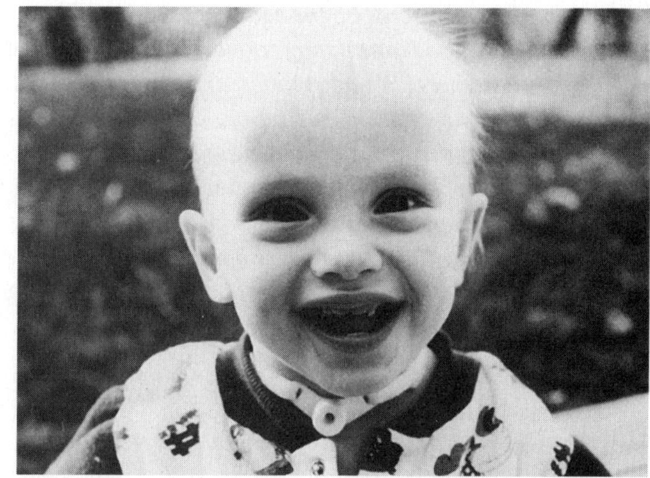

Fifteen-month-old Aaron (a former 26-weeker) doesn't let his trach get in the way of his exploring and learning.

We will never forget the day we went into the hospital and found Aaron in respiratory distress. His little eyes were open wide with fear. As he gasped for breath he seemed to plead with us for help. We felt so helpless as we watched him struggle to breathe. We could hear a tiny squeak coming from him with every breath he took. He was immediately intubated.

It was difficult to remain calm as we listened to the rhythmic sounds of the ventilator breathing for Aaron at the same time the neonatologist talked. Aaron had subglottic stenosis (a narrowing of his airway). The doctor recommended a tracheostomy. The implications of this were enormous. We could not believe they were going to cut our baby's throat. He was so tiny—only four pounds—and so fragile. We felt like we had been punched in the stomach.

Making a decision like this would be difficult under normal circumstances, but we were making it after weeks of little sleep and constant worry. We were forced to depend on the competence and integrity of the medical team. We were putting the life of our tiny precious son in the hands of strangers.

The most difficult part was kissing Aaron good-bye before sending him into the operating room. Part of us wanted to stop the whole thing and just hold him and tell him everything would be all right. Our more rational side handed him to the surgeon and watched tearfully as he was escorted down the hall.

Seeing Aaron for the first time after his surgery brought both relief and trepidation. He looked so much more comfortable: He was not struggling to breathe and he was peaceful. Yet, he had this foreign tube sticking from his throat and many tubes attached to his small body. We wondered, What would be the final outcome? Would he be able to talk? What would our lives be like as we cared for this child? Many of these questions could not be readily answered.

The day before Aaron came home from the hospital, the medical supply company delivered all the equipment we would need to care for him at home. Before we knew it, our living room was full of medical stuff—a suction machine, monitors, oxygen tanks, tubes, and wires. It was all a bit overwhelming.

Once Aaron was home, one of the scariest jobs was our first trach tube change without the backup of the hospital personnel. We were also afraid that his trach tube would become blocked or that a curious child (even Aaron himself) would pull out the tube.

Over time, trach care has become so routine that we often don't think twice about it. To Aaron, the tracheostomy is just another part of him, like his eyes, ears, nose, and belly button. We try to treat Aaron as a typical kid, but with a few added precautions.

—Richard and Cynthia, parents of 26-weeker Aaron, twin to Eric

■ ■ ■

TRACH SAFETY

You and your child's caregivers should review CPR techniques and your family's emergency plan often. Always keep a new trach and suctioning equipment nearby. To prevent an emergency:

- Do not let your child play with small or fuzzy toys (the fuzz could get into the trach). Do not let your child eat small finger foods, such as dry cereal, that might get into the trach and obstruct breathing.
- Avoid smoke, aerosol sprays, dust, lint, chalk, jewelry, sandboxes, animal hair, or using powders around your child. These can get inside the trach and impair breathing.
- During baths, constantly supervise so that water does not get into the trach. Children with trachs should not shower or go swimming.
- Avoid any clothing that may block the trach tube. Use loose cotton bibs.
- Avoid going outside on windy and cold days. The wind and cold can make it difficult for your child with a trach to breathe.

If you need to administer CPR on your child with a trach, remember:

- give puffs of air through the trach;
- make sure the trach is not obstructed by mucus or a foreign object;
- change the trach if it is plugged (Sometimes you cannot see a mucous plug. If no improvement is noted, change the trach); and
- if air leaks from the nose or mouth while giving breaths through the trach, pinch them shut.

Managing a Trach

Home care of a trach is very involved. You will need relief and support from others. Ask family or friends to attend the hospital's education classes with you. Insist on home nursing, at least until you are settled and at ease with your child's care. Do not bring your baby home unless you are comfortable taking care of his needs. The following sections discuss the special needs of your child with a trach.

Changing the trach

Trach tubes are typically changed once a week. Because changing a trach can cause your child to gag and possibly vomit, the best time to do the procedure is right before mealtime or two hours after a meal to prevent aspiration. Always have an assistant when you change the trach, and follow this procedure:

1. Wash your hands. Have the suction machine ready.
2. Cut the new trach ties to the appropriate length, angling them at the ends so they can be easily threaded through the holes.
3. Be sure to keep the new trach tube sterile by leaving it in the package until needed. (Most trach tubes are disposable.) Open the trach tube package and hold the tube

by the end that will remain outside of the trach. Moisten the end of the trach tube with a water-soluble lubricant, such as Surgilube available through your medical supply company. *Do not use Vaseline, as it could cause blockage.* Be sure the obturator (the guide inside the trach tube) is in the new tube. Set the tube back into the package, keeping it sterile, and place it within reaching distance.

4. Wrap your baby in a blanket, securing his arms so he cannot grab the equipment or knock anything over.
5. Holding onto the trach tube, cut the old ties. Never let go until the switch is complete. If you let go, your child can cough it out.
6. With one hand, gently pull the old trach tube out by following the angle of the tube. With the other hand, quickly and gently insert the new trach tube, again following the angle of the tube. *Never force the trach tube.* Immediately remove the obturator, while continuing to hold the tube.
7. Thread the new ties and knot them on one side. Leave enough room so that you can put one finger between your child's neck and the ties.
8. This procedure will cause your child to cough. If necessary, suction with a bulb syringe or suction machine (see steps under "Suctioning" on next page). Keep the suctioning brief, and give your child time to breathe in between suctioning.

You will also need to change the trach ties when they become soiled. When the ties are off, wash around the neck and check the skin for breakdown. If a skin rash develops under the ties or around the trach tube, consult your doctor. Changing trach tube ties should be done with two people.

WARNING SIGNS

Call your doctor immediately if there is:

- bleeding around the trach or with suctioning;
- a foul odor;
- green or yellow drainage around the trach, or with suctioning; and/or
- red and tender skin around the trach.

Call your doctor immediately if your child:

- has a fever;
- is unusually tired or listless;
- has a change in skin color from pink to a pale or bluish color;
- has difficulty breathing;
- is restless; and/or
- is not eating or drinking well.

Suctioning

If coughing does not clear secretions in the tubing, suctioning will be necessary to ensure easier breathing. Because a child with a trach has a high risk of infection, suctioning must be done with care. Use a sterile bulb syringe (boil for twenty minutes daily and keep in a clean area). If you are unable to clear enough mucus with a bulb syringe, use a suction machine and follow this procedure:

1. Wash your hands.
2. Prepare equipment: open suction setup; turn on the machine; have a container with sterile normal saline ready; and connect the catheter to the suction tubing on machine. (A suction catheter may be used more than once if the tip is kept clean inside the package.) Have supplemental oxygen readily available.
3. Put on gloves.
4. Moisten the catheter tip with saline and make sure suction is working.
5. Place 0.5 to 1 cc of saline into the trach tube.
6. Gently insert the suction catheter, keeping your thumb off the opening, for the length of the trach only. (This should be measured in advance and written on a card you keep by the suction machine.) *Be careful: If you suction too deeply, you can damage the trachea.*
7. Put your thumb over the opening in the suction catheter that creates the suction. Using a circular motion, begin to gently suction, then quickly remove the suction catheter.
8. Suction for only five seconds or less. Try holding your breath as you begin to suction. You can judge how long is too long by how you feel. Stop suctioning if your child becomes pale, gray, or dusky, or looks panicked.
9. Run saline through the catheter and repeat until the trach is clear.

Let your child rest at least thirty to sixty seconds between suctionings. If your child needed extra oxygen during the procedure, do not forget to turn the oxygen back down when you are finished.

Humidification

Our nose and mouth moistens, or humidifies, the air we breathe. The air your child with a trach breathes bypasses the nose and mouth and requires artificial humidification. Moisture is administered by a trach collar (or mask) that hangs loosely around the front of the neck and over the trach tube. The collar connects to a tubing that is attached to an air compressor and a bottle of distilled water.

Keeping the tubing free of water to prevent water backup and possible aspiration is important. The trach collar works well at night and before your child is mobile. Once your child crawls, he can use an artificial nose. This device fits over the opening of the trach and humidifies the air.

Skin care

The area around the trach must stay clean and dry to prevent skin breakdown and infection. Wash the skin once a day with either mild soap and water or half-strength hydrogen peroxide (mixed with water), as directed by your doctor. Use Q-Tips or a clean washcloth, then dry thoroughly.

When there is breakdown of the skin, wash areas more often. If there is significant breakdown or an infection, your doctor may recommend placing gauze over the area. Unless prescribed by your doctor, lotions and ointments should not be used. Some parents use stoma adhesive (a thick, pliable, tape-like material) to protect the skin when breakdown becomes a concern.

Eating and speech concerns

The ability to speak depends on how much air releases around the trach and up through the vocal cords. Some children use a tracheostomy speaking valve for speech. Ask your doctor and speech therapist for help in teaching your child to speak.

Most children with trachs can eat normally, but some will have swallowing problems. If you suspect your child has a problem swallowing, consult your child's doctor or a pediatric speech pathologist.

WHEN YOUR PREEMIE NEEDS A VENTILATOR

IN A FEW cases, a child will be discharged on a ventilator. If your health team decides your child needs long-term ventilation, several requirements need to be met before discharge. Typical criteria include:

- a tracheostomy is in place and healed;
- your child weighs at least seven pounds and is consistently gaining weight (this can vary from hospital to hospital);
- your child is stable, without any significant changes for two weeks in his medical status or level of ventilatory support;
- all your child's caregivers are trained in CPR and an emergency plan is in place;
- all caregivers are trained in tracheostomy care, including troubleshooting problems with the ventilator and changing a trach tube;
- arrangements are in place for qualified homecare nurses to cover twenty-four-hour care;
- all medical equipment, from a qualified homecare agency, is in the home;
- insurance has been approved and a case manager has been assigned;
- all follow-up evaluations and rehabilitation services are arranged;

- the local emergency medical service, fire department, utility company, and telephone company have been notified (they will put you on a priority list); and
- transportation is available for medical visits.

Providing your pediatrician is comfortable with the vent, he will take over your child's at-home care. A pulmonologist (a physician specializing in lung problems) should also follow your baby's ventilator management and determine ventilator changes and weaning.

Taking home a child on a vent is like bringing the pediatric intensive care unit into your house. My daughter's bedroom is in our living room.

The hardest part, I think, is never being alone. There is always a home healthcare nurse, a therapist, or an early interventionist in our house. I don't have any more control at home than I did in the hospital.

Another difficult part is not hearing Jorian make any noises. There are no sounds when she cries. Although she doesn't know any different, I can't wait until I can hear her voice.

—Tina, mother of 23-weeker quadruplet Jorian

FINDING SUPPORT

Coping with a technology-dependent child is hard on the entire family. Finding another family who has experienced a similar situation can help. They can provide understanding, guidance, and information. (However, never follow any medical advice from a non-medical person.)

To connect with a family, consult the NICU staff and your baby's specialist. A favorite nurse or doctor who knows your personality and family can match you with a family who has a background similar to yours. National support groups often offer peer support referral services. Logging on to Internet Web sites of national organizations or simply entering your child's medical condition on one of the search tools can also lead you to other families.

Make the effort to find support. Knowing you are not alone can be a great comfort. And learning from others' experiences can assist you on your parenting journey.

CHAPTER FOUR

Getting to Know and Love Your Preemie

TO A GREAT extent, forming a relationship with your baby will come naturally. As you take care of your baby's needs, he learns to trust and rely on you. When you spend time together, you learn about each other and develop a bond. Your parent-child relationship evolves over many years and lasts a lifetime.

You may wonder, however, if the early difficulties of your baby's birth will somehow affect your later relationship. Certainly your baby's introduction to the world and the weeks or months that follow are not ideal circumstances for getting to know one another. The first few years can create some challenges, particularly if your child has ongoing medical and developmental concerns. But you can overcome these early obstacles. By being aware of potential difficulties and by seeking help if needed, you can successfully bond with your child.

OVERCOMING EARLY BONDING OBSTACLES

IF YOU WERE unable to hold your baby after birth (and perhaps for days, weeks, or months afterward), you may worry that the two of you did not bond. Bonding is a term that refers to the feelings and affections a parent feels toward a child; typically this takes time to develop. Bonding often begins during pregnancy and continues after birth (it does not magically occur when you first hold your baby).

Your child's premature birth interrupted important early bonding time. During a full-term pregnancy, Mom and Dad have nine months to physically and mentally prepare for the baby's arrival. Watching Mom's belly grow, feeling or seeing the baby kick, and imagining what life will be like after the delivery, all create an early closeness with the baby. When your baby arrived early, your time together was cut short. You probably felt a sense of loss, and you had to quickly adjust to your role as a parent before you were ready.

The trauma from your baby's early birth created further difficulties. Your baby had to concentrate his energy on survival and recovery, and you needed to cope physically and emotionally with the crisis. Furthermore, NICU conditions are not ideal for relationship-building. Hospital rules and medical concerns may have prevented you from touching, holding, feeding, and sometimes even speaking to your baby. You may have felt like an outsider, rather than a parent. The lack of privacy certainly did not help either.

Some parents overcome NICU obstacles and feel a bond with their baby before homecoming. However, even if you did not feel particularly close to your hospitalized baby, the time you spent with him was important. Getting to know your baby—learning about his personality and his needs—is the first step toward building a healthy relationship. By continuing to learn more about your baby and by taking steps to foster your relationship after homecoming, you can create a strong parent-child closeness.

> *When I was hospitalized at twenty-two weeks gestation, my husband and I were given horrible statistics about the chances for our baby's survival. We asked that everything be done to save our baby as we tried to prepare ourselves for his possible death. Never before was the concept of labor and delivery so filled with dread, tears, and fear. Having a baby was supposed to be a joyous occasion, when tears of happiness are shed. Tears of sadness aren't supposed to be in the picture.*
>
> *When my son was born and the doctors told us he was alive and breathing through intubation, I was stunned. I even thought to myself, This can't be happening. He was supposed to die. I felt like a horrible parent for my thoughts, and haven't ever forgiven myself for thinking them.*
>
> *After he was placed in the NICU, I visited him and went through the motions of talking to the doctors and nurses, but I was numb. It was as if I couldn't feel any emotion or pain. About two weeks later when I received some news from the neonatologist, I broke down and sobbed. I then realized that I did feel deep emotion for my baby, and I began letting myself love him.*
>
> *Although my husband and I originally wondered how our relationship with our son would develop, over time we realized that it is a very natural process. In many ways our relationship with our son is much stronger because we had to really get to know our son much earlier than other parents. We've sat back many times, overwhelmed and consumed by the reality of how strong our love is for our son.*
>
> *Every night I tell my Xavier, "You are the best present God ever gave me." He always returns my sentiment with a kiss and hug, saying, "I know, Mommy. I love you all the way around the world and back again."*
>
> *—Andrea, mother of 23-weeker Xavier*

■

My son and I didn't have an instant bond at birth. I was too consumed with grief and fear. I wasn't sure if I would ever bond with him. During the first months at home, my feelings slowly started changing. I started learning about him, and he started showing me his wonderful personality. It's almost like I had to develop a relationship with him.

—LISA, MOTHER OF 27-WEEKER AUSTIN

■

It took a long time for Devin and me to bond. I don't know if I subconsciously blocked my feelings in order to protect myself from loss, or he didn't trust me because he associated me with painful procedures, rehospitalization, and desertion. As he grew older, he would turn only to his dad when he needed comforting. When I tried to hold him and kiss him, he would physically reject me. This hurt me terribly and bewildered me.

Then suddenly one day, just after he turned two, I picked him up (the same as I had done countless times before) and asked him for a kiss. He put his arms around me and kissed me over and over. That was the turning point, and today we are as close as it is possible to get.

—INA, MOTHER OF 26-WEEKER DEVIN

■

Travis was in the hospital for over ten months. It was weeks before I could touch him and months before I could hold him. I visited him almost every evening after work and every weekend. Others told me it would be difficult once he came home, that he would never be a normal child. I was just so happy to have him home. It didn't matter to me that he had problems.

We were extremely close from the minute he came home, and we have stuck together like Super Glue ever since. I took three months off from my job and have rarely done anything without him other than work. He's thirteen years old now, and we are very close. He tells me he loves me all the time. Travis has some learning disabilities, but he makes up for it in other areas. I think our relationship is strong because I accept him for who he is, and I believe in him.

—DIANE, MOTHER OF 27-WEEKER TRAVIS

■ ■ ■

GETTING TO KNOW YOUR BABY BETTER

ALTHOUGH IT IS often difficult because of the caregiving a preemie requires, one of the best ways to create a closeness with your baby is through touch. Holding your undressed baby against your bare chest, a method called "kangaroo care," creates a physical and emotional closeness. Skin-to-skin contact communicates to your baby that he is important and loved, and it gives you the opportunity to just enjoy him. Experts say that "kangarooing"—by the mother and the father—encourages both the parent-child bond and your baby's growth and early development.

Infant massage is another wonderful way to foster closeness: Massage reassures, soothes, and communicates affection and love. Research shows infant massage may also improve a child's weight gain, enhance his development, and help him transition to sleep more easily. Some experts say massage even improves an older baby's speech development because of the cooing he makes while being massaged. To learn more about infant massage, ask a qualified therapist to teach you massage techniques, and see "infant massage" listed in appendix C.

When your baby is older, around two to three months corrected age, you can begin actual play sessions with him. Playtime is a fun way for you both to deepen your relationship. Not only do you learn about your baby's abilities, but he learns about you. For preemie parents who often feel stressed by their baby's needs, playtimes are critical bonding times.

Your baby is ready to play if he is calm; his color is pink; his breathing is regular; and he is able to focus his eyes on you or an object. When your child shows signs of readiness, offer him one toy or interaction at a time. For example, give him a rattle to hold. If he remains calm and content, quietly talk to him as he plays. If at any time he appears stressed, remove the rattle and help him recover. By making play fun, you will create a special time for closeness. For playing ideas, see chapter 13.

PARENT TIPS:

"KANGAROOING" WITH YOUR BABY

Following are some tips for kangaroo-care sessions:

- Create a sense of privacy. Avoid unwanted interruptions by waiting until siblings are not around or are occupied. Turn off the phone and do not answer the door.
- Pick the right chair. A recliner with a footrest works well. One that rocks is even better. Some parents kangaroo in bed.
- Wear comfortable clothing. A shirt that opens in the front is the most convenient.
- Keep a diaper on your baby to keep you both from becoming wet and uncomfortable.

- Keep the room at a comfortable temperature, between 65° and 72°F. Your body temperature will provide enough warmth for your baby. Be sure there are no breezes flowing near your baby. Place a soft, light blanket over you both.
- Do not limit the time you spend doing kangaroo care—do it for as long as you both like.
- If you are breast-feeding, keep a towel nearby or wear breast pads. Breastmilk often releases during skin-to-skin contact. You may want to nurse your baby during kangaroo care, or you may prefer kangarooing after your baby eats. Experts say skin-to-skin contact can help your baby's digestion.
- Some experts encourage parents to continue practicing kangaroo care until at least three months corrected age. However, many preemie parents continue kangarooing for one or more years. As long as you both enjoy it, continue kangarooing.

When a nurse showed Gary and me how to massage Vincent, I saw how desperate our baby was to feel a loving touch. It was a breakthrough for all of us, and the beginning of my healing from our traumatic separation.

For most of his first year, I massaged him at least once a day. I'm certain this helped him thrive. Massaging Vincent has been good for me, too. I feel like I'm really doing something to make him feel loved and confident, and to help his little body that initially suffered so much.

—ANNE, MOTHER OF 26-WEEKER VINCENT

PARENT TIPS:

MORE WAYS TO CONNECT WITH YOUR BABY

The following are some things you can do to help you and your baby become closer:

- Cuddle your baby frequently. The sound of your heartbeat, warmth from your body, and physical contact will make your baby feel secure and loved.
- Throughout the day, sing or hum songs to your baby. Some songs from the NICU days may be familiar and comforting to him.
- Talk to your baby often, using a soothing, quiet voice.
- Take opportunities to look at each other's faces. Lie on the floor or bed next to your baby. If your baby turns away, remember it is *not* a reaction to you. He just needs to mature more before he can handle the interaction.
- Carry your baby in a front infant carrier or sling whenever you can.
- Forget about the dishes and laundry—spend time with your baby!

In the early days at home, Christine spent much time in our arms. Even as she gets older we continue to hold her a lot. We listen to her needs and try to tune in to her as much as possible. Although her needs change as she becomes more mobile, we still try to keep her nearby so we can make efforts to understand her. My husband and I share everything we learn about her with each other. We work as a team. I believe this is why we've bonded with our daughter.

—*Kathy, mother of 28-weeker Christine*

PARENT TIPS:

Just for Dads

Studies show that children who are securely attached to *both* parents are more confident, competent, and empathetic, but creating this special father-child relationship is not always easy for some men. Dads suggest these relationship-building ideas:

- Become involved with your baby's care as soon as possible. Your preemie is not as fragile as you may think. Attend medical and developmental appointments to learn more about your baby's health and development and what you can do to help.
- Learn your baby's special cues (refer to chapter 1). His cries, smiles, and special faces are all ways of communicating with you.
- Spend time alone with your baby, letting you both get to know one another.
- The old philosophy that "boys don't cry" makes it difficult for some men to show feelings. Breaking this barrier and allowing yourself to feel can bring you closer to your baby. Your baby also needs to know that his dad experiences feelings, such as sadness, happiness, and anger.
- Touch and cuddle your preemie often. Kangaroo care (skin-to-skin contact) is for dads, too!

When Mackenzie was in the hospital, the role that came most naturally for me was to be the protector. I always had to be there and watch over the difficult or painful procedures.

This didn't change when she came home. I didn't know how else to act except as her protector. I guess this was how I dealt with my emotions. It wasn't as though we didn't bond, we just didn't have the casual day-to-day interaction that I shared with my full-term sons. I was always in a crisis mode with her.

I don't think we really connected until I started interacting with her—making her smile, helping her play, and cuddling with her. It took some time before I learned how to not just protect her, but love her too.

—*Jimmy, father of 26-weeker Mackenzie*

Tyler seemed so tiny and helpless in the hospital. The surroundings were so intimidating, and I just wanted him to come home. Once he came home, I realized I had underestimated what it would really be like. I found myself checking on him constantly. I spent a lot of time feeding him at night while my wife pumped breastmilk. This was a time for us to be close and to get to know each other. Although he was still vulnerable, he seemed to take on whatever life gave him without any problem. His easygoing personality and his ability to tolerate life seemed to bring us closer.

—ANDY, FATHER OF 33-WEEKER TYLER

■

WHEN THERE IS MORE THAN ONE BABY TO LOVE

AS A PARENT of multiples, you may be concerned that your children's unique NICU experiences will somehow affect your relationships. One baby may have been hospitalized in a different hospital, making visiting difficult. One may have come home earlier, and you were unable to make frequent visits to see the other(s). Even if your feelings for one child were delayed or altered in some way, you can make up for lost time after homecoming.

Building a relationship with each baby can be quite different. Your children's unique personalities affect how you feel about and interact with them. For instance, one baby may be quiet and adjust easily to life's challenges; another one may be fussy and difficult.

Developmental delays can also affect your feelings toward your babies. You may bond with the child who gives more back, or with the child who demands more. Comparing children, especially if development is quite different, is natural. However, do not let comparisons get in the way of your relationships with your children. Remember, your children may feel your frustration and negativity. Recognize and encourage each child's uniqueness, and try to remain positive.

Once all your babies are home, you will probably only have enough energy to care for their basic needs for at least the first few months. Do not worry if you cannot spend much time alone with each child. By meeting your babies' needs, they are learning to trust and rely on you. As life settles, you can begin to spend quality time with each child and learn to love them individually.

■ ■ ■

PARENT TIPS:

LOVING MULTIPLES

Parents of preemie multiples suggest these ways to help you bond with your babies:

- Have one "special" feeding with each child per day.
- When your infants are about three months corrected age, take showers or baths with each one.
- Enjoy kangaroo care and/or infant massage with each baby.
- When you have adapted to multiple parenting, try to provide separate care schedules (feeding, diapering, and baths) when possible. Be fair with your babies (for example, if you bathe baby John first one day, bathe baby Sue first the next day).
- Do not be too tough on yourself. Parents of preemie multiples often need more time to adjust. When you are feeling bad because you do not have time to spend with your babies, remind yourself that your multiples receive the love they need from each other, too.
- Getting to know your preemies is a slow process that requires time and energy. You need to revitalize your energy every now and then. Give yourself a break *at least* once a week by letting others help.
- Seek professional help if you find yourself feeling unsure of your emotions, or the stress begins to affect your parenting abilities and relationships with your babies.

I was afraid I would never bond with my preemie twins because of their time in the NICU. I wondered if I could ever really love them. I thought I was the world's worst mother! How could I feel this way?

I realize now that bonding with preemies just takes time. Four years later I have such an incredible bond with them—it's indescribable.

—SARA, MOTHER OF 24-WEEKER TWINS JEFF AND ANNA

■

I had an extremely difficult pregnancy. By the time the twins were born, I was already quite depressed. The day after they were born, I had no desire to see them. When I finally did, I felt physically and emotionally detached from them.

I found myself becoming more attached to my son, Nicholas, because he was the sicker of the two. The bond between us seemed to happen so naturally. I couldn't understand why it was more difficult to bond with my daugh-

ter, Hailey. Maybe it was the difficult pregnancy, illness, depression, shock, medications, unanswered questions, lack of sleep, difficulties with pumping and breast-feeding, and fear of my fragile twins. I did have secret fears that something was seriously wrong with Hailey, even though the doctors said she was fine and there was no obvious illness or abnormality.

I have been seeing a therapist, trying to work through all my feelings. She is helping me understand how the entire experience of a premature birth and incidents in my past play into my attachment with my children. The more time passes, the more I understand "why" I've had trouble bonding with the twins.

The twins are three now, and I am finally quite comfortable with the bond between us. The bond is still stronger with Nicholas, but I have accepted that no two bonds with one's children can be exactly the same.

—*Barb, mother of 29-weeker twins Hailey and Nicholas*

IF YOUR FEELINGS CONCERN YOU

THE PREMATURE BIRTH of your child and the crisis that followed can affect how you feel and interact with your child long after the NICU experience. If caregiving makes you feel more like a nurse or doctor than a parent, you may feel "detached" from your child. Even after he is healthy, you may continue to see your child as vulnerable and needing protection. Other unresolved issues in your life, such as a difficult childhood, a divorce or separation, or a death, can also affect how you relate to your child.

It is not unusual for a parent of a preemie to need more time to develop a closeness with his or her child. Nor is it uncommon for a parent to feel overprotective of a medically fragile child. However, if your feelings begin to affect your ability to love, interact with, or discipline your child, or they affect your child's ability to become independent, you should consult your pediatrician or a qualified therapist. How you feel about your child and how you interact with him not only influences your relationship, it also affects your child's self-esteem and trust in others. The sooner you resolve your issues, the more time you can spend focusing on your relationship.

■ ■ ■

Chart 4-1: Is your child's attachment to you "normal"?

During the first months at home, your baby depends solely on you. In time, he will learn to meet some of his own needs independently, such as comforting himself. Stages of alternating between independence and dependence continue naturally throughout childhood. Experts recognize that children exhibit certain behaviors during these stages that indicate a healthy attachment to parents.

The chart below gives examples of these behaviors. Do not be alarmed if your child does not follow the ages and stages exactly. These are only a few of the more common behaviors and not a comprehensive list. If your child has a medical and/or developmental concern, which can affect his behavior, he may take longer to move through these stages. Your child's personality can also affect his behavior. Use the age-specific behaviors listed below as a guide, and discuss any concerns with your pediatrician.

AGE	BEHAVIORS
1 to 3 months corrected age	likes to be held sucks on the breast, bottle, pacifier, fingers, or a blanket for comfort accepts comfort from parent calms when picked up
4 to 5 months corrected age	becomes more social by smiling enjoys being talked to and touched vocalizes to indicate pleasure and displeasure may stop eating briefly to look around at distractions
6 to 9 months corrected age	reaches out for parent follows parent as motor skills improve shows fear of strangers by clinging to parent cries if a parent leaves the room
12 months corrected age	plays alone with parent in the room tries to keep physically close to parent shows distress when separated from parent
18 months corrected age	becomes more interested in the environment and begins to venture away from parent uses parent as a secure base for exploration gradually becomes more comfortable with greater distance from parent as he learns to predict parent's behavior
2 years corrected age	prefers to be held frequently plays alone, but checks on parent often
3 to 4 years actual age	wants to stay close to parent, but usually content holding parent's hand or a comfort item, such as a blanket or favorite toy wants to be held by parent periodically, especially in unsure situations
5 to 7 years actual age	decides it is okay not to hold parent's hand anymore (even though Mom or Dad may not want to let go yet!) develops more independence from parent learns to separate more easily from parent plays with other children without parent present
All ages (before the teen years!)	runs to parent, smiles, or stops crying and clings to parent after a short absence may be quiet or angry for a few days after parent's return from a longer absence

WARNING SIGNS

Your feelings may negatively affect your parent-child relationship if you:

- feel numb or detached from your baby and/or from the outside world most of the time;
- feel overwhelmingly fearful about caring for your baby;
- find yourself just being around your baby but not really interacting with him;
- are having trouble meeting the basic needs of your infant or getting through your daily routine;
- are constantly afraid of hurting or causing harm to your baby;
- are continuously fearful about your baby's health and easily become concerned about mild symptoms, such as circles under the eyes;
- think about calling the doctor frequently;
- check on your child at night often to be sure he is still alive; and/or
- have extreme difficulty leaving your child in the care of someone else.

I spent hours at the hospital, staring at my baby in the isolette, doing everything they would let me do for her. Now she is home and I attend to her every need. But I feel curiously distant from her, disbelieving that she was once a part of me, questioning whether she is really mine.

I am especially aware of this distance I feel when she is crying or getting a shot. It doesn't bother me the way I think it should. I feel somewhat dispassionate—concerned for her, but in an intellectual rather than emotional way. I am still trying to sort through these issues. I have not spoken to anyone about these feelings because they make me feel ashamed and frightened.

—CAROL, MOTHER OF 25-WEEKER EMMA

■

The other night I went in to check on my son because he was crying. Suddenly it struck me that sometimes I don't know if I'm his nurse or his mom. I never get a chance to just hold him and be with him.

It's not that I don't love him more than life itself. It just feels odd sometimes, like I'm confused as to what role I should play. I am sad that our relationship is like this and we have lost this precious time together. My son and I are very close, yet something is missing. I wonder if it will matter in our future relationship.

—TRACY, MOTHER OF 33-WEEKER STEPHEN

■ ■ ■

THE SPECIAL BOND BETWEEN PREEMIES AND THEIR PARENTS

THE EARLY DIFFICULTIES you and your baby faced together can actually lead you to a much closer relationship. Many parents say they feel "emotionally tied" to their infants who overcame such fragile starts.

Preemie parents often try to make up for "lost time" by spending many quality hours with their infants (something full-term parents might not do). The time you also spend nurturing your child who has medical or developmental needs is also time spent getting to know one another. Furthermore, the steps you take to overcome bonding obstacles caused by prematurity continue to create a special closeness. Although it may not seem obvious to you now, you have created the beginnings of an enduring parent-child tie.

PART TWO

Medical Concerns

PART TWO

Introduction

WHEN YOUR BABY comes home, you have to adjust not only to being a parent, but also to your role as a doctor, nurse, and caregiver. Many preemie parents are unaware that medical complications associated with prematurity, such as respiratory difficulties, typically continue beyond the NICU period.

The chapters in part 2 cover the common medical problems of preterm children. Your child will certainly not have all of these problems, and you may at first want to only read about your child's present concerns. It is a good idea, however, to educate yourself about the warning signs of other complications, particularly respiratory illnesses. Being informed should relieve some of your apprehension about caring for your child and allow you more time to just be Mom or Dad.

CHAPTER FIVE

The Lungs

WHEN YOUR BABY was born early, her lungs were immature, and she may have needed breathing support and supplemental oxygen. Depending on her medical condition, she may have required breathing assistance for days, weeks, or even months. This support may have damaged your baby's fragile lungs, making her more susceptible to respiratory illnesses.

Lung-related illnesses are among the most common medical problems premature infants face. These problems can range from mild respiratory distress lasting a few days in the NICU to long-term lung disease requiring months or years of medical attention.

Understanding and dealing with your child's present and potential lung-related concerns are important to her health and future. The following sections discuss the common lung diseases related to prematurity.

> *As frustrating as it is to hear diagnosis after diagnosis attached to Stephen, I do feel better working with answers rather than questions. The hard part is, after fighting so hard to get Stephen through the NICU period, we thought it would be over once we brought him home. We knew there was a chance of asthma since we have other children with it, but never did we think his medical problems would be as complicated as they are.*
>
> *First it was the asthma, then feeding and reflux problems, then immune deficiency, then neurological damage. It seems like every time we see a doctor, some new problem arises. I am adjusting to parenting a special needs child, but I really wish someone in the NICU had warned us of the possibilities.*
>
> —TRACY, MOTHER OF 33-WEEKER STEPHEN

■ ■ ■

RESPIRATORY DISTRESS SYNDROME (RDS)

THE LUNGS ARE among the last organs to completely form in the mother's womb. At about twenty-five weeks gestational age, a baby's lungs are developed enough to begin moving oxygen to the blood. However, they lack an important mucuslike material, called surfactant. Surfactant coats the breathing sacs (alveoli), keeping them open. Without surfactant, the alveoli collapse and oxygen cannot be moved. This results in a breathing disorder called Respiratory Distress Syndrome, or RDS.

Infants typically do not develop enough surfactant to sustain breathing until they reach about thirty-five to thirty-eight weeks gestational age. Babies born without adequate surfactant typically receive a commercially prepared surfactant soon after birth. Introduced into the lungs through an endotracheal tube (a tube placed in the baby's windpipe), this artificial surfactant takes the place of natural surfactant until the baby can produce it on her own.

Commercially prepared surfactant is a common treatment in most NICUs, and it can sometimes successfully prevent or diminish RDS. However, even babies who receive artificial surfactant can develop RDS and may require breathing assistance within the first few days, weeks, or months of life.

Formerly called hyaline membrane disease, RDS is the most common lung disease affecting premature infants. RDS associated with prematurity occurs only in the newborn period. Complications continuing beyond the first month or so are generally a result of RDS and its treatment.

Potential complications of RDS include: chronic lung disease (bronchopulmonary dysplasia), more frequent and long-lasting respiratory illnesses, reactive airways disease, and asthma, as well as sensitivity to environmental and exercise triggers. Preemies who suffered severe RDS are more at risk for developing these long-term complications.

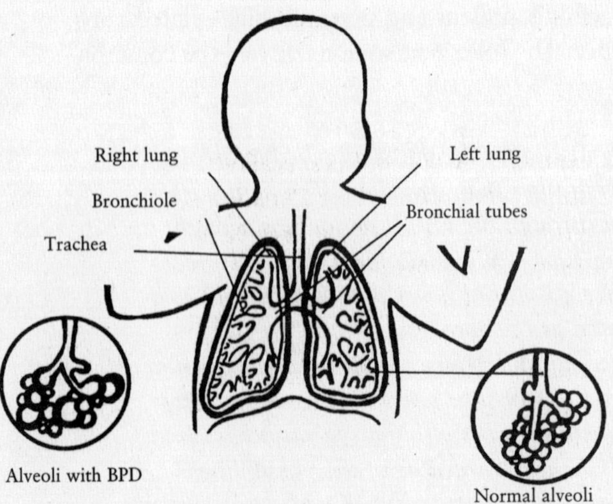

In lungs with BPD, the alveoli (where oxygen is moved from the lungs to the blood) are collapsed from tearing or stretching. They may also be overinflated and/or thickened from scarring.

BRONCHOPULMONARY DYSPLASIA (BPD)

ALL PREMATURE INFANTS are at risk for developing a chronic lung disease called bronchopulmonary dysplasia, or BPD. Very immature lungs, infection, and the need for supplemental oxygen and/or mechanical ventilation can increase this risk.

If your child has BPD, her damaged

lung tissue may make her lungs less compliant (stiffer in their movements). This and other effects on the lungs can cause your child to have BPD symptoms for a few months or for many years. Experts say that most children "outgrow" BPD as new lung tissue develops and takes over the function of damaged tissue. Children continue growing new lung tissue until age eight (some think even longer), but most preemies' lungs heal much sooner. (Even with new lung tissue, some children do continue exhibiting signs of BPD.) Your child has a better chance of overcoming BPD if her lungs are protected with adequate oxygen and good nutrition, and if you take steps to prevent respiratory illness.

I remember when I first heard the words "bronchopulmonary dysplasia." Joseph was still on the ventilator in the hospital. I was devastated. I just knew he would never lead a normal life. As I learned more about what those words meant and as I saw Joe progressing (even though it was at a snail's pace), I realized his life would be different, but BPD was not as horrible as I originally thought.

We brought Joseph home with oxygen, an apnea monitor, a feeding tube in his nose, a feeding pump, a suction machine, and a pulse-oximeter. He took medication and had chest physiotherapy every four hours. When Joseph breathed, his entire body rose. His retractions made his tiny stomach sink into his spine. I could hear him breathing down the hall because he wheezed so loudly. He sweated constantly from working so hard to breathe, as if he were perpetually exercising.

I cried myself to sleep many nights because my son struggled so hard to breathe. I wondered how he kept going day after day. He didn't sit up until he was thirteen months old because he couldn't breathe in a sitting position. He had feeding difficulties. He caught his first cold at ten months and developed pneumonia.

Joseph came off twenty-four-hour oxygen at eighteen months. Today he is still on oxygen at night. He gets breathing treatments twice daily—that's when he's healthy. I still overreact when he's exposed to sick people, especially those with respiratory illnesses. He looks so healthy that others think I'm a lunatic. But I know if I can keep my son from getting sick, his lungs can keep healing.

We have struggled through physical and occupational therapy, oral steroids, feeding problems, breathing treatments, and oxygen for three and a half years. In spite of all that, Joe eats a regular kid diet and is very active. He loves sports, and his doctor says Joe can participate to the extent that he wishes. When people who know about his difficult birth ask me why I let him run with other kids, I say, "Because he can."

—DALE, MOTHER TO 32-WEEKER JOSEPH

■ ■ ■

Diagnosis of BPD

The Bureau of Maternal and Child Health and Resources Development created the following criteria in 1989 for diagnosing BPD. Your preemie may be diagnosed as having BPD if she:

- received positive-pressure ventilation (intubation in the NICU and/or nasal continuous positive airway pressure) during the first two weeks of life for a minimum of three days;
- showed clinical signs of respiratory compromise persisting beyond twenty-eight days of actual age;
- required supplemental oxygen beyond twenty-eight days of actual age; and/or
- had a chest X ray with findings consistent with BPD.

These criteria have recently been modified, making diagnosing BPD much simpler: Any child who continues to have a need for oxygen beyond thirty-six weeks gestational age and/or for more than four weeks after birth is considered to have BPD. Healthcare experts use both definitions.

Signs of BPD

Your at-home preemie with BPD can exhibit a range of symptoms from mild to severe. Following are some common signs of BPD.

Chest retracts when breathing

Stiff lungs can cause the muscles in your child's chest to pull hard with each breath. You may see spaces (a pulling inward of the skin) in between the ribs, below the ribs, and/or at the top of the chest in front of the neck. These are known as *retractions,* which can be mild, moderate, or severe. They can occur occasionally, intermittently with an acute illness, or on a daily basis.

Breathing rate is increased

Your child with BPD may have an increased breathing rate, especially when she has a respiratory illness, a fever, or is kept too warm. You can measure your child's baseline respiratory rate during healthy circumstances by counting her number of breaths for sixty seconds. (Counting for a full minute is important to get an accurate measurement.) For the most accurate recording of your child's breathing rate, count her breaths while she is sleeping.

Requires supplemental oxygen

Your child with BPD may require supplemental oxygen because she cannot keep her oxygen saturation at an adequate level. Her oxygen needs will decrease as her lungs heal.

You were probably told in the NICU that there are side effects from supplemental oxygen, and it may be dangerous for your baby. This was true in the NICU when your baby was on a ventilator, but it is no longer true when your child is on home levels of oxygen. Supplemental oxygen is not only safe but very important for the healing of your baby's lungs and her growth.

Your oxygen supplier or doctor will measure your child's oxygen saturation levels with periodic pulse-oximeter (pulse-ox) tests. This test is done with a device that wraps around your baby's foot or hand and determines the amount of oxygen in her blood. Testing should be done during sleep, alert times, and while eating (oxygen needs can vary in each instance). In rare cases, a hospital will send a preemie home with a pulse-oximeter and teach the parents how to measure oxygen saturation levels themselves. If you do pulse-ox tests, keep a progress report on your baby's oxygen levels and stay in close touch with your doctor. *Never make oxygen changes on your own.*

Wheezes

Wheezing is a high-pitched whistling sound that may occur when your child exhales and her lungs must work hard to push out the air. Wheezing may occur when your preemie is sick, when there is extra fluid or an inflammation in the lungs, or when her lungs are exposed to an irritant, such as cigarette smoke. She may wheeze intermittently or on a daily basis.

Coughs

Coughing helps eliminate excess fluid or mucus that irritates the lungs and impairs the breathing process. Children with BPD do not generally cough on a regular basis. Your child may cough when there is extra fluid or mucus in the lungs, if she is refluxing (see gastroesophageal reflux in chapter 8), or when she has a respiratory infection.

Feeding difficulties

Not all children with BPD have feeding difficulties, but many do. Because your child must work hard to breathe, coordinating breathing and eating at the same time may be difficult. She will need extra calories to compensate for the expended energy.

Treatment for BPD

Your pediatrician's beliefs and practices and your child's individual needs will affect treatment. Common BPD treatments are discussed in this section

Prescribing home oxygen therapy

Babies with more severe BPD who cannot adequately breathe on their own require supplemental oxygen even after homecoming. Your child may need breathing assistance twenty-four hours a day or only when she eats and/or sleeps. In a few cases, children require home oxygen therapy for several years. There is no way to predict how long your child will need supplemental oxygen, but keeping her healthy and helping her gain weight as new lung tissue develops will improve her chances of coming off oxygen sooner.

Some doctors prescribe supplemental oxygen for preemies with BPD who are not growing and gaining weight well. The added oxygen provides breathing support for those children who have difficulty keeping their oxygen saturation at adequate levels and who need extra energy for proper growth.

Prescribing medications

Many preemies with BPD have inflammation in their lungs, causing a narrowing (or blockage) of the airways and a tightening (a constriction) of the smooth muscle that lines the small airways. This tightening is called *bronchoconstriction.* The periodic tightening of the muscle bands around these small airways is called *bronchospasm.*

Bronchodilators, medications taken through breathing treatments or in pill or liquid form, relax the muscle bands and help open up the narrowed airways. Bronchodilators may be prescribed for daily use as a maintenance medication or for intermittent use during a respiratory illness. If your child is on a maintenance bronchodilator, the dosage may be changed or increased during an acute illness.

Diuretics are medications used to remove extra fluid in the lungs, eliminating it through the kidneys. Fluid can accumulate in the alveoli and in the bronchial tubes, making the alveoli stiffer and less able to move oxygen. These medications are taken daily in pill or liquid form.

Steroid and nonsteroid anti-inflammatory medications are commonly used to decrease lung inflammation and the swelling of the lung tissue, improving the lungs' ability to exchange air and making breathing easier. *Steroid* anti-inflammatory medications are given in pill or liquid form or through a hand-held inhaler. Steroids are particularly helpful for reducing the periodic episodes of wheezing and coughing.

Inhaled steroids work best when used on a regular basis; it can take one to six weeks before full effects are seen. Side effects from inhaled steroids can occur. Occasionally, a child develops a dry mouth, hoarseness, or a minor throat irritation. A child can develop thrush, a white film inside the mouth and over the tongue. This is caused by a fungus, which can be treated by oral medications. A few experts think inhaled steroids can cause slower growth, but poorly controlled BPD is actually more likely to do this. Your doctor should carefully select the brand of inhaled steroids and monitor your child for possible growth effects.

Oral steroids are among the most powerful medications available for decreasing lung inflammation. They may be used on a long-term basis (usually every other day) for chronic inflammation, or in a short "burst" of three to seven days for a respiratory infection. Oral steroids may be started immediately after the first signs of a respiratory illness (when a child begins to wheeze and cough with a cold).

The risk for serious side effects is high if oral steroids are given every day on a long-term basis. However, side effects are much less likely to occur if oral steroids are given every other day. Short-term side effects include mood changes, difficulty sleeping, irritability, increased appetite, and weight gain. Long-term side effects include poor or excessive weight gain; poor growth in height; thinning or softening of the bones; cataracts (an eye disease); high blood pressure; high blood sugar; difficulties dealing with stress; increased infections; and thickening of the walls of the heart. Because of these potential side effects, your child on oral steroids should be monitored closely by her doctor.

PARENT TIPS:
How to Give Your Preemie Medicine

Many parents struggle with giving their children medications, and preemie parents are no different. If your child is especially sensitive to objects around her mouth, giving medicines can become even more complicated. Here are some helpful tips:

For Younger Preemies

- Always taste a drop of the medicine before you give it. If it tastes bad, hide the flavor with breastmilk, formula, cereal, or a treat.
- Before a bottle-feeding, remove the top of the bottle and squirt the medication into the nipple, mixing it with a small amount of milk. Let your baby suck the nipple's contents before placing it back on the bottle. Do not mix the medication into the entire bottle—if the bottle is not completely ingested, your infant will not get the prescribed dose.
- If you have a small feeding tube, cut it to about two inches in length. Hook it onto a syringe and put the tubing into the side of your infant's mouth. Slowly squirt the medicine, allowing your child to swallow between squirts.
- When feeding, alternate one spoonful of a favorite food mixed with medication with a spoonful of food without medicine.
- FlavorRx is a liquid you can mix with medications to cover up bad tastes. Check with your pediatrician.
- Try not to show any emotion when giving the medicine—just get it done. You do not want your child to sense your apprehension.
- Give lots of positive feedback during medicine-taking.

For Toddler Preemies

- Starting at about eighteen months corrected age, give your child control by letting her hold the syringe or teaspoon. Practice with water first. *Explain that medicine is only given by an adult.*
- Let your child practice giving "medicine" to a stuffed animal.
- If your child is old enough to eat jelly, chocolate, or peanut butter, try using these to mask the taste of the medicine. Check with your pharmacist about melting a small amount of ice cream, mixing the medication into it, then refreezing to conceal the taste.

- Be careful not to routinely mix medicines into foods that you want your child to like. She may begin to associate the look and texture of that food with the bad taste of the medicine and reject it.
- Do not bargain with your child. Give her one chance to take the medicine and receive a treat. If she does not do it the first time, take away the treat, but give her the medicine. This will help the next time you need to give medication.
- If your child vomits the medicine, ask your doctor if you should give more medication.

Remember to always keep medicine bottles away from children and stored as directed, such as in a cool, dry place. When you pick up your child's prescribed medicine, verify that it is the name and the dosage that your doctor ordered. Always check expiration dates and discard old, unused medication.

Prescribing respiratory treatments

Respiratory treatments improve your preemie's ability to breathe by loosening mucus from the lungs and opening the airways. Such treatments include nebulization (or aerosol) treatments, inhalation through a metered-dose inhaler and spacer, and chest physiotherapy.

Nebulization treatments

To administer nebulized (mist) medications, an electrical air compressor is used. Liquid medicine is put into a plastic cup, called a nebulizer, and the air compressor converts the medication into an aerosol mist. Your child breathes the medicine into her lungs through a mask, attached to tubing and connected to both the nebulizer and the compressor. Children over age four or five may use a mouthpiece in place of a mask.

With a doctor's prescription, your health insurance company may purchase an air compressor and the nebulization setup (purchasing is generally cheaper

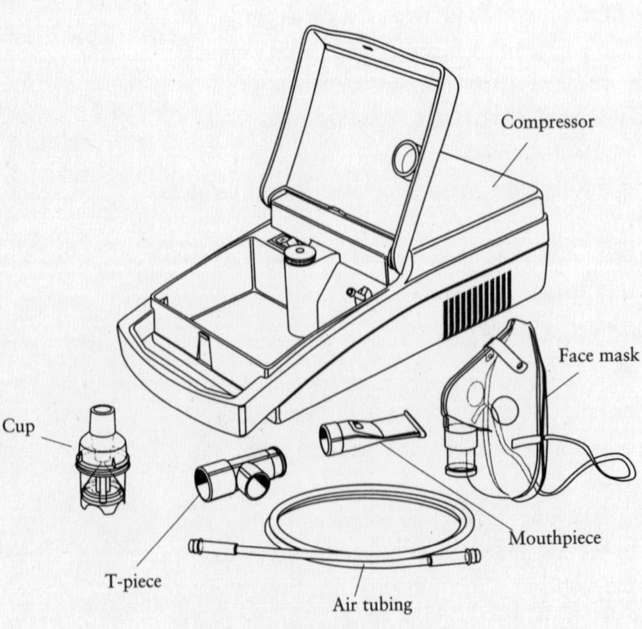

A typical nebulization setup.

than renting). Your doctor will prescribe the type and amount of medication, which is typically mixed with 2 cc's of normal saline. A respiratory therapist, associated with your home oxygen company, or your doctor should instruct you on the proper use of respiratory equipment.

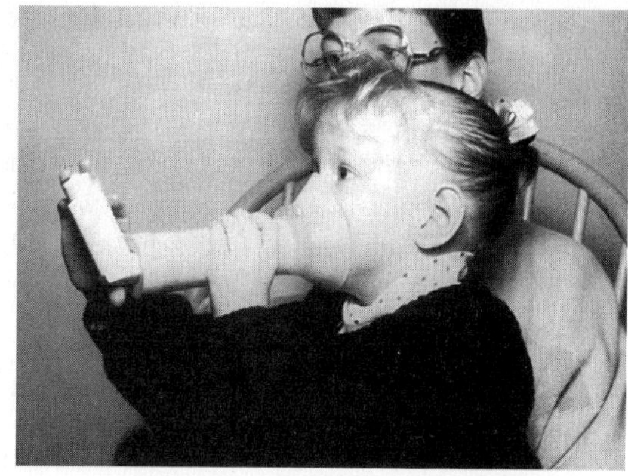

Three-year-old Bethany demonstrates how to use a metered-dose inhaler.

Metered-dose inhaler and spacer

Some medications, including bronchodilators and inhaled steroids, require the use of a metered-dose inhaler (MDI) with a spacer (a clear plastic tube with a mask). The medication is suspended in a dilution and packaged in a pressured canister. Medication is sprayed into the spacer and the child breathes it into her lungs for five to six breaths. This is repeated for as many sprays as are necessary to give the proper dose of medicine (the number of sprays will be prescribed by your doctor).

MDIs are the most commonly used delivery services for asthma medications. Until recently, it was felt that these devices could only be used for older children and adults. It is now believed that babies benefit as much from medication delivered by MDIs as those delivered by nebulization treatments.

Chest physiotherapy (CPT)

Another type of respiratory treatment is called chest physiotherapy (or CPT), also called chest percussion and postural drainage (or PP&D). CPT is performed by placing your child in various positions and either gently tapping on her chest and back for about three to five minutes with a special cup, or by percussing (gently tapping) her chest and back with your cupped hand. The vibrations from the tapping are transmitted through the chest wall, loosening the mucus and moving it from the smaller airways to the large airways. Your child will then cough up the secretions and either spit them out or swallow them.

If your doctor prescribes CPT, she will review techniques and positions with you, as well as prescribe a CPT schedule. *You must learn chest physiotherapy from a medical professional before you perform it on your child.* CPT works best when given after a nebulization or metered-dose inhaler treatment, which opens up airways and allows more efficient mucus clearance. Your doctor may also recommend suctioning your child's nose and mouth after therapy.

Recommending suctioning

As part of the treatment for your child with BPD, your doctor may suggest frequently suctioning your baby's nose and mouth to remove secretions. See suctioning techniques in chapter 2.

Running a cool-mist humidifier

When the air is dry, the mucus in the airways can also become dry, making sneezing and coughing to loosen and remove secretions difficult. If you live in a part of the country where the air is dry (or you have forced-air dry heat), your doctor may suggest running a cool-mist humidifier near your baby to help her breathe more easily. Never use a hot-air humidifier—it can accidentally burn your baby. If your baby is on supplemental oxygen, a water humidifier should be connected to her oxygen tank.

Positioning

Children with BPD may be more comfortable resting in elevated positions, allowing secretions to drain and helping the airways to open. Ask your doctor about positioning your child on her side to allow the lungs to open, helping her breathe more easily. If your child develops a respiratory infection, positioning can be especially important for draining mucus and opening up both lungs. For more on sleep positions, see chapter 2.

Potential Complications of BPD

Children with bronchopulmonary dysplasia are at risk for a wide range of complications, ranging from mild to severe. These include respiratory infections, feeding and nutrition problems, gastroesophageal reflux, high blood pressure, pulmonary hypertension, and other potential complications.

Respiratory infections

Children with BPD are more susceptible to developing serious respiratory illnesses than are their full-term siblings or peers. Upper respiratory infections, or "colds," are more likely to develop into more serious lower respiratory infections, such as pneumonia.

Because your preemie with BPD can develop a serious respiratory infection, it is a good idea to develop an at-home "care plan" with your doctor in advance (see box on page 83). By treating an illness early, you may prevent it from becoming serious and potentially life-threatening.

Feeding and nutrition problems

Your child with BPD uses a great deal of energy and calories to breathe, and she may need special nutrition management. Typically, children with BPD need 1.5 to 2 times more calories than do full-term healthy children. Therefore, it may be necessary to increase the calories of your baby's formula or breastmilk. *This should only be done under the management of your physician.*

Some preemies with severe BPD have trouble coordinating sucking, swallowing, and

GENERAL HOME "CARE PLAN" FOR A PREMATURE INFANT WITH BPD

The following is an example of a home "care plan" designed for a child who has bronchopulmonary dysplasia and who is prone to respiratory difficulties during illness. Ask your pediatrician or specialist to create a plan for your child.

1. With congestion, a cough, or any other symptoms of a respiratory infection, make sure your child has enough oxygen. Some respiratory infections can increase the need for oxygen, especially if the nose is stuffy and less oxygen can be delivered by nasal cannula. Your child who is not presently on oxygen may need supplemental oxygen. You may need to have a pulse-oximetry test performed to determine how much extra oxygen is needed.
2. Special attention should be given to keeping your child's nose and mouth clear of mucus. Suctioning may be necessary if your child is not able to blow her nose.
3. Extra respiratory treatments may be needed because respiratory infections typically cause more mucus and bronchoconstrictions (constrictions of the smooth muscle that lines the small airways of the lungs).
4. Extra fluids may be needed to replace the fluid lost from faster breathing. If your child has a history of fluid overload in her lungs, consult your doctor. Some children need diuretics to rid the lungs of extra fluid, which may accumulate because of the respiratory infection.
5. Your child may need an increase in the inhaled steroids she is taking or be given a "burst" (three to seven days) of oral steroids to treat lung inflammation. Steroids typically work better if given when a cold first starts. If your child has already suffered a severe respiratory infection, starting steroids at the beginning of the next cold could lessen its effects. For your child who is especially vulnerable to colds, steroids should be available at home to give in a timely manner. *Never start steroids without consulting your doctor.*
6. Good hand-washing by all caregivers and siblings is a must to prevent the passing of cold viruses to your child and also to protect family members from contracting a virus.

(Prepared by Susan Brugman, M.D., Associate Professor of Pediatrics, University of Colorado Health Sciences Center, Denver, Colo.)

breathing and need to be fed through a feeding tube. Prolonged feeding problems can result in poor weight gain, delay in lung development, and the development of a resistance to eating (called an oral aversion).

In addition, if your baby is on diuretics, she may have difficulty balancing the salts (sodium, potassium, and chloride) in her blood. These are called electrolytes. Your doctor may need to prescribe additional medications to keep her electrolytes in balance.

Gastroesophageal reflux

Gastroesophageal reflux (or GER), which occurs when food from the stomach "backwashes," is a common problem in children with BPD. A child with BPD works hard to breathe, causing her muscles to pull on her diaphragm. The diaphragm then pulls on the muscle at the top of the stomach (the sphincter), causing it to stay open too frequently and allowing the stomach contents to flow back into the esophagus, mouth, nose, and sometimes the lungs.

The symptoms of GER may or may not be obvious to you or your doctor. It is important for you to understand the signs of GER and its implications. Refer to chapter 8.

High blood pressure

With high blood pressure, the pressure in the arteries throughout the body is higher than average. There are a variety of causes of high blood pressure; however, in preemies with BPD, high blood pressure is most often attributed to the stress hormones these babies make. Some medications, such as steroids, can also increase blood pressure.

Your doctor should monitor your child's blood pressure at each checkup. (You may want to have your own blood pressure checked, too!) If she has a high reading, her blood pressure should be checked several times over a period of a few weeks. If it remains high, medication may be needed.

Pulmonary hypertension and cor pulmonale

Preemies with severe BPD are at risk for developing pulmonary hypertension. When an area of a lung is affected by BPD and is not working properly (it is collapsed or full of mucus or fluid), the vessels that pump blood to the lungs (the pulmonary arteries) must work extra hard because they are pushing against an unnatural resistance. When a large area of the lung is not working properly, it takes even more pressure to push the blood into the lungs, which results in a higher than average pressure in all the pulmonary arteries. This is pulmonary hypertension.

It is the right side of the heart that pumps or pushes the blood through the pulmonary arteries. After a period of time, which varies from child to child, the right side of the heart can become so tired from the increased pressure that the entire heart may begin to enlarge and weaken. This is called cor pulmonale, the most serious of BPD complications. Cor pulmonale can usually be prevented by keeping the lungs free of infection and extra fluid, and keeping a child's oxygen saturation greater than 95 percent at all times (an important reason why your child's oxygen level should be monitored by periodic pulse-oximetry testing).

Potential complications associated with BPD

Children who were mechanically ventilated for a long time are at risk for developing subglottic stenosis, laryngomalacia, tracheomalacia, and bronchomalacia (along with BPD). The breathing tube attached to your baby's ventilator entered her mouth and went down the trachea (the windpipe), which leads to the lungs. This tube can put pressure on the tissue in the large airways (the larynx, the trachea, and the bronchial tubes), causing damage to that tissue. It may scar and narrow the larynx (where the vocal cords are), trachea, or bronchial tubes (this is called stenosis), or it can leave the tissue "floppy," so that it cannot function properly with breathing (this is called laryngomalacia, tracheomalacia, or bronchomalacia).

These problems, combined with bronchopulmonary dysplasia, may prolong the course of BPD. In time, children with these problems generally outgrow them. If your child has a severe problem, she may need a tracheostomy (a plastic breathing tube placed from the outside of the neck into the trachea) to keep her large airways open and help her breathe. Refer to chapter 3.

Potential Long-term Effects of BPD

Since BPD was not even recognized until 1967 and because NICU treatment keeps evolving, there are very few long-term studies showing how BPD affects lung function in adulthood. Most studies were started in the late 1960s and early 1970s, when neonatology was in its infancy. Even the most recent studies conducted in the early 1990s do not necessarily reflect today's significant advances in neonatal lung management.

With so little information, it is difficult to predict what long-term effects BPD will have on former preemies when they are adolescents and adults. It is generally accepted that former preemies with a history of BPD are at greater risk for respiratory complications. Some have early childhood problems, such as reactive airways disease, but outgrow them. Others may develop long-term asthma that persists into adolescence or adulthood. These two lung disorders are discussed later in this chapter.

The most extensive follow-up study on BPD was published by the doctor who first described bronchopulmonary dysplasia in the *New England Journal of Medicine* in 1990. It concluded that most adolescents and adults with a history of BPD (twenty-six subjects, ages fourteen to twenty-three) were leading normal lives. However, there were some concerns. Overall, their size was generally smaller: Their average weight was at the 42nd percentile, and their average height was at the 37th percentile. The participants involved in the study felt that their lung problems consisted mainly of wheezing, frequent episodes of pneumonia, limitation of exercise capacity, and the need for long-term use of medications. They reported that their quality of life was altered, but not significantly. When tested by physicians, the subjects had evidence of increased airway obstruction (blockage in the lungs), airway hyper-reactivity (wheezing that is easily triggered), and lung hyperinflation (the lungs have more air in them than is typical). This study also showed an increased incidence of asthma (by 52 percent) in the group with BPD, compared to the group without BPD. Other long-term studies have shown similar complications, as well as a higher risk of infection and some increase in the incidence of developmental and cognitive (thinking) delays.

These studies strongly suggest that children with a history of BPD should have developmental evaluations, therapy if needed, and at-home intervention to optimize their developmental and learning potential. Any respiratory illness should be monitored carefully to avoid more serious complications. School-aged preemies with BPD may have less endurance when running, playing, and participating in sports. Any unusual symptoms during exercise, such as excessive fatigue, wheezing, or coughing, should be evaluated. As teenagers and adults, former preemies with a history of BPD should not smoke.

RESPIRATORY INFECTIONS

CHILDREN BORN PREMATURELY have fragile lungs that are extrasensitive to respiratory viruses. A typical cold often ends up affecting a preemie's lungs, rather than staying mostly in the nose and throat (as is more common in full-term children). Furthermore, preterm infants, especially those born at less than thirty-three weeks gestation, acquire few or no natural protective antibodies from their mothers before birth. That is why most doctors warn parents to avoid crowded and potentially germ-infested places, such as malls, grocery stores, and childcare centers, for at least the first year or two after discharge. The common types of respiratory infections follow.

> *I counted down the days, weeks, and months of winter. Each week that Jordan stayed well seemed like such an accomplishment. She did get one cold somehow, but we were able to stay on top of it and she handled it fairly well. I'm so glad that winter is behind us. Next winter we will try and keep her away from others, but I don't think we'll need to be quite as cautious.*
>
> —*CINDY, MOTHER OF 28-WEEKER JORDAN*

UPPER RESPIRATORY INFECTIONS (OR "COLDS")

If your child is diagnosed with an upper respiratory infection, it means she has a cold. Because your preemie is more susceptible to a cold's complications, your doctor may aggressively treat a cold at its earliest signs.

Signs of upper respiratory infections

Your child may be getting an upper respiratory infection if she:

- has a stuffy nose with a thin, watery discharge;
- has a fever (but not necessarily);
- is restless or overtired;
- has a decrease in appetite or has difficulty eating;
- is sneezing;
- has watery eyes;
- is breathing faster than is "normal" for her;
- is coughing; and/or
- has an increased need for oxygen (Your child may need to start supplemental oxygen or have her present oxygen increased.)

■ ■ ■

WARNING SIGNS

Call the doctor immediately if your child's cold worsens or she:

- has an increased rate of breathing;
- has difficulty breathing;
- is wheezing;
- has retractions (her chest or rib area "caves in" when she breathes);
- is frequently coughing;
- has a change in color from pink to dusky pale or gray, or there is a blue tone around the lips (even if it is only periodically);
- will not or cannot drink or eat;
- cannot sleep; and/or
- tires easily.

If your child has bronchopulmonary dysplasia, she may exhibit some of these symptoms without a cold. You should still discuss any unusual symptoms or concerns with your pediatrician.

Treatment for upper respiratory infections

How to treat your child's colds needs to be discussed in advance with your doctor. It is a good idea to create a home "care plan" outlining steps to take when your child first exhibits symptoms. The box on page 83 provides an example of a care plan for a child with lung disease. Some other steps your doctor may suggest are:

- giving your child additional clear fluids (providing she is not on fluid restriction). Clear fluids are anything you can see through when they are in a bottle or glass (water, juice, caffeine-free tea, chicken or beef broth, Popsicles, or a commercial supplement such as Pedialyte). Your doctor may also recommend watering down your child's formula for a short period of time. *Do not keep your child on clear fluids for more than twelve hours without consulting your pediatrician;*
- encouraging your child to save her energy for eating and healing by keeping her environment calm and quiet and eliminating excess handling;
- giving infant acetaminophen (such as Tylenol) or infant ibuprofen (such as Motrin) for fever or discomfort. (Always check the dosage with your doctor, and never give your child aspirin without consulting your doctor);

IF YOUR PREEMIE FREQUENTLY WHEEZES

Some pediatric lung experts believe that three or more episodes of wheezing, regardless of the trigger, could mean your child has reactive airways disease (RAD). Some doctors may also diagnose this as asthma. Your child who wheezes frequently may need to be treated as though she has asthma. See "Reactive Airways Disease" and "Asthma" toward the end of this chapter.

- treating nasal congestion with normal saline (commercially prepared saltwater) nose drops or medication, as prescribed or recommended by your doctor; and
- running a cool-mist humidifier close to your baby to keep her secretions moist.

You should never give over-the-counter cold medicines to a child under age one (actual age).

Lower Respiratory Infections

Children born prematurely who have weak, underdeveloped lungs, are small in size, and who have not built up their immune systems often cannot fight off infections. Colds can turn into bronchiolitis or even pneumonia. Either may require hospitalization.

> *I would do everything I could to keep my son's cold under control. Sometimes it worked. Other times he would develop pneumonia. I thought he would never outgrow his preemie lungs and just get a common cold like other kids. Now that he is four, he seems to be able to fight off infection better, but it still takes him a little longer than other kids to get well.*
>
> —*Dani, mother of 31-weeker Josh*

■

YOUR PREEMIE IS IN THE HOSPITAL *AGAIN*

Premature infants are rehospitalized up to 50 percent more often than term children. The most common reason for hospitalization is a respiratory infection. Other reasons include feeding difficulties, poor weight gain, severe gastroesophageal reflux, infection, severe apnea and bradycardia, and surgery (hernia-repair surgeries are the most common).

Hospitalization is an incredibly frightening experience. You not only face the "normal" fears that all parents share, you also must cope with difficult reminders of the past. Walking through those hospital doors can stir up feelings you thought were long buried—anxiety, fear, anger, guilt, and sadness. Family members may experience similar feelings, adding to your own distress.

Hospitalization is an emotional hardship on the entire family. Your ability to cope can positively affect everyone. If you are having an unusually difficult time, seek assistance. Talk with your own or the hospital's chaplain. A social worker or a counselor may help. Find a support group with preemie parents who have experienced rehospitalization. And try to keep in mind that you will get through this—just as you did the first time. For parent tips on hospitalization, see box on page 146.

One week after Devin was discharged, he was readmitted to the NICU. Two months later, he was hospitalized again, but at another hospital. I had managed to keep myself together during his first hospitalization, but with the second, I became unglued. At this new place, I had to get used to a whole new set of rules and get to know an entirely different hospital staff. We had come so far, yet it seemed we were back at square one.

For the first two years of Devin's life, he was hospitalized about every six weeks. It was so hard. I couldn't take off work and was unable to visit him except for my lunch hour. In the evening, I would play with Devin and explain to him that I had to go to work the next day. I tried to keep him on a regular bedtime routine as much as possible. Routines and making the time in the hospital fun must have worked, because Devin now has no anxiety about going into a hospital.

—INA, MOTHER OF 26-WEEKER DEVIN

Bronchiolitis

Bronchiolitis, usually caused by a virus, is an inflammation of the lower small airways of the lungs. If your child has bronchiolitis, her airways are inflamed and swollen, and mucus will collect in them. Airways may become partially or completely blocked, making it difficult for your child to breathe.

Signs of bronchiolitis

Bronchiolitis most often occurs during the first two years of life, but preemies can be susceptible for longer. Depending on the virus causing the illness, it takes three to seven days for symptoms to start after contracting the virus. Bronchiolitis typically lasts for about seven days, but severe cases can last for weeks.

Signs of bronchiolitis typically follow after a day or two of cold-like symptoms. Your child may have bronchiolitis if she:

- has an increased difficulty in breathing;
- has retractions (her chest or rib area "caves in" when she breathes);
- is wheezing;
- has shallow breathing (quick, small panting-type breaths);
- has an increased heart rate;
- has a fever (but not necessarily);
- is frequently coughing;
- shows signs of dehydration (irritability, reduced urine output, dark yellow urine) because breathing problems are preventing her from drinking or eating;
- has a decrease in appetite; and/or
- has a color change to pale or dusky.

Bronchiolitis can be life-threatening. If you suspect your child has bronchiolitis, call your doctor immediately.

Treatment for bronchiolitis

Usually caused by a virus, bronchiolitis cannot be treated with antibiotics. (Antibiotics can only treat infections caused by bacteria.) Treatment is therefore based on minimizing your child's symptoms. If your child can be treated at home, your doctor may recommend:

- increasing fluid intake by giving additional clear liquids or watering down formula;
- running a cool-mist humidifier near your baby to keep her secretions moist;
- giving infant acetaminophen (such as Tylenol) or infant ibuprofen (such as Motrin) for fever or discomfort (Always check the dosage with your doctor, and never give aspirin without consulting your doctor.);
- giving respiratory treatments, such as a nebulization treatment and/or chest physiotherapy;
- prescribing medications, such as bronchodilators or steroids (inhaled or oral);
- prescribing supplemental oxygen or increasing present oxygen level; and
- encouraging your child to rest.

Pneumonia

Pneumonia is an infection within the lung tissue; the infection could be in one small area of the lung, all over one lung, or throughout both lungs. Pneumonia may be caused by a variety of microorganisms. Viruses or bacteria that cause pneumonia are found in the mucus from the mouth and the nose of the infected person. Pneumonia spreads by coughs and sneezes, by sharing the same eating materials or drinking glass, and by touching something the infected person has just touched. Depending on the germ involved, the incubation period is from eighteen hours to six days; this means it can take less than a day or as many as six days for symptoms to appear after contact.

Your pediatrician will diagnose pneumonia by examining your child, possibly taking an X ray of her chest, performing blood tests, and/or running lab tests of the mucus produced by coughing.

Signs of pneumonia

Signs and symptoms of pneumonia usually begin two or three days after cold symptoms (or a sore throat in older children) start. However, pneumonia can occur without any signs of an upper respiratory infection. Symptoms vary depending on what germ caused the illness and how prone your child is to an infection in the lungs. Pneumonia caused by bacteria will often make a child sick faster, with a sudden high fever and an increased rate of breathing. Your child may be evaluated for pneumonia if she:

- has a high fever;
- exhibits chills;
- has rapid breathing;
- is wheezing and/or making grunt-like sounds;
- is frequently coughing;
- has retractions (the chest or rib area "caves in" when she breathes);
- has bluish or gray color in lips or fingernails;
- is vomiting;
- has pain in her chest, abdomen, or shoulder area;
- is unusually tired or listless; and/or
- has a decreased appetite.

Pneumonia can be life-threatening. If you suspect your child has pneumonia, call your doctor immediately.

Treatment for pneumonia

If your child has bacterial pneumonia, your doctor will prescribe antibiotics. For viral pneumonia, your doctor will treat your child's symptoms. If your child can be treated at home, your doctor may suggest:

- increasing fluid intake by giving clear liquids or watering down formula;
- running a cool-mist humidifier near your baby to keep her secretions moist;
- giving infant acetaminophen (such as Tylenol) or infant ibuprofen (such as Motrin) for fever or discomfort (Always check the dosage with your doctor, and never give your child aspirin without consulting your doctor.);
- giving respiratory treatments, such as nebulization treatments and/or chest physiotherapy;
- prescribing medications, such as bronchodilators;
- prescribing supplemental oxygen or increasing present oxygen level;
- recommending a heating pad or warm compress to be placed on the area of pain; and
- encouraging your child to rest.

Other Critical Respiratory Infections

Two specific viral respiratory infections—respiratory syncytial virus and influenza—can be life-threatening for children born prematurely. You should learn the symptoms of these illnesses in order to recognize when treatment may be needed. Equally important is learning and taking the preventative measures discussed in this section.

■ ■ ■

Respiratory syncytial virus (RSV)

Respiratory syncytial virus (or RSV) is the major cause of lower respiratory infections in young children: It causes up to 70 percent of bronchiolitis cases and 25 percent of pneumonia cases. For adults and children over the age of three, RSV presents itself just like a cold. For very young babies and preemies with any type of respiratory compromise, RSV can become life-threatening.

RSV is in the same virus family as influenza, measles, and mumps. Epidemics in the United States typically begin between late October and mid-December, peak in January and February, and end in April or May. In the southern hemisphere, RSV peaks in June through August.

Two major strains of RSV have been identified: type A and type B. The predominant strain varies each year, but both strains can be quickly identified in the laboratory. After an RSV infection, the body forms some immunity to the virus, but that immunity is not complete or long-lasting. If a healthy child gets a second RSV infection, it is usually less severe than the first infection. However, if your child still has lung disease, a second or even a third RSV infection can be severe.

Children become infected with RSV through direct contact with the virus. Your preemie must touch the virus, then touch her mouth, eyes, or nose to contract it. This virus can live for several hours on objects, such as countertops and tissues, and for about thirty minutes on human skin.

A person with RSV is most contagious during the first two to four days, but RSV can continue to spread for up to two weeks after a stuffy nose begins. The incubation period is four to six days; once your child has come in contact with the virus, it takes four to six days for symptoms to appear.

Andrew has had RSV three times in his first seventeen months of life. The first time he was only seven months old. We thought it was just a cold, but it kept getting worse. Just when we thought our lives were becoming normal, reality hit. It was clear Andrew was never going to be that perfect healthy baby, and we'd always have to be on the lookout for signs of illness.

That's when we began our life of seclusion. We didn't take Andrew anywhere that wasn't absolutely necessary. If anybody had a sniffle, he stayed home and they stayed away. Hand-washing was on the verge of compulsiveness.

I had a lot of guilt about working and having to take Andrew to daycare. After all, it was our choice to have him, and shouldn't we be willing to go without anything for our child? But we couldn't afford to give up my income and keep our house and car. We felt a home daycare was the best choice. The daycare provider was not allowed to take him anywhere, although we couldn't control exposure to her other children.

During the second episode of RSV, he was rushed to the hospital by ambulance. The third time we were on vacation. I continue to worry and wonder when our lives will ever be normal.

—*Renea, mother of 28-weeker Andrew*

Signs of RSV

It is impossible to tell if an adult's or older child's cold is caused by RSV or another less-threatening virus. However, if it occurs during the RSV season, RSV is most likely the cause. In preemies and other infants, RSV can be diagnosed by testing the nasal secretions.

Your child with RSV will exhibit "cold" symptoms, which then may develop into lower respiratory infection symptoms, such as those associated with bronchiolitis and pneumonia.

Your child may be evaluated for RSV if she:

- has large amounts of clear secretions from the nose (These may be difficult for her to clear.);
- has a fever (It may or may not be indicative of the severity of the illness.);
- has episodes of apnea (more commonly in infants under two months corrected age);
- exhibits signs of a lower respiratory infection (a frequent cough, difficulty in breathing and/or rapid breathing, retractions, wheezing, and/or a decreased appetite);
- has an increased need for oxygen (Your child may need to start supplemental oxygen or have her present oxygen increased.); and/or
- has an ear infection (Ear infections occur frequently with RSV).

If you suspect your child has RSV, consult your pediatrician immediately.

Treatment for RSV

Antibiotics will not treat RSV, because it is a virus. A drug called Ribavirin is sometimes used to treat RSV in severe cases, but many experts feel it is ineffective. If your child is diagnosed with RSV, your physician will base treatment on your child's needs. This may include:

- prescribing supplemental oxygen or increasing her current oxygen level (one or more pulse-oximeter studies are needed);
- increasing fluid intake by giving clear liquids or watering down formula;
- running a cool-mist humidifier near your baby to keep her secretions moist;
- prescribing respiratory treatments, such as nebulization treatments and/or chest physiotherapy;
- giving infant acetaminophen (such as Tylenol) or infant ibuprofen (such as Motrin) for fever or discomfort (Always check the dosage with your doctor, and never give your child aspirin without consulting your doctor.);
- prescribing an antibiotic for an ear infection; and
- encouraging your child to rest.

Some preemies, especially those who are smaller and younger and those with more severe BPD, are hospitalized for RSV treatment. Discuss your doctor's requirements for hospitalization in advance so you will know what to expect if your child contracts RSV.

Prevention of RSV

Keeping your premature infant from contracting RSV is critical to her future health. Being vigilant about avoiding crowds and smoke, washing hands, and screening visitors during RSV season are important. You should also actively discourage hospitalization for elective surgery to prevent your baby from contracting RSV within the hospital.

Some doctors use preventative treatments during RSV season. A drug called Respigam has been proven to significantly decrease the incidence and severity of RSV in preemies. It is administered through an IV every month during RSV season. A new drug called Synagis, which is an antibody against RSV, is given as a shot during RSV season. Ask your doctor if your preemie qualifies for Respigam or Synagis.

Potential long-term effects of RSV

RSV is a serious illness during the first years of a preemie's life. Your baby's lungs are still healing, and another insult to her lungs may damage the new, healthy lung tissue she has developed.

The more serious the infection, the more likely it is your child will have long-term damage. One-quarter to one-third of infants who had RSV develop asthma-like symptoms during their first three years. Experts disagree whether RSV causes asthma, accentuates an existing problem, or unmasks an asthmatic tendency.

Influenza (the "flu")

Influenza, commonly known as the "flu," is a highly contagious respiratory infection caused by the influenza virus. Influenza outbreaks generally occur in the winter and early spring. There are three types of the influenza virus, but only two affect humans: type A (the most common) and type B. Both types are always changing, resulting in a new epidemic every few years. Like other respiratory viruses, the flu can be difficult for premature infants to handle.

Signs of influenza

Flu symptoms usually appear one to four days after your child is exposed to the virus, and the initial symptoms usually disappear after about five days. However, your child may still be weak and/or have a persistent cough for up to fourteen days, possibly longer. Your child may have the flu, if she:

- has a high fever;
- is irritable;
- exhibits chills;
- has a decreased appetite;
- has a runny nose;
- is frequently coughing;

- is breathing rapidly with retractions (the chest or rib area "caves in" when she breathes);
- is unusually tired or listless; and/or
- is vomiting.

Your older child may have a sore throat and complain of a headache and/or muscle aches. If you suspect your child has influenza, consult your pediatrician immediately.

Treatment for influenza

Antibiotics will not help the flu, because it is caused by a virus. There is a medication for type-A influenza, but it is not approved for infants. Treatment is generally based on minimizing your child's symptoms. Your doctor may recommend:

- increasing fluid intake by giving clear liquids or watering down formula;
- running a cool-mist humidifier near your baby to keep secretions moist;
- giving infant acetaminophen (such as Tylenol) or infant ibuprofen (such as Motrin) for fever or discomfort (Always check the dosage with your doctor *and never give aspirin, as it is associated with a rare condition known as Reye's Syndrome, particularly in children with the flu.*);
- prescribing respiratory treatments, such as a nebulization treatment and/or chest physiotherapy; and
- encouraging your child to rest.

If your child is improving from the flu after three to five days and then suddenly her cough worsens, her breathing becomes more difficult, and she develops a high fever, immediately call your doctor. Influenza predisposes babies to contract some serious, life-threatening infections, such as bacterial tracheitis (an infection in the windpipe) and bacterial pneumonia.

Prevention of influenza

The American Academy of Pediatrics recommends that any child with chronic lung disease should receive a flu vaccination after six months of age (actual age for preemies). This vaccination reduces the likelihood of your child contracting the flu by 60 to 80 percent. In addition, all siblings and caretakers of your child should be immunized to decrease their chances of contracting the flu and passing it on to your child. If your vaccinated child does develop the flu, her symptoms should be fewer and milder.

During your child's first three years, the flu vaccine should be given in two doses—spaced one month apart—in the early fall. All subsequent immunizations require only one shot. The influenza vaccine does not cause the flu, as some people believe. It also will not prevent flu-like illnesses caused by other viruses.

■ ■ ■

COMMON PREEMIE LUNG DISORDERS

CHILDREN BORN PREMATURELY are at risk for developing two lung disorders—reactive airways disease (RAD) and asthma—both discussed below.

REACTIVE AIRWAYS DISEASE (RAD)

Reactive airways disease (or RAD) has become a common term referring to how the lungs react, by wheezing, to an environmental or illness-related trigger. Your child with RAD may wheeze when she breathes cold air, exercises, or when she has a respiratory infection. While this does not necessarily mean she has asthma, the wheezing is usually treated like asthma (with bronchodilators inhaled from a metered-dose inhaler or a nebulizer). Many children outgrow RAD, but approximately 50 percent of infants and young children who continue to have wheezing episodes beyond three years of age will be diagnosed with asthma.

ASTHMA

Asthma is a lung disorder included in the group of reactive airways diseases. Wheezing is a prominent symptom. Preemies are more at risk for developing asthma, especially if they had chronic lung disease and/or a family history of asthma or allergies. Children with asthma have recurrent breathing difficulties. During an asthma "attack," the air flow coming in and out of the lungs is decreased or blocked by swelling, increased mucus, and muscle squeezing of the airways (bronchospasm or bronchoconstriction).

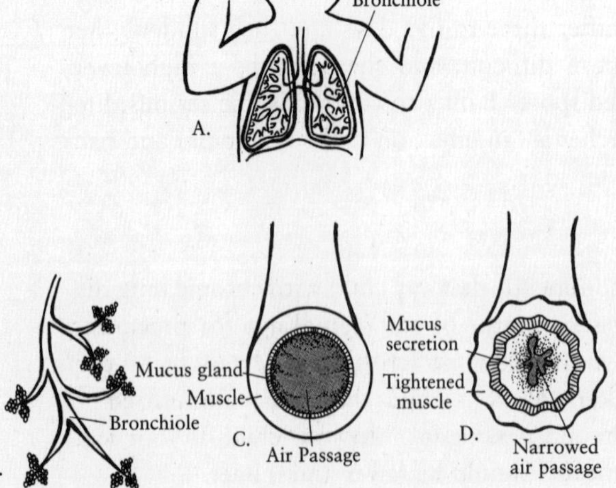

What happens during an asthma "attack":

A. Lungs
B. Bronchiole
C. Bronchiole that is clear and relaxed
D. Bronchiole during an asthma "attack"; it is clogged with mucus and has tightened muscles that narrow the airway, making breathing difficult

Diagnosis of asthma

After several episodes of wheezing, your pediatrician may suspect asthma. If your child is under six years of age, your doctor may be reluctant to diagnose her with asthma and may prefer to call it reactive airways disease until she is older. The difference between RAD and asthma is how long the wheezing episodes last. (RAD tends to disappear by age six, while asthma is more persistent and may last through adulthood.)

An accurate diagnosis of asthma is often difficult because symptoms can be similar to other respiratory illnesses. Your doctor will rely on your observations, your preemie's medical history, and a physical exam. Allergy testing, a chest X ray, blood tests, and pulmonary function testing (if your child is able) may also be done. During a pulmonary function test, a child breathes into and out of a small inhaler-type machine that measures the lungs' abilities. It evaluates the type and amount of lung problem, as well as the response to treatments. Your doctor may refer you to a pediatric pulmonologist and/or an asthma-allergy specialist.

Signs of asthma

About 90 percent of asthma "attacks" in very young children are triggered by a respiratory illness. Symptoms can also be triggered by environmental factors, such as cold air, dry air, cigarette or fireplace smoke, pollen, and other airborne substances, as well as by exercise. Asthma in young children does not always present itself through wheezing. Other symptoms in infants and small children include:

- retractions (the chest or rib area "caves in" during breathing);
- coughing; and/or
- an increased rate of breathing.

If your child frequently has these symptoms, consult your doctor or an asthma-allergy specialist.

Treatment and prevention of asthma

Typical treatment and prevention of asthma includes medications (such as bronchodilators and/or steroids) and respiratory treatments (such as nebulization treatments and the use of a metered-dose inhaler to administer medications). Minimizing environmental triggers and learning to manage asthma at home are also important.

One way to manage asthma in an older child is by using a peak flow meter, a handheld instrument designed to measure the flow of air through the airways. A peak flow meter can determine whether your child's lung function is abnormal, help predict the onset of an attack, and determine which medicine is helping. You can also prevent or lessen the frequency and severity of asthma episodes by:

- helping your child avoid irritants and/or allergens that may cause asthma attacks, including cigarette smoke and furry animals;
- making sure your child eats a well-balanced diet;

- offering your child liquids frequently;
- administering medications to your child as ordered and *never* giving nonprescription drugs without your doctor's approval; and
- encouraging your family to wash their hands frequently to prevent the spread of infection.

Support groups for parents of children with asthma can be helpful for learning about and coping with asthma.

Potential long-term effects of asthma

A large percentage of young children with asthma, particularly those who have a history of chronic lung disease, continue to have symptoms into adulthood.

ALLERGIES

RESEARCH SHOWS THAT preterm infants are *not* at increased risk for allergies. In fact, some studies show that preemies may actually be at less risk for certain allergic symptoms, such as eczema (a skin disorder). A family history of allergies may increase your child's risk for allergies, however. In addition, your child with a lung complication, such as BPD, may develop "allergic-appearing" reactions to viruses and foreign substances (pollen, dust, animal dander, or smoke) because her lungs are more susceptible to the effects of these irritants. Such a reaction usually takes the form of bronchospasm (a "tightening" of the airways) and wheezing—symptoms that closely mimic asthma. If you suspect your child has allergies, talk with your doctor about further investigation by a pediatric allergist.

COPING WITH ISOLATION

DURING YOUR PREEMIE'S first year, and maybe for one or two more years, it is critical to keep your child healthy by staying away from germ-carrying people. At times, you may feel as though you are missing a part of your baby's childhood. You cannot do things or go places with your baby that a parent of a term infant can—shopping at the mall, trips to indoor or outdoor playgrounds, or even lunch with friends. Isolation can be incredibly lonely.

One way to combat loneliness is by getting together with other parents of preterm infants—parents who know the importance of illness prevention. You can even start a preemie parents' group or playgroup. If you did not connect with any parents in the NICU and there is no preemie parent support group in your community, ask for referrals from developmental specialists, the hospital, or a community organization that serves parents of children with special needs.

Communicating by phone with those who understand can also help those long days pass. If you have access to a computer, hook up to one of the preemie parent lists, such as Preemie-l.

Try and remember that the sacrifices you are making today to keep your preemie healthy are investments in your child's future health. The need to stay isolated *will* pass, and soon you and your child can venture out.

CHAPTER SIX

The Brain

OF ALL THE complications associated with a premature birth, a diagnosis of a neurological (brain) problem is one of the most devastating for parents. The majority of preemies "outgrow" their lung illnesses and feeding problems, catch up in size, and overcome their developmental delays, but neurological problems can last a lifetime.

Learning about, living with, and accepting your child's neurological condition is a process that will take time. Do not be afraid to seek and accept help from others during this difficult journey. Developing a support network with other families who have children with similar neurological problems can be beneficial. You will also need support while coping with other medical problems, doctors' visits, surgeries, and therapies.

This chapter will introduce you to your preemie's neurological condition.

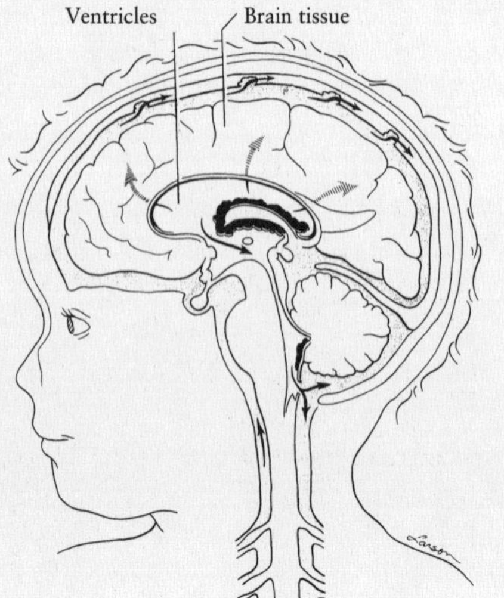

The brain

WHEN THE BRAIN IS PREMATURE

NORMAL DEVELOPMENT OF the brain and central nervous system allows a typical baby to grow and develop skills she needs for everyday life. A term baby's brain is resilient: It can withstand many insults without any long-term effects. When a baby is born prematurely, however, the brain is less resilient because it is not fully developed. A traumatic event before, during, or soon after a premature birth can cause long-term complications.

The ventricles and the brain tissue around them are the most common areas that are adversely affected by trauma in a preterm infant. The ventricles are channels of fluid deep inside the brain that produce and hold cerebral spinal fluid (CSF, also termed "water"). CSF circulates and "cushions" the brain and spinal cord, while also providing essential nutrients for the central nervous system. The ventricles are surrounded by brain tissue that contains many nerves that tell the body's muscles how to function. The location and extent of damage to the brain determines how the baby is affected. The following sections discuss the common brain problems of preemies.

INTRAVENTRICULAR HEMORRHAGE (IVH)

BLEEDING IN OR around the ventricles of the brain is called an intraventricular hemorrhage (IVH, or sometimes referred to as a "bleed"). An IVH is most common in preemies born before thirty-two weeks gestational age. Before thirty-two weeks, the blood vessels in a baby's brain are not well protected by tissue surrounding them, leaving them at risk for damage from trauma. These tiny blood vessels can break when injury occurs, and they can bleed into the ventricles. Changes in an infant's blood pressure is the most frequent cause of trauma to the vessels. However, there are a number of other insults, which can occur at any gestational age, that cause bleeding in the brain.

Damage to brain function occurs when the excess blood causes an enlargement of the ventricles or, in more severe cases, when the blood flows into the brain tissue outside of the ventricles. Blood is a foreign substance to this tissue and will destroy it. Some experts believe it is not only the blood in the brain tissue that destroys brain cells, but the lack of blood flow to the brain because of the bleed that causes long-term damage.

A head ultrasound, CAT scan, or MRI is used to diagnose an IVH. An IVH is graded by its level of severity. It is impossible to predict how an IVH will affect your child, and the "wait and see" approach can be difficult. In general, a mild IVH can cause few or no problems; a more severe IVH (grade 3 or 4) can lead to long-term complications. If you are told that your child's IVH has "resolved," it means that the blood is no longer visible on ultrasound. Damage and long-term effects are still possible, even if the IVH has "resolved."

Some preemies with an IVH are also diagnosed with periventricular leukomalacia or hydrocephalus, discussed later in this chapter.

■ ■ ■

IVH LEVELS

The amount of hemorrhage or "bleed" in the brain can vary and is graded by either a head ultrasound or a CAT scan.

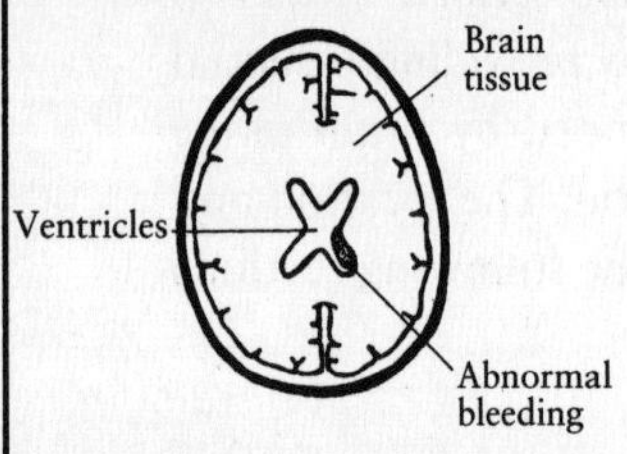

Grade 1: The blood is in the lining of the ventricles.

Grade 2: The blood is in the ventricles.

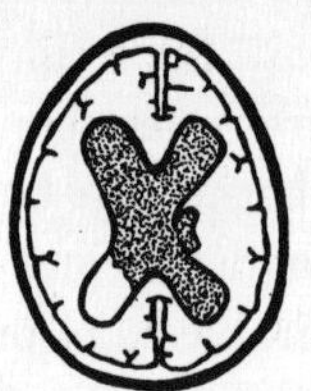

Grade 3: The blood is in the ventricles, which are somewhat enlarged.

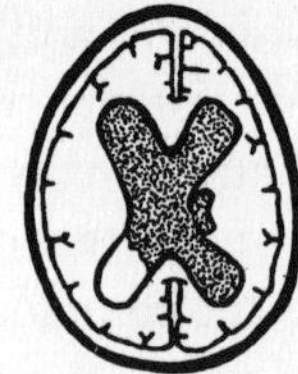

Grade 4: The bleeding is occurring in the ventricles and in the tissue of the brain.

Jack was less than forty-eight hours old when we were hit with another bombshell—Jack had an intraventricular hemorrhage. The first ultrasounds showed grade 2, which then slightly worsened before starting to resolve.

Jack's IVH was the most frightening part of his NICU course. With just about every other preemie problem, his doctors could be very specific and tell us about potential outcomes. But with this brain bleed, there was no way to know. We were told we would have to "wait and see."

I went from feeling numb, to worried, to scared. What would this IVH mean to my child? I could handle the supplemental oxygen. I could cope with any eyesight problems. But the thought of something being wrong with my child's brain—his mind and his intellect—really frightened me.

Every developmental checkup we attended was full of uncertainty. What would the doctors discover? I have never really felt excitement or joy when Jack has reached a milestone. Instead, I have felt relief—one more milestone to check off the list.

It turns out that the brain is really an amazing organ. Jack is now four years old and is developmentally right on track or even ahead. He loves books, jokes, and is a great storyteller. In just about all ways, Jack is a "normal" little boy. As for me, I am much more tired and older than I was four years ago, but also much wiser.

—*Kerri, mother of 24-weeker Jack*

■ ■ ■

A NEUROLOGICAL EXAM: WHAT TO EXPECT

A neurological exam is an overall evaluation of your child's physical and cognitive abilities. The questions and assessments will change slightly as your child grows, but the general intent remains the same. Your child will be assessed based on her corrected age until approximately two and one-half years, when the developmental difference becomes insignificant. Common screening questions include:

- Does your child react when family members or friends talk and play with her?
- Do you have concerns about your child's attention, concentration, and learning abilities?
- Are your child's gross motor skills (rolling, walking, running, etc.) and fine motor skills (hand use) delayed beyond her corrected age?
- Do you see any unusual movements in your child's arms, legs, or eyes? If so, what are the movements like, how long do they last, and when do they happen? Do the movements in her limbs stop if you hold them?

Your physician will also perform a general physical assessment evaluating your child's:

- consciousness (state of alertness or arousal ability);
- cognitive abilities (attention, speech, self-help skills, memory, play, and understanding of questions);
- the movement of all her body parts, including her face and her reflexes;
- sensory abilities (vision, hearing, taste, smell, and awareness of touch and pain);
- regulatory functions (breathing, heart rate, temperature, and bowel and bladder habits); and
- head circumference (if your child is under four).

Other testing may include:

A computed tomography (CT or CAT scan). A special type of X ray that visualizes the structures of the brain. A CAT scan takes about twenty minutes and the child is usually sedated. Sometimes a special fluid (a contrast material) is injected into a vein in the child's arm and eventually flows into the vessels of the brain. This contrast material helps to visualize certain structures of the brain.

A magnetic resonance imaging (MRI). A magnetic field is used instead of an X ray to visualize tissue. An MRI takes about thirty minutes, and the child is usually sedated.

A head ultrasound. A smooth and rounded probe is placed on the head near the fontanel (the "soft spot"). Sound-wave pictures of the ventricles are transmitted onto a screen for the doctor, who then examines the size of the ventricles. This procedure is gentle and the child often sleeps through it.

An electroencephalogram (EEG). Eight to twenty-one probes are placed on the child's head and body to record atypical electrical activity in the brain, especially if there are any concerns about possible seizures. For a child who experiences seizures, this test is often ordered to see if it is safe to begin weaning the child off her seizure medication. An EEG takes about forty-five minutes, and the child may or may not be sedated.

When you are shown your child's CAT scan, X ray, MRI, or EEG, ask to see a normal one, giving you a basis for comparison.

Potential Complications and Long-Term Effects of an IVH

Preemies with any level of intraventricular hemorrhage, but particularly those with a grade 3 or grade 4 IVH, are at greater risk for cognitive (thinking), physical, and behavioral problems. These include difficulties with memory, speech, vision, fine and gross motor skills, attention, and learning.

Generally, the younger in gestational age and the more severe the IVH, the more significant the long-term problems. Early and ongoing assessments are extremely important. Your child with long-term complications from an intraventricular hemorrhage can benefit greatly from activities that help her develop her weak areas and accelerate her strengths. Refer to chapter 13.

PERIVENTRICULAR LEUKOMALACIA (PVL)

PERIVENTRICULAR LEUKOMALACIA (OR PVL) is a type of brain injury specific to preemies. *Periventricular* means "surrounding the ventricles" and *leukomalacia* refers to the softening of the brain tissue surrounding the ventricles. This softening results from a temporary decrease in blood flow to the brain, which causes the tissue to die. Eventually, holes or "cysts" develop and replace the healthy brain tissue with fluid. The loss of this important brain tissue and the nerve fibers that run through the brain tissue (which greatly control muscle movement) can cause long-term damage.

Happy and healthy two-year-old Eric (a former 26-weeker) with PVL and cerebral palsy loves to meet people.

When your baby was hospitalized, your neonatologist tried to avoid any trauma that might have caused the development of PVL. (However, most events occur without warning, making prevention difficult.) The reason for decreased blood flow resulting in PVL is often unknown, but some causes include:

- extreme prematurity;
- an intraventricular hemorrhage (IVH). (It is not uncommon for babies who have a grade 3 or grade 4 IVH to have PVL, but even a preemie without an IVH can have PVL.);
- a temporary lack of oxygen;
- a brain infection, such as meningitis;
- a seizure disorder;
- abnormalities in the blood; and/or
- a significant pause in breathing and/or drop in heart rate (apnea and bradycardia).

Periventricular leukomalacia . . . even in my nursing career, I had never heard of this diagnosis. I only knew it didn't sound good. When I asked Eric's neonatologist what this meant, he answered simply, "Cerebral palsy."

Eric and his identical twin brother, Aaron, were born on July 28, 1993, at 26 weeks gestation. Both had many of the common complications of prematurity. Eric's most serious complication was and is periventricular leukomalacia, or PVL.

When I first learned of Eric's condition, I attempted to find out everything there was to know about the subject. I wanted an exact portrait of how this diagnosis would affect my son. I quickly learned a lesson that all families raising a child with a disability learn—there are no clearly defined borders in relation to outcome. We only knew that Eric was at high risk for cerebral palsy.

But what did that mean? Would he walk with a limp? Would he be severely disabled? My spirit grieved for Eric and my mind created negative caricatures of Eric's future. Not knowing exactly what I was grieving for made it all the worse. Seeing a person in a wheelchair affirmed my worst fears. Seeing a typical child running and playing outside gave me a glimpse of what Eric had lost. As I looked upon this beautiful, tiny baby it seemed impossible that his brain was not perfect. I cried for what Eric had lost at such a young age. I also wept for the loss of Eric as I had imagined he would be. In many ways, the unknown was the hardest part of Eric's diagnosis of PVL.

Children come into this world innocent, carefree, and full of life. At least that is how it's supposed to be. What possibly could have gone so wrong that my child would never have the same advantages as typical children? Questions such as this constantly went through my mind. I struggled with feelings of guilt, sadness, anger, and jealousy. Guilt for maybe having done something that caused the twins to be born too soon. Sadness at the loss of the usual joys of pregnancy, childbirth, and twins. Anger because this happened to our family and jealousy toward people with "normal" children.

Now that Eric has actually been diagnosed with cerebral palsy, I am slowly gaining insights into his full potential. At least I can begin to cope. I try not to mourn what was lost, but accept and acknowledge what has been found. I realize that although things could have turned out better, they could also be much worse.

I am thankful for Eric and his brother. Eric has an infectious smile and a belly laugh that is contagious. He has brought tremendous joy into our lives and into the lives around him. He has taught me patience and to take nothing for granted. He has taught me what is truly important in life. When I first learned of his diagnosis, all I could think about was his disability. Now I see that he is "Eric," a child similar in most ways to any other child. His disability is only a small part of who he is.

—CINDY, MOTHER OF 26-WEEKER ERIC, TWIN TO AARON

■

On day three of Alexandra's life, we got the good news that her grade 1 IVH [intraventricular hemorrhage] was resolving. Then, almost as an afterthought, the doctor said that Alex had some areas of her brain that looked "suspicious." In my naïveté of the medical world, I had no idea what this meant and ignored its importance.

After a CAT scan just before discharge, the doctor finally put a name to it—periventricular leukomalacia. The explanation of this diagnosis was simple; the prognosis was devastating. Every problem seemed to have the word "major" in front of it: major learning disabilities, major speech problems, and major physical disabilities.

During Alex's first years home, I didn't think about her PVL much. I was just happy to have her home and happy she was healthy.

By the time Alex was three years old, I began to notice how behind she was in development. Her pediatrician made me feel as if I was overreacting, but I couldn't ignore my instincts. I had her evaluated, and I remember sitting there in the conference room as they explained how significantly she was delayed. I thought, How could I have not noticed this earlier? I knew then how uncertain her future was.

I began educating myself. I fear her PVL more today than I did three years ago. I fear the unknown. Will she always need special education classes? Will other kids make fun of her? Will she ever be able to marry?

I become frustrated when I try to relay my fears to others—people don't understand. I get angry when people say I'm being pessimistic, because I think I am anything but that. I rejoice at everything Alex does.

Somehow I have learned to love her for who she is and not for who Alexandra was "supposed" to be. If she never progresses beyond this point, that's okay, because I really love her like she is . . . yet I never give up hope.

—*Kathie, mother of 28-weeker Alexandra*

Diagnosis of PVL

Head ultrasounds are typically done for preemies at risk for PVL within two to four weeks following birth. Your baby was labeled "at risk" if she exhibited any PVL symptoms and/or had an extremely traumatic birth. Although an initial ultrasound was performed early, the damage from PVL takes about two to eight weeks to be detectable, and more than one ultrasound may have been needed prior to discharge. Your baby may also need a follow-up head ultrasound after homecoming. Occasionally, a suspicious area detected by head ultrasound turns out not to be PVL.

Potential Complications and Long-term Effects of PVL

For parents, the future of their child with periventricular leukomalacia is a great concern. Unfortunately, there is no way to predict potential problems. Not knowing can be the hardest part.

The more severe the PVL, the more likely it is that there will be significant cognitive and/or motor problems. The area of the brain affected determines the extent and type of damage. Tissue damage in the back of the brain may affect vision. Cysts in the front of the brain can impair intellectual function. Movement can be affected by damage around the sides of the ventricles. Trauma to the nerve fibers can affect communication between different parts of the brain, as well as affecting movement and coordination. Children with PVL are at risk for the development of hydrocephalus and cerebral palsy, discussed later in this chapter.

If your child was diagnosed with periventricular leukomalacia—even a mild "suspicious area"—she should be watched closely by her physician and evaluated by developmental specialists. Early and ongoing intervention, including physical, occupational, and speech therapy, can enhance your child's outcome. Early intervention services may not "cure" your child's problems, but they can build on her strengths, as well as empower you to enhance her life.

WARNING SIGNS

If your preemie was diagnosed with any level IVH or PVL in the NICU, healthcare professionals should have advised you of potential problems and their warning signs. Early signs, such as excessive irritability and developmental delays, do not necessarily mean your child will have future significant problems. (These symptoms can also be caused by other problems besides IVH and PVL.)

On the other hand, not showing any early warning signs does not always mean your child will be without future problems. Because of this uncertainty, your child should have ongoing regular evaluations with her doctor and developmental specialists.

Motor Problems

Consult your doctor if your child:

- has tight or stiff muscles;
- has difficulty and/or dislikes being on her abdomen;
- exhibits delays in rolling over, crawling, standing, or walking, beyond her corrected age;
- exhibits atypical crawling;
- starts to walk on her toes;

- moves one side more than the other;
- frequently arches her back (not just when she is angry or at play);
- has difficulty eliciting reflexes (for example, she has difficulty turning her head or moving her arm in response to a need);
- has problems with moving (for example, she turns her head and is unable to return it forward); and/or
- has poor coordination or balance.

Cognitive (Thinking) Problems

Consult your doctor if your preemie:

- does not listen to your voice by three to four months corrected age;
- does not make different sounds by eight to nine months corrected age;
- does not understand or say any words by twelve to thirteen months corrected age;
- has difficulty tolerating average amounts of light, touch, or sound;
- does not react to a change in her environment;
- exhibits visual difficulties, including difficulty following an object;
- is fussy, difficult to console, unable to adapt to new situations, and/or shows unpredictable behavior; and/or
- does not cry or move around like most babies her age.

HYDROCEPHALUS

Hydrocephalus occurs when too much cerebral spinal fluid (CSF, or "water") is in the ventricles of the brain. Excess CSF causes a baby's head to grow too quickly and creates pressure on the brain.

If your child's hydrocephalus is *congenital,* some type of brain structure abnormality interfered with the reabsorption of CSF while she was developing in the womb. If your child has *acquired* hydrocephalus, this means that a hemorrhage, an injury, or an infection caused an interference in CSF reabsorption or an abnormally large production of CSF. This may have occurred before, during, or soon after delivery.

In preterm infants, the most common causes of hydrocephalus are intraventricular hemorrhage (IVH) and periventricular leukomalacia (PVL). IVH hydrocephalus develops when the ventricles are blocked by a blood clot or scar tissue. Hydrocephalus associated with PVL develops when the ventricles enlarge to fill the collapsed cysts in the brain tissue.

> *My daughter Leah was diagnosed with hydrocephalus three to four weeks after the diagnosis of an IVH. For the first few weeks, her head growth was stable. As time progressed, her head circumference increased at an unacceptable rate. She had serial lumbar punctures to remove the fluid in her brain every other day for two weeks.*

During this time, my anxiety level skyrocketed. I had so many questions about her future. The technical information was easy to come by, but alarming. I read about cerebral palsy, learning disabilities, shunt infections and malfunctions, and difficulties obtaining developmental support services. When I read about the difficulty of obtaining medical insurance, the potential for a severe financial impact added to my distress.

I felt I understood the technical and physiological aspects of hydrocephalus, but I wanted information on what it took to parent a child with hydrocephalus. I desperately needed to do whatever was necessary to improve the situation. I felt helpless. I worried that if my daughter had a shunt, I would never know what or who she would become.

A couple of days before discharge, Leah's head growth stabilized. I measured her head circumference every day for the first two weeks after she came home. I had extreme anxiety before each doctor's exam, followed by great relief after the visit ended. Once I found others who had children with hydrocephalus and educated myself on how our lives could be "normal" despite these problems, I relaxed a little.

Leah is now two years and five months old, and we continue to worry, but the anxiety has tapered. We are fortunate that Leah has not needed a shunt. She is developing appropriately in all areas, except for some hint of a speech delay. As for me, I have deep scars from the whole experience. I feel that I am stronger from the experience and have a much greater appreciation for my kids, family, and friends.

Steve, father of 27-weeker Leah, twin to Caleb

Diagnosis and Signs of Hydrocephalus

Hydrocephalus is typically diagnosed within four months following birth by a head ultrasound, CAT scan, or MRI. A baby can be diagnosed with hydrocephalus up to one year of age; therefore, all at-risk infants should be watched closely for the first twelve months of life. Your infant will be evaluated for hydrocephalus if she:

- has an enlarged head;
- is quiet and the fontanel (the "soft spot" on top of her head) is tense and full;
- has separated sutures (where the bones that meet at the top of your baby's head are separated due to the pressure from the expanded ventricles);
- is vomiting;
- is eating poorly;
- is unusually sleepy;
- is irritable;
- has a downward deviation of the eyes ("sunset eyes"); and/or
- has a seizure.

Treatment for Hydrocephalus

In very mild cases, hydrocephalus can resolve itself: The body reabsorbs the excess fluid, the ventricles in the brain stop growing, and the symptoms cease. A future infection can cause resolved hydrocephalus to occur again, but this is rare. In more severe cases, the increased size of the ventricles will cause further problems requiring treatment. Treatment involves removing excess fluid from the ventricles. This is done by one of three ways:

Serial lumbar punctures. The doctor inserts a needle into the child's back and into the spinal canal, then withdraws CSF fluid. This procedure may be done periodically when the pressure from too much CSF is more than what the child can tolerate.

A reservoir. An approximately one-inch-round metal or plastic chamber is placed under the skin in the child's head. The chamber connects to a tube in the ventricle. When necessary, fluid can be removed periodically from the ventricles by placing a needle in the chamber under sterile conditions.

A shunt. A tube is surgically placed in one of the ventricles. The tube is attached to a longer piece of tubing placed under the skin. It travels behind the ear, down the neck and chest, and ends where the CSF fluid can drain either into the abdomen or into the heart. Once the shunt is in place, the ventricle size usually decreases (generally within three to five days of placement) and the head should begin to grow normally. Until there are further advances in medicine, a shunt is needed for life. If your child needs a shunt, ask to see one before it is placed.

For older children, there is a medication that in some cases can decrease the production of cerebral spinal fluid.

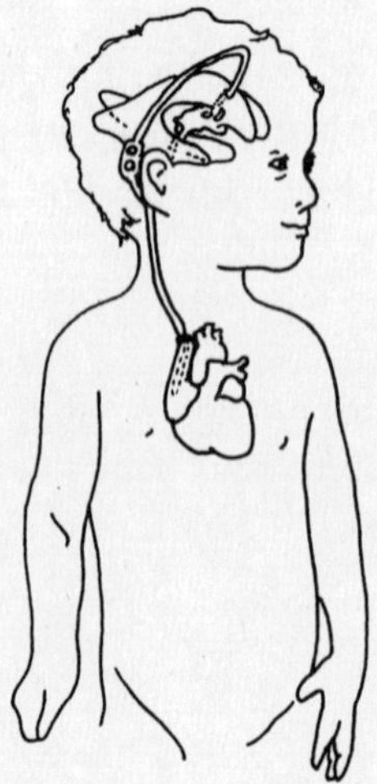

A. This shunt moves the excess cerebral spinal fluid from the ventricles into the heart.

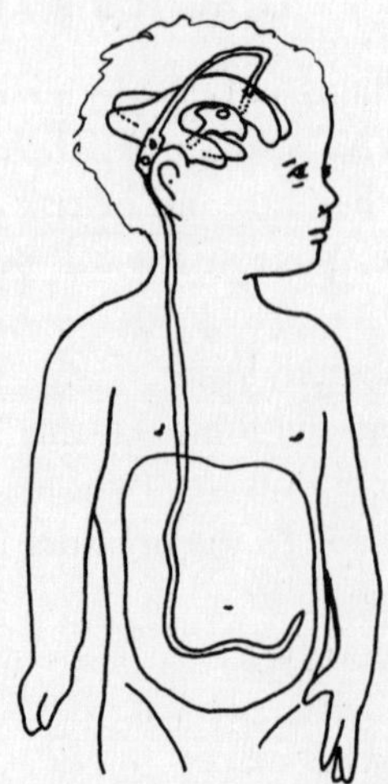

B. This shunt moves the excess cerebral spinal fluid from the ventricles into the stomach.

WARNING SIGNS OF SHUNT COMPLICATIONS

Your child's shunt will need replacing if it stops working. A malfunction can be caused by an obstruction, a mechanical flaw, or when your child outgrows the shunt. An X ray may be needed to evaluate the shunt's position and working ability. A CAT scan or MRI may be required to assess the size of your child's ventricles. If your child gets an infection in the shunt or near the shunt's tubing, the shunt may need replacing (and your child will need antibiotics). Infections are most often associated with the placement or revision of a shunt, but can occur from another infection in the body.

Consult your doctor or neurologist immediately if your *infant* with a shunt:

- has an enlarging head;
- is quiet and the fontanel (the "soft spot" on top of the head) is tense and full;
- has a fever;
- is eating poorly;
- is vomiting;
- has swelling or redness near the shunt's tubing under the skin;
- is irritable;
- is unusually listless or sleepy;
- has a downward deviation of the eyes ("sunset eyes"); and/or
- has a seizure.

Consult your doctor or neurologist immediately if your *toddler* with a shunt:

- has an enlarging head;
- has a fever;
- is eating poorly;
- is vomiting;
- complains of a headache;
- is irritable;
- is unusually sleepy;
- has swelling or redness around the shunt's tubing under the skin;
- exhibits a loss of motor function; and/or
- has a seizure.

Consult your doctor or neurologist immediately if your *school-aged preemie* with a shunt:

- has a fever;
- is eating poorly;
- is vomiting;

- complains of a headache;
- has vision problems;
- is irritable;
- is overtired;
- exhibits a personality change;
- has a loss of coordination or balance;
- has swelling or redness around the shunt's tubing under the skin;
- has difficulty waking up or staying awake;
- has a seizure; and/or
- has a decline in academic performance.

Bailey had to have a shunt at three weeks of age when she weighed just three pounds. It was terrifying to watch such a fragile child head to the operating room. We were not sure if she would return.

Bailey got a second shunt at five months of age. I guess I have to say that living with a "shunted" child is like watching a ticking bomb. We are never sure when there might be a problem or a shunt failure. I'm afraid of missing a symptom and not catching a problem in time, leading to even more damage. At this point, Bailey is not able to tell us that her head hurts or that she can't see very well. We just trust our instincts and insist on being seen by our specialist, even if we aren't sure.

Sometimes I feel like a neurotic parent, but thinking about the alternative puts everything into perspective. With each new day, it gets easier. Watching Bailey laugh and play reminds me that she is a happy, healthy little girl.

—*Kim, mother of 29-weeker Bailey, twin to Brett*

Potential Complications and Long-term Effects of Hydrocephalus

Long-term outcomes of children with hydrocephalus vary according to its severity. Some children will develop normally; others will have significant motor problems. Delays in vision, intellect, speech, and social abilities are also possible. Your child with hydrocephalus needs to be evaluated early to establish a record (a baseline) of what is considered normal for your child. This baseline can be used in the future as a basis for comparison.

■ ■ ■

SEIZURES

A SMALL PERCENTAGE of children born prematurely experience seizures (atypical, repetitive, and uncontrollable movements of the muscles). A seizure disorder often exists with another neurological problem, such as a brain hemorrhage or periventricular leukomalacia. Other causes of seizures in preemies include trauma at birth, significant lack of oxygen, genetic abnormalities, infection, and metabolic disturbances (such as low blood sugar or a high fever).

When Brayden began having seizures at eight months of age, my husband and I seemed to be the only ones caught off guard. It was as if the neurologist had known all along that Brayden would develop seizures at some point because of his brain bleed.

The first two seizures were not all that frightening. He just stared into space, and his right arm twitched for about a minute. He was totally unresponsive to visual or auditory stimuli. His neurologist decided to put Brayden on seizure medication.

A few weeks after starting the medicine, Brayden had significant seizures. These were much more involved and concerning. He went completely limp, his eyes were fixed and glazed, and his whole body began to move. It is so difficult to sit and watch helplessly as your child has a seizure. Some seizures seem to last an eternity.

As I sit and think about Brayden's future, I think of all the things he will not be allowed to do, such as participate in contact sports. I will worry every time he goes out to play or spends the night at someone's house. I want to treat him as normally as possible, but I feel I must protect him from potential danger.

It is hard on us, too. We cannot find baby-sitters, even for an hour, because everyone is afraid of his seizures. Most people who do not live with seizures do not understand them. Parents of children with seizure disorders live with a stress that most other parents cannot understand.

—*Jayna, mother of 29-weeker Brayden*

Diagnosis and Signs of Seizures

Diagnosis of a seizure disorder involves a neurological examination, including an EEG and/or a CAT scan or MRI. Blood tests are often used to evaluate any possible blood imbalances in other areas of the body that might be contributing to the seizures.

In infants, the most common type of seizures are subtle seizures: tiny jerking motions in the arms or legs that cannot be stopped with holding. Toddlers and older children exhibit more obvious movements and symptoms.

Your *infant* may be evaluated for a seizure disorder if she:

- has unusual eye movements (staring, repeated blinking or fluttering of the eyelids, or a forced movement of both eyes in one direction);
- drools excessively;
- sucks excessively;
- twitches her arms or legs; and/or
- exhibits "rowing" movements of the arms or "bicycling" movements of the legs.

Your *toddler* may be evaluated for a seizure disorder if she:

- exhibits atypical movements in the arms or legs;
- twists her head or holds her head in a rigid position;
- turns or rolls her eyes;
- drools and/or smacks her lips excessively;
- loses bladder or bowel control;
- bites her tongue or cheek; and/or
- loses consciousness.

An older child might even experience an "aura," a feeling that a seizure is going to happen before the onset of any seizure activity.

Treatment for Seizures

Medication can usually control seizures. Over time, parents often learn what particular situations (such as a stimulating environment) may trigger a seizure. By avoiding those situations, seizures can sometimes be controlled more easily.

If your child has a seizure, there is nothing you can do to stop it, but you need to keep her safe from trauma. Do not restrain your child or place anything in her mouth, and turn her on her side to prevent choking. Once your child is safe, call your doctor.

Potential Long-term Effects of Seizures

The long-term outcome of children with seizures is difficult to predict. As with other problems associated with the brain, the earlier the problem begins and the more severe the problem, the more likely it is there will be future effects. Recurrent seizures as well as motor and cognitive delays are potential complications.

■ ■ ■

CEREBRAL PALSY (CP)

AN INJURY TO the brain before, during, or shortly after birth can cause cerebral palsy (CP), a disorder affecting muscle tone and movement. In children born prematurely, the most common causes of CP are lack of oxygen at birth, a brain hemorrhage, or periventricular leukomalacia. Recent research also suggests a possible link between low levels of a thyroid hormone in some preemies and CP. About 6 to 7 percent of all premature infants are diagnosed with CP; multiples and those under two pounds are at greater risk.

The extent and location of the brain insult determines the type and severity of cerebral palsy. Some preemies may show serious symptoms at birth; others are not diagnosed for several years.

The reason it can be so difficult to detect mild to moderate cerebral palsy in children born prematurely is because many of its early signs are similar to typical preemie development—sleeping difficulties, feeding problems, difficulties coordinating sucking and swallowing, jittery or jumpy actions, and even stiffness. Clear signs of CP may not be evident until after a preemie's nervous system is more mature. For these reasons, physicians often do not make a diagnosis of CP until twelve to eighteen months corrected age.

After Emily had been home for only a short while, I realized that things were much different than they had been with our son, who was also a preemie. Feeding Emily was a big problem. She barely took an ounce of formula every two hours. After a few months, she finally took a good amount of formula, but she projectile-vomited after every eating.

Emily also cried a lot. I thought it was colic, but the crying was not at any particular time, nor for any regular duration. She constantly startled herself into seemingly endless crying jags.

During well-preemie checkups, the doctor or nurse would ask about milestones. Although I sensed that Emily was behind, I kept reminding myself that I had been told by NICU personnel that Emily would start out slow, but would eventually catch up.

When Emily was ten months old, her doctor told us he thought we should have Emily evaluated for "possible mild cerebral palsy." I suddenly found myself at the beginning of a whole new emotional roller-coaster ride. My jaw dropped, my face felt immediately on fire, my eyes filled with tears, and my body began to shake all over. I clung tightly to my precious girl as I heard his words.

I've always seen problems as challenges—find all the possible solutions, then make an informed choice. But I felt completely helpless when I was first told that my child might have a lifelong disability. The only thing that was within my power was to learn about cerebral palsy. Like a sponge, I began soaking up information.

Emily's doctor made the referral to early intervention, and I was contacted by them in a matter of days. The next step was to meet with Emily's service coordinator, appointed by the public health department's early intervention program. The following week a physical therapist visited our home to evaluate Emily. We then had Emily evaluated by a neurologist and an orthopedic specialist, and she had a developmental evaluation.

Everything was going at such a horrendous speed that I sometimes had to hold up my hands and say, "Slow down for a bit!" Much like the NICU experience, I found myself going through the motions that were necessary for the good of my child—but none of it really made sense at the time.

—Sandra, mother of 30-weeker Emily

Signs of CP

Throughout your preemie's first year, your doctor will watch closely for signs of CP by monitoring milestone achievements and examining muscles and coordination. If your doctor becomes concerned, she will do an evaluation, including a neurological exam, to help identify possible brain abnormalities. Your physician may suspect CP if your child:

- retains her baby reflexes, such as grasping like a newborn;
- is "floppy";
- moves one side more than the other;
- assumes atypical, awkward positions;
- has poor muscle control and is uncoordinated;
- has problems sucking, chewing, and/or swallowing;
- is unusually tense and irritable; and/or
- has other problems with the senses, especially hearing and vision.

It is important to note again that many preemies exhibit characteristics of CP, such as poor muscle tone and irritability. These characteristics may be "transient," meaning they will improve over time and disappear by twelve to eighteen months corrected age. The majority of preemies do not have CP, but you should always discuss any concerns with your pediatrician.

Treatment for CP

Cerebral palsy is not a progressive disorder—it will not get worse over time. There is no cure for cerebral palsy, but physical, occupational, and speech therapy can help your child achieve her potential. If your child is diagnosed with CP, you will be referred to an early intervention program.

Biofeedback—in which an electrical machine gives your child information about the functioning of a particular part of the body—can help. Through biofeedback, your child with CP can gain increased control over movements.

Types of CP

Doctors classify cerebral palsy in two ways: by the affected limbs and by the nature of the movement disturbance. Your child with cerebral palsy can be affected in several areas, and more than one term may be used to describe her condition.

By affected limbs

Diplegia. Two similar limbs on opposite sides are affected, such as both legs (as opposed to one arm and one leg on opposite sides).

Hemiplegia or hemiparesis. The arm and leg on one side are affected.

Paraplegia. The legs only are affected.

Quadriplegia or quadriparesis. Both arms and both legs are affected.

By the nature of the movement disturbance

Spastic. Muscles are tense and resistant to movement. *This is the most common form of cerebral palsy in preemies.*

Athetoid. The affected parts of the body perform involuntary movements, such as turning, twisting, facial grimacing, and drooling.

Ataxic. The main characteristics are lack of balance and coordination and disturbed depth perception.

Drugs, including muscle relaxants for spastic muscles, are sometimes also used. Surgery is done when it can help certain specific problems affecting the eyes, ears, or muscles involved in walking. Orthopedic devices such as splints, wheelchairs, walkers, and page-turners, may also help your child with CP.

Potential Complications and Long-term Effects of CP

Children with cerebral palsy have difficulty with movement and positioning of the body. They are also at risk for physical problems, such as joint contractures (stiffness), hip dislocation, and scoliosis (curvature of the spine). Problems associated with damage to the central nervous system are common in children with CP. These include difficulties with communication, feeding, vision, hearing, behavior, and learning.

In many cases, intellectual abilities are normal, although learning disabilities may appear later in school. Spastic diplegia, the most common form of cerebral palsy associated with prematurity, has a good intellectual outcome. With severe CP, significant mental delays may occur. A child with CP is also at risk for developing a seizure disorder.

EDUCATION IS EMPOWERING

This chapter introduced you to your child's brain-related problem, but there is much more you need to know in order to effectively parent your child and help your family.

Your preemie's specialist can refer you to recent books and articles written about your child's brain condition. A visit to a medical library at a university or hospital, or accessing an on-line medical library on the Internet, can also provide you with valuable information. (If you do not have a computer, most libraries do.) National parent organizations typically offer parent-friendly literature, too.

Do not hesitate to ask healthcare professionals and parents any questions. The more you know, the better prepared you are to advocate for and parent your child.

CHAPTER SEVEN

Eyes and Ears

YOUR PRETERM INFANT, especially if born under three pounds, is more at risk for vision and hearing problems than a term infant. Vision is one of the most important senses for helping your baby learn about the world around her. The sense of hearing teaches your child about language and communication. When your child has a vision or hearing loss, her development and learning are affected, and early diagnosis and treatment are critical for her future. This chapter will teach you about the common eye and ear problems of preemies and their warning signs, helping you identify any concerns.

YOUR PREEMIE'S EYES

Retinopathy of Prematurity (ROP)

THE MORE COMMON eye and vision problems of children born prematurely are typically the result of retinopathy of prematurity (ROP). ROP is an eye disease caused by an abnormal growth of blood vessels in the retina (the membrane that lines the inside of the eye and receives visual images). Blood vessels within the retina begin to develop around sixteen weeks gestational age and continue until shortly after a term birth. A premature birth causes the blood vessel development to stop briefly and abnormal vessels to start growing. If these abnormal vessels follow a typical growth pattern, ROP will not develop. If the new vessels develop atypically, ROP will develop. If ROP is accompanied by scar tissue (caused by blood and fluid leaking from the vessels into parts of the eye), ROP can become more serious.

ROP is believed to be caused by prolonged and high concentrations of supplemental oxygen in the NICU (however, there are other theories regarding causes). Home oxygen therapy does not cause ROP. ROP develops around thirty-seven weeks gestation, regard-

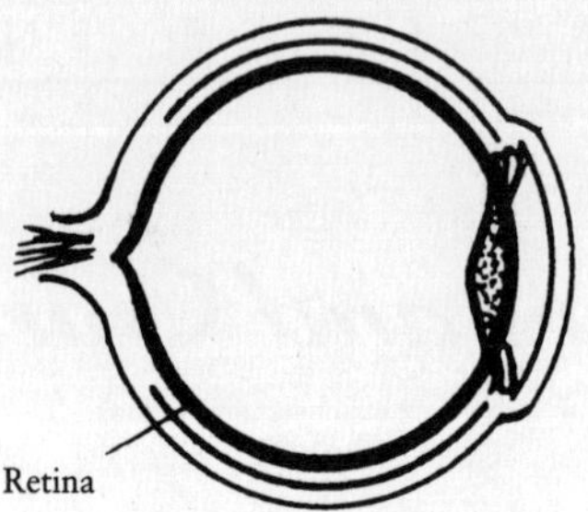

Cross-section of the eye

less of the number of weeks born early. In other words, a baby born at twenty-four weeks and another born at thirty weeks may both develop ROP around thirty-seven weeks gestational age.

Birthweight is a more significant indicator for ROP than gestational age: The smaller the preemie, the greater risk of developing ROP. Of preemies born under two pounds, twelve ounces, 66 percent develop ROP, and 20 percent of those need treatment. Of preemies born under one pound, ten and a half ounces, 90 percent develop ROP, and 37 percent of those require treatment.

Retinopathy of prematurity can lead to mild or severe eye and vision problems. Mild ROP typically "resolves" or causes minor vision difficulties, such as nearsightedness or crossed eyes. In more severe cases, the scar tissue may retract, or tighten, pulling on the retina. If the scar tissue is severe enough to detach the retina, blindness can result.

WARNING SIGNS
of Vision Problems for Preemies with or without ROP

Even preterm children without a history of ROP are at a slightly higher risk for vision problems, such as crossed eyes (strabismus) and poor color vision, than term children. Any vision problem can affect your child's development and self-esteem.

Consult your pediatrician or pediatric ophthalmologist if your *infant:*

- cannot keep her eyes on an object or face, or follow it as it moves (beyond six weeks corrected age);
- moves her eyes constantly, even when she is trying to look at an object (eyes "wander" without paying attention);
- tilts or turns her head abnormally;
- crosses eyes frequently (beyond three months corrected age);
- pokes at her eyes or waves her hand in front of her face often;
- does not blink when a camera flashes in front of her face;
- cries or turns away from normal lighting;

- has chronic tearing in one or both eyes;
- has an eyelid that droops and covers the pupil of the eye; and/or
- has one eye that points inward or outward most of the time.

Consult your pediatrician or pediatric ophthalmologist if your *school-aged child:*

- complains about headaches;
- has difficulty adjusting to different lighting conditions;
- holds objects close to eyes or sits close to the television;
- rubs her eyes frequently;
- tilts her head in various directions to observe objects;
- has difficulty with eye-to-eye contact;
- frequently looks downward;
- jerks her eyes when she is visually following an object in a horizontal, vertical, or circular path; and/or
- has difficulty with or is reluctant to read.

Diagnosis of ROP

If your premature infant was born weighing under three pounds, five ounces, she should have been routinely screened for ROP in the NICU by an ophthalmologist. The bigger preemie who is very sick in the NICU or is on oxygen is also screened for ROP. If ROP was detected in the hospital, your discharged baby will need ongoing follow-up exams with a pediatric ophthalmologist until the ROP is completely resolved. She should also be routinely evaluated for potential vision problems resulting from ROP.

John Henry was born at 24 weeks and is now three years old. Due to a heart defect, he was on a ventilator for three and a half months, often on high amounts of oxygen. He endured many life-threatening illnesses in the NICU. After surviving his heart surgery, we thought we could stop holding our breath, but then the ophthalmologist told us that John Henry had ROP. It progressed from stage 2 to stage 3 very quickly. He needed surgery within a few days. We were told the surgery might prevent impaired vision, but there was a possibility that even with surgery, John Henry could lose his eyesight.

After the surgery, I wished I had a crystal ball to see a glimpse of the future—a glimpse of whether John Henry would be able to enjoy the things that had meant so much to me as a young child, like reading a favorite book or seeing grandma's face.

At seven months corrected age, John Henry got his first pair of glasses. He looked like a smart little professor. He didn't like them at first, but once he realized he could see with them, he decided they were okay. His second pair of glasses were very cute and fit him perfectly. He wore those all the time.

STAGES OF ROP

An ophthalmologist classifies ROP by four stages, indicating the degree of severity:

Stage 1: In a normal eye, there are areas of the retina with blood vessels and areas without; these are separated by a thin line.

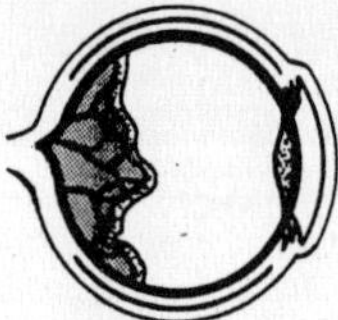

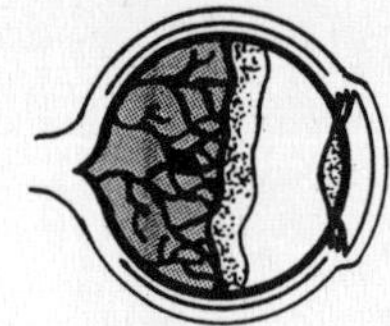

Stage 2: Blood vessels are growing and the thin line becomes a ridge.

Stage 3: Blood vessels are outside the ridge and retina.

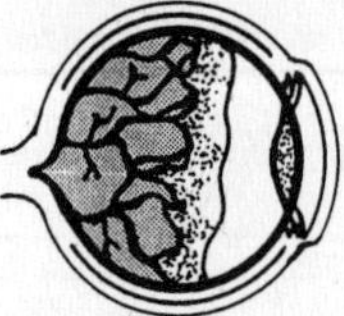

Stage 4: The scar tissue pulls on the retina and it detaches.

John Henry is now doing exceptionally well. He can see letters in children's books and already reads and writes simple words. He loves to draw pictures of our family with crowns on our heads because he believes he is the King of the whole wide world. Still, I doubt if the worry will ever completely go away.

—*Suzanne, mother of 24-weeker John Henry*

Treatment for ROP

Your pediatric ophthalmologist will watch for any progression of ROP. If your child's ROP reaches stage 3 (the doctor may use the term "at threshold"), very close monitoring is necessary and surgery may be considered.

Surgical treatment for ROP involves stopping abnormal growth of the blood vessels. One option may be laser therapy, which destroys abnormal blood vessel growth with a beam of light. Another may be cryotherapy, which uses nitrogen to freeze the abnormal blood vessels to stop their growth. Both are usually done under general anesthesia. Consult your ophthalmologist regarding your surgical choices.

When Hunter was in the hospital, the ophthalmologist told us he had developed ROP and should be watched closely. At his first follow-up eye appointment after discharge, we were told he needed immediate surgery or he would most likely go blind in both eyes. We scheduled laser surgery for the following day.

Here we finally had our baby home, he was adapting to his new pain-free environment, and now we had to go back to where we had started. My heart sank as they wheeled my baby away for surgery.

Surgery took two and a half hours. Hunter had to be intubated, and it was really hard to see him with that tube again. His eyes were swollen and red. When he woke up, we could tell that he was wondering what in the world was going on. He had such a sad look.

Six months later, we went for a checkup and the ophthalmologist said Hunter had the best-looking "lasered" eyes she had ever seen. We were so happy. The pain of the surgery and hospital stay were worth it because our baby can see perfectly today.

—*HEATHER, MOTHER OF 26-WEEKER HUNTER*

Potential Long-term Effects of ROP

Eye problems associated with ROP include:

Progressive myopia (nearsightedness). Between 40 and 80 percent of preemies who showed signs of ROP develop nearsightedness around two to six months actual age. The degree of nearsightedness is correlated with the severity of ROP. Some children born prematurely without ROP can develop nearsightedness, too.

Amblyopia ("lazy eye"). Approximately 6 percent of children with ROP, compared to 1.4 percent of the full-term population, will develop a dimness of sight, often referred to as "lazy eye."

Retinal detachment (holes in the retina). Holes may form in areas of regressed ROP and lead to a retinal detachment. This is associated with nearsightedness and is more commonly seen in the teenage years.

Cataracts (when the eye's lens becomes cloudy, causing partial or total blindness). Preemies who were treated with laser surgery for ROP have an increased risk of developing cataracts as teens or adults.

Glaucoma (an eye disorder caused by increased pressure in the eye). Between the ages of twelve and forty-five, former preemies with ROP have a low to moderate risk of developing glaucoma.

Blindness. In a very small percentage of children with ROP, blindness can result when the retina detaches.

■ ■ ■

LATER VISION PROBLEMS NOT ASSOCIATED WITH ROP

Preterm infants have shown a higher incidence of visual-motor and visual-spatial problems at five years of age in some preliminary studies. *Visual-motor* function is the actual movement of the hands and coordination of eye and hand movements. This function is important in learning to read, spell, and write. *Visual-spatial* function is the ability to draw forms or figures and is important in learning math and adapting to school. These problems are associated with the brain, rather than with the eye itself.

Diagnosis of Later Problems

Your pediatrician should examine your child's eyes at each routine checkup. Using an instrument called an ophthalmoscope, your doctor will check your child's blink response, the presence of the red reflex inside the pupil, and the pupil's response to light. At about six months corrected age, your doctor will also observe visual development using a variety of methods.

At your child's three-year (corrected age) checkup, your child's vision can be evaluated using a symbol chart, a letter-matching test, or picture cards, and the doctor will check for color blindness. Once your child learns the alphabet, she can be tested using a standard alphabet chart.

Treatment for Later Eye Problems

Treatment of eye and visual problems depends on the child's age as well as the type and severity of the problem. Nearsightedness, amblyopia, and strabismus are typically treated with glasses. Amblyopia, with the presence of strabismus, is sometimes treated by using an eye patch. The patch is placed over the "good" eye to encourage the use of the deviating eye. Cataracts and retinal detachment usually require surgery.

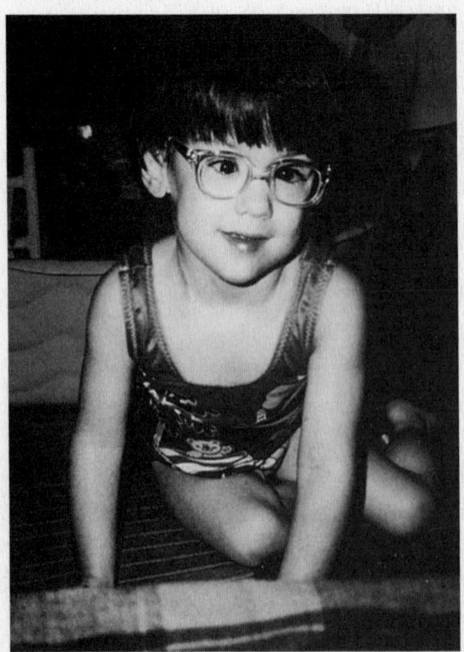

Curious three-year-old Seleste (a former 25-weeker) sees something she wants.

If your child requires glasses, she will most likely need a new pair every one to two years to compensate for vision changes. If the glasses have heavy or thick lenses, soft contacts may be prescribed, even at a very young age.

BLINDNESS

A child who loses her vision will need to learn alternative ways of interacting with the world: Loss of sight can affect all areas of your child's development, as well as her relationships with others and her self-esteem. Early contact with organizations for the blind, as well as early and ongoing developmental evaluations and support, are critical in helping your child adapt and succeed.

> *I remember the first time the doctor said, "We have a problem with Jacob's eyes." We had been through so much that I thought surely they can fix this too. The doctor assured me that laser surgery usually did the trick with no problems. After the third surgery, he told me that Jacob had lost sight in the left eye. I remember thinking that it was okay because he still had the other eye.*
>
> *After the next surgery, the doctor said, "We lost total vision in the right eye, and now the left eye is the better eye, but poor vision is expected." We were confused by the diagnosis because it had changed so drastically and quickly.*
>
> *When I found out that his vision would not be good enough to read, I thought about all of the tools available to help with reading and learning. When I found out that he probably wouldn't be able to see color, I was crushed and thought how much I wanted him to see the blue of the sky.*
>
> *I became the researcher and teacher to our nurses, doctors, and family about dealing with blind infants. It kept me busy. I thought I was doing okay, until one night my husband took Jacob's hand and brought it to his face to show Jacob his daddy. It was at that moment that I realized I could never fix Jacob's situation, and our lives would never be the same.*
>
> *Jacob's left eye has improved with surgery. Every time he sees something, we rejoice. When he achieves something that is hard to accomplish due to blindness, we are so proud. The first smiles were more precious than gold.*
>
> —*Tamara, mother of 24-weeker Jacob, twin to Aaron*

YOUR PREEMIE'S EARS

CHILDREN BORN PREMATURELY are at risk for two ear-related problems: ear infections and hearing loss.

Ear Infections

Most children will have one or more ear infections during childhood. Children born prematurely, particularly those who were on a ventilator, those who have frequent colds, and those with a family history of ear infections, are at greater risk for more frequent ear infections.

Infants and young children are more prone to ear infections because the eustachian tube (the tube that connects the middle ear to the back of the throat) is narrower and shorter. This keeps fluid that is produced in the middle ear from draining, and leaves the ear more susceptible to bacteria that are in the nose and throat. If these germs make their way into the middle ear, they multiply and create buildup of fluid behind the eardrum, and an infection will result. A child can experience pain with an infection when there is buildup of fluid and pressure in the ear.

Signs and diagnosis of ear infections

Your child may have an ear infection if she:

- is irritable (especially when lying flat);
- pulls, tugs, or rubs her ear;
- has a poor appetite or trouble sucking on the bottle or breast;
- sleeps poorly or wakes up frequently (especially when lying flat);
- has a fever;
- has drainage from the ear (this happens only after the eardrum has ruptured);
- exhibits cold symptoms along with conjunctivitis ("pink eye");
- has temporary hearing loss; and/or
- has a stabbing pain in the ear (a symptom of older children).

If your child exhibits any of these symptoms, call your doctor. A physician or a qualified nurse will examine your child's ear to determine if it is infected.

Treatment for ear infections

Ear infections are usually treated with a seven- to ten-day prescription of an antibiotic. Although your child should feel better in one to two days, the full course of antibiotics is needed to completely kill the infection-causing bacteria. Most physicians will reexamine the ear to ensure that the treatment worked. Decongestants and antihistamines will not help an ear infection.

If your child's symptoms do not improve within two to three days after the start of an antibiotic, call your doctor. She may need to prescribe a different medication. Your doctor may also recommend an acetaminophen (such as Tylenol) or ibuprofen (such as Motrin) to relieve your child's discomfort (never give your child aspirin without consulting your doctor). A warm, moist washcloth or a heating pad next to the ear may also help.

To help fluid drain out of the ear and to ease pain, prop your baby upright in an infant seat, and keep her elevated during feedings. Use pillows to keep an older child upright. Ask your doctor about using vegetable oil or prescription eardrops for reducing pain.

If your child's eardrum breaks and leaks fluid or a small amount of blood, do not panic. It is generally caused by a small tear, which will quickly repair itself. The tear will relieve built-up pressure, making your child more comfortable. You should, however, consult your physician if the drainage persists beyond one or two days.

If your child has more than three ear infections in six months, she may need further treatment. Your physician may prescribe a continuous course of antibiotics throughout the cold and flu season. If your doctor is concerned about your child's ear's ability to drain fluid, or your child experiences prolonged hearing loss, your physician may refer you to a pediatric ear, nose, and throat (ENT) specialist. This specialist will evaluate the need for further antibiotics or surgery.

Surgery requires a small incision inside the ear, which allows fluid to drain. A small tube that allows future fluid to drain is placed inside the eardrum. The tube remains in place until it falls out on its own (usually between six months and one year).

Prevention of ear infections

Ear infections are not contagious, but colds that cause ear infections are. If your child is prone to ear infections, keep her away from other children and adults with colds and from large crowds. Also, make sure she:

- eats a proper diet;
- gets adequate sleep;
- is evaluated for allergies (if she exhibits symptoms);
- drinks plenty of fluids;
- gets a flu shot; and
- does not take a bottle while lying flat. (This may encourage bacteria to move into the ear.)

Potential complications of ear infections

Meningitis (an infection in the fluid covering the brain and spinal cord) and mastoiditis (a serious infection in the bone behind the middle ear) are two rare, but serious, complications of ear infections. This is why a full treatment of antibiotics to completely cure an infection is important.

Call your doctor if your child:

- has a high or prolonged fever;
- has severe ear pain;
- has a stiff neck or severe headache;
- starts acting very sick;
- has redness, swelling, or tenderness behind the ear;
- has pus-like drainage from the ear; and/or
- cannot walk normally.

Hearing Loss

Hearing loss affects thousands of children each year, and premature infants, especially those who weighed less than three pounds, five ounces, are at increased risk. At even higher risk are those babies who were born very early, extremely tiny, and/or who were on ventilator support for a long time.

If your child has a hearing loss and it goes undetected, a speech delay is likely. Your child's language can be permanently impaired, and later learning and social development can be affected. *It is critical for your baby to get a hearing screening by three months corrected age and for you to watch for the warning signs of possible hearing loss.*

WARNING SIGNS OF HEARING LOSS

Even if your baby showed no hearing loss during initial testing, you should continue watching for signs of hearing difficulties. Mild and sometimes moderate hearing loss may be more difficult to detect, especially if your child has developed some coping strategies, such as lip-reading.

From Birth to 6 Months Corrected Age

Have your child retested if she:

- does not startle, awaken, or react to loud noises;
- does not respond to the sound of your voice;
- starts the cooing milestone but then stops; and/or
- does not move her eyes in the direction of a new sound.

From 6 to 12 Months Corrected Age

Have your child retested if she:

- is delayed in babbling, or babbling has slowed down or stopped (However, infants with a hearing loss may babble);
- does not turn her head in the direction of a voice or a new sound;
- does not point to objects or familiar people when asked;
- does not make consonant sounds ("dada," "baba") after 11 months corrected age; and/or
- does not respond to clapping or waving good-bye.

From 12 Months to 2 Years Corrected Age

Have your child retested if she:

- does not respond to simple requests;
- does not imitate simple words;
- does not have a way of indicating "no" or other simple gestures (either verbally or nonverbally);
- does not listen to music or television at normal levels;
- does not respond accurately to where sounds are coming from; and/or
- does not use speech like other children of the same corrected age.

Diagnosis of a hearing loss

Your child may or may not have had a hearing screening before discharge. If your baby was not tested in the hospital, make an appointment for a screening immediately. Consult your pediatrician, the Department of Health and Human Services, your school district, or the county health department for information. The screening should be done under the supervision of an audiologist. Be sure to obtain written results of any testing performed, including the date and type of exam that was given.

If your baby tested positive for a hearing loss in the hospital, it is your responsibility to make sure she is retested after coming home. After testing positive, your child should be rechecked within six to eight weeks. Various factors, such as fluid in the ear, can sometimes create a false-positive outcome. If the hearing loss is confirmed, your child should be regularly seen by a pediatric audiologist and a pediatrician, or a pediatric audiologist and an ENT specialist. It is recommended that children who test positive for a hearing loss be reevaluated every three months for one year after the initial diagnosis; every six months during the preschool years; and yearly when in school. More frequent evaluations may be necessary for fluctuating or progressive hearing losses.

Three types of hearing tests are commonly used for children:

An objective or physiological/electrophysiological test. This type of test evaluates the functioning of the middle and inner ear and determines the significance of the hearing loss. The most common of these tests are the auditory brain-stem response (ABR) and the otacoustic emissions (OAE). The ABR uses an earphone to transmit the noise, while electrodes placed on the skin by the ear measure the infant's response. An OAE uses a probe or earplug-like instrument that makes sounds or "clicks" while measuring the infant's response.

A tympanometer test. Middle ear function is assessed using a tympanometer, a small probe or plug that is placed in the child's ear. The information from this test is helpful in determining the presence of middle-ear dysfunction and the type of hearing loss.

Behavioral testing. An audiologist can begin behavioral testing starting around six to eight months corrected age. The audiologist observes the infant's or child's response to different sounds, and she gathers information about the child's ability to hear. Various tones, noises, and speech are presented through speakers, headphones, and/or earphones.

During behavioral testing, an infant, toddler, or preschooler will typically sit in a small room with her parent, and the audiologist will observe from another room. Using speakers and/or headphones, the audiologist will train a child to look at a light or toy each time she hears a sound. The sounds tested are the most common pitches, or frequencies, used in speech. The audiologist observes infants and smaller children for head turns as different pitches are given. If a child loses interest in the lights or toys and if she is developmentally ready for play, the audiologist may encourage her to play a game by placing a toy in a container each time she hears a sound. An older child can point, clap, or raise her hand when she hears a sound.

The results of most hearing tests are recorded on an audiogram, a chart that tracks the pitch and loudness of sounds that elicit a child's response. For those children who have a hearing loss, an audiogram helps map what the child can and cannot hear.

My daughter tested positive for a hearing loss two days before she left the hospital. The news left me devastated. I cried at the thought of her never hearing me say "I love you." One month after her discharge, Jill was tested again. The results were unclear, but the news wasn't good. Another test one month later couldn't give us any better results, and the doctors still seemed unsure of her hearing ability.

Jill got her first set of hearing aids when she was six months old. This was quite a challenge. Once I finally got them in, she would pull them out! Things became easier once we began to transition her slowly to the hearing aids. She began by wearing them five minutes every hour, and we very slowly increased her to ten minutes per hour, then fifteen, and so on, until she was wearing them all the time. I decided I didn't want to be ashamed of her hearing loss and bought her the most colorful hearing aids there were! They fit who she is perfectly.

Her hearing loss can be challenging, with the daily management of keeping the hearing aids in, as well as managing the appointments with the speech therapist and teacher of the deaf. (At age two, she is learning to sign.) I always remind myself of the light at the end of the tunnel. She is happy, healthy, and communicating with me now. She is always showing me how life is worth living and how truly special she is.

—*PHYLLIS, MOTHER OF 24-WEEKER JILL*

TYPES OF HEARING LOSSES

Conductive hearing loss. A stiffness or malfunction in the middle ear creates the hearing problem. This hearing loss may be correctable. Frequently, a child will have a temporary conductive hearing loss during and for several weeks after an ear infection.

Sensorineural hearing loss. A malfunction or damage in the inner ear causes the hearing problem. This hearing loss is permanent and may range from mild to profound levels.

Mixed hearing loss. A combination of conductive and sensorineural hearing loss. This is often seen with birth defects.

When your preemie has a hearing loss

There are different types of hearing losses, each of which can range in severity from mild to profound. The type and degree of hearing loss your child has affects the sounds she can and cannot hear. Even a mild hearing loss can delay a child's speech and language development, especially if it goes undetected for some time.

There is no "treatment" for hearing loss caused by nerve damage, but there are many helpful hearing and communication aids. Some hearing losses not caused by nerve damage are correctable. Work closely with a pediatric audiologist to find the best options for your child.

Discovering your child has a hearing loss creates many difficult decisions and tasks for you and your family. Connecting with community and parent support groups quickly is important. Other parents can share the paths they have taken.

SELF-ESTEEM BUILDING FOR YOUR CHILD WITH A HEARING OR VISION LOSS

When your child with a vision or hearing loss recognizes she is different from other children, she may fear rejection and hesitate to join social play. Her lack of self-confidence may make it difficult for her to develop important social skills. By building your child's self-esteem, you will give her the courage to join in playtime and learn from other children.

To build your child's self-image, give her positive feedback often. Also expose her to other people (who are not family members) who will support her. Other parents with children who have hearing or vision loss can offer more ideas for promoting your child's socialization skills.

Other Concerns

As a parent of a child born prematurely, you will often wonder if your child's medical and physical problems are related to her early birth. Some of your concerns cannot be directly pinpointed to a preterm birth, but others, such as digestive difficulties, scarring, and dental problems, are unquestionably the results of prematurity.

The previous three chapters discussed the lungs, the brain, and the eyes and ears of premature infants. This chapter addresses the remaining complications and concerns associated with prematurity. What you need to know if your child needs surgery is also discussed.

YOUR PREEMIE'S DIGESTIVE SYSTEM

Gastroesophageal Reflux (GER)

Gastroesophageal reflux (GER, or "reflux") is one of the most common gastrointestinal problems in infants, and preemies have a higher incidence than term infants. GER occurs when the muscle that attaches the esophagus (the food pipe) to the stomach is open too frequently, allowing stomach acid and partially digested food to flow back up, or reflux, into the esophagus. This muscle, called the lower esophageal sphincter (LES), naturally opens and closes for swallowing, burping, and vomiting. Periodic refluxing after eating is normal in adults and children, but when refluxing occurs too often, more serious problems can result.

Preterm infants are more likely to develop GER because of their lung problems. When a baby has to work hard to breathe or breathes rapidly, the muscles in the diaphragm can pull on the sphincter and cause it to open. The stomach contents will then inappropriately flow back up the esophagus, often causing the baby to regurgitate.

Premature infants without any lung problems can also develop GER. Weak or immature muscle development in the esophagus and around the sphincter can cause GER symptoms. The muscles in the esophagus may be too weak to move food adequately from the mouth to the stomach, and/or the muscles around the sphincter may be too weak to control the sphincter appropriately. Other factors that may cause reflux include certain physical abnormalities and some medications.

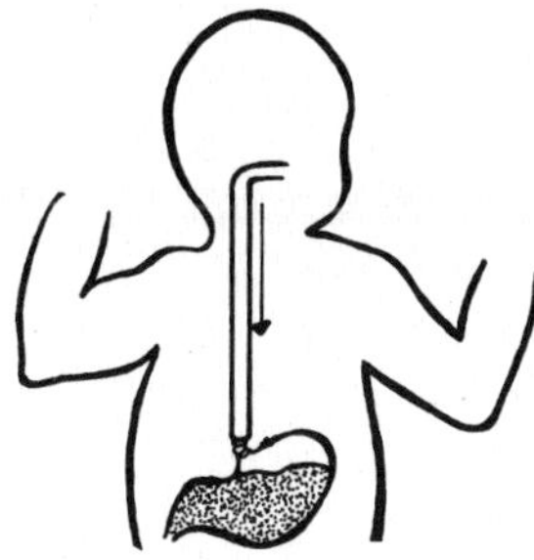

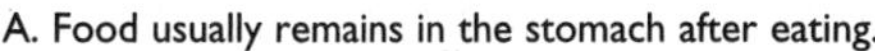

A. Food usually remains in the stomach after eating.

B. When refluxing, the lower esophageal sphincter opens too frequently and food flows back up into the esophagus.

Mackenzie began refluxing just a few days after coming home from the hospital. I told her pediatrician I thought she was refluxing, but he wouldn't listen. He thought I was just being an overanxious nurse and mom. We had to see a specialist before she received any treatment. By then she had stopped eating about 60 percent of her feedings! It's very difficult to have a child that won't eat—it affects the lives of the entire family.

Although surgery is a drastic measure, I was relieved when she finally had the surgical repair to stop the refluxing. She had been so miserable with pain from the heartburn and esophagitis. Even though the repair helped, she still had feeding problems for a long time. At age three, she has overcome most of these problems and is eating and gaining weight well.

—DIANNE, MOTHER OF 26-WEEKER MACKENZIE

■

It was hard seeing one twin eat so well and the other having so much trouble. Andrew's feedings became horrible, disappointing events that happened too often. After every feeding, Andrew would throw up over half of what he just ate. We had plastic sheets all over the house and cleaning was constant.

It was a painful life for him and for me to watch. I couldn't sleep because

I was afraid he would spit up and choke. It's funny how you worry about your baby having the right number of toes and fingers. You don't think you have to worry about whether your baby will be able to eat on his own.

—AMBER, MOTHER OF 29-WEEKER ANDREW, TWIN TO BLAKE

Signs of GER

Although most preemies will outgrow GER by one year corrected age, GER should never be left untreated—severe complications can result. Your baby should be evaluated if she:

- frequently spits up;
- is often fussy after feedings;
- seems unusually fussy throughout the day;
- refuses to eat or fights feedings;
- eats only small amounts and seems to get full quickly;
- arches during feedings;
- chokes or stops breathing, even for less than five seconds;
- loses weight or has difficulty gaining weight; and/or
- has frequent respiratory infections.

If your pediatrician suspects GER, she may refer you to a pediatric gastrointestinal specialist for further evaluation and treatment.

Diagnosis of GER

GER may be diagnosed by a simple doctor's visit and/or by a variety of tests. If your preemie is evaluated for reflux, make sure you understand the tests used and why they were chosen, and do not be afraid to ask questions. Testing may include:

An upper GI (UGI). A UGI is one of the first tests performed to ensure there are no underlying physical problems causing symptoms similar to reflux. A liquid drink, called barium, is given orally or by a tube threaded through the mouth into the stomach. X rays are taken to check for any narrowing or blockage in the gastrointestinal tract and to see if the barium "backwashes" into the esophagus. A UGI is only about 50 percent accurate because the baby might not reflux during the X ray (or if she does, it may represent a normal reflux episode).

A twenty-four-hour pH probe. A good but more difficult diagnostic tool is the twenty-four-hour pH probe. For this test, a small tube is threaded into a child's nose and down into the esophagus. The tube is attached to a machine that reads the level of acid (which should not be there) in the esophagus. The acid level is recorded after each feeding during a twenty-four-hour period. A baby may or may not need hospitalization for this test.

A milk scan. A milk scan also examines how food moves down the esophagus and into and out of the stomach. A child is fed formula containing a safe chemical, called technetium, which will appear on a special scanning device. The physician then examines the scan, watching for both slow emptying of the stomach as well as for refluxing. She will also look to see if the reflux gets high enough in the esophagus to enter the lungs.

An endoscopy. The most aggressive and least common test given is an endoscopy. Under sedation in a doctor's office or in the hospital, a flexible tube is placed down the child's throat into the esophagus. This allows the specialist to look directly at the tissue in the esophagus to see if there is any obvious damage or alteration in the tissue.

Treatment for GER

Treatment for GER varies from home management techniques to surgery. Your child's treatment plan may include:

Prescribing home management techniques

Some simple things your doctor may suggest doing include:

- thickening your baby's formula or breastmilk with rice or oat cereal;
- giving your child smaller but more frequent feedings;
- burping your infant frequently (every one-half to one ounce) during feedings;
- encouraging your infant to suck on a pacifier between feedings;
- keeping your child's head elevated most of the time and especially during the first hour after eating; and/or
- refraining from holding your infant in positions that put pressure on the abdomen (such as on your hip with your arm wrapped around her stomach).

Prescribing medications

To help improve the emptying of stomach contents and relieve pain and inflammation of the esophagus, medication is often prescribed. More than one drug may be used at the same time. Your pediatrician may have to experiment to find which medicine works best for your child. Always tell your doctor if your child is taking an antibiotic; some drug combinations are inadvisable. Also, be aware that some dosages may need adjusting as your child gains weight.

Antacids are commonly used to neutralize, or decrease, the stomach acid: When the stomach contents flow back up the esophagus, the damage to the tissue is minimized with antacids. Side effects include diarrhea and irritability. Other medications are used to completely block the production of acid in the stomach, helping in the same manner as antacids. Side effects include diarrhea, irritability, and nausea.

To increase the digestive tract's ability to pass food and improve the emptying of the stomach, certain medications can help. If food passes from the stomach and through the intestines more quickly, there is less chance of reflux. Side effects from these medications include diarrhea, restlessness, irritability, nausea, muscle control problems, and (in rare cases) changes in the functioning of the heart.

REFLUX SURGERY: MAKING THE RIGHT CHOICE FOR YOUR CHILD

Deciding whether GER surgery is necessary for your child—weighing the benefits against the risks—can be difficult. Answering these questions may help:

- Have I tried all other medical treatment options with which I am comfortable?
- Will taking away the pain of reflux be important to my child's present and future development?
- Could the surgical complications outweigh the benefits?
- If a feeding tube is placed with GER surgery, can I handle its management and care?
- Will I still be able to feed my baby by mouth with the feeding tube in place?
- Will the surgery improve my child's weight gain?

Recommending surgery

If your child's reflux persists for a prolonged period of time, despite adequate medical management, and/or your child's reflux is causing significant difficulties (choking, apnea, difficulty eating, and/or inadequate weight gain), surgery may be necessary. Surgery is required in only about 10 percent of all reflux cases. When a child has surgery for GER, a feeding tube is often placed in the stomach. For more information on feeding tubes, see chapter 11.

There are a few variations of GER surgery, and the general purpose is to wrap a small portion of the top of the stomach around the esophagus, thus creating an artificial sphincter. A few surgeons perform this surgery laparoscopically. Ask your doctor to explain all of your choices.

Complications can arise from GER surgery. Some infants and children gag or retch with feedings after surgery is performed. Because of the alteration of the stomach's anatomy around the esophagus and the slight decrease in the size of the stomach, the feeling of fullness after eating can be exaggerated and can trigger a gag reflex. Even if your child cannot actually vomit, she may begin retching.

You can help the gagging or retching by feeding your child slowly. Make sure she is burped well before, during, and soon after feedings. If your child's gagging or retching is severe, your doctor may prescribe Benadryl (an antihistamine) to help relax muscles and decrease the gagging reflex. Your child needs time to outgrow the tight feeling from the surgery for the gagging to stop. However, if you are concerned that gagging is excessive, consult your doctor.

Potential complications of GER

Reflux can cause additional problems that vary in severity. These include:

- frequent vomiting;
- failure to gain weight or grow because food and nutrients are lost from vomiting;
- apnea (when the child stops breathing for twenty seconds or more);

- the development of lower respiratory infections because bacteria from food and stomach acid may move high up the esophagus and be aspirated into the lungs;
- inflammation and ulcers in the esophagus (esophagitis);
- an irritated esophagus can bleed and cause anemia; and
- in some rare cases, reflux can severely damage the tissue in the esophagus and create precancerous cells (Barrett's Esophagus).

Consult your pediatrician if your child exhibits any unusual symptoms.

Potential long-term effects of GER

Preemies with chronic reflux are at risk for ongoing feeding problems. These children learn early that it hurts to eat and the pain from eating creates negative reinforcement. They may become afraid to put anything in or near their mouths, or they may eat only enough to satisfy their hunger. Some children stop eating altogether.

If your child shows any of these behaviors, she needs immediate evaluation and treatment by a specialist. Her reflux may not be under control, or you may need assistance in helping your child cope with her eating issues.

VOMITING AND DIARRHEA

Vomiting and diarrhea are common childhood illnesses that can quickly cause dehydration for your premature infant, especially if she is medically fragile. Both vomiting and diarrhea are usually caused by a virus, with symptoms lasting from two to seven days. If your child has a compromised immune system or has had previous trauma to her intestines, it may take her longer to recover. You must monitor lost fluids and watch for signs of dehydration (see box on page 138).

It may be difficult for you to know if your child is simply spitting up or vomiting. If your baby does not usually spit up after or in between feedings and she begins to do so, a stomach virus is most likely the cause. If your infant often spits up during or after feedings but other signs indicate illness (for instance, a fever or diarrhea), try measuring the lost food's contents.

Take a cloth containing the lost food and lay it next to a similar clean one. Pour a measured amount of formula or fluid onto the clean cloth until it looks equal to the amount on the soiled cloth. This helps you get a better idea of how much food your infant is losing. Losing more than one-third of a feeding two times in a twenty-four- to forty-eight-hour period is too much, and you should consult your pediatrician.

Diagnosing diarrhea is usually much easier. Three or more episodes of loose, watery stools per day should be discussed with your doctor. Bowel movements of normal consistency, occurring as often as every feeding, can be normal for a child. It is not only the frequency but the consistency that is important.

WARNING SIGNS
OF DEHYDRATION

Your child may be dehydrated if she:

- is unusually thirsty;
- has decreased urination;
- has sunken eyes;
- has dark yellow urine;
- acts irritable;
- is listless; and/or
- exhibits dry skin that wrinkles easily.

If your child exhibits any of these signs, immediately consult your pediatrician.

The fluid and electrolytes lost from vomiting or loose stools can cause dehydration and electrolyte imbalances. At the onset of *vomiting,* give your child one teaspoon of a clear liquid every few minutes. Clear liquids are anything you can see through when they are in a bottle or a glass. To prevent electrolyte imbalances, use commercially prepared fluids, such as Pedialyte or Infalyte, which contain balanced amounts of water, sugar, and electrolytes.

Once your child can handle fluids, give her an ounce or two of liquids every thirty minutes. Formula and solids can be slowly introduced when vomiting has completely stopped. Some pediatricians recommend diluting formula or breastmilk with commercially prepared fluids before giving full-strength milk. Clear liquids alone should not be given for more than tweleve hours without consulting your doctor.

WARNING SIGNS

If your child is vomiting and/or has diarrhea, immediately call your doctor if she:

- has vomit or stool that is red, dark, black, or has pus in it (Green stools are normal, especially during a viral illness);
- is not improving after four to six hours of taking clear liquids;
- is on fluid restriction;
- exhibits signs of dehydration;
- refuses to drink;
- complains of abdominal pain for more than two hours;
- vomits excessively; and/or
- has a fever over 100.5°F.

Never give your child any medication for vomiting or diarrhea without consulting your pediatrician.

If your baby is not vomiting and has *diarrhea,* continue to feed her by breast or bottle—unless the diarrhea worsens with continued feedings. If your child is taking solid foods, choose foods that are nutritious but bland and with little sugar. Cooked carrots, bananas, crackers, pasta, breads, oatmeal, rice, yogurt, or bland meats are good choices. Your child with water-loss diarrhea may need twice as much fluid as she typically takes in one day. Use Pedialyte or Infalyte to replace lost fluids. Try to avoid apple juice: It may complicate the diarrhea. If your child is taking formula and has diarrhea often, your pediatrician may suggest changing her formula to one that is more easily digested.

Constipation

Some infants and children have bowel movements once or twice a day; others have one bowel movement every two to three days. The consistency of your child's stool is a better indicator of constipation. If your child does not seem uncomfortable, is eating well, and her stools are soft, she may naturally have more infrequent bowel movements. If the stools are hard and difficult to pass, she is constipated.

The best remedy for constipation is additional fluids. Whether breast- or bottle-feeding, offer your child small amounts of water in between feedings. (If your child is on fluid restriction, consult your pediatrician before offering additional liquids.) Also, if you are breast-feeding, do not forget to drink plenty of fluids yourself—at least eight glasses a day.

Your child on solid foods should have more high-fiber foods, such as fresh fruits and vegetables, bran, prunes, or baked beans. (Always be aware of small foods that may cause choking.) Slowly increase high-fiber foods to prevent gas and bloating. Avoid constipation-causing foods, such as milk, bananas, and cheese, but remember to replace the protein and calcium found in these foods through a supplementary vitamin or other foods.

Resolving constipation is important: You do not want your child to become afraid of the pain associated with passing a hard stool. Physicians recommend a variety of remedies, including stool softeners, corn syrup, and mineral oil. These are only temporary solutions until your child's diet works. Discuss methods with your doctor.

Short-Bowel Syndrome (SBS)

A small percentage of premature infants develop complications in the NICU that can result in the death of part of the bowel. When a section of the bowel dies, it needs to be surgically removed, which leads to a condition called Short-Bowel Syndrome (SBS, or also called Short-Gut Syndrome).

If your child has SBS, she was very sick during her NICU stay. At home, her complex medical and nutritional management requires a pediatrician with SBS expertise and/or a pediatric gastrointestinal specialist. Nutrition, medication, and vitamin and mineral requirements vary according to the amount and location of bowel removed. Your infant needs a constantly updated and individualized medical care plan to meet her unique needs.

Hernias

Premature infants, especially those born very early, are at greater risk for developing umbilical and inguinal hernias. An *umbilical* hernia results when the muscle around the umbilical cord (belly button area) is weak or does not close properly. An umbilical hernia may be visible all the time or only during crying.

The majority of umbilical hernias correct themselves by the time a child is two. An umbilical hernia that does not resolve can be repaired surgically. Some physicians repair umbilical hernias is another surgery is done. Never attempt to "treat" your child's umbilical hernia by taping it or holding it down in some type of binder.

An *inguinal* hernia develops when air, fluid, or the intestine protrudes through a hole in the child's groin muscle. Inguinal hernias are more common in boys, but girls can develop them, too. If your infant has an unusual lump or bulge in the groin area or has an enlarged testicle, consult your pediatrician.

Inguinal hernias always require surgical repair. Immediate surgery is needed if the hernia cannot be reduced (gently pushed back into the muscle opening). *Never try to reduce your child's hernia without a doctor's demonstration.* If the hernia is reducible and not causing any concerns, the surgery can be scheduled at an agreed-upon time with a pediatric surgeon.

In older preemies without lung disease, hernia surgery is often done without overnight hospitalization. A smaller preemie or one with lung disease will need to stay at least one night. A preterm child who has had an inguinal hernia repair is more at risk for it to return than a term child is. A small infant with a large hernia has an even higher risk of recurrence.

WARNING SIGNS FOR HERNIA

Your doctor will show you how to reduce your child's inguinal hernia. If you cannot push the hernia back into the groin area and past the muscle, immediately call your pediatrician. A hernia can become incarcerated (trapped) in the sack outside the muscle lining, requiring immediate surgery. Also call your doctor if:

- the area around the hernia is tender;
- there is redness or a bluish color in the groin or near the hernia;
- your child is crying inconsolably in pain; and/or
- your child is vomiting for no obvious cause.

YOUR PREEMIE'S SKIN

EVEN THOUGH THERE are no specific skin conditions associated with prematurity, preterm infants can have sensitive and fragile skin. At the time of discharge, your baby may not have formed a good top layer of skin, called the epidermal layer. This layer coats and protects the rest of the skin.

Topical medications, such as hydrocortisone cream, and chemicals found in some lotions and soaps can penetrate your baby's fragile skin and be abnormally absorbed into the body. Topical medications should only be used under the supervision of your physician. Also, you should use only soaps and lotions that are mild and naturally based (without any added chemicals).

In most cases, a baby's skin rash is painless and does not require medical treatment. If your infant gets a rash (other than a diaper rash), it may be caused by dry skin, and Vaseline or a mild lotion without perfume will help. Consult your doctor if the rash becomes reddened and the skin begins to break down. *If your child has a fever with a rash, call your pediatrician immediately.*

Diaper rashes are commonly caused by dampness and the interaction of urine and the skin. To prevent and treat a diaper rash, try to keep your baby's skin dry. When possible, leave diapers off (or loose) for short periods of time. When a rash is present, temporarily stop using baby wipes that might further irritate the skin. There are a variety of ointments you can try for your baby's diaper rash, such as Desitin, A & D, and Bag Balm. You can also make your own ointment by combining 50 percent zinc oxide with 50 percent Maalox. *Never use talc powder on or near your baby—it can irritate her lungs.*

A diaper rash should show improvement within seventy-two hours. If not, call your pediatrician. If your baby's diaper rash becomes reddened with small raised bumps, consult your pediatrician.

YOUR PREEMIE'S SCARS

MANY PRETERM INFANTS come home with physical scars from hospital procedures. For parents, they can be a reminder of the difficult NICU experience. The most common areas for scars are on the hands and feet, caused mainly by needle sticks and IV placements. Some preemies have scars on the insides of their elbows and upper arms from IVs, on their abdomens following surgery, or on their chests from chest tubes or surgery.

There are no scientifically proven treatments for completely eliminating scars, but there are methods to help them fade. If your child's scar is especially bad, topical gels and creams, laser surgery, or steroid injections may help. Special reconstructive surgery can sometimes lessen or change the appearance of a scar. Consult a dermatologist or plastic surgeon to learn about your options.

Scars are not physically harmful to your child, but they can impact her self-image. At around preschool age, your former preemie may ask you about her scars. Answer her questions honestly and in simple terms she can understand. Do not make the cause of the scars or the scars themselves sound scary or "bad." Your child may interpret that she is bad for having them. Help your child feel good about herself by telling her the scars do not change who she is—they only make her more special to you.

My daughter has scars on her chest, hands, feet, nose, and head. She also has large scars on one ankle and one hand from IVs that slipped out of the veins. The IV solution "ate" some of the tissue. The scars on her chest are not raised up, but blotches are shades darker than the rest of her skin. They seem to grow and get darker as she grows. I was told that the scars can be fixed as she gets older, but I don't like the idea of causing my daughter any more pain.

—CHRISTA, MOTHER OF 27-WEEKER SARAH

YOUR PREEMIE'S TEETH

SOME DENTAL ABNORMALITIES are associated with preterm birth; others are not. The dental concerns preemie parents most often ask about are discussed in this section.

My daughter's two front teeth came in looking like the enamel had been scraped off the lower parts. It's almost as if someone took a file and tried to sharpen them! Our dentist thought it might be due to her premature birth.

—SHELLY, MOTHER OF 30-WEEKER STERLING

■

My twins have grooves in the roofs of their mouths. Our dentist said they are from the ventilator tubes, even though they were only intubated for seven days. He said they will need braces after they get all their permanent teeth.

—CHUCK, FATHER OF 24-WEEKER TWINS HAILEY AND RYAN

ENAMEL HYPOPLASIA

Enamel hypoplasia is an abnormal formation of enamel (the white outer coating of a tooth). Teeth with this problem are usually discolored or opaque and can have uneven surfaces or abnormal shapes. Enamel hypoplasia is a fairly common childhood dental problem, but is more prevalent in preemies. The lower your child's birthweight, the more at risk she is for developing enamel hypoplasia.

Causes of enamel hypoplasia

During the fourth month of pregnancy and continuing until late into the first year of life, a baby develops her primary, or "baby," teeth. When a child is born prematurely, life-sustaining factors, such as nutrition and intubation, can affect teeth formation.

The intravenous fluids given in the NICU may have inadequate amounts of important nutrients, such as calcium and phosphorus, needed for tooth formation. Without adequate amounts of these nutrients, the cells that form the enamel layer of the tooth can be physically disrupted and hypoplasia can result. Changes in enamel can occur on any tooth, but the upper front primary teeth are more commonly affected. A preemie's permanent teeth may also be affected (most notably the six-year molars but usually to a lesser degree).

Teeth enamel can also be affected by intubation, particularly on the left-side teeth. Many experts believe the left side is commonly affected because the laryngoscope (the tool used for intubation) presses against the left-side gums during the intubation process. However, experts disagree whether it is the extended length of time the breathing tube is in place or the trauma of inserting the tube that causes enamel problems.

Complications of enamel hypoplasia

If your child has enamel hypoplasia, her teeth are not as well protected, and she is at greater risk for cavities. You can help keep her teeth healthy by:

- visiting a pediatric dentist by her first birthday;
- brushing your infant's teeth twice a day (in the morning and at the end of the day) using a soft cloth or pediatric toothbrush. Use only a very small amount of toothpaste on the toothbrush. If your child refuses to let you brush her teeth, ask your dentist about alternative ways to provide oral hygiene. An occupational therapist may also have useful information;
- never putting your child to bed with a bottle—this can cause severe tooth decay that destroys the teeth;
- encouraging good dental hygiene throughout childhood; and
- asking your dentist about fluoride treatments and sealants that protect the teeth (these vary by dentist and area of the country).

Delayed Tooth Eruption

Many dentists believe that birth is the stimulus for tooth eruption, yet many preemies are several months behind term children in developing their teeth (even after correcting age). Experts believe the lack of sufficient nutrients from NICU fluids may delay teeth development and eruption. Children who were born earlier and those who had difficult NICU courses are more likely to have delayed tooth eruption.

Chart 8-1: Tooth formation and eruption

A dental chart showing teeth formation and eruption in children born prematurely has not yet been created. Parents and dental professionals must use a schedule for term children and adjust for gestational age. Remember, many preemies have slower tooth eruption. For most preterm children, "catch-up" dental growth occurs by nine years of age or sooner.

PRIMARY TEETH

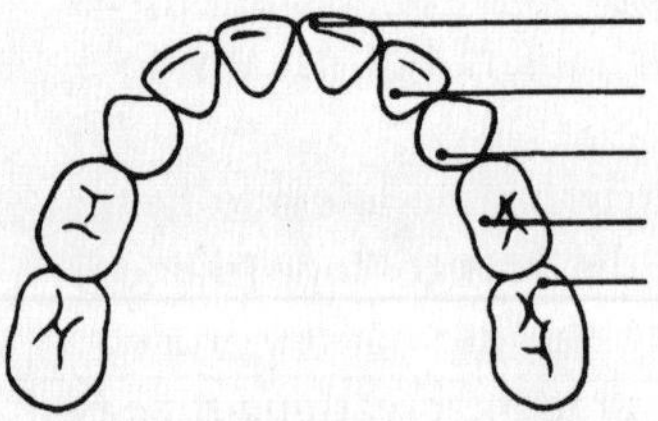

Upper Teeth	Erupt	Shed
Central incisor	8–12 mos.	6–7 yrs.
Lateral incisor	9–13 mos.	7–8 yrs.
Canine (cuspid)	16–22 mos.	10–12 yrs.
First molar	13–19 mos.	9–11 yrs.
Second molar	25–33 mos.	10–12 yrs.

Lower Teeth	Erupt	Shed
Second molar	23–31 mos.	10–12 yrs.
First molar	14–18 mos.	9–11 yrs.
Canine (cuspid)	17–23 mos.	9–12 yrs.
Lateral incisor	10–16 mos.	7–8 yrs.
Central Incisor	6–10 mos.	6–7 yrs.

PERMANENT TEETH

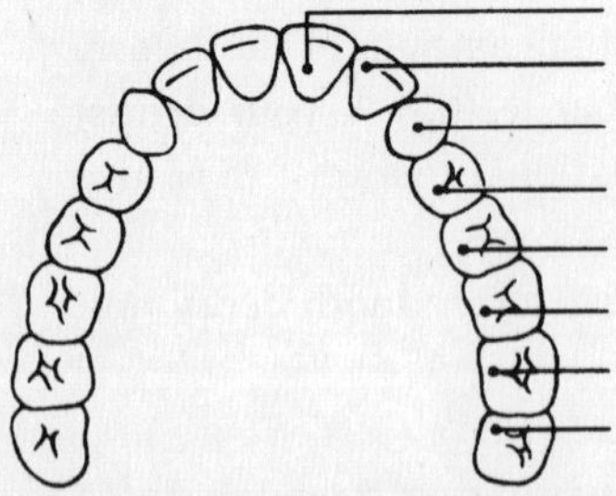

Upper Teeth	Erupt
Central incisor	7–8 yrs.
Lateral incisor	8–9 yrs.
Canine (cuspid)	11–12 yrs.
First premolar (first bicuspid)	10–11 yrs.
Second premolar (second bicuspid)	10–12 yrs.
First molar	6–7 yrs.
Second molar	12–13 yrs.
Third molar (wisdom tooth)	17–21 yrs.

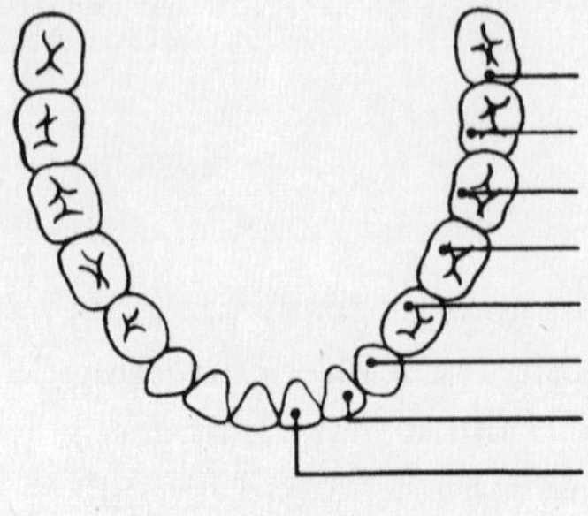

Lower Teeth	Erupt
Third molar (wisdom tooth)	17–21 yrs.
Second molar	11–13 yrs.
First molar	6–7 yrs.
Second premolar (second bicuspid)	11–12 yrs.
First premolar (first bicuspid)	10–12 yrs.
Canine (cuspid)	9–10 yrs.
Lateral incisor	7–8 yrs.
Central incisor	6–7 yrs.

Slow tooth eruption is not a serious problem as long as no teeth are missing (a problem not specific to prematurity). Consult your dentist if your child's teeth erupt out of order or one is missing (see chart 8-1). Problems with teeth spacing can result.

Grooves in the Palate and Dental Arch

A premature infant who was intubated, even for a short period of time, can develop a narrow groove in the palate (the roof of the mouth) and the dental arch (where the teeth erupt). The breathing tube places pressure against the soft bone of the palate, resulting in an indentation. This indentation can cause a narrowing of the palate and/or dental arch and a decrease in the width of the upper bone of the jaw. Crowding of the teeth can result.

Complications of palatal and dental arch grooves

As a preemie grows, the palatal groove typically decreases in size and is less prominent by two years corrected age. Children with grooves sometimes have trouble eating foods like peanut butter, which can stick to the roofs of their mouths.

If the palate remains narrow, a child's bite can be affected. Cross-bite, when the top back teeth touch the middle or inside of the lower teeth, occurs in about one-fourth of children who were once intubated. Children who have cross-bites often bite their cheeks when eating or chewing, and they sometimes have headaches, jaw muscle tenderness, ear stuffiness, and pain.

If your child has a cross-bite or overcrowding of the primary teeth, the problem does not necessarily need immediate treatment. Your dentist may wait until your child's permanent teeth are in and her jaw is more developed (around seven to eight years of age) before reevaluating and treating.

A groove in the dental arch can affect tooth eruption, teeth and jaw alignment, and possibly your child's speech. Dental eruption problems should be monitored and treated by your dentist. If you have any questions about your child's speech, refer to chapter 12 and consult a pediatric speech pathologist.

Braces

Many pediatric dentists and orthodontists believe preemies, even those with palatal grooves, are not more prone to needing braces than are term children (although this has not been studied extensively). The need for braces is based solely on upper jaw width and cannot be determined until a child's permanent six-year molars have erupted.

■ ■ ■

Discolored Teeth

Preemies who developed high bilirubin levels (jaundice) can have a yellow or brown discoloration of their primary teeth. This does not affect the permanent teeth. This type of staining cannot be removed by routine brushing or cleaning by the dentist.

WHEN YOUR PREEMIE NEEDS SURGERY

Fear often overcomes a parent of a child facing surgery. You worry about how your child will tolerate the surgical procedure, the anesthesia, the pain, and the recovery. As a parent of a once medically fragile infant, this fear is often compounded by memories of the NICU. As one mother says, "My daughter has been through so much in her short life. I almost can't bear the thought of putting her through more pain and the trauma of being in the hospital again."

For a planned surgery, education and understanding can relieve some anxiety. Learn all you can about the procedure, the anesthesia, and post-surgery care. Educate your child according to her age and ability to understand. Of course, if the surgery is an emergency, you will not be prepared, and coping with the trauma may take some time.

PARENT TIPS:

Preparing for Your Preemie's Surgery

To help you and your child cope with a surgery, try these suggestions from parents.

For Parents

- Visit the hospital's medical library and ask for assistance in finding information on your child's condition and surgery. The Internet offers extensive medical information, too.
- Keep a notebook of any questions you want to ask the doctors or nurses. Write down the answers.
- Ask if your child will need any medicines or respiratory treatments before surgery, and obtain medications at least three days prior to surgery.
- If it is RSV season, ask if the surgery can be delayed.
- Ask if your child's surgery can be scheduled at a time best for your child and your family.
- A list of things to pack for your child's hospitalization will help you remember important items during a stressful time.
- Arrange for family or friends to handle whatever is needed at home while you are gone.

- Arrive at the hospital with plenty of time to check in, preventing additional anxiety.
- When the staff allows, assist with any medical care that you are comfortable with and trained to do.
- Educate the medical personnel about your child's medications, likes, dislikes, schedule, and personality. Do not hesitate to express any concerns about your child's care to the medical staff. Remember, *you* are the expert on your child.

For Children

- Depending on your child's age, explain what will happen in the hospital: Describe the hospital and surgery rooms, the hospital gown, the staff, and the masks healthcare professionals wear. Read some children's books about hospitalization.
- If possible and if your child is old enough, take a tour of the hospital together.
- Puppets or dolls can help explain the hospital and surgery to your child. Some hospitals have programs for children to help prepare them for surgery.
- When talking about the surgery to your child, do not say words or phrases like "cut," "open you up," or "put you to sleep."
- Remain calm—your child may sense your concern and become even more frightened.
- Be honest about the pain. Try to compare it to something your child can understand, such as the pain from a pinched finger.
- Explain to your child how she will be different after the surgery (stitches, an IV, tubings) so she knows what to expect. Children can imagine terrible things. Encourage your child to talk or draw pictures about her feelings and concerns.
- If you know an older child who has had a surgery, discuss how well that child did. If appropriate, have the older child talk to your child while you listen.
- To make your child's adjustment to the hospital easier, take familiar comfort items, such as crib bumper pads, a tape recorder and tape with favorite songs, a special blanket, or a favorite stuffed animal. Make sure you mark these items with your child's name.
- If possible, try to stick to a daily routine in the hospital, similar to the one followed at home.
- Buy your child a special toy or treat to add some fun to the hospital stay.
- Give your child reassurance that you will not leave the hospital when she is in surgery. Insist on being with your child before the anesthesia works and when she wakes up from surgery.
- Treat your child as if she is someone very special for having surgery!

Surgery is a traumatic event for your child, and she may have developmental setbacks. You will need to give your child time and encouragement to catch up to her former level of development.

It was very hard for us to decide to go ahead with Jacqueline's surgery. We knew our decision could affect the rest of her life. One day she would ask us why she had scars. I only hope when that day comes, I can explain why we made the decision to go ahead with the surgery and how it helped her.

—KAREN, MOTHER OF 27-WEEKER JACQUELINE

■

Taking Lauren back to the hospital for surgery after being home for five weeks was very hard. Even though I knew the surgery was important and necessary for her to get well, I had an awful time deciding to go through with it. When we walked through the hospital door, all the feelings from the NICU came rushing back. Another preemie mom told me to stay calm and make sure I had confidence in the doctor. Lauren did well and I remained calm until we came home, then I cried out of relief and exhaustion.

—MICHELLE, MOTHER OF 26-WEEKER LAUREN

WHEN SURGERY IS A CHOICE

Before agreeing to surgery for your child, you should understand what treatment options are available for your child's condition. You should also get adequate answers to your questions.

If your child's potential surgery has significant risks, ensure that you have exhausted all other medical treatments. On the other hand, a simple surgery, which will not compromise your child's health, may be a better alternative than medical treatment (especially if it involves painful procedures or potential long-term complications). Before consenting to surgery, some questions you might want to ask are offered below.

WHAT IS LAPAROSCOPIC SURGERY?

Laparoscopic surgery involves making one or more one-half inch incisions near the area needing surgical repair. Reflux surgery, for instance, requires four tiny incisions in the abdomen. A large microscope-type instrument is placed through the incisions so the surgeon can visualize the area under the skin. These instruments are also used to do the required surgery.

Laparoscopic surgery eliminates a larger incision; requires less manipulation of the muscles and tissues around the surgical site (thus decreasing recovery time); produces less scarring; and minimizes pain. The disadvantages are that laparoscopic surgery is more difficult to perform than the traditional approach, and expertise varies among surgeons. Laparoscopic surgery may or may not be the appropriate choice for your child's surgery, particularly if your surgeon has not had extensive experience doing laparoscopic surgery.

Regarding surgery

- What is the surgical procedure in simple terms? Ask the surgeon to draw a picture.

- How long will the procedure take?
- Who will do the surgery, and who will assist?
- How many times has the surgeon performed this surgery?
- Is it possible to do the surgery laparoscopically?
- Will my child need more than one surgery?
- Will my child need any tests before or after the surgery?
- Will my child need respiratory preparation prior to the surgery?

Regarding anesthesia

- Who is the anesthesiologist?
- Is the anesthesiologist educated in pediatrics?
- Will she be the only anesthesiologist at the surgery?
- What type of anesthesia will be used and what are the potential side effects?
- Will my child need a ventilator during surgery?
- Can I be in the surgery room while my child falls asleep?
- How long will it take for the anesthesia to wear off?
- Will my child need oxygen after anesthesia?

WHAT IS ANESTHESIA?

During a surgical procedure, anesthesia is used to block partial or total feeling in the affected area. With every type of anesthesia, a medication to sedate (to help the child relax) is typically used. Sedation medications are administered through an injection, an IV, or a pill. Sedation will often keep the child from remembering the surgical event clearly and help with any pain she might experience.

Types of anesthesia include:

Topical. A cream or spray is used on the skin or tissue to numb the area. A topical cream can lessen the pain of an IV placement. Some lung and digestive procedures are done with a spray anesthetic while the child is awake, but sedated.

Local. When using a local anesthetic, the area needing surgical repair is numbed by an injection at the site of the surgery. Local anesthesia is most often used when the surgical treatment needed is minimal and brief in time. The area remains numb for six to twelve hours after the procedure.

Spinal block. Medication is injected with a needle through the covering of the spinal cord, numbing the lower half of the body.

Epidural block. Using a catheter, medication is injected into the space outside the covering of the spinal cord.

General. Medication is given through a vein and/or inhaled through the lungs, making the child fall into a deep sleep and unable to remember anything later. A breathing tube is placed in the throat and connected to a ventilator during the surgery.

■ ■ ■

Regarding post-surgery care

- What will my child's recovery be like?
- Where will the incisions be made, and how big will they be?
- If there are stitches, when can they be removed?
- Will my child have an IV? If so, for how long?
- Will my child receive any medications after surgery?
- Will my child need oxygen or an increase in her present oxygen needs after the surgery?
- How soon can my child eat, and what can she eat?
- How long will my child be in the hospital?
- Who will teach me how to take care of my child's post-surgery needs?
- Will anyone be sent to my home to follow my child's progress?

IS IT A "PREEMIE THING"?

THIS CHAPTER, AND the chapters before it, covered the common medical complications associated with prematurity. But because medicine quickly changes and new discoveries in the care of preterm infants are being made every day, these chapters cannot be complete.

If you find yourself wondering if your child's uniqueness is a "preemie thing," do not hesitate to ask your doctor or specialist. Consult up-to-date medical journals and Internet medical sites for new preemie-related information. Knowledge is empowering. The more you know about prematurity and its effects, the better parent you will be.

PART THREE

Feeding Your Preemie

PART THREE

Introduction

LIKE MOST PARENTS, you eagerly anticipated feeding your baby. Whether by bottle or breast, feeding a baby is one of life's precious experiences. But your baby's premature birth may have created some feeding challenges and growth concerns that interfere with these special times of closeness. You and your baby need to overcome these obstacles before feeding times can be enjoyable.

Part 3 will answer many of your growth, nutrition, and feeding questions. With the proper direction (and perhaps some professional assistance), you *can* successfully feed your baby and create those happy memories.

CHAPTER NINE

Growth, Nutrition, and Bottle-feeding

SINCE THE DAY your baby was born, growth has been a concern, and it is only natural for you to closely monitor your child's food intake and physical development after homecoming. If your child has eating or growing concerns, worries can linger for weeks, months, and even years. After all, your child's health and strength depend on his ability to eat and grow.

This chapter discusses your baby's growth and nutritional sources during the first years. Ways to optimize growth are also included. As you read, remember that food and nutrition are essential to your child's growth—but the nurturing you do as a parent is equally important.

YOUR PREEMIE'S GROWTH

CHILDREN BORN PREMATURELY, especially those who had more severe medical complications, often take longer to catch up in size to their full-term peers. By eighteen months corrected age, about half of all preterm babies are above the 10th percentile for weight on the standard growth chart (the same one used for term children). By eight years of age, about 80 percent of former preemies are above the 10th percentile.

Most former preemies eventually reach their "genetic potential" for growth. This means their adult weight and height are similar to their adult siblings' and parents' sizes. Catching up typically takes time, however, and there is no way to predict how quickly your preemie will grow. Your pediatrician should carefully monitor your baby's growth by measuring him frequently during the first year. If there are any problems with weight gain, your child's growth should be measured at least once a month. After one year corrected age and if your baby is growing adequately, measurements will be done less often. Your doctor will specifically examine weight, length, and head circumference.

Chart 9-1: Average weight gain for premature infants during first year

When your preemie came home from the hospital, he had already doubled or tripled (maybe even quadrupled!) his birthweight. This is quite an accomplishment when you consider that full-term babies usually do not triple their weight until their first birthday.

Still, it is hard not to worry about your baby's size. The following chart indicates about how much your premature baby should gain during his first year (and hopefully relieve some of your concern):

CORRECTED AGE	AVERAGE WEIGHT GAIN
0–3 months	25–35 grams per day
3–6 months	15–20 grams per day
6–12 months	10–15 grams per day

Note: 15 grams = 0.5 ounces; 30 grams = 1 ounce. Beyond twelve months corrected age, physicians typically monitor a preemie's growth curve, rather than calculate average weight gain.

My five-year-old seems small. He's not the smallest in his class, but he is still very skinny. He has finally made the growth chart for height, but still is not even close for weight. I think it is up to the individual preemie and depends on how rough a start he had that determines when he hits the chart.

I have learned not to panic when a checkup comes and my son has not grown much in between visits. Instead, I try to find the best way to help him. For example, I am more conscious about increasing his calories while still giving him a balanced diet.

—*ANDREA, MOTHER OF 23-WEEKER XAVIER*

YOUR PREEMIE'S WEIGHT

During your baby's first years, your pediatrician will look for a continuous weight gain, indicating good growth. Your baby's weight will be plotted on a growth chart at each visit. If your child stops gaining weight or starts losing weight, your doctor will do an evaluation and discuss any concerns with you.

YOUR PREEMIE'S LENGTH

Your pediatrician will measure your baby's length (the distance from his heel to the top of his head) and plot it on a growth chart. Plotting the ratio of weight to length will help determine if your preemie is growing at a proper rate. An upward sloping curve suggests your baby is growing adequately. A downward sloping or "flattened" curve indicates further evaluation is needed. After three years of age, your child's height will be measured in the standing position using his actual age.

Your Preemie's Head Circumference

Tracking your baby's head circumference measurements tells your pediatrician if your baby's brain and skull are growing normally. Head circumference measurements can also detect concerns: A sudden increase in growth may indicate an abnormal amount of fluid in the brain (or it may be "catch up" growth); a slow or stopped head growth may mean poor overall growth.

Discuss any concerns regarding your child's growth with your pediatrician. Parental input can be a valuable tool for diagnosis and treatment of growth problems.

WORRIED ABOUT YOUR PREEMIE'S HEAD SHAPE?

You may worry that your baby's head, which may be unusually shaped or appear large in relation to his body size, is an indicator that something is wrong. Many infants born prematurely have what is sometimes referred to as "preemie head." The head often achieves catch-up growth before the body, making it appear unusually large. Your child's body will eventually "grow into" his head size.

If your baby has an elongated head, it may have been caused by prolonged periods of time lying on his side in the NICU. Lying on his back with his head turned to the side to accommodate the breathing tube or feedings will also "flatten" the soft, pliable skull bones. You can help "mold" your baby's head to a rounder shape by laying him on his back, or reclining him in an infant seat, and propping his head straight using rolled blankets or cloth diapers.

Charts 9-2 to 9-5: Growth charts

Growth measurements for preterm infants are typically plotted by corrected age on growth charts designed specifically for premature infants. These charts are for preterm children up to age three, and are based on the average weights of preemies.

Some doctors use term infant growth charts for preemies and plot by corrected age (but these charts may not give an accurate assessment). The most important reason for tracking on a chart is to monitor your child's *growth curve*—the line that is drawn from point to point on the chart each time your baby is measured. An adequate growth curve is one that slopes upward following the normal curve for advancing age, indicating a consistent growth pattern. Weight, length, and head circumference should be proportional. (However, head circumference often plots in a higher percentile early on.)

Examples of preterm infant growth charts follow (you may want to plot your baby's measurements after each doctor's appointment for your own record; ask your doctor to convert pounds and ounces to grams and inches to centimeters):

■ ■ ■

Chart 9-2: Growth charts for premature boys less than 1,500 grams

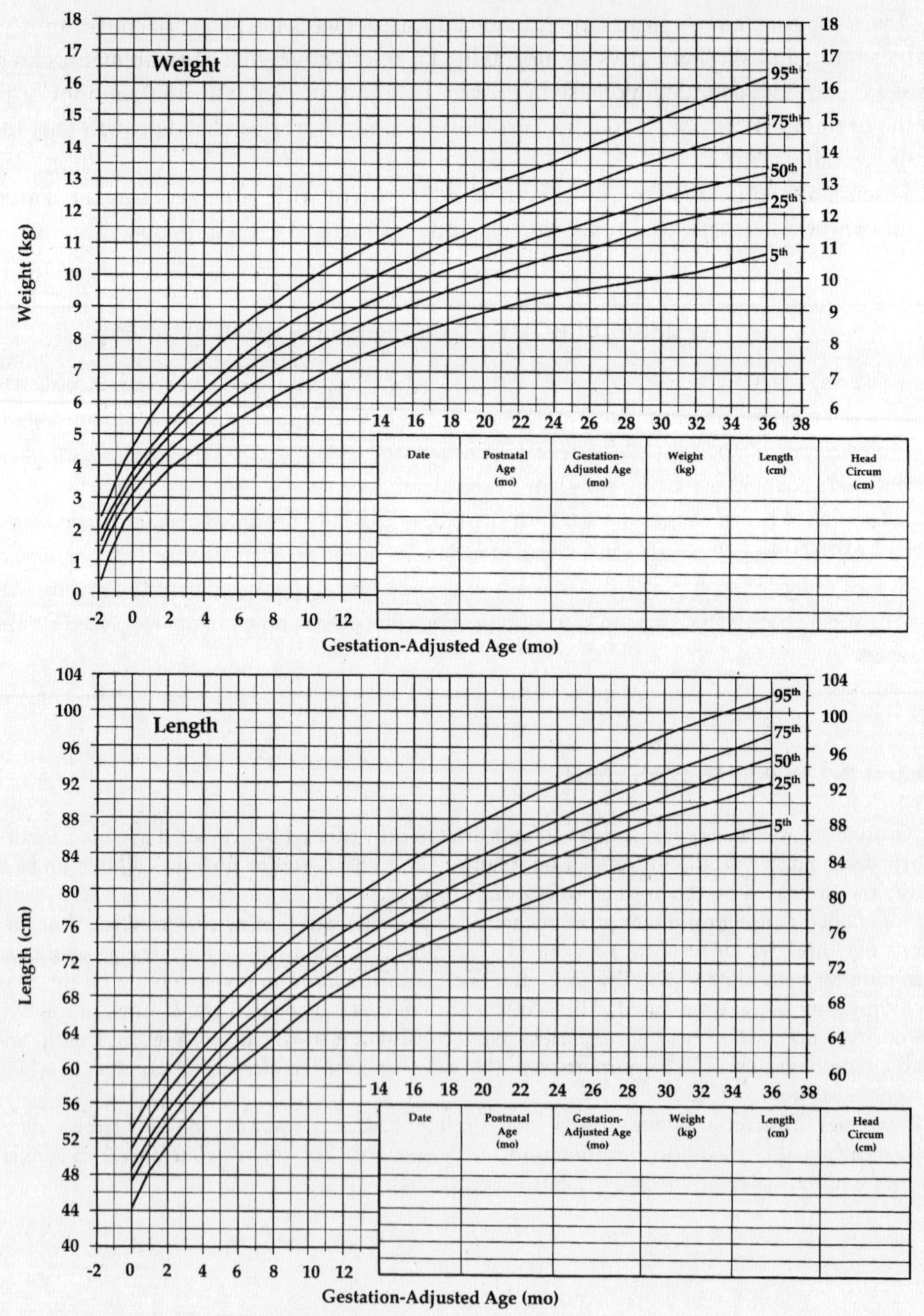

(Charts on pages 158-165 used with permission from Ross Products Divison, Abbott Laboratories Inc., Columbus, OH 43216. From HDP Growth Percentiles copyright © 1998 Ross Products Division, Abbott Laboratories Inc.)

Chart 9-2: (cont.)

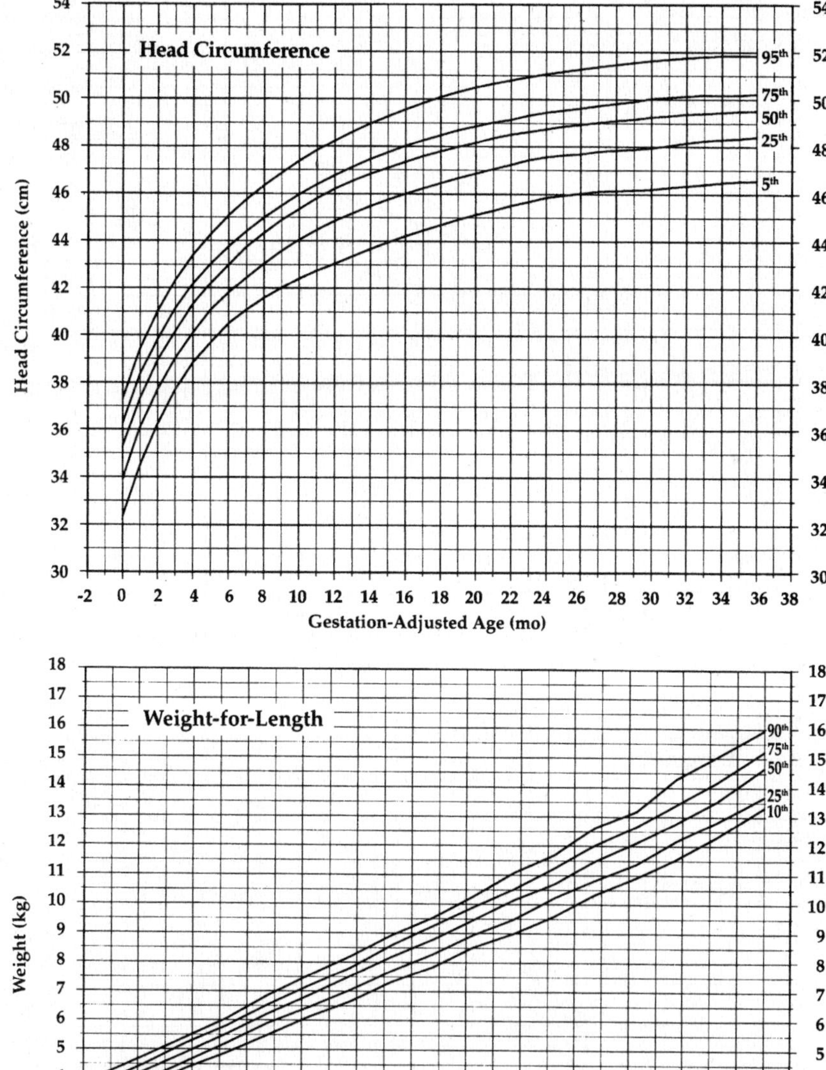

Chart 9-3: Growth charts for premature boys 1,500 to 2,500 grams

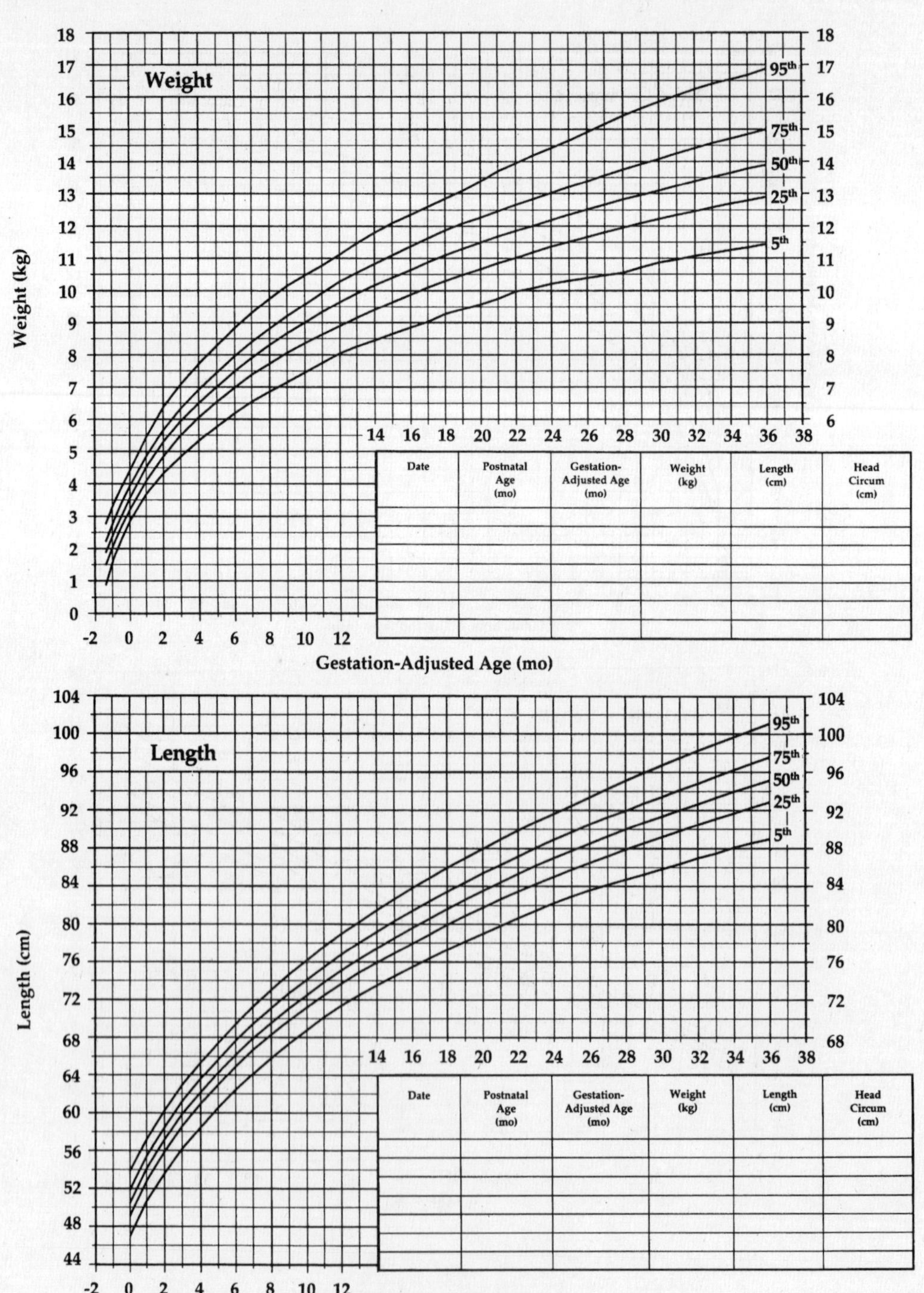

Chart 9-3: (cont.)

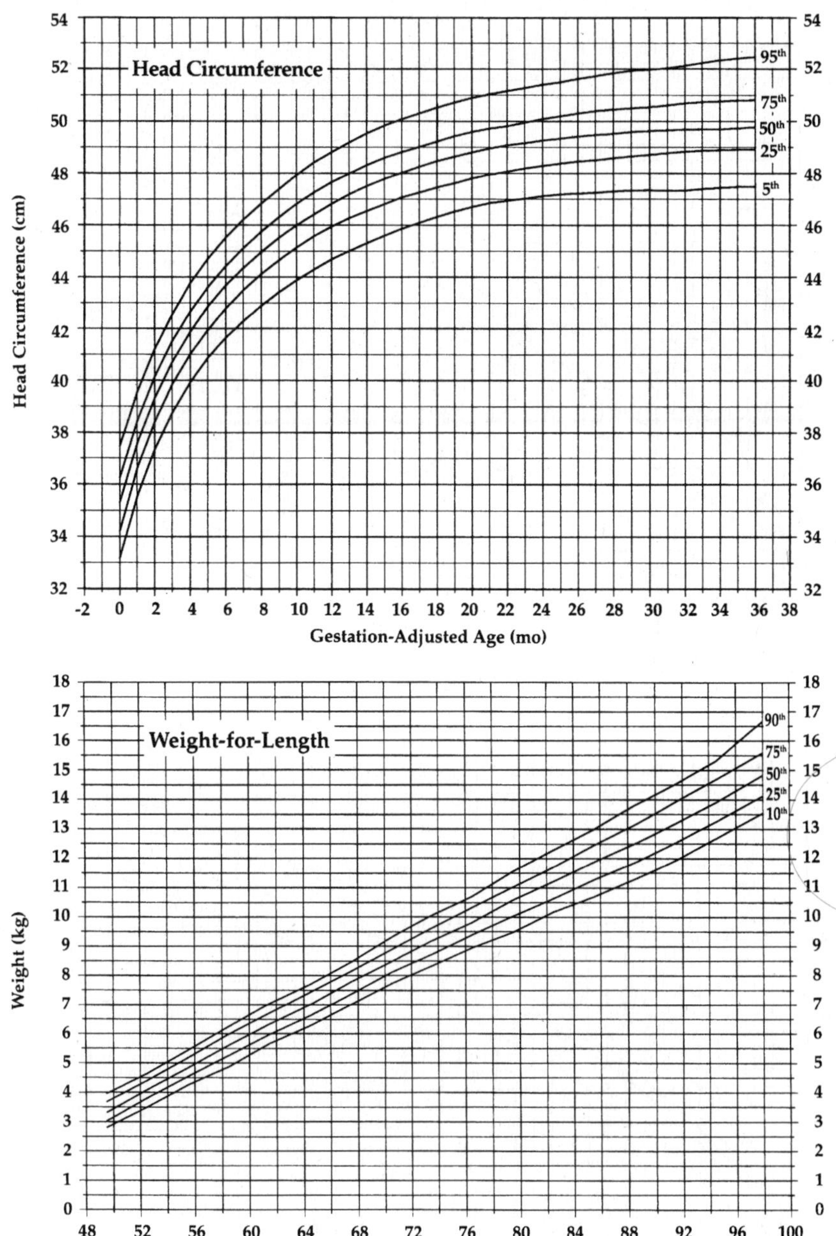

Chart 9-4: Growth charts for premature girls less than 1,500 grams

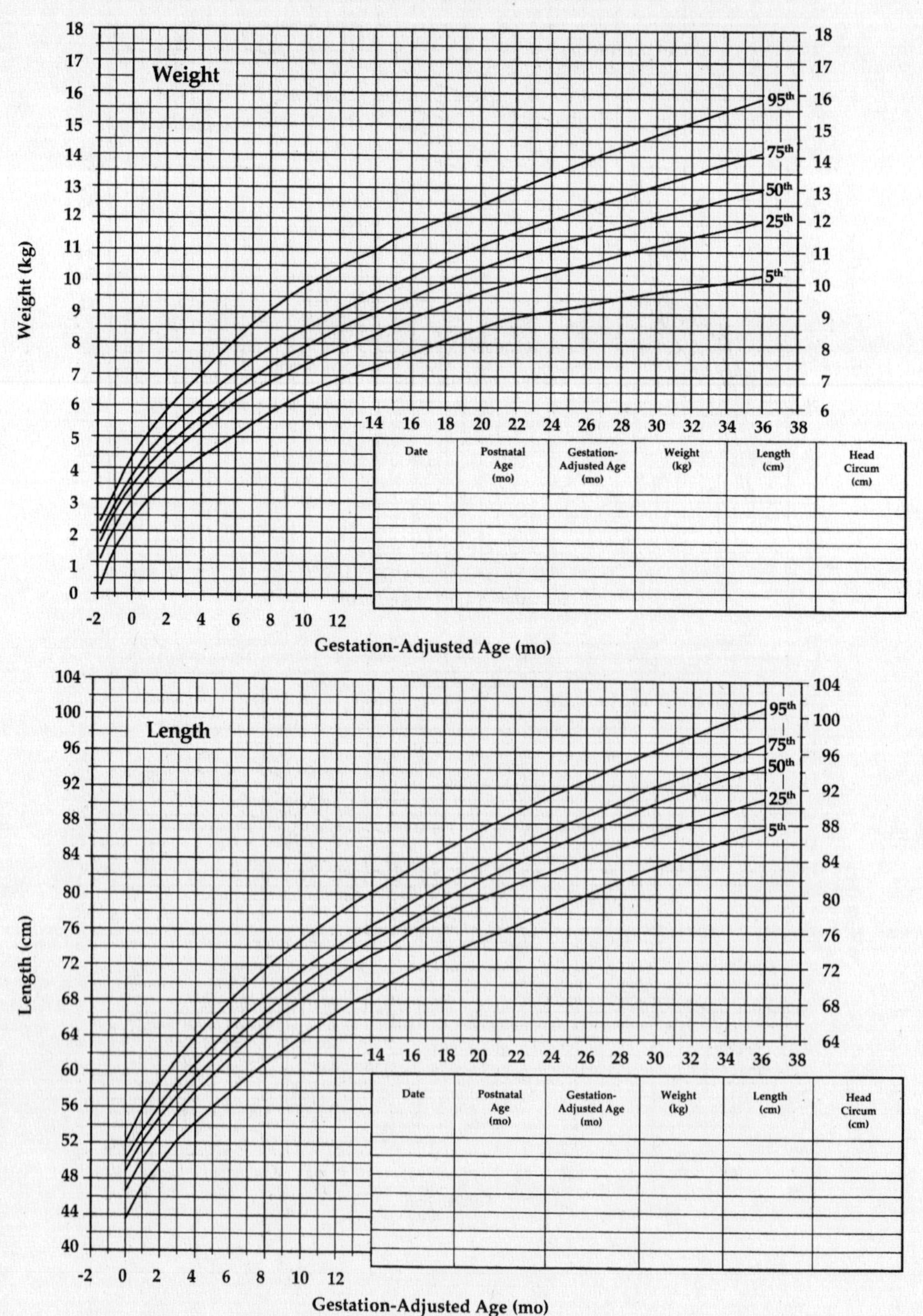

Chart 9-4: (cont.)

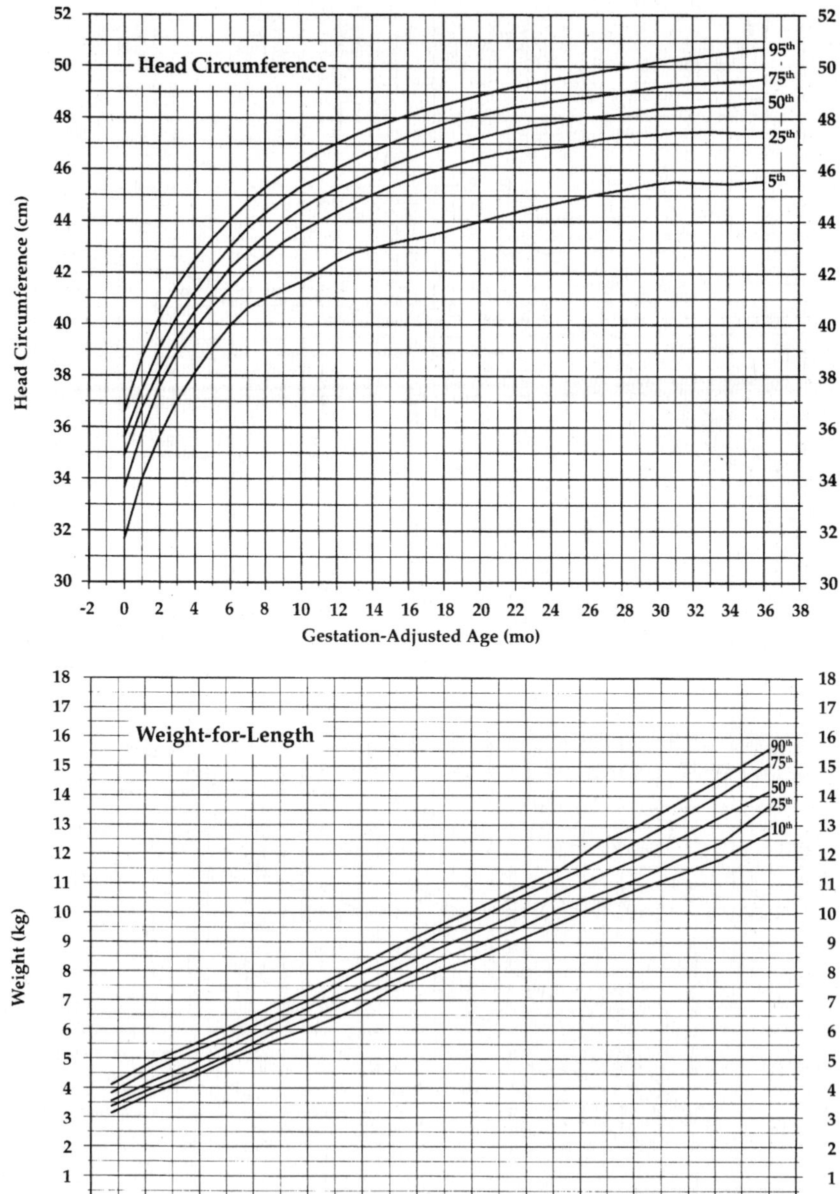

Chart 9-5: Growth charts for premature girls 1,500 to 2,500 grams

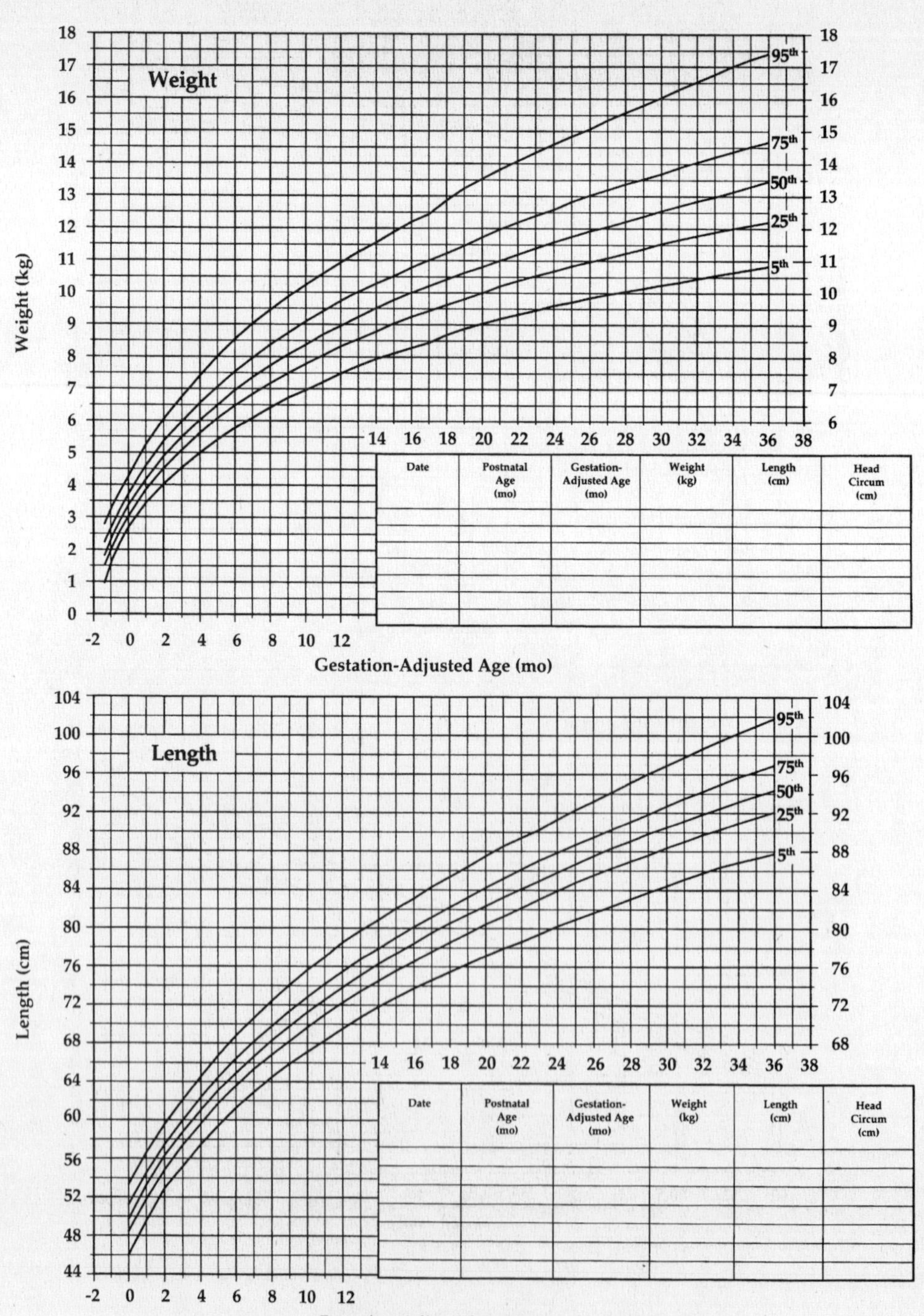

Chart 9-5: (cont.)

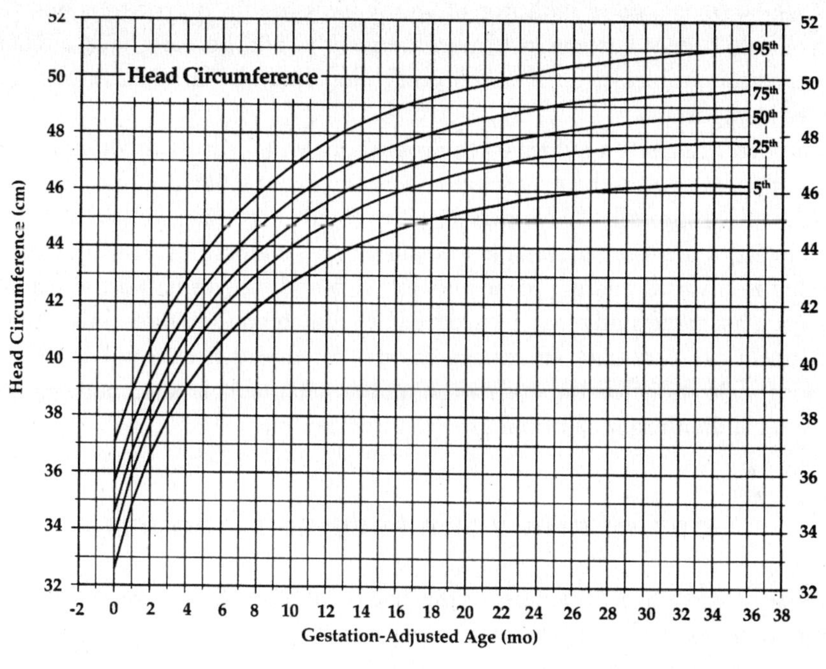

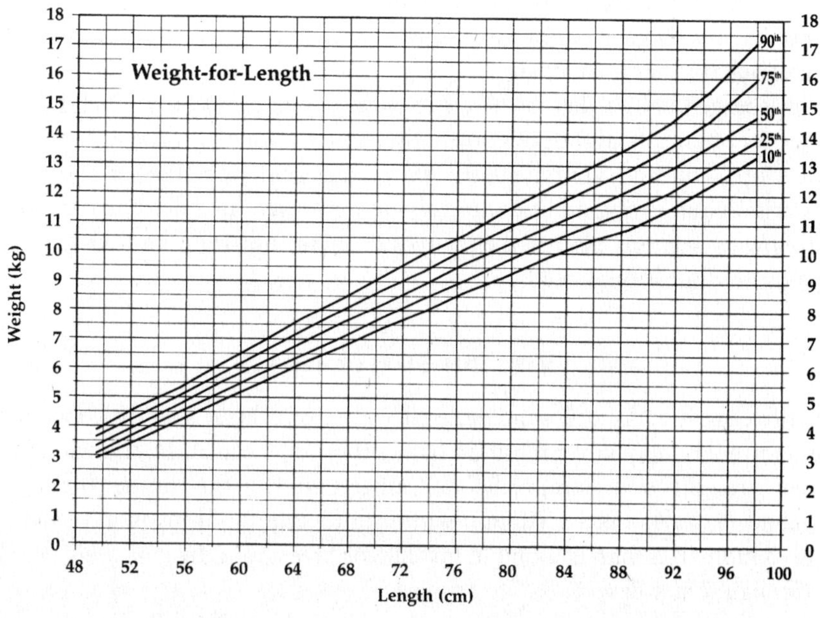

IF YOUR PREEMIE HAS DELAYED GROWTH

PROPER GROWTH IS a good indicator of your child's health. If growth is poor or inadequate, your child may become sick more frequently, and he may have difficulty overcoming medical problems, such as chronic lung disease. Early treatment of growth difficulties is important.

If your doctor suspects a mild growth problem, he will do an evaluation of your child's diet and eating habits, and he may suggest increasing your child's calories or changing his eating schedule. If growth delays persist, your doctor may refer you to a pediatric gastroenterologist, a dietitian, a feeding specialist, or an endocrinologist (a medical doctor specializing in diseases relating to hormones). A blood test, urinalysis, thyroid function test, and/or a hormone study may be needed. Depending on the cause of the growth problem, treatment can vary from increasing calories to various behavioral or medical treatments. Hospitalization for the evaluation and/or treatment is sometimes necessary. In most cases, children resume normal growth after treatment.

OPTIMIZING YOUR PREEMIE'S GROWTH

FULL-TERM INFANTS ACQUIRE most of their body fat, as well as vitamins, iron, and minerals important for bone growth and strength, during the last trimester of pregnancy. Your baby born prematurely missed important weeks or months of critical growth inside the womb. Even with early strict nutritional management in the NICU, your baby may have been discharged at a small size.

Your discharged baby's diet is therefore critical. What and how much he eats affects how he grows physically and developmentally, how healthy he stays, and how strong his bones develop. You and your pediatrician should work together to ensure that your child's nutrition and eating abilities are helping him reach his fullest growth potential.

The following sections discuss the sources of infant nutrition and what to do if your baby has greater nutritional needs.

VITAMIN SUPPLEMENTS

Some preterm infants need supplemental vitamins; others, such as those on preemie follow-up formulas, may not. Breast-fed babies typically need additional vitamin D. Your doctor may prescribe a vitamin, or he may suggest an over-the-counter brand.

Your child may also need a vitamin with iron to help build his blood. Many preterm infants need more iron than is found in formula or breastmilk. Iron may also be given separately through infant drops.

■ ■ ■

"YOUR CHILD IS SOOOO SMALL!"

I worry about what message my daughter is getting when she is constantly told how small she is.

—*ANNE, MOTHER OF 32-WEEKER ELIZABETH*

A mother at the playground wants to know your child's age. You cringe, swallow, then announce your preemie's actual age. "Really?" *the woman squeals. "But she's soooo tiny!"*

You probably have heard similar remarks at the grocery store's checkout line, at the park, even in the doctor's office. Maybe you give your child's corrected age, trying to avoid unwanted comments. Perhaps you tell the whole birth story, letting people know your child's miraculous beginning. One mom says she typically retorts: "My daughter is just the right size for her."

If you deal with size comments often, you may wonder how they will affect your child's self-esteem. What message is he receiving by constantly being told he is small? Will he grow up thinking bigger is better and feel poorly about himself? Counteracting any negative messages with positive ones is important. Let your child know it is the person inside who truly matters. Read books that stress this lesson.

Reinforce the skills your child is good at—a sport, coloring, or being a good friend. Remind your child that he is strong: "You fought so hard in the hospital. How strong you are!" A good self-image is one of the best gifts you can give your petite child. By feeling good about himself, your child will have the confidence to think and act "big."

BREASTMILK

If you are breast-feeding your preterm infant, you are giving him nutrients designed especially for his unique needs. You are also providing him with important antibodies that help fight infection. (Although the milk produced during the first few days after birth has the highest amount of antibodies, later breastmilk continues to have anti-infection cells.) Breastmilk is also easier for your baby to digest; it protects against allergies; it may reduce the risk of Sudden Infant Death Syndrome (SIDS); and it is less stressful on your child's kidneys.

Your pediatrician and/or lactation consultant should give you guidelines for breast-feeding, including how often to nurse, how long the sessions should last, and how many supplemental bottles your baby may need. Your doctor and/or lactation consultant may recommend nursing at least every two to three hours, particularly if your baby often falls asleep while eating. Some doctors and breast-feeding experts suggest waking babies to eat; some feel sleep is equally important for growth and health. Make sure you discuss breast-feeding philosophies and your goals with your doctor and/or lactation consultant. Refer to chapter 10 for more on breast-feeding.

■ ■ ■

When breastmilk is not enough

Preterm infants who have not yet mastered breast-feeding (and even some who are skilled feeders) may require extra calories for adequate growth. Those infants with chronic lung disease who burn calories quickly because they work hard to breathe may need additional calories, too. Having to increase the calories of your breastmilk does not mean your milk is inadequate—it is simply a method to help your baby grow.

Your pediatrician will develop a plan with you to increase your child's calories. *Never increase the caloric content of your breastmilk without a doctor's order—serious imbalances with your baby's vitamins, minerals, fluids, protein, and carbohydrates can result.* Your baby may need a bottle with higher-calorie formula, or he may need breastmilk mixed with a powdered preemie formula or a human-milk fortifier (a powder that is made specifically for increasing the calories of breastmilk) for some or all feedings. Supplemental calories will be needed until you and your doctor are satisfied with your child's growth.

FORMULA

Some parents wonder if their discharged baby can continue to eat the higher-calorie formula given in the NICU. The special formula used in the hospital has higher amounts of protein that can be harmful to your child if not closely monitored. Instead, your doctor should advise you regarding the type of formula to feed your baby. He may recommend regular formula with twenty calories per ounce; suggest increasing the calories of regular formula; or prescribe a formula designed specifically for preterm infants (Similac NeoSure or Enfamil 22).

Your doctor should also tell you how much and how often to feed your baby. Ask him to recommend specific volume amounts for several feeding schedules. For example, how much should you feed your baby every three hours? Every four to five hours? Within a twenty-four-hour period? Knowing how much formula your baby needs to consume within twenty-four hours allows you some flexibility with your baby's feeding schedule. However, your doctor may recommend following a strict schedule and even waking your infant for feedings.

Most preemies take baby formula until they are twelve months corrected age, when cows' milk is started. If a child still needs more calories for growth after age one, special formulas, such as Pediasure and Kindercal, have thirty calories per ounce and can be given up to age ten.

■ ■ ■

Chart 9-6: Increasing the calories of breastmilk

If your doctor has prescribed increasing the caloric content of your breastmilk, use this guide to help you.

USING REGULAR POWDER FORMULA (SUCH AS IMPROVED SIMILAC OR ENFAMIL)

Calories per ounce	Formula	Breastmilk
22	1 teaspoon	180 cc's
24	2 teaspoon	180 cc's

USING HUMAN MILK FORTIFIER

Calories per ounce	Fortifier	Breastmilk
22	1 packet	50 cc's
24	1 packet	25 cc's

Note: Human milk fortifier is only recommended for infants up to forty weeks gestational age because it is too high in some nutrients for large infants, and it is expensive and difficult to obtain.

USING SIMILAC NEOSURE

Calories per ounce	Powder Formula	Breastmilk
22	1 teaspoon	130 cc's
24	1 teaspoon	70 cc's
27	1 teaspoon	40 cc's

USING ENFAMIL 22

Calories per ounce	Powder Formula	Breastmilk
22	1/3 teaspoon	45 cc's
24	1/2 teaspoon	45 cc's
27	1 teaspoon	45 cc's

Note: 30 cc's = 1 ounce

Chart 9-7: Average formula intake for preterm infants

As your baby grows, he should increase the amount of formula he consumes. Use the following chart as a guide to see if your infant is eating within the average volume range. If your baby has lung disease or another medical problem, he may consume less.

Remember, the volume your baby consumes is not as important as the amount of calories he eats and his ability to gain adequate weight.

WEIGHT	TOTAL DAILY FORMULA INTAKE	FEEDING FREQUENCY
4–5 pounds	11–14 ounces	Every 2–4 hours
5–6 pounds	14–16 ounces	Every 2–4 hours
6–8 pounds	15–20 ounces	Every 2–4 hours
8–10 pounds	15–24 ounces	Every 3–4 hours
10–12 pounds	24–30 ounces	Every 3–5 hours

Note: This chart is based on standard twenty-calorie-per-ounce formula. Many preemies require more calories per ounce.

During the first weeks at home, your baby may consume small amounts of formula at each feeding, and you should measure volume by cc's, rather than ounces (30 cc's equal one ounce). As your baby grows and eats more, start converting to ounces. By the time your baby is eating three ounces (or 90 cc's) per feeding, you should be measuring ounces only.

(Prepared by Lyn Stevenson, R.D., C.S.P., Clinical Dietician, Children's Hospital of Denver, Denver, Colo.)

When regular formula is not enough

Consuming an adequate amount of formula is necessary for any baby (full-term and preterm), but infants born prematurely often require additional calories for adequate growth. If your baby does not grow well on the amount of formula he is taking, he may need the calories in his formula increased (rather than increasing volume at each feeding). Both the special twenty-two-calorie follow-up formulas designed for preterm infants (Similac NeoSure and Enfamil 22) and the twenty-calorie-regular infant formulas can be mixed as high as twenty-eight-calories per ounce.

The decision to increase your baby's calories should be based on his growth curve. If you are concerned about your child's growth, discuss increasing calories with your pediatrician. *Never increase the caloric concentration of your baby's formula without a doctor's order—serious imbalances with vitamins, minerals, fluids, protein, and carbohydrates can result.*

■ ■ ■

Chart 9-8: Increasing calories of baby formulas

If your doctor has prescribed increasing the caloric content of formula, use this guide to help you.

USING REGULAR POWDER FORMULA (SUCH AS IMPROVED SIMILAC OR ENFAMIL)

Calories per ounce	Formula	Water
20	1 scoop	2 ounces
20	4 scoops	8 ounces
20	1 cup	29 ounces
22	1 scoop	55 cc's
22	3 scoops	5.5 ounces
24	1 scoop	50 cc's
24	2 scoops	98 cc's
24	3 scoops	5 ounces

USING CONCENTRATED LIQUID FORMULA (SUCH AS IMPROVED SIMILAC OR ENFAMIL)

Calories per ounce	Formula*	Water
20	13 ounces	13 ounces
22	13 ounces	10.5 ounces
24	13 ounces	8.5 ounces

*Concentrated liquid formula comes in 13-ounce cans, and it is easier to mix using the entire can.

Note: Powdered and liquid formula can be increased to 25, 26, 27, and 28 calories per ounce by adding Polycose and/or vegetable oil. Polycose is a fine powder that increases calories by adding carbohydrates. MCT (a special easily digested oil used for children with digestive problems) and vegetable oils add fat calories. Your doctor or a pediatric dietitian will determine the best way to create higher calories for your baby.

Chart 9-8: (cont.)

USING SIMILAC NEOSURE

Calories per ounce	Formula	Water
20	3 scoops	5.5 ounces
22	3 scoops	5 ounces
24	3 scoops	4.5 ounces

USING ENFAMIL 22

Calories per ounce	Formula	Water
20	2 scoops	4.5 ounces
22	1 scoop	2 ounces
24	2 scoops	3.5 ounces

Note: 30 cc's = 1 ounce

I knew Caroline would have some difficulty taking a bottle when she came home from the hospital—she never was an aggressive eater. But I never thought feeding would be so hard for so long. It seemed we had to try everything to keep her growing. We tried every different nipple, we increased her calories, and we changed her schedule. Finally we got help from a speech-language pathologist.

I guess I wanted her to eat like other "normal" babies, but that wasn't what she wanted to do. I still mourn the loss of holding her and feeding her, and putting food in front of her without worrying about every bite.

—*Janet, mother of 27-weeker Caroline*

How to Prepare Formula

For mixing formula during the first months after homecoming, boil water for twenty-five minutes or use bottled water. Your baby's digestive system needs time to mature before it can tolerate the impurities of tap water.

You also need to sterilize new bottles, nipples, and pacifiers by boiling them in water for twenty-five minutes in a large, covered pot. After initial boiling, wash them in the dishwasher and use the heat-drying cycle to kill germs. Make sure the nipple's hole remains open after washing, by running water through it or by inserting a toothpick.

Always wash your hands before making your baby's bottles, and follow the manufacturer's directions on the formula label.

YOUR BABY'S HUNGER CUES

Preterm infants do not always cry the way term babies often do when they are hungry. Instead, your preemie may be ready to eat if he:

- opens his mouth and moves his head from side to side;
- begins waking and wriggles around while still in a sleepy state;
- sucks more vigorously on a pacifier;
- sucks on his fingers or on a blanket; and/or
- smacks his lips.

How to Bottle-feed

Even though you bottle-fed your infant in the NICU, it will take time and practice for you both to feel comfortable with at-home feedings. As your baby adjusts to his new surroundings and establishes a schedule, and as you learn how to care for your baby, feeding times will get easier. Soon, they will even become routine.

Follow these steps for smoother bottle-feedings:

1. Vigorously wash your hands in soapy water before feeding your baby (your hands may carry germs that could pass to your baby).

WARNING SIGNS

While your baby is adapting to home or if he is ill, some feedings will not go smoothly. If your baby often eats poorly (for more than three feedings a day for two days), consult your pediatrician. Your doctor may recommend an evaluation with a feeding specialist. You should also consult your doctor if your baby:

- takes longer than forty minutes to complete a feeding for three or more feedings in a day;
- becomes stressed during at least 50 percent of his feedings (his color becomes mottled; his lips are pale; he breathes quickly or pants; he "shuts down" by falling asleep; he has an apnea or bradycardia episode);
- takes longer than five minutes to recover from the stress eating causes;
- does not begin to eat more as he gets older (for example, your baby continues to take two ounces every three hours, even though your doctor says he should be eating about three ounces);
- is excessively fussy after most feedings;
- vomits frequently during or after feedings; and/or
- gags often during or between feedings.

2. Set your baby's bottle in hot water or a bottle warmer until the milk feels warm (test the temperature on your wrist). *Never microwave a bottle—it may cause "hot spots" that can burn your baby.*
3. If your baby is on supplemental oxygen, you may need to increase the level before giving a bottle (eating can require extra oxygen).
4. Remember that your baby needs a lot of energy to suck, swallow, and breathe. He needs to stay calm and focused. Minimize stimulation by picking a quiet room where the lighting is dim, and try to keep siblings busy in another room.
5. Find a comfortable chair and position yourself and your baby so that you are both relaxed. Make sure you have a cloth diaper, kitchen towel, or receiving blanket for burping. Wrap and hold your baby snugly, but make sure his hands are free to touch his mouth or grasp your finger while he is sucking.
6. Hold your baby's head slightly elevated and put a few drops of milk on his bottom lip or on a pacifier. The flavor will help him recognize that food is coming.
7. Now gently introduce the nipple into your baby's mouth, making sure it is on top of his tongue. Let your baby establish a synchronized pattern of sucking, swallowing, and breathing. He may need to pause and breathe in between "bursts" of sucking. If he shows signs of stress (becomes pale, mottled, or dusky, drools, or pants), remove the bottle and let him recover. Do not jiggle the nipple in his mouth—this will only add to his stress. As your baby matures, his eating pattern will become more natural and require less exertion.
8. Some babies need frequent burping; others do not. If you stop your baby to burp before he is ready, he may become disorganized, making it difficult for him to restart the eating process. Your baby may need burping if he begins to gag, slows down his sucking, or stops sucking altogether. With time, you will instinctively know your baby's feeding needs.
9. Your baby is finished eating when he is very sleepy or refuses the bottle. Remove the bottle and take some time to snuggle and relax together.

PARENT TIPS:
Best Bets for Bottle-Feeding

To help your baby eat better from a bottle, try these suggestions from parents and feeding specialists:

- Do not be overly concerned about keeping a strict feeding schedule during the first few weeks—it will only cause your family additional stress. Instead, monitor the volume your baby consumes within twenty-four hours, rather than every three hours. Schedules are important for babies, but your baby must adjust to home first.
- Find a nipple that lets your baby control the flow of formula. Begin by using store-bought nipples that closely resemble the size, style, and firmness of the

nipple used in the hospital. As your baby grows, you may need to change nipples to fit his needs.

- Never feed your baby when he is lying completely flat—it can cause ear infections and increase his risk of choking. Your child should also never suck on a bottle while he is sleeping. In addition to possible choking, it can result in severe tooth decay.
- Never prop your baby's bottle. You need to monitor his sucking and swallowing while you hold him and enjoy some time together. Face-to-face interaction will also set the stage for later spoon-feeding.
- To avoid unnecessary stimulation while feeding your baby, try not to wipe his mouth until he is finished eating. Gentle burping will also be less disruptive and fatiguing.
- If your baby gets too sleepy during a feeding and has not consumed enough, try gently changing his diaper to wake him; then resume feeding.

Weaning from the Bottle

While most pediatricians recommend weaning a child from the bottle between one and two years of age, your preemie may or may not be ready for weaning. To evaluate your child's readiness to give up the bottle, try answering the following questions:

- Are my child's nutritional needs being met from sources other than formula? (This is an especially important question if your child is having difficulty gaining weight.)
- Is my child's bottle a source of nutrition or a source of emotional security?
- Does my child seem ready to make the transition away from the bottle? (Children who are healthy, on a feeding schedule, not teething, and seem happy overall are more likely to wean successfully.)
- Does my child have the developmental ability to successfully drink from a cup or straw?
- Is my child willing to use some type of cup?
- Does my child have sensory issues that need addressing before we start the weaning process?

If you cannot answer some of these questions, consult an expert who can. Weaning is a personal decision, but one that should be made based on your child's unique needs and readiness.

When you are ready to begin weaning, discuss methods with your doctor. Some experts recommend that you introduce the cup before you make any attempt to wean your child from the bottle. One way is a graduated-feeding system, which offers a cup with a nipple, then one with a soft spout, and finally the cup alone or with a straw. An alternative strategy, which can be helpful for a child with a strong allegiance to routines or who is easily distressed by change, is reducing the volume of bottles by one ounce each week. This allows for a more gradual transition off the bottle.

PARENT TIPS:

TAKING AWAY THE BOTTLE

As you begin weaning, remember these important tips:

- Create a bedtime routine that does not emphasize the bottle. Also, lessen the emphasis on the bottle as a means of security. For example, instead of giving your baby a bottle, read a story, give a kiss and hug, then let your child cuddle with her favorite stuffed animal or blanket. When your child is upset and wants a bottle, find another way to comfort him, such as rubbing his back. If your child wakes in the middle of the night, offer him a drink of water from a cup, instead of a bottle.
- Give your baby opportunities to drink appropriate liquids from your cup. This gives him a chance to try an alternative means of drinking liquids and "sharing" with you.
- When your child is successfully eating solids (around eight to ten months corrected age), offer him the cup in the middle or toward the end of every meal.
- Communicate your bottle-weaning plan with all your child's caregivers. One person can unintentionally undermine the entire weaning process.

THE IMPORTANCE OF SUCCESSFUL FEEDINGS

SUCCESSFUL EATING IS important not only to your child's growth but to your parent-child relationship as well. As you learn how to feed your baby and your baby learns to eat, you are sharing a special interaction. Your baby begins to trust and rely on you, the person who is providing not only food but also a comfortable and secure place. As a parent, you are spending time getting to know your baby away from the NICU. This interaction during mealtimes continues throughout childhood.

CHAPTER TEN

Breast-feeding

AS YOU PROBABLY already know, nursing a preterm infant is not an easy process. Preemies have weaker sucks, they tire more easily, and they can become confused by the introduction of various nipples. A low milk supply can add to feeding difficulties. Even with all these obstacles, your baby can successfully breast-feed—he just needs a little more time and some extra support.

This chapter provides information to help you and your baby make the transition to full-time breast-feeding. During your breast-feeding journey, always remember: Whatever amount of breastmilk you provide your baby (in the NICU and at home) is a wonderful gift. You should feel good about any pumping and nursing you do.

Having a premature baby is not what every mom anticipates or expects. Initially, I was very disappointed and depressed that I was not able to carry to term. However, soon after Christine was born, I found myself engorged and realized that I could provide something that no one else could give our daughter—my milk. With the help of very understanding nurses at the hospital, I was able to learn to pump my milk and became proficient very quickly.

My breast-feeding journey had many highs and lows, but fortunately I sought support and as much information as I could. I was persistent about seeking information on breast-feeding that was accurate and compatible with my own mothering philosophy. I always kept in mind that whatever time I shared with my daughter while nursing and whatever amount of breastmilk I provided her was beneficial. Now that our daughter is two years old, I have many precious memories of special feeding times.

—KATHY, MOTHER OF 28-WEEKER CHRISTINE

■

After rooming-in at the hospital with Tyler for two nights, I knew breast-feeding was going to take a lot more patience than I had previously anticipated. He was still struggling after four weeks of nursing, and my milk was low.

After Tyler came home, I still had hopes for breast-feeding. Unfortunately, he had a medical complication on his fourth day home. He needed supplemental oxygen and he couldn't nurse effectively. I was crushed. Here was this little baby I wanted to cuddle and nurse as much as he needed, yet he was too sick to eat.

I tried everything I could think of as well as suggestions from others. Nothing worked and I felt horrible guilt. I walked around with these stupid pumping attachments strapped to my bras, and I felt like a zombie from the fatiguing two-hour cycles of pumping, nursing, and supplemental feedings. I became obsessed with breast-feeding. It was an endless feeling of blame, failure, doubt, and sadness.

I was afraid to consult a lactation consultant or La Leche League for fear of embarrassment and of not living up to their expectations. I was also afraid they might not understand about the special needs of a preemie. When a friend told me that I should do what was in my heart, I quit pumping and began only nursing. Within three weeks, Tyler stopped nursing due to my dwindling supply.

I felt sad and relieved at the same time. I finally was able to spend each feeding holding, cuddling, and enjoying my baby. I do have some regrets, but I know I gave Tyler four months of precious breastmilk. I did the best I could.

If I had to do it over again, I would have asked others who had experience in nursing a preemie for more advice. I would also recognize my body's and my baby's limitations without a cloud of failure resting on my shoulders.

—KERRY, MOTHER OF 31-WEEKER TYLER

■

My milk really only came in on one side and that was pitiful. The breast-feeding literature I read made me feel inadequate because I would pump and pump, especially on the "off" side, and I barely increased my supply.

It seemed to take a long time, but I did succeed in getting my son to nurse. For about three weeks, my milk wouldn't let down unless I put some milk on my nipple and my son nursed for a while. I would then feed him his bottle and pump my breasts for the next feeding. Jonny was never a good eater, and I don't think I went to four-ounce bottles until he was nearly six months corrected age.

—JULIE, MOTHER OF 30-WEEKER JONNY

HOW BREAST-FEEDING WORKS

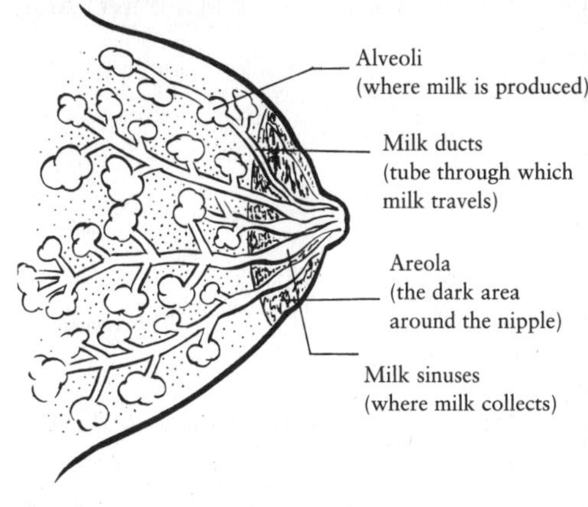

The breast

DEEP INSIDE YOUR breasts are milk-producing glands, called alveoli, that resemble small clusters of grapes. The alveoli collect nutrients from your blood and turn them into milk. The milk then travels through the milk ducts to collecting areas, called milk sinuses, which sit behind the areola (the darkened area around your nipples). The milk is stored there until needed. Your breastmilk is released through dozens of milk sinus openings in your nipples.

When your baby nurses, your brain releases two hormones: prolactin and oxytocin. *Prolactin* tells the alveoli to begin producing breastmilk. *Oxytocin*, the same hormone that causes the uterus to contract, causes the alveoli to eject, or "let down," milk into the milk ducts. The more often you put your baby to the breast, the more your milk supply will increase.

HOMECOMING AND BREAST-FEEDING

THE FIRST FEW weeks at home can be very difficult for preemie moms who are breast-feeding, even for those who successfully nursed in the hospital. Your baby must adjust to his new surroundings before he can really concentrate on eating. At times, it may seem as though he is rejecting breast-feeding (and you may think he is rejecting you, too). Keep in mind that he is only coping with the stress of homecoming (just as you are) and needs a little time before he can focus on feeding. Use this time to get to know your baby better—learn his cues, likes, and dislikes—making the transition to full-time breast-feeding easier.

During the homecoming week it is imperative that you try to nurse whenever your baby shows signs of hunger. Your baby may be ready to eat if he starts stirring during his sleep, begins sucking on a pacifier or his fingers, or moves his hands toward his face. Do not wait until your infant is really hungry; it is easier to feed a calm, slightly hungry infant than a "starving," irritable one. When your baby shows a hunger cue, speak to him softly and gently pick him up (be careful not to overstimulate). If possible, try to nurse your baby for about five minutes on each breast.

If your baby was on a breast-feeding schedule in the hospital, attempt to continue it at home, but do not get locked into set feeding times. Let your baby tell you when he wants to eat. This may be as often as every one or two hours during the first weeks at home, especially if he often falls asleep while eating.

If a feeding is going well, continue to nurse for as long as your baby likes. If your baby

PUMPING AND STORING BREASTMILK

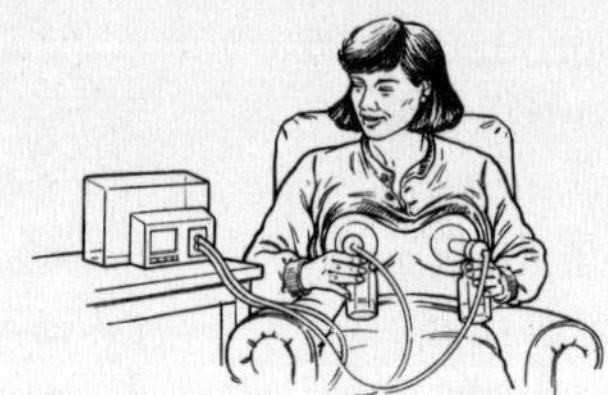

This woman is using an electric breastpump.

Mothers of preterm infants typically find that an electric breastpump is the most efficient way to express milk. Electric pumps, including portable ones, are available to rent at most medical supply companies or through lactation consultants. Ask your health insurance provider if they will cover the rental of a breastpump.

Other breastpump options include: manual pumps, battery-operated pumps, and semiautomatic electric pumps. Any pump you use should come with complete instructions. Of course, you can also express your milk the old-fashioned way—by hand. Consult a lactation expert, or one of the many good books on breast-feeding, for proper hand-expression techniques.

Follow these suggestions for proper handling and storage of breastmilk:

- Your breastpump may come with a container attached to it for storing milk in the refrigerator. You can also store pumped breastmilk in a clean container, such as a glass or plastic bottle, or in disposable plastic bottle liners. Pour a little bit more than your baby typically eats at a feeding.
- If you are freezing breastmilk, disposable plastic bottle liners work best. Double-bag them to prevent tearing and close with rubber bands. Place multiple bottle liners into a large plastic freezer bag to prevent individual bags from tearing and from sticking to the freezer. Label each bag with the date and time of pumping.
- Breastmilk can be stored within the refrigerator for up to forty-eight hours after expressing or twenty-four hours after thawing. Breastmilk can be kept in a freezer within a refrigerator for up to three weeks; in a seprate-door freezer for up to three months; and in a deep freezer for up to six months. You should verify these storage times with your pediatrician or lactation consultant.
- The best way to thaw breastmilk is slowly in the refrigerator. If you need to thaw breastmilk quickly, run warm water over the container or place it in a bowl of warm water. (Do not microwave, as this can cause "hot spots" that might burn your infant's mouth.) Make sure no water seeps into the breastmilk.
- Wash all breastpump parts that come in contact with milk in hot soapy water after each use.

becomes frustrated or sleepy, stop nursing and pump. Your baby will eventually learn to regulate feeding times, and he will create a schedule.

Until your baby is breast-feeding full-time, you need to give him supplemental bottles with pumped breastmilk (or formula if your supply is low). After each breast-feeding, pump your breastmilk. Pumping keeps your milk supply plentiful while your baby is learning to eat. It also keeps your breasts soft, decreasing the chances of engorgement. In addition, the milk that is released late into a feeding and is pumped immediately after nursing, called hindmilk, has more fat calories than milk produced early. You should save this high-calorie milk to use in your baby's bottles.

You may be tempted to bottle-feed your baby pumped breastmilk frequently to prevent the frustration of difficult nursing. Giving bottles of breastmilk too often will only prolong the transition to full-time breast-feeding. Again, you should attempt breast-feeding for most feedings.

Give yourself and your baby at least several weeks to make the transition to full-time breast-feeding. As your baby becomes a more skilled eater—and if he is growing adequately—slowly decrease bottle-feedings and pumping, and increase breast-feeding times.

> *You know you're a true preemie mom when you've finished a middle-of-the-night breast-feeding/supplementing session with the little darling, then you hook yourself up to your double-breast pump and fall asleep for forty-five minutes. Milk overflowing everywhere! The pump's motor overheating! And you wonder why the sensation of being "milked" didn't wake you.*
>
> —*Leslie, mother of 29-weeker Bryce*

ARE THE STRUGGLES OF BREAST-FEEDING WORTH IT?

Sometimes the grueling nursing-pumping-supplementing sessions make you wonder if breast-feeding is really worth it. You may be encouraged to persevere by learning that recent studies show nursing is physically easier on infants born prematurely (although this is not always recognized by medical professionals). Your preemie can more easily regulate the flow of breastmilk, making eating less stressful. Less stress means he can focus on coordinating sucking, swallowing, and breathing. The skin-to-skin contact during nursing also feels good and gives your child an important sense of trust and closeness.

When you become frustrated, remember that even mothers of full-term infants struggle with what is sometimes called a "natural process." As a mother of a preterm infant, you know this process is certainly not as natural as many would like to believe. Many factors can affect your breast-feeding success: your baby's health and development; your own health; life circumstances; family dynamics; and the amount of support you receive.

Breast-feeding is a personal experience, but one that often requires advice and encouragement from an expert. If you are having difficulty with nursing or with your breastmilk supply, do not hesitate to seek help. A feeding specialist, such as a certified lactation consultant or an occupational therapist educated in feeding issues, can provide you with information on breast-feeding methods and devices. An occupational therapist can also assess any developmental concerns. Your doctor or county's health department can give you a referral. Ask potential support persons about their experience, education, and breast-feeding philosophy—you need to find someone you are comfortable with and can trust.

A local breast-feeding support group can also help, but make sure support persons understand the uniqueness of preterm infants. Ask your NICU or preemie parent support group for names and phone numbers.

> *I was never able to nurse Drew in the NICU. I tried after he came home, but I wasn't successful. My husband and I were both up all night with the feeding routine. He would feed Drew while I pumped.*
>
> *Daytime feedings were even more difficult. I would feed Drew previously pumped breastmilk, then I'd pump. My milk supply was low, and I barely filled the tiny bottles. I felt like all I accomplished during the day was feeding Drew and hooking myself up to a pump.*
>
> *Although the routine was tiring and frustrating, I felt it was important for me to continue. I believed Drew needed what little milk I could provide him. We continued to follow this routine for about five or six weeks, when my pediatrician suggested I stop and go full-time with formula. This decision was extremely frustrating and emotional for me. I wanted to nurse and couldn't, and now I was being told to stop pumping. In retrospect, I wish I had asked for help with nursing from someone who knows about breast-feeding preemies.*
>
> —SUZI, MOTHER OF 33-WEEKER DREW

HOW TO BREAST-FEED YOUR PREEMIE

TIME, PATIENCE, AND practice are the keys to successful breast-feeding. The following steps will make the nursing process a little easier:

1. *Wash your hands vigorously in soapy water before breastfeeding.* Your hands may carry germs that you could pass to your baby.
2. *Increase your baby's supplemental oxygen.* If on extra oxygen support, your baby may need a higher level while nursing (ask your pediatrician).
3. *Position yourself.* Before you begin breast-feeding, it is important that you are positioned properly. Find a comfortable chair in a quiet place where you can concentrate and relax. Your back should be straight, not bent over your baby. Use a footstool to support your feet and lift your knees, reducing the strain on your back and hips. A pillow on your lap will support your baby and bring him closer to you.
4. *Position your baby.* There are two breast-feeding positions recommended for premature infants: the *chest-to-chest hold* (also called the *across-the-lap* or *cross-cradle hold*) and the *football hold.* For the *chest-to-chest hold,* support your infant's head and body with

Mother and baby demonstrating the "chest-to-chest" breast-feeding position.

Mother and baby demonstrating the "football-hold" breast-feeding position.

the arm on the same side as the breast he is nursing from, and use the opposite hand to hold your breast. Your baby lays across the pillow, almost chest-to-chest with you.

For the *football hold* (which is also good for nursing twins), rest a pillow on your lap and position your baby on it with your upper arm underneath his back and head. He should be looking up at you. Continue supporting your baby's head with the hand that is on the same side as the breast you are using. With the opposite hand, support your breast.

In either position, it is important to prevent your baby's head and neck from twisting or turning. His body should be aligned with his head, and his head should not be bent too far forward. Your preemie has less head control than a term infant does, so help him by guiding his head to your breast. Having him hold on to your finger or bra may help him feel more secure as you position him.

If your baby tends to gulp and choke a lot, try positioning his head so that the back of his neck and throat are higher than your nipple. You can also stop nursing momentarily and hand-express your milk until the milk flow slows down. This will lessen the speed and force of your milk flow.

5. *Release a little milk from your breast.* The smell and taste of milk will invite your baby to latch on to your breast. will Express or pump some breastmilk before feeding. (This also helps large-breasted women or women with inverted nipples prepare for nursing.) Pumping helps milk "let down" so that your baby has immediate gratification when he begins to suck. It also makes your nipple somewhat longer and easier for your baby to grasp. You may want to pump one breast to help with the let-down process while your baby nurses on the other.
6. *Encourage your baby to latch on to the breast.* Because breastmilk is stored in the ducts that sit behind the areola (the dark area around the nipples), your infant needs to latch on to about one-half to one inch of the areola—*not just the nipple.* By compressing the

milk sinuses located behind the areola, your baby will get more milk for his efforts.

Until your baby has practiced breast-feeding for a while, getting him to latch on can be challenging. The best way to do this is by encouraging him to open his mouth as wide as his typical yawn. While supporting your breast with one hand (thumb on top and four fingers beneath), gently stroke his lower lip with your nipple to cause him to naturally open. When he opens his mouth, quickly and gently bring his head toward your nipple and push your breast inside his mouth. Make sure his tongue is under your nipple and the areola is centered in his mouth. Another pair of hands may be helpful in supporting your baby's head.

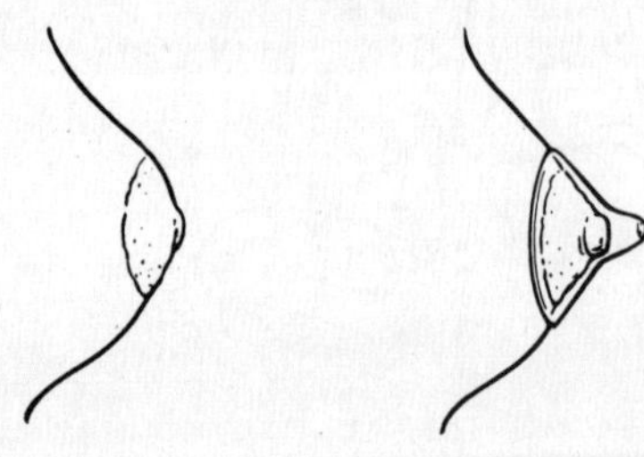

A. A mother's breast without a nipple shield. B. A mother's breast with a nipple shield.

The shield may help your infant nurse, even if you have flat or inverted nipples.

If nursing ever becomes painful, stop your baby's sucking by inserting your little finger (with a filed fingernail) into the corner of your infant's mouth and gently pull down on his jaw to break the suction. Not having enough of the breast in your baby's mouth can sometimes cause discomfort. Try getting him to nurse again by using the above method.

If your baby is having problems latching on, try using a nipple shield, available from a lactation consultant. Nipple shields work well for flat or inverted nipples, and for babies who become very frustrated from the latch-on process. Use nipple shields only with the supervision of your physician or lactation consultant.

7. *Continue feeding.* Once your baby begins feeding, let him nurse for about twenty minutes per side (if he can). Your baby may eat more efficiently if he sucks from one breast at a feeding (but do not forget to pump your other breast after he is done).

   If your baby tends to fall asleep during nursing, it may help to change breasts during feedings, even as often as every five minutes. When you notice a change in his sucking pattern and you think he may be getting sleepy, stop the feeding, burp him, and resume feeding on the other breast. Of course, falling asleep can mean your baby is finished eating—rely on your instincts.
8. *Snuggle and relax with your baby after the feeding.* Your preemie is finished eating when he is very sleepy or refuses the breast.

WARNING SIGNS

DO NOT BREAST-FEED IF:

- you are on any medication that may transfer to your baby through breastmilk (inform your pediatrician about any medicine you are taking); or
- you have a serious illness, such as HIV or tuberculosis, that can be transmitted to your baby through breastmilk.

A. Nursing twins using the "chest-to-chest" position

B. Nursing twins using the "football hold" position

BREAST-FEEDING MULTIPLES

MOTHERS OF MULTIPLES often say the emotional perks from breast-feeding are multiplied by having more than one baby to nurse and love. On the other hand, nursing two or more can be stressful.

When your babies first come home, you may need to nurse individually while they learn to breast-feed, especially if one or more is having trouble with the process. Getting both babies to wake up and nurse around the same time will be less stressful, but this is not always possible. As you and your babies become more skilled, you can nurse two babies at the same time (using the "football hold"), or you may decide to continue nursing individually. Try both ways before choosing the method that feels most comfortable.

If you nurse two babies at the same time, lay them on a pillow and place a small rolled washcloth or cloth diaper under your babies' necks to support their heads. An extra set of hands to assist during the latch-on process can be helpful.

Your body should naturally produce enough milk for twins, but may not produce enough for triplets or more. Furthermore, the stress of parenting more than one baby, particularly if one or more has ongoing special needs, can affect breastmilk production. To maintain your milk supply, take care of yourself by eating well, drinking plenty of fluids, and resting. Seek the help of a lactation consultant or another feeding specialist, if needed.

If you are unable to breast-feed your babies full-time, try not to feel guilty or inadequate. Any amount of breastmilk you give your babies by nursing (or pumping and bottle-feeding) will help your babies' growth and health.

I had a typical early experience with breast-feeding my preemie twins, Layla and Gavriella. That is to say, I mostly pumped and was confronted by screaming, frustrated, angry babies whenever I tried to nurse them. It was the most demoralizing thing I have ever experienced. I was so frustrated and depressed.

About a month after they came home, they both suddenly just "got it." I couldn't believe it! I even managed to feed them simultaneously (on my bed) once or twice. It was exactly what I had imagined during my pregnancy.

Unfortunately, I didn't have the support and information I needed, and I made one critical mistake. I had out-of-town company for two days and I didn't nurse (just pumped and gave them bottles) while they visited. When the company left, the girls were horrified at the thought of nursing again. I was devastated. I was angry at myself for being so stupid. I couldn't believe that no one had told me that babies could "forget" how to nurse once they seemed to know how to do it. I tried and tried, but only managed to get Layla to breast-feed again.

Now, at twenty-two months, Layla is still nursing. I continue to pump for her sister. It's important to me that both girls get breastmilk. As long as one is nursing, I want the other to have breastmilk, too. I am extremely lucky and grateful to have an abundant milk supply.

I am reluctant to wean Layla. I enjoy the cuddling, and she seems to need the nursing. One of the things I mourn the most is the loss of nursing Gavriella. I blame myself for the loss. I messed it up. I am so sad when she looks at Layla nursing and announces it's "num-num" but doesn't want it herself. I worry about what this means to our relationship down the line. Maybe that's why I am still pumping after all these months.

With preemie twins there is so much to balance. They are so individual, and they both need you. I wonder if their different temperaments had anything to do with Layla's willingness and ability to return to nursing and Gavriella's difficulty. I tell myself that they each took what was best for them.

—MARA, MOTHER OF 30-WEEKER TWINS GAVRIELLA AND LAYLA

▪

Even before the twins were born, I had the expectation that I would nurse my babies as I had with my firstborn. So, after their birth, I started pumping and taking my milk to the hospital. When I was given the "go ahead" to nurse, I was able to put them, one at a time, to the breast in a kangaroo-care hold. They each took to nursing immediately.

The girls continued to successfully nurse at home. I tried every method—alternating who ate first, switching positions, feeding simultaneously, and nursing individually. This kept my breasts from becoming sore and emptied all my milk ducts. I preferred nursing in tandem because it was less cumbersome; more importantly, it gave me time to focus on each daughter separately.

—EMILY, MOTHER OF 32-WEEKER TWINS CHLOE AND MADELINE

IS YOUR BABY GETTING ENOUGH MILK?

ONE SIMPLE WAY to tell if your baby is getting any breastmilk at all is by listening for swallowing while he eats. If you hear him swallow, you know he is consuming something. Another indicator is if your breasts feel softer (but not necessarily "empty") after your baby nurses. (If you have an abundant milk supply, your breasts may not become noticeably softer.)

If there are signs that your baby is getting some milk, the question then is: How much milk? To determine if your baby needs supplemental bottles and to alleviate your worry, some breast-feeding experts suggest using an infant scale. Companies or organizations that rent breastpumps usually rent baby scales, too. Make sure it is a reputable company—it is important that the baby scale be balanced properly. You can use a scale until breast-feeding is well established, and you and your doctor are comfortable with your baby's growth.

To use an infant scale, weigh your baby fully dressed just before a feeding. After eating, weigh him again without changing his diaper or removing any clothing he had on during the first weighing. Keep in mind that items such as monitor leads or pacifiers can alter weights.

The difference between the two weights is the amount your baby consumed. For example, if your baby weighs twenty grams more after a feeding, he consumed twenty cc's (one gram equals one cc). When your baby is eating well, you can begin measuring by ounces (thirty cc's equal one ounce).

You can also weigh your baby frequently at your doctor's office until breast-feeding is well established. You must get an early first weight on your doctor's scale for a baseline measurement. Because scales can vary greatly, make sure your baby is always weighed naked on the same scale.

Another way to assess whether your baby is getting enough breastmilk is by monitoring his wet and soiled diapers. Breast-fed babies typically wet six to eight diapers and soil two to three diapers daily. Any less than this may mean your baby is not getting enough breastmilk, and he can become dehydrated. Watch for other signs of dehydration (irritability, listlessness, and dark yellow urine). If you are still concerned after using these methods to evaluate your baby's consumption, consult your pediatrician.

PARENT TIPS:

STIMULATING YOUR MILK SUPPLY

Some women naturally have low milk supplies; others have more milk than their babies need. Follow these suggestions from moms and professionals for increasing your breastmilk supply:

- The more your baby nurses, the more milk you will produce. Keep time between feedings to a three-hour minimum, with a longer stretch at night.

- Pump for five to ten minutes after *every* feeding until your baby is nursing full-time.
- Alternate which breast your baby starts feeding on with each feeding. If you have a particularly low milk supply on one side, letting your child with a weak suck nurse only on that side will not help. You will need to pump that breast with a breastpump that has a good suction.
- Drink at least eight glasses of water daily. Try drinking a glass each time you nurse. Water keeps you healthy and well hydrated, which helps increase your supply.
- Get as much rest as possible. Your milk supply will increase faster if you are well rested.
- Eat a well-balanced diet that increases your calories by an extra 500 to 600 calories per day. Consume lots of calcium (from milk or soy) and iron, and take a supplemental vitamin, all of which will help your baby grow.
- Massage your breasts as your baby feeds to release breast-feeding hormones and encourage a higher yield.
- Take a bath or shower before nursing to help you relax. Your milk will "let down" more easily and you will increase production if you are relaxed.
- Apply a hot towel to your breasts for a few minutes before feeding and take deep breaths to help with let-down and increase of milk production.
- Some herbal teas, such as raspberry leaf and fenugreek, are thought to help nursing mothers. Fenugreek can also be taken in pill form; check with a lactation consultant or your health professional.
- A prescription medication called Metoclopramide has a side effect of increasing milk. Discuss the use of this medication with your doctor.

WEANING FROM THE BREAST

THE AMERICAN ACADEMY of Pediatrics suggests breast-feeding for at least twelve months (when possible and supplemented with baby food starting around six months corrected age). Nursing beyond a year is up to you. Your baby may naturally wean himself, or you may decide to stop. (Make sure that stopping is *your* choice, and do not let others persuade you. After all, you are the one who persevered through the NICU experience and homecoming difficulties.)

Your decision to wean may be influenced by life circumstances, such as returning to work or having another baby. If you never make the transition to full-time breast-feeding, the physical exhaustion and time commitment of nursing, pumping, and bottle-feeding may play a big part in your decision. You may also stop nursing if your child suddenly refuses to breast-feed, or your milk supply drops too low and attempts to increase it do not work.

You may feel sad when your baby begins to wean from the breast, particularly if disappointing circumstances influence the process. Breast-feeding is a special interaction between mother and child, and it is normal to feel a loss. Remind yourself that any breastmilk you provided your premature baby was a precious gift that has lifetime benefits. And the early mother-child bond that nursing helped create is only the beginning of your relationship.

CHAPTER ELEVEN

Later Eating and Your Concerns

WHEN YOUR BABY is around four to six months corrected age, you may notice he is becoming interested in new foods. He may intently watch you eat, reach toward your meal, smack his lips at the sight of food, or bring his hands toward his mouth at the family dinner table. These are all signs that your child may be eager to try something new.

Introducing foods to your baby can be exciting and fun, but when your child has feeding issues, it can also be frustrating. Knowing what and how much to feed your child, as well as recognizing any early signs of eating difficulties, are important to your child's growth. This chapter discusses feeding milestones, the progression of starting solid foods, and the common feeding problems associated with prematurity.

INTRODUCING SOLID FOODS

BEFORE YOU START feeding your baby solid foods, ask your pediatrician or occupational therapist to evaluate your child's readiness. Introducing certain solids too early can contribute to food allergies and can also influence atypical oral-motor development (the development of the muscles in the mouth used for speech and eating).

In addition, your child's health, developmental delays, or nutritional concerns can affect the timing of food introductions and the way your child should be fed. For example, a child with chronic lung disease who has difficulty breathing while eating may need his lungs to mature before he can attempt solids. A child with weak head control may need his head supported when introduced to the spoon. Some doctors postpone starting solids until a baby is gaining adequate weight on formula or breastmilk.

FEEDING MILESTONES

Just as there are milestones for physical abilities, such as walking, there are developmental milestones for eating. Each milestone is important in the development of lifelong eating, communication, and social skills (although some children may skip steps and continue to develop appropriately). Use the following common milestones as a guide and discuss any concerns with your pediatrician and/or occupational therapist.

BY 6 MONTHS CORRECTED AGE, YOUR BABY SHOULD

- be increasing the amount of formula or breastmilk he consumes as he grows;
- demonstrate an ability to hold his head steady in an unsupported position; and
- be attempting smooth pureed solids, such as rice or barley baby cereal and/or stage-1 commercial baby food.

BY 12 MONTHS CORRECTED AGE, YOUR BABY SHOULD

- have mastered (removing the food from a spoon and swallowing) pureed vegetables and fruit and/or stage-2 commercial baby food;
- eat finger foods, such as soft crackers and dry cereal;
- be comfortable with soft solids, such as mashed potatoes (although he may not have mastered them yet);
- show interest in table foods; and
- drink formula, breastmilk, or juice from a cup (although he may still spill a lot).

BY 18 MONTHS CORRECTED AGE, YOUR BABY SHOULD

- have mastered drinking from a cup;
- use utensils (although he will drop plenty of food);
- eat coarsely chopped cooked table food, such as soft meats (chicken, slivered pork) and steamed vegetables;
- be able to clean off his lips with his tongue; and
- be making the transition to eating with less trunk support (eating in a booster chair instead of a high chair).

BY 24 MONTHS CORRECTED AGE, YOUR BABY SHOULD

- be eating chewy meats and raw vegetables;
- have mastered a variety of textures and consistencies of food; and
- have mastered eating without excessive trunk support.

When your pediatrician or occupational therapist feels your baby is ready to begin solids, use a blender or food processor to puree rice or barley baby cereal (mixed with a little formula or breastmilk for a familiar flavor). By blending rice or baby cereal, the food will have less texture and should make the transition easier for your baby. The pureed cereal should be a thin and smooth consistency, like baby food applesauce. If the food is too thick, it will be difficult for your baby to move it toward the back of his mouth and to swallow. If needed, add more breastmilk or formula to make it thinner. Feed your baby cereal once a day between breast- or bottle-feedings.

After your baby succeeds with cereal (it may take several days or even weeks), try a smooth pureed single vegetable or fruit or stage 1 commercial baby food. If weight gain

WARNING SIGNS

Children can have reactions to certain foods. Consult your pediatrician if your child:

- becomes constipated, or his stomach is extended and hard;
- has diarrhea;
- vomits or spits up frequently;
- is gassy;
- wheezes;
- frequently sneezes, coughs, and/or has a runny nose;
- is irritable and/or has behavioral problems;
- has frequent colds and/or ear infections;
- develops dark circles under the eyes;
- has frequent skin rashes or develops hives; and/or
- has swelling of the lips.

is a concern, consult your pediatrician about whether your baby should start on high-calorie pureed food. Single foods should be added no more frequently than once every three days so that you can determine if a certain food causes an allergic reaction. Continue feeding a solid once a day between breast- or bottle-feedings. When using a commercial baby food, make sure you feed your baby from a bowl (not the jar) to prevent contamination from the bacteria in your baby's mouth.

After your baby successfully eats pureed solids, a soft solid or stage 2 commercial baby food follows. Soft solids include thick rice cereal or mashed potatoes.

For the first month or two of beginning solids, your baby should continue to eat normal amounts of formula or breastmilk. In the beginning, feeding solids is primarily a way to introduce the feeding process and different textures, and to help your baby develop feeding skills. The nutritional value is less important. A three-meal-a-day schedule is not generally recommended until your baby is around eight to twelve months corrected age.

WARNING

As you introduce new solids, always be careful about the types and sizes of foods that may cause choking. Never feed your child peanuts, raisins, popcorn, grapes, or hard candy. If your family has a history of food allergies, consult your pediatrician regarding when to introduce commonly allergenic foods, such as dairy, eggs, wheat, corn, and peanut butter.

When you introduce a certain texture, such as oatmeal, your baby may gag or refuse it. Many preemies are "sensitive" to textured foods. Try waiting three to four days before reintroducing the food. If after two weeks your infant is still not accepting the new food, try a more gradual approach. Combine a familiar, favorite food with the textured food: use three parts favorite food with one part textured food, then half favorite food with half textured food, and finally one part favorite food with three parts textured food. Some infants with chronic illnesses or developmental delays are very slow to make the transition. Consult your pediatrician or a feeding specialist if problems persist.

As hand-to-mouth coordination develops, introduce finger foods (usually around seven to nine months corrected age). Begin with infant biter biscuits or zwieback toast that cannot easily be broken into pieces and cause choking. Foods that quickly turn to "mush" are generally well accepted once your baby can more easily move foods around in his mouth.

Your child may be ready at around twelve months corrected age to try soft table foods, such as macaroni or French fries. At around sixteen to eighteen months corrected age (and if your child is developmentally ready), he can try coarsely chopped cooked food, such as chicken, slivered pork, and steamed vegetables. Once he has mastered these, you can try chewy meats and raw vegetables. However, before you move on to these more difficult foods, consult your pediatrician or occupational therapist to ensure your child's readiness.

Chart 11-1: Feeding schedule for solid foods

If your child is small-sized, still not on the growth chart, or a poor eater, you probably wonder if he is eating enough of the right foods. Use the following chart as a *guide* for introducing and measuring solid foods. Always discuss the introduction of new foods with your pediatrician.

Age	Food	Typical serving size
4 to 6 months corrected age	Breastmilk or formula	6–8 ounces
	Baby cereal	1–2 tablespoons
	Stage 1 baby food	1–2 tablespoons
6 to 8 months corrected age	Breastmilk/formula	6–8 ounces
	Baby cereal	2–4 tablespoons
	Fruit juice*	2–4 ounces
	Pureed fruit/vegetable	2–4 tablespoons
	Crackers/teething biscuits	1–2
	Stage 2 baby food	1/2–1 jar
8 to 12 months corrected age	Breastmilk/formula	6–8 ounces
	Cheese	1/2 single slice
	Yogurt/cottage cheese	1/4–1/2 cup
	Baby cereal	1/4–1/2 cup
	Crackers/teething biscuits	2
	Bread/donut/bagel	1/2 slice
	Pasta/rice	2–4 tablespoons
	Pureed fruit/vegetable	1/4–1/2 cup
	Soft fruit/vegetable	2–4 tablespoons
	Soft meats	2–4 tablespoons
	Fruit juice*	2–4 ounces
	Beans/egg	2–4 tablespoons
	Stage-3 baby food	1/2–1 jar
12 to 18 months corrected age	Whole milk	4–6 ounces
	Cheese	1/2 single slice
	Yogurt/cottage cheese	1/4–1/2 cup

Chart 11-1: (cont.)

AGE	FOOD	TYPICAL SERVING SIZE
12 to 18 months corrected age (cont.)	Hot cereal	1/4–1/2 cup
	Dry cereal	1/4 cup
	Crackers	2
	Bread/bagels/pancakes	1/2 slice
	Pasta/rice	2–4 tablespoons
	Soft fruit/vegetable	2–4 tablespoons
	Fruit juice*	4 ounces
	Beans/egg	2–4 tablespoons
	Steamed vegetables	2–4 tablespoons
	Coarsely chopped meats	2–4 tablespoons
18 to 24 months corrected age	Whole milk	4–6 ounces
	Cheese	1/2 slice
	Yogurt/cottage cheese	1/2 cup
	Hot cereal	1/4–1/2 cup
	Dry cereal	1/4–1/2 cup
	Crackers	2–4
	Bread	1/2 slice
	Pasta/rice	3–4 tablespoons
	Soft fruit/vegetable	3–4 tablespoons
	Fruit juice*	4 ounces
	Beans/egg	3–4 tablespoons
	Steamed vegetables	3–4 tablespoons
	Coarsely chopped meats	2–4 tablespoons
	Chewy meats	2–4 tablespoons
	Raw vegetables	2–4 tablespoons

*Your doctor may recommend not giving fruit juice if your baby is not gaining weight well or is not taking adequate formula.

(Prepared by Lyn Stevenson, R.D., C.S.P., Clinical Dietitian, Children's Hospital of Denver, Denver, Colo.)

PARENT TIPS:

INCREASING YOUR CHILD'S CALORIES

Some toddlers and older children born prematurely need extra calories to help them gain adequate weight. Here are some suggestions for increasing your child's calories once he is eating mostly solid foods:

- Add butter, margarine, or vegetable oil to foods.
- Add tofu to pureed foods.
- Add Jell-O or instant hot cereal to blended fruits.
- Add finely chopped hard-boiled eggs to a variety of foods.
- Replace butter or margarine with peanut butter.
- Add brown sugar to fruits or sweet vegetables.
- If your child tolerates milk and special flavorings, mix Carnation Instant Break-

fast powder with whole milk. One-third cup of instant breakfast adds 130 calories.

- Add sweetened condensed milk, half and half, dry milk powder, or evaporated whole milk to foods.
- Do not be "low-fat conscious" when preparing foods.
- When it is in season, let your child drink eggnog.
- Your child should drink whole milk. You can add cream or half and half for added calories.
- Add cheese sauce to cooked vegetables.
- Add butter, margarine, cream cheese, mayonnaise, or cheese spread to crackers.
- Use dips, such as salad dressing, guacamole, and yogurt, for vegetables; whipped cream or caramel dip for fresh fruits.

PARENT TIPS:
Starting Solids

Spooning pureed solids into your child's mouth requires patience—and a good sense of humor. Try these tips for making feeding times easier:

- Begin introducing pureed solids at a quiet time of day and avoid busy family mealtimes. Your attention needs to be focused on your baby's needs.
- Your attitude is critical. Act as if you enjoy all of your baby's food (even if you do not). Maintain a happy facial expression and never make a negative comment about the food. Try not to show any apprehension.
- Introduce solids when your baby is alert and happy, not when he is crying or overly hungry.
- When introducing the spoon, place it on your baby's lower lip, encouraging him to suck the cereal off the spoon. At first, he may use his tongue to push the food out of his mouth. This behavior will continue until his eating skills are more developed.
- Avoid the tendency to push food into your baby's mouth. Let him explore the food with his tongue. When first introducing pureed solids, the feeding experience is more important than the volume consumed.

WHEN YOUR PREEMIE STRUGGLES WITH EATING

Most families anticipate mealtimes as happy social events, times of good food and conversation. When your child has eating concerns, much of that enjoyment is lost. You can help your child and family by learning about the common eating issues associated with prematurity. The earlier you recognize a problem and the more quickly your child receives professional support, the sooner you can all enjoy those family meals.

I kept asking the doctors and therapists why my daughter wouldn't eat and why she only said one word—"ba"—for everything. She was still on stage-2 baby foods at age three. Chandler had a great appetite, but wouldn't eat anything with texture. The therapists working with her made very little progress. They told me about her sensory problems, but they never fully diagnosed her.

It wasn't until she was four years old that we found a speech-language pathologist who had experience with children like Chandler. Chandler finally began to make real progress. She was diagnosed with oral-motor and sensory problems. She was seen weekly, and we were given exercises for her tongue and mouth. We also worked with the behavioral part of eating—lots of praise and hand-clapping followed any attempt Chandler made to chew food.

Getting Chandler to eat was a very long process. She is now almost six years old, and while she steadily adds textured foods to her diet, she still prefers soft foods. At least we can now feed her peanut butter and jelly sandwiches. And, this past Halloween we felt tremendous joy when she ate a candy bar!

—L.J., MOTHER OF 26-WEEKER CHANDLER

■

Feeding is probably the biggest problem we faced with our son Taylor. He saw many different doctors and therapists and had a variety of diagnoses. Some seemed appropriate; others seemed uncaring, even insinuating that we as parents were the problem.

At first Taylor's problem was a weak suck. Switching to the disposable bottles and an orthodontic nipple helped. When it was time to move on to solid foods, the problems really began. We added "chunks," and Taylor gagged and threw up. He fought every bite. For nearly three years his problem was treated strictly as an aversion to things in his mouth. We were given instructions on how to decrease his sensitivity to textures by slowly increasing unusual textures. They said he would eventually figure it out. To me, he seemed to be contentedly starving.

We "force-fed" Taylor for a long time. Then we found out force-feeding was controversial and only works when there is strictly a behavioral problem. My justification for force-feeding was that I was "saving" Taylor from a feeding tube surgery. Looking back, I wish I had let him get a feeding tube so he could have gained weight and become stronger, then tackled learning to eat. Instead, I may have created another phobia by forcing him to eat.

After three years of therapy, we were no further along. Taylor was afraid of food, and he had no idea what to do with it once it was in his mouth. No one listened to me, until we found a wonderful speech-language pathologist who was well trained and immediately understood Taylor's problem. She addressed his muscle and tongue control as well as jaw-position issues. Basically, he did not have the strength in his tongue, jaw, cheeks, and lips to manipulate the food and control it.

We continue to nag him to finish his food, but we do not force him. Thanks to the wonderful knowledge of his therapist, Taylor is starting to eat solids. On his fifth birthday he even ate some of his birthday cake! My best advice for other parents facing feeding problems is to insist on seeing a feeding specialist and trust your gut instincts.

—*Tammy, mother of 28-weeker Taylor*

The Common Causes of Feeding Problems

When trying to understand your child's feeding difficulties, it is important to keep in mind that other developmental areas besides his oral abilities—his cognitive and physical abilities—affect how he eats. Any developmental delays can affect when milestones are reached. If your child's problem is affecting his ability to eat, an evaluation is critical. Other causes of feeding issues are discussed below.

Sensory difficulties

Just as a child may not like different textures touching his hands or feet, he may not like textures touching his face or mouth. He may even dislike other sensory input, such as various smells or tastes. Excessive stimulation from the environment, such as too much noise during mealtime, may also affect his ability to eat.

Oral aversions

Problems can develop from too much negative input around an infant's mouth. Tubes, suctioning, tape, smells, and even tastes can have an undesirable impact. A child may remember these unpleasant experiences and respond negatively to stimulation in and around his mouth.

PARENT TIPS:

Coping with a Picky Eater

Parents sometimes find themselves coping with a child who will eat only certain foods or who refuses to eat anything at all. Some children do not have a hearty appetite, and they need to be reminded to eat, even when they are older. Here are some helpful hints for dealing with your picky eater:

For Infants and Toddlers

- Try making your own baby food—some infants like the flavor better than store-bought baby food. Prepare large amounts (avoid using salt or extra sweeteners), place in ice cube trays, and freeze in dated bags for later use. When you need a meal, simply thaw.
- Let your child have fun playing with his food, making eating a positive experience. If he thinks mealtimes are work, he will not want to eat. Do not worry about a messy face and hands until mealtime is over.
- Give your child food options. For example, place three foods on a tray including at least one favorite food (more than three may be overwhelming). Feed your child one tablespoon of each food for every year of age (for example, a two-year-old gets two tablespoons of mashed potatoes).
- Your child may need to take several small steps before accepting a new food. For example, he may need to taste the food at one sitting, touch it at the next, and lick it at the third before he actually eats it.
- Do not feel your child must conquer one texture before he can move on to another. Many children with oral sensory issues go from smooth purees to chewables, skipping the lumpy foods, such as macaroni and cheese or stage-3 baby foods. They do this because the combination of smooth and lumpy textures is too difficult for them to move around their mouths, or it is too unpleasant from a sensory standpoint.

For Toddlers and Preschoolers

- Create a schedule that includes three meals and two to three snacks each day. To avoid power struggles, limit meals to thirty minutes and snacks to fifteen minutes. It is okay to let your child learn the feeling of hunger in between meals. This will help him learn to eat more at scheduled times.
- Keep mealtime conversation light and focused away from the food.
- If your child does not eat a reasonable amount of food at a meal, do not start a battle. Do not criticize, yell, or punish your child for not eating. This will only make mealtimes negative experiences. Offer the same food or another food later.
- Do not let your child "graze," or snack between meals too often. Children who graze eat less overall than those who adhere to structured meals. They are often not hungry at mealtimes and miss the social part of eating, too. Mealtimes are opportunities for your child to try different foods. "Grazers" tend to eat finger foods and get more of their calories from liquids and sweets. Juice and sweets should be saved for after-meal treats.
- Experiment with different flavors. Children with sensory issues may enjoy more strongly flavored foods. Your child may prefer more spicy foods or foods that can be dipped into ranch dressing, catsup, or salsa. Your child may not like cucumbers but love pickles.

Oral-motor issues

The tongue, jaw, lips, cheeks, and palate all work together to move food into and through the mouth. If one or more of these body parts does not work properly, the ability to eat can be affected. Muscle control might be weakened or abnormally stronger in certain areas; coordination of swallowing may be altered; or the synchronization of sucking, swallowing, and breathing may be difficult. These are only a few of the many, sometimes complicated, oral-motor problems associated with prematurity.

Medical problems

Medical problems (such as chronic lung disease, reflux, and the need for a tracheostomy) and physical problems (such as a groove in the palate) can influence an infant's ability to eat. For example, an infant with lung disease may have a poorly coordinated or weak suck because of prolonged intubation, or he may have difficulty breathing while eating. Some medical problems that create feeding difficulties can easily be corrected; others require more time and treatment.

Behavioral issues

Just as infants learn how to eat, they can also learn how not to eat, especially if there are issues of pain (as is common with reflux); problems with coordinating sucking, swallowing, and breathing; or fatigue. Sometimes when the amount a baby eats becomes such a strong focus, the family and child lose the ability to enjoy mealtimes and behavioral problems can result.

If eating or growth problems continue during childhood, the dynamics between parent and child are often affected. The parent may push the child to eat, causing the child to feel he has little or no control. The only way the child then feels he can gain control of his environment is by regulating how much or what he eats.

Every feeding problem is treatable. The less complicated issues may take only a few weeks or several months to resolve; more complicated issues can take many months or even years of treatment by a feeding specialist. The earlier treatment is started, the better.

Diagnosis of Feeding Problems

Your pediatrician may diagnose and treat a less complicated feeding issue, such as a weak suck. If your doctor suspects a more complicated problem, he should refer your child to a feeding specialist. Some areas of the country have clinics specializing in feeding issues; ask your doctor if there is one near you.

WHO ARE FEEDING SPECIALISTS?

The following are healthcare professionals who can help with the unique feeding problems of preterm infants:

An occupational therapist (OT). An OT examines the sensory aspects of eating, as well as how the muscles of the mouth, jaw, hands, neck, and trunk are working. She oversees the child's ability to self-feed, remain calm, and stay organized during feedings.

A speech-language pathologist (SLP). When dealing with feeding problems, an SLP does many of the same things an OT does. She also closely examines the child's coordination of sucking, swallowing, and breathing. A child can begin seeing an SLP as soon as he exhibits feeding difficulties; he does not have to wait for language to develop.

A developmental psychologist. Some psychologists specialize in the treatment of children who are "picky eaters," or who exhibit aversions or food-refusal behaviors. A developmental psychologist examines learned behaviors and interaction patterns around feeding.

A pediatrician. Some pediatricians who are specially trained in developmental issues manage feeding problems. Such a pediatrician assists in ensuring there are no medical problems affecting feeding or growth.

A nurse specialist. Nurses who have special training in feeding behavioral problems assist in reviewing medical issues and provide parents with information and support.

A dietitian. A dietitian's role is to monitor a child's calorie intake, nutrients (protein, fat, vitamins, minerals, and fluids), weight gain, and growth. A dietitian will review what a child is eating and recommend changes if necessary.

If your child is referred to a feeding specialist, an evaluation will be performed. The evaluation may take place in a clinic, a medical office, or your home. First, the specialist will gather a thorough history of your child's medical background and feeding patterns, including information from his doctor and observations from you. Make sure you give the specialist an overall picture of your child's everyday feeding habits and patterns, including his difficulties and successes. (Some parents document their child's eating habits for several days.) The information you provide will make it easier for the specialist to diagnose and treat your child.

The feeding specialist will also observe your child when he eats. He will watch you hold and feed your infant, or watch your child feed himself. Even if your child is older, the specialist may want to observe your participation in the feeding process. Try not to feel intimidated—the therapist is only gathering important information that will help your child. The specialist will observe how your child:

- sucks, swallows, and breathes together;
- uses his eating-related muscles;
- chews;
- uses utensils;
- reacts to the environment;
- interacts with you (or another person who feeds him); and/or
- responds to the stress of eating.

WARNING SIGNS

The following are signs of possible feeding problems. Consult your pediatrician if your child exhibits any of the signs listed below at the ages indicated.

Birth to 6 Months Corrected Age

- has difficulty synchronizing sucking, swallowing, and breathing while breast- or bottle-feeding;
- turns pale, gray, or bluish when bottle- or breast-feeding;
- sets off his home monitor more than twice per feeding;
- coughs, gags, or spits up frequently during or shortly after feedings;
- fatigues easily during feedings; and/or
- has difficulty showing hunger or fullness cues.

6 to 9 Months Corrected Age

- has difficulty making the transition to pureed foods;
- is resistant to touching foods with his tongue or hands;
- does not like to be spoon-fed; and/or
- turns away, arches, or cries when offered food at times he should be hungry.

9 to 12 Months Corrected Age

- lacks any self-feeding skills;
- is not yet on solid foods;
- is picky regarding textures and/or tastes;
- has a low food volume intake; and/or
- turns away, arches, or cries when offered food at times he should be hungry.

12 to 15 Months Corrected Age

- has difficulty touching or handling foods for self-feeding;
- "pockets" food in his mouth for long periods of time;
- has not made the transition to table foods; and/or
- cannot focus on eating or cannot stay at the table during mealtimes.

15 to 18 Months Corrected Age

- is unable to chew soft solids, such as muffins or French fries, or small pieces of hard solids, such as raw carrots;
- chokes on or swallows foods whole often;
- is not slowly making the transition to hard solids; and/or
- prefers to "graze" or eat sweets (sweets turn off the appetite).

18 to 24 Months Corrected Age

- refuses many types of foods;
- seems to lack pleasure in eating;
- seems unaware of being hungry or full; and/or
- gags or vomits when given certain textures.

Note: The warning signs between 12 to 15 months and 15 to 18 months may overlap, as well as 15 to 18 months and 18 to 24 months.

The therapist may want to see your child eat in different settings or at different times of the day. An evaluation using an oxygen or home monitor may be needed. In rare cases, other tests are performed to determine if a medical or physical problem is affecting the ability to eat. Last, the therapist may recommend a consultation from another specialist, such as a pediatric gastroenterologist. Once all this information is collected, the feeding specialist will compile a written evaluation, and he should present it to both you and your doctor.

Treatment for Feeding Problems

After the specialist has an understanding of your child's feeding problem, the specialist will create a treatment plan. The plan may be simple or complex, depending on your child's needs. Your child's health, safety, and optimal nutrition should be its primary focus. Specific steps addressing your child's immediate issues, such as nutritional needs, as well as long-term goals, such as ways to strengthen weakened muscles or help coordination problems, should be included.

WHEN TREATING YOUR CHILD'S FEEDING PROBLEM: IMPORTANT THINGS TO REMEMBER

The problematic issues involving feeding may require a healing process for both you and your child. This healing process is different for each family. Your child's early feedings may have been difficult experiences, and you may still be mourning the loss of special feeding times you had anticipated during your pregnancy. You may need to overcome feelings of guilt or inadequacy that often come from having a child with eating problems. Your child may have issues to cope with too. He may need to overcome the negativity he associates with eating.

As a parent of a child with a feeding problem, you may need to change how you approach feeding, a mindset that may have been formulated for decades. For example, you may feel that food volume is the key to a successful meal. Feeding success is really based on your child's enjoyment of eating, rather than the quantity he consumes. If your child needs more volume to keep growing, try increasing the calories, instead of concentrating on volume. The following approach to feeding your child may help you reformulate your thinking:

1. Address anything that might be negatively affecting your child's eating, such as reflux, bad-tasting medicine, or unneeded pressure to eat.
2. Remember that feeding is a shared interaction within your family and should be a positive, happy event. This does not mean you should do back handsprings and jump up and down to get your child to eat, but make mealtimes enjoyable for everyone.
3. Let your child have as much control over eating as possible. For example, let him slow down his feeding when he wants, or let him put something new in his mouth when he is ready. Forcing your child to eat only works in specific situations and should be managed by trained professionals in a hospital environment.
4. Finally, remember that developing feeding skills and changing existing patterns will take time. Try to see the big picture: Look for progress over periods of time, rather than on a daily basis.

Your child's feeding plan should also:

- be individualized to meet your child's unique needs;
- include calorie goals based on your child's age and weight;
- include fluid needs;
- have a schedule for meals, snacks, and/or tube feedings; and/or
- have time limits for feeding sessions.

The plan should also be designed to help your child safely progress through feeding milestones. Because a step that works now may not work in the future, your child's progress and plan should be evaluated often. Be leery of the "quick fix": The feeding process includes many skills that will take time to develop.

Your child's treatment plan should be carried out by all persons who feed your child, including both parents, school personnel, daycare providers, and grandparents. Mealtimes should be made as normal as possible, with your child sitting at the table (even if he has a feeding tube). Avoid talking about feeding issues and growth concerns in front of your child.

Does Your Preemie Need a Feeding Tube?

A feeding tube, called a gastrostomy tube or "g-tube," is one way to provide nutrition to a small percentage of preemies who have feeding difficulties or poor growth. The child receives part or all of his food through the feeding tube, surgically placed from the outside of the abdomen to the stomach (or the intestine, in some rare cases). In most instances, a child can continue to take some feedings by mouth. If a child takes longer than thirty minutes per g-tube feeding, a special pump can be attached to the feeding tube to provide a continuous feeding.

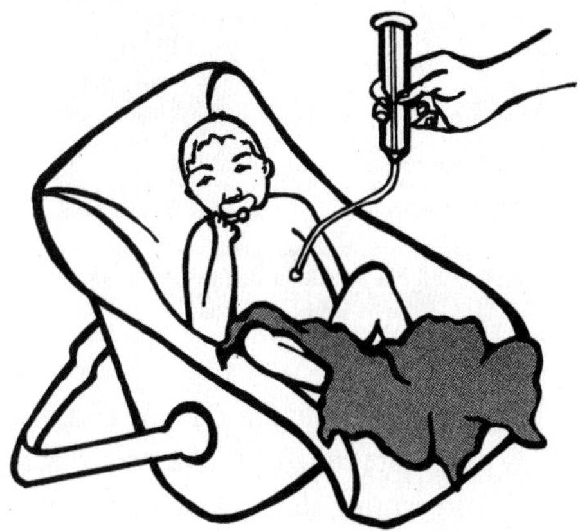

This baby is being fed through a gastronomy button.

> *When the doctor said my child needed a feeding tube through her stomach so that she could start growing, I was very sad. We tried for six months to get her to gain weight and grow but without progress. I thought about the pain, the scar, and the outcome before I consented to surgery. I didn't want my child to hurt, but I didn't want to see my child slowly starve to death either.*
>
> *I wish I had talked to someone that had been through the same thing and how they survived. That might have helped.*

I don't like the way the feeding tube looks, but I do like the way my child has grown because of it. I also can't wait for the day the feeding tube is removed.

—KRISTINA, MOTHER OF 25-WEEKER FAITH

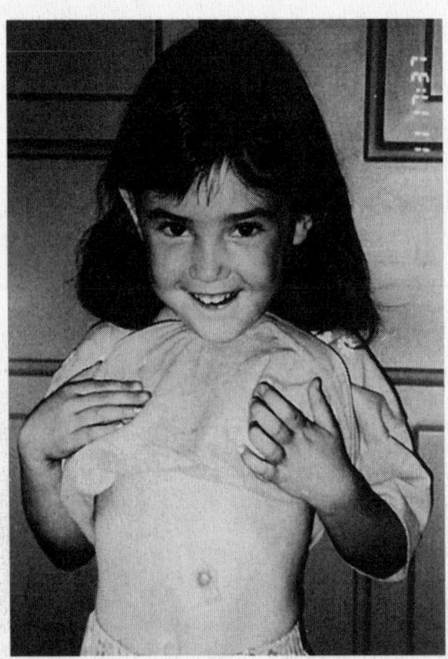

Five-year-old Mackenzie (a former 26-weeker) shows off her button.

Types of feeding tubes

A gastrostomy tube is a plastic tubing that is about twelve inches long. An opening on one end is placed inside the stomach; the larger end attaches to a syringe where formula or breastmilk is poured into during feedings. A g-tube requires only one tubing, can quickly be changed, and helps the child burp easily. A disadvantage is that a g-tube can slip out or become clogged, both requiring replacement. It is also aesthetically unpleasant because it hangs out of the stomach; however, it can be camouflaged when the child is fully dressed.

A gastrostomy tube that shows only a small part of the tube outside of the abdomen is called a "button." It can be placed six weeks after a g-tube placement or without a prior g-tube placement. Two brands, the MIC-KEY and the Bard (also called Surgitek), are the most common brands used. Each is about two inches long. The end inside the stomach looks like a mushroom and stays against the wall of the stomach, keeping the button in place. On the flat outside end, there is a one-way valve that works like a trap door. When a separate tube is in place for feedings, the valve is open. When it is removed, the valve closes, preventing the stomach contents from flowing out. These buttons also come with a special decompression tube used for venting (artificially burping) the stomach. The feeding tubes are simple to use, and the button can easily be concealed under clothing.

The advantage of a button is that it is more aesthetically appealing for children and parents. (The Bard button lies closer to the skin than the MIC-KEY.) The disadvantages are that placement is more difficult, and problems with completely venting air from the stomach can occur. (Ventilation is sometimes easier with the MIC-KEY button.) If you have a problem with your child's button and your health insurance will not pay for a replacement, contact the manufacturer about possible financial reimbursement.

Percutaneous endoscopic gastrostomy tube (PEG tube)

A g-tube or button is often placed while a child is having another surgery, such as a GER repair. However, if another surgery is not needed, a g-tube or button can be placed

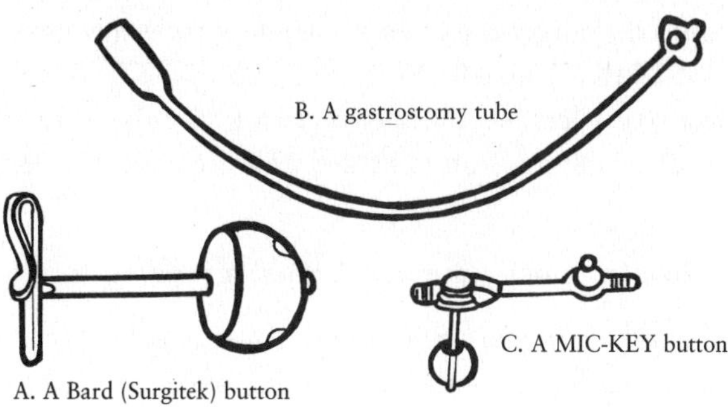

Different types of tubes and buttons

under general anesthesia using an endoscope (a long tube-like scope placed down the throat into the stomach). If endoscopy is used for placement, the g-tube or button is labeled a PEG, or a percutaneous endoscopic gastrostomy tube.

FEEDING TUBE SURGERY: WHAT TO CONSIDER

Making the decision to have a feeding tube placed in your child is not easy. You may wonder how long your child will need the tube, if you can handle its management, what it will look like, and if other children will make fun of him.

Talking with medical experts, including your pediatrician, a pediatric gastroenterologist, and a pediatric surgeon, can help. Get a second opinion, if needed. Discuss your concerns with a family who has a child with a g-tube or button who can offer first-hand experience and insight. Ask to see the child's feeding tube so you will know what one looks like after placement. You may want to discuss your concerns and feelings with family members, but you and your child's primary caregivers should make the final decision.

Asking yourself the following questions may help during the decision-making process. If you cannot answer some, consult your medical team.

- How will my child benefit from a feeding tube?
- Will my child continue to take some food by mouth?
- What difficulties will a feeding tube cause for my child?
- How much will my child's nutrition change after a feeding tube?
- Is the surgery too risky for his present medical condition?
- Can I manage the daily needs of a feeding tube?
- Can all his caregivers, including daycare providers or teachers, care for a feeding tube and its associated needs?
- How long should I expect my child to have the tube or button in place?
- What does the tube or button mean to my cultural beliefs?
- Will the feeding tube change my feelings toward my child?

If some of these questions are difficult to answer, wait a few weeks and reevaluate. Ask your pediatrician how long you can postpone placement of the feeding tube.

Using an endoscope, the surgeon passes the feeding tube through the mouth and into the stomach, then out of the stomach through a small hole in the abdomen. Many surgeons and gastrointestinal specialists initially place a PEG tube, then replace it with a button in a few months (after the incision is healed and the child is tolerating his feedings).

How long will your child need a feeding tube?

Your child's feeding tube will be removed when he learns to eat well, does not stop eating with a minor illness, can burp without the tube, and is growing adequately without the need for supplemental g-tube feedings. After a doctor removes the tube, the hole will close and heal on its own within a few weeks. A small percentage of children will need the hole surgically closed (sometimes done by laser).

PARENT TIPS:

Coping with a Feeding Tube

Your pediatrician or feeding specialist will teach you how to feed your child through a feeding tube, how to clean and care for the equipment, and how to recognize signs of potential problems. The following are some additional tips from parents:

- Until the area around the tube is completely healed, keep the tube secured to the abdomen, preventing it from pulling and irritating the skin. Secure the tube with medical tape, such as Tegaderm or Op-site, available at most medical supply stores. Leave the tube loose enough to not irritate the skin, but tight enough that it does not get pulled.
- If the button or tube leaks, you will need to protect the skin from any irritation caused by acid in the stomach fluids. Try putting an ointment, such as Desitin, Bag Balm, or Neosporin, on the skin, then cover with a gauze dressing, especially at night. Occasional leakage around the site may mean your child needs a new button, a spacer under the button to make it fit properly, or treatment from your doctor. Consult your pediatrician.
- If there is a red rash around the button, it may be an infection. Consult your pediatrician.
- Granulation tissue is the buildup of abnormal skin cells around the button or tubing—it looks similar to a bad scar. Granulation tissue can interfere with the development of a good seal around the tube and may cause leaking. Consult your pediatrician for treatment.
- Once any breakdown of skin heals, it will return to looking like "normal" skin. (Your problems will not last forever!)
- Ask your doctor if you can give your child through the feeding tube a small amount of white grape juice or cranberry juice (the acidity of the juice cleans

the inside of the button.) Juice should *not* be used if there is leakage around the tube—its acidity can contribute to skin breakdown.

- If you are having difficulties burping your child, lay him on his back and gently rock him from side to side with the ventilation tube in place. The air should rise. If the surgery site is healed, gently push on his stomach to release air.
- If your child is on continuous feedings at night, tape the feeding tube to his abdomen, run it through the front of his outfit, and tape the tube to his back. If there is still a chance of him pulling on the tubing, run the tubing down through the bottom of his pajamas. Securing the tubing in two different places should prevent it from pulling out.
- Buy clothes that open in the front for easy access to the feeding tube.
- If a feeding tube is pulled out, it is not a medical emergency, but the hole can close within six hours. If you do not know how to replace the tube or do not have an extra one, tape a piece of gauze over the hole and call your doctor or the emergency room.
- If your child is older, let him show off his button and be proud of it!

FEEDINGS *WILL* GET EASIER

LEARNING HOW TO feed a baby is difficult for any parent—even those of full-term infants. Your preemie's special needs understandably add to your concerns. By reaching out to others who are knowledgeable about preterm infants, you can help your child overcome any obstacles. Mealtimes will become relaxing, intimate moments of family togetherness—with a little time and patience.

PART FOUR

Your Growing Preemie

PART FOUR

Introduction

YOU MAY HAVE many questions about your preemie's development: Will she eventually catch up, and if so, when? How can her developmental growth be encouraged? What are the warning signs of developmental problems? The lack of information on preterm infant development can be frustrating. Most child development books are written for full-term children and do not take into consideration the differences an early birth causes. Once again, you feel alone in a world full of term children and their parents.

Each preemie is unique (just as no two full-term children are alike), but there are some important developmental characteristics common to children born prematurely. Chapter 12 educates you about these differences. By understanding "normal" preemie development, you can monitor your child's progress and seek professional help if needed. Chapter 13 provides an overview of early intervention services that can promote your child's developmental growth and describes developmental activities you can do at home.

CHAPTER TWELVE

Your Preemie's Early Development

YOUR PRETERM CHILD'S development—her physical, intellectual, communication, and social abilities—may be much different from a term child's development. An early birth will most likely affect your baby's sleep patterns, feeding schedule, activity level, even her temperament for *at least* the first year after homecoming. Later developmental milestones, such as walking and talking, may also be delayed.

Most preemies overcome delays within the first two to three years, but some have longer-lasting problems. Those children who were born earlier, had more severe complications, and required extensive medical interventions are more likely to have prolonged delays. Some cognitive (thinking) delays may not be identified until a child is school-aged, when more complicated learning processes begin.

Ideally, your baby was followed by developmental specialists in the NICU and will continue to have developmental evaluations after homecoming. Experts recommend evaluations every four to six months during the first two years of life. Preterm children with severe problems should be followed even more closely. Developmental tests are often used to help identify problem areas. If needed, physical, occupational, and/or speech therapy and a home program involving "exercises" and play activities should be arranged.

"CORRECTING" YOUR PREEMIE'S AGE

Your child born early had a different developmental starting point from most children's. For example, if born eight weeks early, your one-year-old probably has the developmental abilities of a ten-month-old term baby (although some areas, such as mental and social skills, may be age-appropriate). When considering your child's developmental progress, correct or adjust her age for weeks or months born prematurely (see box on page 224). Your doctor and developmental specialist should evaluate your child according to her corrected age until she is two or three years old.

If your child is not receiving follow-up care and you are concerned about her development, ask your pediatrician for a referral to a developmental follow-up program. Intervening early can optimize your child's development by promoting the most efficient use of her muscles and learning experiences and by minimizing her (and your) frustration.

My preemie didn't do anything in normal sequence. I couldn't follow the books on typical child development. The doctors kept telling me he'd catch up. It took years, but eventually he did.

—SARAH, MOTHER OF 27-WEEKER ADAM

■

I knew I should be grateful to even have my child, but I kept wondering if there would be any developmental problems ahead. There were all those follow-up appointments and therapy sessions. It seemed as though he'd make progress in one area, then slow down in another. I had to do exercises with him every day. I kept wondering when it would all end and I could finally enjoy my family.

—LINDA, MOTHER OF 30-WEEKER ERIC

■

Just before my daughter turned two, she finally caught up. For so long she seemed frustrated because her mind wanted to do what her body was not yet capable of doing. Then, all of a sudden, it was as though her muscles developed and new skills began to "clump" together. She had waited so long to explore her world, and she was finally doing so.

—MARTIN, FATHER OF 26-WEEKER JENNA

DEVELOPMENTAL MILESTONES

WHEN YOUR CHILD becomes interested in her surroundings, you will eagerly anticipate developmental milestones, such as sitting up, crawling, walking, and talking. While you should celebrate these achievements, keep in mind that your preemie's development is a process, not a race for developmental goals. Because your baby was born with immature nervous and muscular systems, she may take longer to reach milestones. Also remember that your child is unique and will develop at her own pace and in her own way. Her health and personality, as well as your family's cultural and educational background, can all influence her development.

The following sections will explain the tests that may be used to evaluate your child's development, the specialists your child may see, terms you may hear, and your preterm child may develop differently from a full-term child. Physical (gross and fine motor), cognitive (thinking), communication, and social development are discussed.

> *Every time my son reaches a developmental milestone, I applaud. I applaud not only to let him know how proud I am of his accomplishment, but because it is a sign to me that my son is "normal."*
>
> *My son was born three months early. He weighed under two pounds. He spent his first three and a half months of life in the neonatal intensive care nursery. Among numerous problems, he suffered severe respiratory distress, a mild intracranial brain hemorrhage, numerous infections, and bilateral inguinal hernias. It's amazing how one sentence can summarize months of terror and heartache.*
>
> *But my son was one of the lucky ones. He came home. And after many follow-up examinations, he appears to be healthy . . . healthy except for "mild developmental delays." While I rejoice at his will to live and our positive outcome, I can't help but wonder what impact these developmental delays might have on my son's future and, since modern medicine has just recently started saving tiny babies like my son, what unidentified concerns might lie ahead?*
>
> *Like a soldier, I'm always on guard, trying to anticipate disaster before it hits. I've been told by well-meaning friends and doctors to stop looking for problems. This is not easy. From the day my baby arrived, I was conditioned to expect the worst.*
>
> *We were told after his birth that he had a 50-50 chance of survival. No one could tell us what kind of life he would live if he did survive. They told us to expect the negative and be grateful for the positive. During the first weeks in the NICU, we were warned about severe intracranial brain bleeds leading to brain damage. We were told about possible eye damage caused by continuous high pressures of oxygen. Our son's hernias could rupture at any time, demanding emergency surgery. The numerous infections he caught were life-threatening.*
>
> *This day-to-day fear of the unknown didn't end after the doctors discharged our four-pound baby. Although I was elated to even have a baby to take home, I couldn't help but be apprehensive about caring for him. Would I panic the first time the apnea monitor sounded? If he stopped breathing, would I remember CPR? Would I recognize the signs of a serious cold?*
>
> *All parents worry about their children, about illnesses and accidents. But parents of children who have already endured life-threatening obstacles are particularly fearful. I'm not trying to create problems. I just want to give my child the best possible future.*
>
> *And so, I take my son to therapy—physical, occupational, and speech. I hope that my son will overcome his delays and that new problems aren't identified. I try not to compare him to term babies the same age, or even to other*

preemies. And, while I still note each one of my son's milestones as signs of a "normal" child, I've begun to spend more time focusing on the traits that make him unique. After all, my preemie isn't only special because of his early birth, but in so many other ways, too.

—AMY, MOTHER OF 28-WEEKER DANIEL

WHAT ARE DEVELOPMENTAL TESTS?

DEVELOPMENTAL TESTS TELL healthcare providers if your child is developing at the same speed and order as "typical" children. These tests do not tell *why* your child develops in a certain way, nor can they predict how "smart" your child will ultimately become. The test (or tests) chosen for your child depends on what she is being evaluated for and which one the evaluator is most familiar with. Your pediatrician and developmental specialists will interpret test results and assess the causes of any developmental delays. The following are the most common developmental tests used:

Bayley Scales of Infant Development, second edition (BSID, 2 ed.). Two scales that measure a child's (age 2–42 months) current level of cognitive, language, social, and fine and gross motor development.

Peabody Developmental Motor Scales (PDMS). Two scales that measure development of 1) fine motor skills (use of small muscles for eye-hand coordination, as well as problem-solving and attention, and 2) gross motor skills (use of large muscles for sitting, rolling, crawling, and walking) in children ages 0–83 months.

Alberta Infant Motor Scales (AIMS). Used to identify infants up to 18 months of age who have normal patterns of movement, but demonstrate immature motor skills for their age, and infants who exhibit atypical patterns of movement suggestive of a specific motor disorder, such as cerebral palsy.

DeGangi Test of Motor and Neurological Functions. Measures the quality of a baby's posture (the positioning of the body) and her movements. For example, it evaluates how a baby moves or holds a position as opposed to simply looking at whether she can perform the skill.

Clinical observation. Assessments of a baby's development made by experienced developmental specialists and/or doctors in conjunction with standardized tests, such as those listed above.

WHO ARE DEVELOPMENTAL SPECIALISTS?

EACH AREA OF development overlaps and greatly affects other areas, requiring developmental specialists to work closely with each other as well as with you and your child.

Your developmental specialists should consult your pediatrician and other doctors to provide a "team approach" for treatment. Your child's developmental specialists may include any of the following professionals:

A physical therapist (PT). A PT helps a child learn better ways to move, coordinate her movements, and use her balance, and assists with the creation or purchase of adaptive equipment (for example, constructing splints, modifying chairs, and using walkers and wheelchairs).

An occupational therapist (OT). An OT helps a child work on better ways to use her upper body—arms, hands, eyes, mouth, and tongue—for play, eating, and self-care skills. An OT may also suggest or make the right special equipment to assist development (for example, equipment for bathing, dressing, eating, playing, or going to school).

A speech-language pathologist (SLP). An SLP helps a child with the use of the muscles in the mouth that are important for eating and speaking. She can help your child understand words, as well as how to use words and sentences. An SLP also assists in selecting alternative methods of communication if your child is unable to develop the use of words or intelligible speech. As your child grows, an SLP can help her interpret and use more complex language skills required for school.

A neurologist. A neurologist diagnoses and treats diseases of the nervous system.

A psychologist. A psychologist is a doctor specializing in behavioral and emotional needs.

An orthopedist. A doctor who diagnoses and treats problems with muscles, bones, and joints is an orthopedist.

A developmental pediatrician. A developmental pediatrician, who specializes in the motor, cognitive, behavioral, and emotional development of children, may coordinate your child's therapy program (developed by therapists) and integrate it with your child's medical needs.

Terms You Should Know

When a developmental specialist describes your child's motor development, ask for simple explanations and drawings or pictures. Ask a therapist to explain what "normal" development is and how your child differs, and do not hesitate to ask any questions. Listed below are some developmental terms professionals may use.

Cerebral palsy. This is a broad term used to describe a number of sensory-motor disorders, resulting from damage to the brain. In premature infants, cerebral palsy is typically caused by severe hypoxia (low oxygen supply), a bleed in the brain, or periventricular leukomalacia. It is a diagnosis rarely made before twelve months corrected age and is used to describe anything from mild to severe abnormalities of muscle tone that affect the development of gross motor skills.

Extension. When a baby is in an extended position, her arms and legs are straight, her head goes back, and her trunk (body) is straight. If she arches her back and neck, she is "hyper-extended."

Fine (small) motor skills. The ability to use the small muscles of the hands and fingers, which is often dependent on the quality of eye-hand coordination. Examples include picking up objects, manipulating objects in the hand, and drawing.

Flexion. When a baby is flexed, her arms and legs bend forward and in toward the chest or abdomen, her head and neck come forward with the chin tucked down toward the chest, and the trunk (body) is rounded forward.

Fluctuating muscle tone. When a preemie's tone changes between low and high ranges beyond what is considered normal, she has fluctuating muscle tone. Babies with fluctuating tone often seem "tight" at times and "loose" at other times.

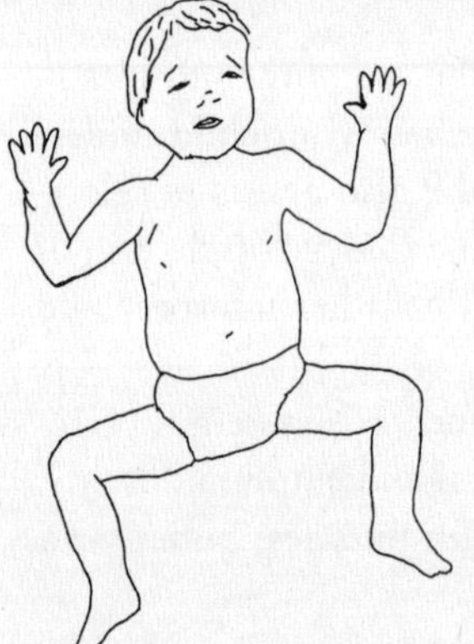
A child with "frog legs"

Gross (large) motor skills. The ability to hold the body up against gravity and to move between positions. Examples include crawling, sitting, standing, and walking.

Hypertonus (or hypertonia). Abnormally high tone, which in the most severe form is referred to as "spasticity." It usually does not become significant until four to six months corrected age. Hypertonic babies have increased resistance to movement of the muscles and limited motion in the joints. Their muscles seem "tight." This prevents smooth, coordinated, and energy-efficient movements, and their movements often appear stiff and jerky.

Hypotonus (or hypotonia). Abnormally low tone. Decreased tone does not support the joints well, and the baby may feel unusually "floppy" or double-jointed. Hypotonic babies often seem weak and slow to respond. This muscle tone is frequently present early in a preemie's development and may be prolonged when medical problems, such as lung disease, or when neurological immaturity are present.

Midline of body. Bringing arms to the midchest area.

Muscle tone. Responsiveness of muscles to adjust to gravity during position changes and movement.

Prone. Lying on the stomach.

Supine. Lying on the back.

PHYSICAL (GROSS AND FINE MOTOR) DEVELOPMENT OF PRETERM INFANTS

A TERM BABY SPENDS the last few months of pregnancy in a flexed position and moving in a very cushioned environment. Pushing against fluid and the uterus helps develop

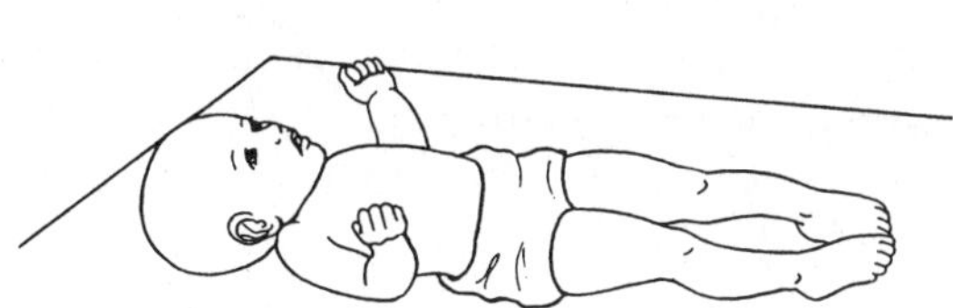

A hypertonic infant lying on her back

A hypertonic child in standing position

proper muscle tone. An infant born prematurely, however, spends weeks or months outside the womb in a very loose, uncontrolled environment. Even if the best care was taken to swaddle and create a "natural" fetal position, the womb cannot be completely duplicated.

A hypotonic infant lying on her stomach

The NICU environment can influence the development of your child's muscle strength and tone. For instance, if your baby was swaddled on her tummy, her feet and hips may have been extended or pushed flat (instead of being flexed) and her shoulders may have been slightly flattened and elevated (rather than rounded). If your baby's hand was restrained for an IV, the muscle use in that hand or arm may have been affected. When your baby moved or reacted to a sound, she pushed against hard surfaces, rather than the soft surfaces of the womb.

Furthermore, your preterm baby's brain did not have enough time within the womb to learn how to process movement responses. Therefore, when your baby was born, her brain was less equipped to handle the outside world. (Experts believe there are critical times in a baby's development when the brain should be exposed to light, sounds, and vibration. If exposed too early or too late, brain development may be altered.) If your baby's brain experienced some trauma, such as a hemorrhage, signals from the brain telling the muscles how to work can also be affected.

As your baby grows and develops at home, atypical muscle strength or tone will make it more difficult for her to move against gravity and control her movements. She may have

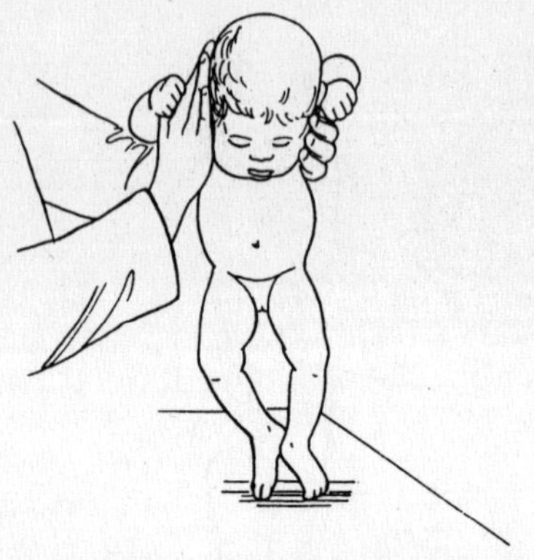

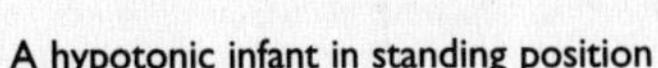

A hypotonic infant in standing position

A baby in flexed position

difficulty holding her head up, or she may have trouble bringing her hands together. If your baby's legs that are "naturally" in a frog position, this can prevent her from shifting her weight to the side and rolling.

If your baby's shoulder muscles are weak, making it difficult for her to push up on her elbows and lift her head (which may also be larger in comparison to her body), she may not like to play on her stomach. Low muscle tone in her neck and trunk (body), or a "tightness" in specific muscle groups, may also make your baby stiffen her legs or arms.

While all this may sound overwhelming at first, much can be done to improve atypical muscle strength and tone and enhance your child's motor development. A developmental

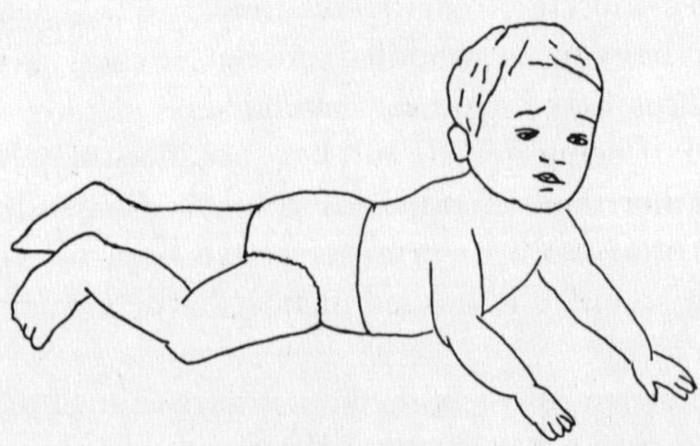

A baby in extended position

specialist can teach you simple positioning techniques (how to lay or sit your baby) and motor games that can help. Intervening early is important. Make sure your baby is evaluated regularly. If your child with motor delays is not being followed by a developmental specialist, ask for a referral from your pediatrician immediately.

■ ■ ■

All preemies, while not necessarily truly disabled, could be labeled as "special needs child." Their needs—oxygen, medication, monitors, therapy—could be loosely termed "disabilities," even if the special needs disappear within the first few years. One could say that many preemies have "temporary disabilities."

This unique situation is difficult to explain to full-term parents. They tend to either not treat our babies as having special needs, or they err on the opposite side and treat them as permanently disabled. Unlike parents of truly disabled children, preemie parents are given hope that our children's disabilities will resolve.

The great majority of preemie parents must wait and see if their children will develop disabilities beyond developmental delays. There is a combination of hope and fear that comes with the unknown. Parents carry, in the backs of their minds, a lingering fear of discovering a prematurity-caused disability later in life, as well as the hope that their children will grow up to be perfectly normal.

Sure, full-term parents worry about their children's development, but not to the degree that preemie parents do. Full-term parents have the expectation that their children will progress without difficulty. Preemie parents do not. The fear of the unexpected and the unknown continues to creep into our lives long after the NICU experience is over.

—Kerry, mother of 31-weeker Tyler

COGNITIVE (THINKING) DEVELOPMENT OF PRETERM INFANTS

Your baby's early learning comes from her environment—through information gained by what she sees, hears, smells, tastes, and touches, and by moving to explore her world. Thinking abilities develop as she learns to imitate and problem-solve (find, sort, and use information). An example of early problem-solving is finding a toy hidden under one of two cups.

More mature learning occurs through childhood play involving discovery, sorting, and remembering information. The process of developing cognitive skills requires trial and error and repetition (for example, trying to put shapes into a shape sorter again and again). Preemies who have delayed learning skills, impaired visual perception, or weak eye-hand coordination may need more repetitive play. Fortunately, in the early years of a child's life, the brain has the remarkable ability to use information gained through repetition to reorganize brain connections (even rebuild damaged connections).

Most healthy preemies catch up to their full-term peers in intellectual abilities by two or three years of age. Those with long-term medical problems, significant sensory difficulties (see box on page 223), or disabilities may continue to have cognitive difficulties of varying degrees throughout life.

COMMUNICATION DEVELOPMENT OF PRETERM INFANTS

Full-term infants begin communicating with their first cry, and they continue to express themselves through various vocalizations—crying, cooing and squealing. At around four months, their cooing becomes babbling. When children are around nine months to one year of age, they begin to say words like "mama" and "dada."

Children born prematurely often take longer to reach these communication milestones. Medical problems, such as respiratory difficulties, can affect the start of early speech and language skills. Feeding disorders and oral defensiveness (hypersensitivity in and around the mouth) can also hinder speech development. Extended hospitalization or rehospitalization, the presence of a tracheostomy, and hearing loss are other possible causes of delays.

Some communication delays associated with prematurity include:

Voice problems. Preemies with voice problems were usually intubated for a prolonged period of time. They have either high-pitched, light voices or hoarse, harsh-sounding speech. Some even speak in a whisper. Their voice quality usually improves over time, but some children may still continue having voice problems at school age.

Dysfluency (stuttering). Many preterm and term children stutter when they learn more words than their motor abilities allow them to say. However, signs of repetition of initial sounds in words ("babababa" for "baby") and/or tension in the face, neck, and/or shoulders may indicate a more serious problem.

Deficit in comprehension. Children with deficits in comprehension may not answer questions appropriately or understand word or sentence meanings. For example, when asked, "What is your name?" she may answer, "Three" (her age). When told to put the block on the chair, she may put it on the table.

Delayed sound production. Producing sounds is crucial to the development of language. Some preemies may be slower in producing sounds and, therefore, slower to develop recognizable words.

Delayed use of words. Sometimes a child's use of vocabulary or grammar does not match her age or her understanding of language (she may understand more words than she uses). She may use nonspecific words ("it," "that," and "thing"), instead of the object's name. Her use of sentences or grammar may also fall below her level of understanding. For example, she may use a two- or three-year-old's sentence level when her understanding is at a four-year-old's ability.

Delays in communication can affect your child's future social and academic development. If you have concerns regarding your child's speech or language, discuss them with your pediatrician or a speech-language pathologist.

■ ■ ■

WHAT IS SENSORY INTEGRATION DYSFUNCTION?

Approximately 10 percent of *all* children are diagnosed with sensory integration (SI) dysfunction. Some studies indicate that preemies, especially those with very low birthweights, are at greater risk for a sensory integration disorder.

Children with SI disorders have difficulty coping with experiences involving their senses. While you are probably familiar with the five basic senses (taste, touch, sight, hearing, and smell), experts recognize other senses as well: movement (sliding down a slide); body position (combing hair); the pull of gravity (swinging); and balance (sitting in a chair).

For most children, their brains organize and interpret information coming from the senses (sensory integration) without any effort or problems. When they ride a bike or build a snowman, they have fun because their bodies and brains work together smoothly. For children with sensory integration dysfunction, the connection from the mind to the body is not as smooth. These children become easily frustrated and can experience much anxiety. If these children do not receive therapy, sensory difficulties can lead to learning or behavioral problems.

There are different levels of sensory integration dysfunction. Some children experience one or two problems, while others cope with many issues. Typical treatment involves therapy, ideally by an occupational or physical therapist trained in sensory integration dysfunction. Therapy improves a child's self-concept by helping her learn and achieve new skills she otherwise would not try. If you think your child may have an SI disorder, consult your pediatrician or local pediatric developmental therapy clinic.

Social Development of Preterm Infants

How your baby communicates her needs, how she responds to you and others, and how she controls her moods and feelings are all part of her social development. Later, these skills will play an important part in her personal relationships and social behavior.

Children born prematurely are often described as "hyper" by their parents. Many say their preemies are sensitive children who have intense personalities, are strong-willed, and tend to overreact. Once upset, these children often have difficulty calming down. These behaviors often last into early childhood.

According to some experts, your highly active preemie may become a more calm person as she matures. Your guidance can also help. As you teach her appropriate behaviors, be patient and encouraging—how you react to your child also affects her social development.

If your child's personality makes parenting difficult, you may need to seek professional help through parenting classes or a family counselor. Sensory difficulties can sometimes contribute to a child's active behavior. A physical, occupational, or speech therapist familiar with sensory integration can assess your child and provide treatment, if needed.

■ ■ ■

Chart 12-1: Overview of typical preemie developmental milestones

By understanding the common ages and stages of child development, you can monitor your preemie's progress and identify the first signs of any problems. It is important that developmental delays, even slight

(Adapted with permission from *Primary Care of the Preterm Infant,* Judy C. Bernbaum, M.D., and Marsha Hoffman-Williamson, Ph.D., St. Louis, Mo.: Mosby-Year Book, Inc., 1991, p. 181.)

AGE	GROSS MOTOR	FINE MOTOR
1 month corrected age	Lifts head for a few seconds when lying on stomach	Hands usually fisted with random opening and closing; brings hands to mouth; stares at objects and lights
3 months corrected age	Fairly good head control on tummy and in supported position; lifts head and chest when lying on stomach; thrust arms and legs in play with both sides appearing the same	Holds on to a rattle; follows slow-moving objects with eyes; brings hands together at midchest area
6 months corrected age	Rolls and is beginning to sit well without support; supports self on one forearm while lying on side; pulls forward with arms while lying on stomach	Reaches and grasps with both hands; moves toys from hand to hand
9 months corrected age	Gets into and out of sitting position on all fours independently; crawls on hands and knees	Points with index finger
12 months corrected age	Walks alone (may take up to 15 months)	Uses thumb and pointer finger to grasp small finger foods; drops objects into a small container
18 months corrected age	Walks up steps while holding on to support; "runs"	Builds tower with 3–4 blocks
24 months corrected age	Alternates feet while going up stairs; kicks ball	Stacks 6 cubes; turns individual book pages
30 months corrected age	Jumps with both feet	Strings beads; holds pencil in hand, not fist
36 months corrected age	Balances on one foot for 5 seconds; rides tricycle	Imitates building a block bridge

ones, are not overlooked. Some children with delays skip steps in learning (they will learn A, then C, and skip B). These "gaps" in learning may or may not affect later learning, but should be assessed. Think of your child's early learning development like building a house—a solid foundation is essential.

Use the following chart as a *guide* for monitoring your child's development and discuss any concerns with your pediatrician or developmental specialist.

Cognitive	Communication	Social
Begins to handle different sensory inputs (however, most movement is random and a reflex to the environment)	Cries to make needs known; listens and soothes to voice; gives eye contact	Regards face; enjoys being talked to and held
Begins to realize body movements affect surroundings (bats at mobile, bounces in infant seat); begins the effort to repeat movements that create a response	Coos and laughs; has different cries for different needs (hungry, hurt, bored)	Smiles easily and spontaneously
Shakes rattle; starts to imitate gestures that self can see and engage in (smiling and frowning); has an increased interest in surroundings and in the results of actions	Babbles, laughs, coos; turns to look at new sounds	Awareness of strangers; smiles at self in mirror
Takes toys in and out of containers	Begins to use 2-syllable sounds together ("dada" or "mama")	Anxious response to strangers; strong attachment to parents
Begins to use objects for specific functions (comb to comb hair); begins to anticipate behavior will have a consequence	Says at least 2 words in addition to "mama" and "dada"; recognizes own name; imitates familiar words	Shy, but enjoys attention and play; gives affection and cuddles
Begins trial-and-error thinking; begins to understand reasoning	Points to three basic body parts; follows simple requests; knows and names 2–5 familiar objects; uses 10–20 words including names; combines 2 words ("all gone" or "bye-bye")	Helps with simple tasks; imitates others' actions spontaneously
Matches circle, square, triangle; understands the use of many objects; understands self is separate from environment	Uses 2-word phrases; understands simple questions and commands; asks for a drink	Washes and dries hands; helps get dressed
Knows simple songs with hand gestures; completes simple puzzles; begins to understand basic instructions	Uses pronouns "I," "you," and "me" correctly; states full name; may say "no" when means "yes"	Plays tag; asserts personality
Knows big and little; understands basic instructions; believes all objects are related to her somehow	Can match primary colors; can sing songs; asks "what" questions	Plays with children; takes turns hand gestures; completes

WARNING SIGNS

Consult your pediatrician or a developmental specialist if your child exhibits any of the signs listed below at the ages indicated.

At 6 Months Corrected Age

- has difficulty lifting her hand and pushing up on her arms while lying on her stomach;
- cannot stay lying on her side to play with toys;
- is not sitting, even with support;
- is not rolling or is rolling by arching her neck and back;
- makes no effort to reach or bat at objects;
- does not move her head toward a sound or search for objects with her eyes;
- grasps an object weakly or holds only for a moment;
- keeps her hands fisted and/or keeps her thumb inside her fist;
- is not able to get her hands to her mouth or together;
- continues to have trouble taking a bottle or first solids; and/or
- does not coo or babble.

At 12 Months Corrected Age

- is sitting but not able to sit independently;
- is crawling or "bunny hopping" by moving both legs forward at the same time;
- is not easily able to pick up small objects, such as finger foods;
- does not search for a hidden object;
- does not vocalize consonant and vowel combinations ("ba");
- does not look at books for short periods of time. (Keep in mind that if she is busy learning to crawl and walk, she may not have much interest in sit-down activities. Encourage her to spend some time doing "quiet" activities, such as looking at books.);
- does not respond to simple familiar speech routines, such as pat-a-cake; and/or
- uses one side of her body much more often than the other.

At 18 Months Corrected Age

- does not walk, or constantly walks up on her toes;
- does not imitate sounds or produce any sound combinations that represent a word ("doodie" for cookie);
- cannot build a tower with blocks;
- is most interested in putting toys in her mouth during play, rather than more purposeful play using her hands; and/or
- understands fewer than eight words.

■ ■ ■

At 24 Months Corrected Age

- does not put two words together in speech;
- does not identify basic objects or pictures of basic objects;
- has play skills that remain primarily imitative, and does not initiate play on her own;
- has large motor skills that are lacking in balance and control (falls or trips a lot more than other children her age);
- cannot complete a simple puzzle or shape sorter;
- does not follow simple commands, such as "give me"; and/or
- cannot identify basic body parts.

At 36 Months Actual Age

- does not use prepositions ("in," "by" and "to") in speech;
- cannot copy a circle (or attempt to);
- has such poor speech that it is impossible for others to understand;
- does not follow commands that use "in," "on," and "under";
- does not answer simple "yes" or "no" questions correctly;
- does not jump with both feet off the ground; and/or
- cannot feed herself with a spoon.

(Adapted with permission from *Primary Care of the Preterm Infant*, Judy C. Bernbaum, M.D., and Marsha Hoffman-Williamson, Ph.D., St. Louis, Mo.: Mosby-Year Book, Inc., 1991.)

KEEPING TRACK OF YOUR PREEMIE'S PROGRESS

Using a baby book created for term children and their families for your preemie can be discouraging. Weeks or months may pass before you can actually record a developmental milestone. Many of the items listed may not even apply to your preterm baby.

You can create an individualized preemie baby book by using a blank scrapbook or inserting heavy blank pages into a binder. Write celebrations and paste photos and keepsakes onto pages (do not forget that tiny disposable diaper or blood pressure cup). You can keep track of firsts (first smile, first crawl, first word) by corrected age and actual age.

Recording your preemie's developmental achievements can help you see how your child develops over time (rather than just focusing on day-to-day progress, which can sometimes be disappointing). Your homemade "preemie book" will also help you tell your child someday about her special birth.

■ ■ ■

CHAPTER THIRTEEN

Early Intervention

Your child with developmental delays can benefit from early intervention. Early intervention includes government-funded services, therapy by developmental experts, and support at home. This chapter addresses how to find and work with early intervention programs and specialists; it also provides specific activities you can do at home to optimize your child's developmental growth. Remember: All babies learn through daily activities, and the best intervention for your child is what you do every day as a family.

FINDING EARLY INTERVENTION SERVICES

In 1986 the Handicapped Infants and Toddlers Program was added to the Education of the Handicapped Act (EHA) of 1970. (EHA was updated and renamed the Individuals with Disabilities Education Act, or IDEA, in 1990.) This program encourages states to establish early intervention services for eligible infants and toddlers from birth to age three. These are often called "birth-to-three programs."

Your premature infant up to age three may qualify for free early intervention services under IDEA, but eligibility requirements and services vary from state to state. If your state serves children "at risk," the qualifying criteria may be birthweight, gestational age at birth, or other medical conditions. If your state serves only children identified as having a delay, it may be difficult for your child to qualify if she is not delayed beyond her corrected age.

Your pediatrician, another healthcare professional, or a social worker may refer you to an early intervention program. You can also seek help yourself. To find out more about your state's early intervention services, contact your state's lead agency, the agency chosen by the governor to "lead" the development of early intervention services. The National Information Center for Children and Youth with Disabilities at (800) 695-0285 can provide you with a recent list of lead agencies and early intervention contacts for your state.

If you live in a large community, you may have a Child Find office, directed by your state's department of education (or lead agency), to identify and diagnose children with disabilities. Your community or state may also have a government-funded parent center for families with children who have special needs. Contact the National Parent Network on Disabilities at (202) 463-2299 for a parent center near you.

THE EARLY INTERVENTION PROCESS

BEING BORN PREMATURELY should automatically qualify your child for an evaluation to determine if she is eligible for early intervention services. Conducted by a multidisciplinary team, the evaluation should take place within a few months after homecoming. In addition to you, the team may include: your child's doctor; early intervention specialists; occupational, physical, and speech therapists; a psychologist; a social worker; a home healthcare nurse; and anyone else you want (such as a daycare provider). Along with your observations about your child, other information used may include: your child's hospital records, your child's and your own medical reports, results from developmental tests, and observations and feedback from your child's healthcare providers.

If your child is found eligible, a service coordinator should be assigned to your family. This person can help you understand the early intervention programs and services in your community, coordinate these services, and assist in the transition to a preschool program when your child turns three.

THE INDIVIDUALIZED FAMILY SERVICE PLAN (IFSP)

Your child who qualifies for early intervention must have an Individualized Family Service Plan (IFSP), a written plan for a child (birth through age three) who has developmental delays. Those involved in its development and writing may include: your family, relatives, and friends; your service coordinator; your child's doctor; early intervention specialists; physical, occupational, and speech therapists; a psychologist; a social worker; and a home healthcare nurse. Your child's IFSP will include:

- a statement about your child's present levels of development (cognitive, speech and language, social, motor, and self-help);
- a statement about your family's priorities for your child's needs as well as for your family;
- a statement about your family's strengths and needs relating to the enhancement of your child's development;

- a statement of major outcomes, or goals, to be achieved for your child and family;
- the criteria, procedures, and timelines for determining progress;
- the specific early intervention services necessary to meet the unique needs of your child and family, including the method, frequency, and intensity of services;
- the projected dates for the start and expected end of services;
- the name of your service coordinator; and
- procedures for making the transition from early intervention services into a preschool program (if your child is two or older).

Your child's IFSP is not just another piece of paper—it is the cornerstone of her early intervention program. Family-centered early intervention is a process, requiring commitment from both your family and your child's service providers. By actively participating in the process, you can create a better future for your child and family.

Barely a month had passed since Emily's doctor made the referral to early intervention when we had our first Individual Family Service Plan (IFSP) meeting. I was a bit nervous about it since everything still seemed so surreal to me. While it was convenient to have this meeting in our home, I was frantic about having the house clean and tidy for the three professional women who were coming.

This first meeting evoked many emotions, and I didn't have the time to examine my feelings. I just attended to business. I remember feeling judged even though I knew logically this wasn't the case at all. When I was asked questions about our family, I felt incredibly cornered and defensive. I thought, Why are they asking these questions?

Fortunately, the IFSP team picked up on my nonverbal cues. When they explained they needed to ask questions to better understand our family's strengths and to help our family support Emily, I was so relieved.

After six months of being in the early intervention system, the second IFSP meeting was much different. I knew the service providers quite well, and I was beginning to understand the system. Although I did put extra effort into cleaning prior to the meeting, I was relaxed and even served beverages!

—SANDY, MOTHER OF 30-WEEKER EMILY

Developing an IFSP

Your initial meeting with your child's service providers might be overwhelming and confusing. You can more actively participate by coming prepared with a written list of questions, suggestions, and concerns you want addressed.

To begin, think about what is important to your child and family. Try answering these questions:

- What are the biggest challenges you are facing right now?
- At night, when you cannot sleep, what are you worrying about?
- What would you like to do with your baby now and in the future?
- When you were pregnant and dreaming about what your life would be like when your baby was the age she is now, how did you imagine that you would spend your days?
- How can other support systems (churches, respite care organizations, or parent support groups) help you?

The answers to these questions can give you a better idea about what your future expectations and hopes are for your child and family. Share them with IFSP team members, helping them to better understand your needs, expectations, and your family.

When developing the IFSP, it is important not to focus on what your child cannot do. Instead, look at your child as a whole person and examine what she can do. Before the meeting, try finishing these sentences:

I love the way my child . . .
My child is good at . . .
I would like my child to be able to . . .
My child's favorite things are . . .
My child does not like . . .
My child needs help with . . .
Some important things I would like the other IFSP people to know about my child are . . .

Let the IFSP team know about your family's strengths and resources, as well as the things with which your family needs help. Try finishing these sentences:

Our family's strengths are . . .
Our family's resources are . . .
Our family's weaknesses are . . .
Our family's most important concerns are . . .
The most important things we would like addressed on our IFSP regarding our family are . . .

Developing outcomes, or goals, is an important part of the IFSP process. Share what you would like to see happen in the next six months to one year for your child and your family. The team can then brainstorm ways to help you and your child attain these goals. To identify outcomes, think about what is going on right now in your family. Is it hard to feed your baby? Is your child having trouble playing with her siblings because of delayed motor abilities? Does your family want to participate in an activity but cannot? What would you like to learn to do with your child? Are finances an issue?

Also, think about where you take your child and where you would like to go, but cannot because of her special needs. Your child's early intervention program should take place in "natural environments." This means at places in the community where your child would go if she did not have delays.

Make a list of where you go with your child now (the library, restaurants, a community center, stores, the church nursery, or on public transportation). Make another list of places you would like to go and activities you would like to participate in, but cannot. Your child's early intervention services should involve the places and activities that are important to you as a family.

All this information can help the IFSP team determine what supports and services your child and family need. The team must also determine where and how this help will be provided and who will pay for it. (The initial evaluation and coordination of services are free. However, unless your county has money available, your health insurance or you must pay for subsequent services.)

Developing an IFSP can be time-consuming and tiring, but parents often say the results are well worth it. A good IFSP will not only help your child reach her fullest potential but offer your family tremendous support, too. One mother calls her child's early intervention program "a port in the storm."

EARLY INTERVENTION AT HOME

YOUR CHILD'S EARLY intervention services may include support from developmental specialists, such as physical, occupational, or speech therapists. These experts should work with you and your doctor to optimize your child's development by suggesting daily "exercises" for you to do with your child. Try to incorporate these developmental exercises and activities into everyday playtime, making learning fun rather than "work." Your child will develop best in a patient, loving, encouraging, and relaxed environment.

The following suggestions, listed by age and developmental area, can further enhance your child's abilities. Remember to use your child's corrected age (subtract weeks or months born early).

ENCOURAGING YOUR PREEMIE'S DEVELOPMENT

0 to 3 months corrected age

Gross motor

- When you hold and feed your baby, encourage her to curl up into a flexed position, keeping her chin tucked down, her arms forward, and her back and hips rounded.
- Encourage your baby to lift her head: Sit her up when burping; keep your face at the level of your baby's face (or slightly above) when holding her upright at your shoulder; help your baby raise her head and support herself on her forearms when she is lying on her tummy against you.
- Relax tight muscle tone in your baby's legs by gently and rhythmically rocking her bent hips and knees from side to side during diaper changes.

- Encourage equal muscle development on both sides of your baby's body by feeding her alternately from one side, then the other. Be sure to lay her on her left side, right side, tummy, and back during playtimes, but provide the support she needs, *especially on her tummy.*

Fine Motor

- Many preemies like to hold their arms in a "high guard" position (with arms up and out to the sides) to help substitute for trunk muscle weakness. Help your baby learn to move her hands closer together by providing adequate body support and gently bringing the shoulders forward.
- Stroke the back of your baby's hands, fingers to wrist, to encourage her to open them. Gently massage the palms, beginning at the center of the palm and stroking firmly out toward the base of the fingers and thumb.
- Let your baby feel different textures, such as stuffed animals and rubber and plastic toys. Encourage her to hold on to a variety of lightweight toys with her thumb around the toys, instead of tucked into the palm or at the side.

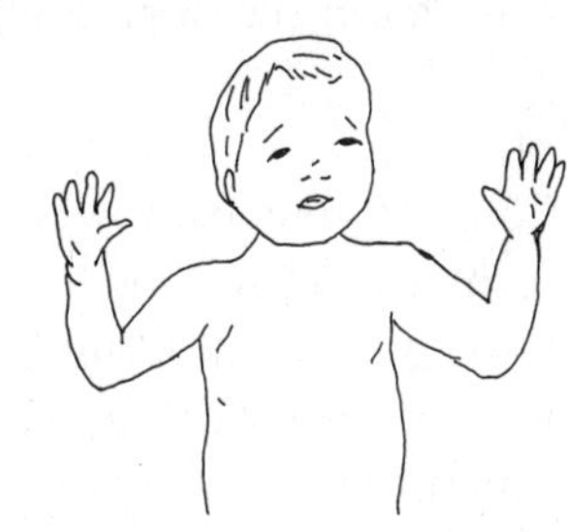

Baby in "high guard" position

You can support your baby while you feed her by keeping her shoulders rounded, her arms flexed, and her hands midline. She may like grasping your finger or a blanket.

Communication

- Sing and talk to your baby often—during caregiving, playtime, even when doing household chores.
- Try to be comfortable and relaxed when handling your baby, and smile frequently.
- When your baby can tolerate more stimulation, let her hear a variety of sounds (music, bells, TV). Watch for signs of overstimulation (looking away, startling, color changes, yawning, and tremors). If your baby is frightened by a sound, calm her, then try to reintroduce the sound while holding and comforting her.
- Imitate your baby's cooing to her.
- Give your baby time to respond to your sounds.

Cognitive

- Provide your baby with quiet time to visually explore her world.
- Encourage your baby to turn her head toward sounds.
- If your baby makes a sound, imitate it and encourage spontaneous imitation (however, the imitation of sounds is not always done at this age).

- Expose your baby to a variety of visual inputs (pictures, toys, faces), one at a time. Begin with contrasts such as black and white or red and yellow, then graduate to more variety.
- Read to your infant. Begin with board books that have colorful photographs or drawings. When she stops being interested, move on to something else.

Social

- Comfort your baby when she is fussy or stressed. Teach her self-comforting skills, such as hand-sucking.
- Carry your baby around with you often, talking to her in a soothing voice.
- Infant massage can be a positive social interaction between baby and parent. Ask an expert to show you how to massage your baby, or refer to the resources in the back of this book.
- When your baby shows signs of wanting to interact, look into her eyes and smile. Do not be distressed if she does not look back or smile at first. It will take time for her to process this new stimulation and to respond.

3 to 6 months corrected age

Gross Motor

- When your baby is awake, continue to encourage her to spend time on her tummy. Give her adequate support by placing a rolled blanket under her chest (at the nipple level) and start with short periods of time (1–2 minutes). Try getting down on the floor with her so she will lift her head to see you, or lay her on your chest so that she can look up at you.
- While your baby is lying on her back, gently pedal her feet. Help your baby raise her bottom 2–3 inches off the surface while keeping her legs bent at the hips and knees (this helps to round out the neck, shoulder, and trunk muscles, which are often tight in preemies).
- To get your baby to pay attention to both her right and left sides, offer visual and auditory (sounds) activities on both sides. Also offer interesting objects to encourage reaching. You may need to change your baby's crib or seating position periodically so that the interesting objects (a window, a picture on the wall, or an activity in the room) are not always on the same side.
- To encourage rolling, place a toy in front of your baby while she lies on her back, then slowly move the toy toward the side and back. When your baby stretches to see the toy, she will start to roll. You can help her by gently rolling her arms, hips, and legs to the side.

■ ■ ■

Fine Motor

- Give your baby playthings she can touch, squeeze, pull, push, and grasp. Encourage her to reach for dangling toys placed in front of her at chest level.
- Encourage batting by placing a crib gym or a row of toys that stretch across the crib. *Do not use strings or ties that could get wrapped around your baby's neck.*
- Play pat-a-cake.
- When your baby lies on her side, bring her hands together. Place a toy at midchest level. Do not place it at head level as it will cause her to arch.
- Tie bells to your baby's booties to encourage her to reach toward her feet.
- Put a toy in your baby's hand and encourage her to change it to the other hand. Offer your baby two objects—one for each hand—at the same time.

Communication

- Continue to sing and talk to your baby often.
- Continue imitating your baby's cooing and babbling sounds.
- Encourage your baby to locate sounds by helping her turn her head toward a sound.
- As you talk to your baby, repeat her sounds back to her to encourage back-and-forth sound play. Occasionally interject a new sound (such as "baba") to see if she will imitate you.
- Read to your infant often. Make sounds for the pictures (a horn's "beep," a telephone's "ring," a cow's "moo"). Allow grabbing, rubbing, and scratching at books.
- Encourage your baby to play with her lips, cheeks, and tongue by showing her kisses, "raspberries," and blowing.

Cognitive

- Provide your baby with quiet time to explore her world.
- Introduce new objects and let your baby thoroughly explore them to stimulate curiosity.
- Expose your baby to a variety of visual inputs (pictures, toys, and faces), one at a time.
- Partially hide a favorite toy and help your baby find it.
- Begin playing social games, such as peek-a-boo.

Social

- Show your baby herself in a mirror.
- Interact with your baby by smiling, talking, and singing to her often.
- Carry your baby around the room and tell her about different objects.
- Infant massage is beneficial at this age to help your infant become more aware of her body. Ask an expert to show you how to massage your baby.

■ ■ ■

6 to 9 Months Corrected Age

Gross Motor

- Do not use an infant walker, as it will slow down walking skills and can be dangerous. Instead, offer lots of playtime on the floor. Encourage play on tummy, back, when sitting, on hands and knees, and in kneeling position, working all of the body's muscles.
- Use pillows to support your baby in a sitting position until she can sit unsupported. When your baby can keep her back somewhat straight, move the pillows an inch or two away, providing a little less support but still close enough to soften a fall.
- Encourage your baby by exciting her with your voice or a toy to push up on her arms (so her chest lifts off the floor) and really look around.
- Place a toy out of reach and encourage your baby to get the toy by crawling on her hands and knees. At first you will need to give her support to maintain a hands-and-knees position. Gentle rocking back and forth in this position will activate hip and shoulder muscles.

Fine Motor

- Encourage your baby to place smaller objects inside larger ones, such as nesting cups.
- Provide your baby with stacking toys or large blocks.
- Let your baby bang a pot with a spoon.
- Encourage play with two-handed toys that require holding with one hand and manipulating with the other.

Communication

- Expose your baby to many different sounds and help her locate them.
- Talk to your baby often, using short simple sentences.
- Interpret your baby's body language. For example, when your child acts angry, say something like, "You're mad because you want your bottle. Mommy is hurrying. Here's your bottle." When your child reaches for you say, "Do you want up?"
- Continue to imitate your baby's sounds and encourage your baby to make the sounds back to you.
- Recite nursery rhymes and simple songs.
- Point to and name objects as your baby looks at a picture book.
- Use the names of familiar people, and identify everyday items and actions so your baby will begin to connect words with meanings.

Cognitive

- Your baby should now be able to sit still for a few minutes to look at picture books. Do not worry if your child seems uninterested in books. You can start "reading" or talking about the book as your child chews on it. Gradually increase reading times as your child becomes more attentive.

- Introduce toys that have a reaction to her manipulation, such as a busy box.
- Let your baby play with small plastic cups in the bathtub.
- Hide or drop toys or objects and retrieve them while talking to your baby. ("Here's the ball under the chair.")
- Play simple "hide and seek" games with siblings or another adult while you carry your infant.

Social

- Play social games, such as pat-a-cake and peek-a-boo.
- Call your baby by her name, and show her herself and other family members in photographs.
- Encourage waving in response to "bye-bye."

9 to 12 months corrected age

Gross Motor

- When your baby is in her crib, encourage her to pull up to a kneeling position and then to standing.
- When your baby starts showing signs of wanting to stand and step, place toys slightly out of reach on low tables or chairs to encourage her to walk by holding on to furniture.
- When she is ready, hold your baby's hands or trunk and help her walk.
- Roll a large ball to your baby and encourage her to roll it back to you.
- Encourage your baby to toss a small (tennis-sized) ball.

Fine Motor

- Let your baby explore ribbons and different textured materials with her fingers.
- Encourage your baby to pick up small objects between her thumb and index finger (make sure they are safe items, such as dry cereal).
- Show your baby how to put action figures on small chairs or in toy cars.
- While you read to your baby, demonstrate how to turn individual pages of a book.

Communication

- Continue talking to your baby often and responding to the sounds she makes. Your baby may now be ready to imitate new sounds you produce.
- Look at picture books and name the pictures.
- Do not interrupt when you hear your baby "talking" early in the morning or after a nap.
- Pause and listen when you "converse" with your baby, who may need extra time to respond.
- Have your baby give you familiar objects when you ask for them with an outstretched hand.

- Talk about what your baby is doing. ("You are pushing the truck. The truck goes fast.")
- Sing songs and read nursery rhymes.
- Talk about your actions. ("I'm stirring the pancake mix.")
- Talk about other activities your child is observing. ("There goes a fire truck. The truck is fast!")
- Use hand gestures as you describe something. For example, turn your hand when you say "open."

Cognitive

- Make a book out of magazine pictures and talk to your baby about the pictures.
- Show your baby what some things can do: a toy car rolls, a horse walks, a telephone rings.
- Play stacking, nesting, or ring games, showing your baby how to play the game first.

Social

- Spend time interacting with your baby, such as showing her how to pull a pull-toy.
- Let your baby sit near your family during meals and eat some of the safe food you are eating.
- Make a silly face and encourage your baby to imitate it. Have your baby make a silly face and you imitate it. You can also begin showing your baby "feeling" faces, such as angry, sad, and happy looks.

12 to 15 Months Corrected Age

Gross Motor

- Let your child walk with a push-toy on wheels. Be sure the toy has a wide base so that it does not tip over easily.
- Help your child crawl up, turn around, and crawl back down steps. Down is hardest and often comes after your baby has mastered going up.
- Show your child how to catch a large ball and how to throw it back to you. Then use a smaller ball overhand.

Fine Motor

- Encourage your child to feed herself with a spoon and drink from a cup. Spoons with a large handle usually work best.
- Show your child how to stack large blocks, line them up, and play with them.
- Encourage your child to put items into containers, then have her dump them out and start again. Plastic formula cans work well and make a "clunk" sound. Later, cut square holes in the top to make the game more challenging.
- Encourage your child to "catch" bubbles blown high into the air.

Communication

- Imitate the sounds, gestures, and words your child tries to use, making it fun so she will try to copy you.
- Name the objects or actions your child shows interest in but does not yet know how to say. For example, if she likes bananas, say "Banana, yum-yum."
- Continue to look at and read picture books together.
- When you talk to your child, use key words, that she knows (table, bottle, dog). Encourage and reward her efforts at producing words, and acknowledge any attempt to name an object, even if the sounds used are not quite right ("goggie" for doggie).
- Model the correct form of words. For example, if your child says "wa," you should say "water."
- When bathing and dressing your child, point to and name body parts.
- Talk to your child, using short sentences.

Cognitive

- Let your child scribble with crayons on paper.
- Encourage your child to match objects (sock with sock, spoon with spoon).
- Continue to let your child stack blocks or plastic containers. Encourage your child to find new ways to stack and knock them over.
- Allow your child to help with basic tasks around the house and explore what chores you do. She can wash the table or sweep with a broom.
- Ask your child to go get her shoes or a favorite toy.

Social

- Always emphasize manners.
- Your child will begin to "test" what is right and what is wrong. When she does something wrong, state that it is "not okay" and distract her by doing something she likes.
- Give your child a doll to feed and love.
- When you go out with your child, talk about the things you see and do.

15 to 18 months corrected age

Gross Motor

- Encourage your child to climb onto chairs while you supervise. She can learn spatial concepts by climbing up, on, under, over, and through various safe and stable household objects.
- Help your child play on outdoor playground equipment, such as slides and swings, as you supervise.
- Show your child how to kick a large ball.
- Let your child play on a safe rocking horse.

■ ■ ■

Fine Motor

- Give your child crayons and paper to scribble.
- Let your child dial on an unplugged telephone, or push buttons on a pretend remote control.
- Have your child string large macaroni on a piece of yarn.

Communication

- Talk to your child often and describe in short sentences what you see and do. Speak simply, clearly, and slowly to your child. Use statements, rather than questions. ("You are rolling the ball," rather than "What are you doing?")
- Describe what you and your child are doing when you play games, such as tossing a ball or hiding a stuffed animal.
- Always praise your child's efforts at communication.
- Have fun talking to your child on a toy telephone.
- Ask your child to point to 3–5 familiar pictures in favorite books.
- Enjoy rhymes and finger plays with your child.
- Use "shadowing." If your child is interacting with another person, stand just behind or next to your child and "help" her to say things.
- Avoid pressuring your child to talk.

Cognitive

- Give your child plenty of opportunities to put one object into another (for example, a ball into a cup).
- Allow your child to try new ways to control situations, such as throwing toys for you to retrieve.
- Let your child "experiment" with trial and error to see what happens, such as opening and closing doors.

Social

- Hug and kiss your child often, and try to get her to hug and kiss you back. (However, you should respect your child's contact preference. If she does not like to hug or kiss, find alternative ways of touching and expressing affection.)
- Hide and have your child look for you. Make it easy for her to find you.

18 to 24 Months Corrected Age

Gross Motor

- Show your child how to jump, getting both feet off the floor at the same time. If she needs help, hold her hands.
- Show your child how to stand on one foot, then the other. She can hold onto your hand or a chair.
- Have your child sway, clap, and dance to music.

Fine Motor

- Cut holes of different sizes and shapes into the top of a shoe box or plastic formula can lid. Give your child things to put through these holes.
- Make clay and let your child play. (Mix 1 tablespoon of salad oil with a cup of water; stir in 2 cups of flour and 3/4 cup of salt. If you wish, add food color.)
- Play with simple three- or four-piece puzzles.

Communication

- Have your child practice following simple commands, such as "in," "on," "up," "out," and "down."
- Read together often. Talk about the story and pictures.
- As you talk with your child, begin to give simple directions. ("Please bring me the cup.") Repeat and correct what your child says. For instance, if your child says, "Daddy go," you should say, "Daddy is going to work."
- Expand what your child says. For instance, if your child says, "Daddy go," you should say, "Daddy is going to work. He is driving his car."
- If your child is slow to add new words to her vocabulary, consider these strategies:

1. Ask for word imitation only periodically, not excessively (a few times a day to start).
2. Ask your child to repeat words you know she is capable of saying.
3. Request imitation only when your child really wants something and is motivated to get it. (For example, when she is thirsty, encourage her to say "juice.")
4. Reward your child's speech attempt immediately (even if it is not accurate) by giving or doing what your child asks or says (within reason, of course).
5. Do not pressure your child to talk! Avoid withholding things. Resist the advice of well-meaning friends and relatives who say you should "make" your child talk.

Cognitive

- Give your child simple directions, such as "Please bring me a cup."
- Your child will now begin to learn there are solutions and consequences to her actions. She will stack toys and leave them or push a toy somewhere for a purpose.
- Help your child categorize objects, such as putting all the balls in one bucket and all the cars in another.

Social

- Let your child imitate what you are doing (for example, stirring or pushing a play lawn-mower).
- Take your child on outings that stimulate conversation, such as walks to see the animals or flowers, trips to the zoo, or shopping.
- Play interactive games, such as hide-and-seek.
- Show your child how to cooperate when building with blocks or decorating cookies.

2 to 3 Years of Age

Gross Motor

- Encourage your child to go through homemade obstacle courses: crawl through large packing boxes, walk on a chalk line, roll up and down a grassy hill.
- Have your child ride a tricycle.
- Play bounce and catch with a large ball.
- Encourage your child to throw a ball at a target on the wall.

Fine Motor

- Let your child unscrew the lid of a plastic jar.
- "Finger-paint" using shaving cream on the bathtub walls.
- Let your child cut with rounded-tip scissors.
- Provide your child with washable watercolors for painting.
- Make sewing cards out of cardboard and let your preemie practice sewing with yarn.

Communication

- With your child as the main character, tell make-believe or true stories.
- Repeat new words over and over.
- Talk with your child often. ("I like this kind of ice cream!")
- Read together every day, and let your child see you read often.
- To increase vocabulary, use specific names for things and feelings. Do not overuse pronouns, such as "it," "they," "that," and "this."
- Be descriptive. ("Let's put this thermometer in your mouth and see if you are too hot," instead of, "Put this in your mouth.")
- Avoid asking too many questions that may overwhelm your child.

Cognitive

- Encourage your child to match pictures with real objects, such as a picture of a ball with a real ball.
- Encourage simple associations, such as putting toothpaste with toothbrush or sock with shoe.
- Have your child sort objects, such as things to eat in one bucket and items to wear in another.
- Show your child how to draw a circle by holding her hand and making a circular motion.
- Stand back and let your child try over and over to complete a task until she completes it herself.

Social

- Encourage your child to dress without help.
- Let your child play dress-up and pretend to be an imaginary person.

- Have playmates over and encourage sharing.
- Help your child imitate things you do, such as "shaving" or "cooking."

YOUR IMPORTANT ROLE

RESEARCH SHOWS THAT parent involvement is the most important element for enhancing a preterm infant's development. When assisting your child with needed exercises and during playtime, you learn about your child's strengths and weaknesses as well as likes and dislikes. Only a parent can develop this unique insight—you see your child as a whole little person, whereas professionals often focus on specific healthcare needs.

Communicating your knowledge about your child can help doctors and therapists better understand her. With your assistance, specialists can create a complete developmental plan for your child that encompasses all her individual needs and encourages her to reach her fullest potential.

PART FIVE

Your School-aged Preemie

PART FIVE

Introduction

FOR YOUR CHILD who had such a fragile beginning and for you who lovingly helped your child grow and develop, the first day of school should be celebrated. Starting school is a big milestone for any parent and child, but you have the right to feel especially proud.

When school starts, you may feel as if you are closing the door to your child's "preemie-hood" and can finally move forward. Or you may have difficulty letting go of the past, particularly if there are ongoing concerns. The best thing you can do for your school-aged preemie (with or without special needs) is to get involved in the classroom and become an equal partner with his educators. The chapters in part 5 will help you do this. Chapter 14 addresses the common concerns of parents whose preemies are entering the preschool and kindergarten years. Chapter 15 focuses on the special education process. Both chapters can help you start your child's education off right.

CHAPTER FOURTEEN

Off to School He Goes

YOUR FORMER PREEMIE is almost old enough to begin preschool—you both have come a long way since those early homecoming days. Now you have new questions and concerns regarding your child's education and future. Many of your questions are probably not much different from those of term parents: Is a prekindergarten program necessary? Is my child developmentally ready to begin school? What type of classroom would be best for my preschooler? For your child who may have lingering effects from his preterm birth, the answers to these questions can be more complicated.

Your child may have special concerns (such as difficulties fighting off respiratory illnesses or easily becoming overstimulated) that may affect when or where to start preschool. Perhaps you wonder if other children will tease your developmentally delayed or petite child and if you should postpone the start of school. Many once medically fragile children have difficulty separating from their parents, and this may concern you.

When wondering whether to start a preschool program, consider the benefits. If your child was kept apart from other children during his germ-susceptible years, a preschool environment can teach him important social skills. Your child may also benefit from a little time away from you, especially if he suffers from mild separation anxiety. (If you are an overly protective parent, short separations may be good for you, too.) Some doctors even say exposing your child to common childhood germs found in preschools can help your former preemie build his immunities prior to the more important kindergarten year.

You should also consider that many educational experts believe prekindergarten programs have become the "equalizers" of skill development for children. A good preschool can help your delayed child develop skills, and preschool teachers may identify problem areas before elementary school. It is easier to get help in the preschool years, or postpone the start of elementary school, than it is to redo a grade later.

If you choose not to send your child to preschool, he can learn prekindergarten social and intellectual skills through other activities. A developmental therapist can also suggest activities. By exposing your child to other children (in addition to siblings), he can learn important social skills.

The following pages provide answers to some other questions you may have regarding preschool.

I know that sending my preemie to school is a move I'm making for the good of my child. However, I feel as if I'm standing at the edge of an Olympic-sized swimming pool with my toes curled desperately over the edge. I'm scared of what I might find after I dive in. I must dive though. I know this. And I know that doing so will not be half as bad as the anguish I'm experiencing standing on the edge, contemplating all that I might encounter.

—*Sandy, mother of 34-weeker Jimbo*

■

My three-year-old preemie started a prekindergarten program three days a week for two hours a day. She has learned to count to ten, writes and colors with her left hand, and can cut straight lines with her right hand. She has memorized two fairy tales. I can remember so vividly how my only hope was for her to breathe on her own.

—*Jessica, mother of 26-weeker Carolyn*

At what age should my former preemie start preschool?

By three and four years of age all children—preterm and full-term—vary greatly in their development. Deciding preschool readiness by correcting your child's age (deducting the number of weeks or months born early) is not recommended. A three-year-old former preemie born in September may be socially and developmentally prepared to start preschool, while his four-year-old term neighbor may not be ready.

Later in this chapter you will find lists of developmental skills preschoolers learn. Use these as *guides* for deciding if your child is ready to start preschool or needs an extra year of learning at home. You can also discuss preschool readiness with your child's doctor and developmental specialist, an early childhood educator, and family and friends.

If your child has significant health or developmental concerns, you may want to consider postponing preschool for a year. He may need an extra year of growing and learning at home before starting school.

I debated whether to start my daughter in preschool when she was eligible or put it off for a year. The big clincher for me was something my pediatrician said: "Except in cases where there is an actual physical or mental delay due to an early start, please do not hold your child's prematurity against her." Since preschool is hardly a high-pressured learning experience, I decided to start preschool at age two and a half. I'll decide in two years if she's ready for kindergarten.

—MONICA, MOTHER OF 33-WEEKER ELAINE

■

I chose to start Paul in preschool a year later than he was eligible because he didn't seem emotionally or developmentally ready when he was three. He also caught colds every other week and I knew starting preschool would expose him to even more illnesses. I thought it would be an advantage if he was one of the older kids in kindergarten. As it turned out, he missed a lot of preschool due to illness. When he entered kindergarten, he fought colds off and seemed right on track developmentally. He wasn't the smallest kid in the class either!

—WENDY, MOTHER OF 28-WEEKER PAUL

What type of preschool would be best for my former preemie?

There are many different kinds of preschools in various settings, including those operated by local schools, those sponsored by federal agencies, such as Head Start and early intervention preschools, and those run by nonprofit organizations, such as churches. Some employers offer preschools, some are owned and operated by individuals or franchises, and still others are run by parents. Daycare centers sometimes offer morning preschool programs, too. With so many to choose from, you should find one suited to your child.

When selecting a preschool, consider your child's personality. Does your child feel uncomfortable in a large group? Then perhaps a small home preschool would suit him. Does your child need a lot of active time with outdoor activities? Then you will want to make sure the preschool offers playground equipment and plenty of free playtime. If your child does not like a lot of noise and stimulation, a small parent-run preschool may be a better choice.

You should make sure the preschool teacher is qualified to care for any of your child's health or developmental needs and is comfortable doing so. Children who have more severe special needs and are receiving early intervention services will most likely be referred to a special education preschool, discussed in the next chapter.

You should visit any preschool you are considering and talk with the teacher. Visiting a class and observing the teacher and students can tell you a lot about the classroom. Asking parents who have children in the program about their experiences can also help in your decision.

TEN SIGNS OF A GREAT PRESCHOOL

The National Association for the Education of Young Children (NAEYC) suggests you look for these signs of a good preschool classroom:

1. Children spend most of their time playing and working with materials or other children. They do not wander aimlessly, and they are not expected to sit quietly for long periods of time.
2. Children have access to various activities throughout the day. Look for assorted building blocks and other construction materials, props for pretend play, picture books, paints, and other art materials, and table toys, such as matching games, pegboards, and puzzles. Children should not all be doing the same thing at the same time.
3. Teachers work with individual children, small groups, and the whole group at different times during the day. They do not spend all their time with the whole group.
4. The classroom is decorated with children's original artwork.
5. Children learn numbers and the alphabet in the context of their everyday experiences. The natural world of plants and animals and meaningful activities like cooking, taking attendance, or serving snack provide the basis for learning activities.
6. Children work on projects and have long periods of time (at least one hour) to play and explore. Worksheets are used little if at all.
7. Children have an opportunity to play outside every day. Outdoor play is never sacrificed for more instruction time.
8. Teachers read books to children individually or in small groups throughout the day, not just at group storytime.
9. Curriculum is adapted for those who are ahead as well as those who need additional help. Teachers recognize that children's different backgrounds and experiences mean that they do not learn the same things at the same time in the same way.
10. Children and their parents look forward to school. Parents feel secure about sending their children to the preschool. Children are happy to attend; they do not cry regularly or complain of feeling sick.

My former preemie and I have not been separated much. How can I make the transition easier for both of us?

Children with past or present special needs often have difficulty separating from their parents, and parents of once medically fragile infants can have anxieties about entrusting their child's care to another adult. To make the transition to preschool easier, try the following tips from parents and educators.

Before school starts

- Read books about starting preschool.
- Play out a preschool day at home so your child will know what to expect: have free playtime, a lesson, snack time, and quiet time.
- Get to know at least one classmate.

- Provide opportunities for your child to interact with other children in community settings, such as the library, the pool, or the playground.
- Drive by the preschool often and point out the building to your child. If possible, let your child play on the school's playground.
- Encourage your preschooler to share his concerns or fears about starting school.
- Help your child develop appropriate self-help skills, such as putting on his own coat and shoes.
- If possible, visit the preschool together and meet the teacher. Talk to the teacher about any concerns you or your child have.
- If your child has not been left with a sitter much, or has not attended daycare, hire a suitable childcare provider for a few hours a week about a month before preschool starts. This will help your child get used to being apart from you and help you get accustomed to another adult caregiver.

After school starts

- Encourage your child to take a special comfort item, such as a stuffed animal or family picture, to preschool.
- Let the teacher know about any of your concerns, then follow up often on your child's progress.
- Spend some time in the classroom observing.
- Always act positive about school and expect your child to do well.

YOUR PRESCHOOL PREEMIE'S ABILITIES

TAKING INTO CONSIDERATION that the average range for three- to five-year-old development is wide, many preemies are developmentally equal to their full-term peers by preschool age. In other words, their communication, thinking, physical, and social abilities are within the guidelines of "normal" preschool development.

Former preemies who are slower in catching up to their full-term peers usually have had more severe medical problems. These children may take longer to speak clearly, to toilet-train, or to hold a pencil. If your child is delayed below what is considered developmentally "normal" for his age, or in the low range of "normal," he can benefit from added support. For example, if he has poor fine motor skills, you can provide him with at-home activities or professional help from a developmental specialist.

To evaluate your child's development, it is helpful to know what most preschoolers do. Following are typical preschool abilities, common warning signs you should know, and suggestions for enhancing your preschooler's development. Use these lists as *guides,* keeping in mind that your child may not be doing all the tasks listed.

I know that all kids have quite a range in the development of different types of skills—motor, social, and mental—but I feel that my twins have an even greater range. Their physical size and muscle strength prevent them from doing some things that other kids their age can do.

—JESSICA, MOTHER OF 26-WEEKER TWINS MICHAEL AND MICHELLE

COMMUNICATION SKILLS

At preschool age, some former preemies have speech and language delays, including difficulties with articulation (producing sounds), expressing their thoughts, creating complex sentences, and controlling the volume of their voices. Sometimes a child will speak well at home, yet have difficulties at school. A child can become very frustrated, even angry, because of his inability to communicate appropriately.

At about three to four years of age, your child should be able to:

- tell you about everyday happenings or tell you a short story;
- name one color;
- point to "big," "little," "full," and "empty";
- follow simple directions, such as "put the block under the table";
- ask questions to get information;
- repeat rhymes, songs, or commercial jingles;
- answer simple questions, such as "What are you doing?" or "What are you wearing?"
- answer slightly more complex questions, such as "What do you do when your hands are dirty?" and
- ask for help when needed.

WARNING SIGNS

Consult your doctor or a speech therapist if your four-year-old:

- has difficulty remembering various sounds;
- uses a vague vocabulary (He often says "thing" or "you know" instead of using the specific word);
- uses a lot of gestures in place of words;
- uses very short sentences or no sentences at all;
- has trouble detecting differences and similarities in sounds;
- has difficulty understanding directions;
- has difficulty answering simple questions; and/or
- speaks in such a way that only you can understand him.

At about four to five years of age, your child should be able to:

- understand more complex questions, such as "Why do you brush your teeth?";
- ask "who" and "why" questions;
- use contractions ("aren't") and the past tense correctly;
- begin to use complex sentences;
- name the colors red, blue, yellow, and green;
- say sentences with four to five words;
- tell stories;
- understand "behind," "beside," and "in front of";
- recognize similarities and differences in pictures;
- speak about imaginary conditions, such as "I hope" or "When I grow up"; and
- follow directions with two to three steps.

You can help your three- to five-year-old's language development by:

- strengthening his vocabulary by talking with him often;
- modeling good speech to your child;
- taking trips to the library each week;
- providing books at home and in the car;
- letting your child see you read books, magazines, and newspapers;
- asking your child questions;
- encouraging your child to verbally request things, rather than just pointing;
- reading stories every day and writing down letters that your child dictates (This will help him build his vocabulary and show him the relationship between printed and spoken words.);
- making up silly poems with your child, helping him recognize similar sounds;
- weaving the meanings of letters into daily activities (For example, ask your child, "Do you want to play with the toy that starts with a *B*?"); and
- playing "I Spy" or "I'm thinking of" using a real object, then a picture of an object, then by describing the object ("I'm thinking of something yellow. Monkeys like to eat it. What is it?").

■ ■ ■

Thinking Skills and General Knowledge

Former preemies may have difficulty with cognitive (thinking) abilities at preschool age. They may have trouble making associations between words and objects, problems with short-term or long-term memory, and difficulty with organizational skills.

At about three years of age, your child should be able to:

- draw circles and copy a cross or square;
- do simple puzzles and group things according to size, color, or use (eating versus wearing);
- count a few items, such as steps or blocks;
- recognize colors by name ("Find your blue pants");
- respond to "why" questions;
- use sentences in conversations;
- talk about things he sees in a book or tell you about a recent experience; and
- create short pretend play sequences (take the food out, "cook" the food, and serve it).

You can help your three-year-old's thinking abilities by:

- showing him shapes in pictures and items found around the house;
- having him sort small toys or objects by size, color, or use (foods versus clothing);
- letting your child explain pictures in books;
- encouraging your child to tell you a story about a recent experience;
- playing with your child to create longer sequences of pretend play (an order to the play, rather than random playing); and
- practicing puzzle skills using a talk-out-loud approach ("Here is the car. The car goes here. Just move it a little").

WARNING SIGNS

Consult your doctor or a developmental specialist if your five-year-old:

- has not learned basic preschool concepts, such as colors, counting, and shapes;
- cannot answer simple questions related to his own experiences ("What did you do at the park today?");
- seems to forget learned concepts easily or has difficulty retaining information; and/or
- plays randomly and rarely engages in sequence play (taking out the food, "cooking" it, and serving it).

At about four years of age, your child should be able to:

- draw circles, squares, straight lines, and possibly triangles;
- do puzzles involving several shapes that are mixed up with others;
- compare sizes (smaller, larger, bigger, same);
- count items (Slowly increase the number of objects up to ten);
- talk about stories, pictures and everyday experiences (Ask your child to tell you about something that recently happened in the same order in which it occurred.);
- retell stories and practice nursery rhymes and songs; and
- create more complex pretend play by having your child assume roles or characters in a play.

You can encourage your four-year-old's thinking abilities and knowledge by:

- practicing with more difficult puzzles using the talk-out-loud approach ("Here are kitty's eyes. Put her eyes here. Move them just a little.");
- helping your child identify various sizes of stuffed animals, pots and pans, and trees;
- letting your child help you prepare meals by measuring cups of water and teaspoons of sugar;
- encouraging your child to count items, such as fruit or cans at the grocery store;
- letting your child sort socks (teaches sorting and classification);
- encouraging left-to-right movement during drawing (an important skill for later reading and writing);
- teaching similarities and differences by asking questions ("How are these two cups the same? Mommy thinks it's because you can use them both for drinking. Do you think Mommy's right? How are they different? Is one big and one little?");
- helping your child identify what does not belong in a group ("Does this shoe belong with pots and pans?");
- encouraging your child to pretend to be a character from a book or help him plan out a skit; and
- taking educational trips to the fire station, nature center, or local children's museum.

Physical Skills

Physical (gross and fine motor) skill delays in the early school years are common in children born prematurely. Your child may have trouble holding a pencil or crayon in the correct manner, stringing beads, or carrying a cup. He may be slower than his peers at riding a bicycle, kicking a ball, or using playground equipment.

▪ ▪ ▪

Gross (large) motor skills

At about four years of age, your child should be able to:

- climb jungle gyms and other appropriately sized playground equipment;
- alternate feet while climbing stairs without support;
- jump up to two inches (but may have trouble coordinating the act of jumping with the act of reaching up with one hand to touch an object);
- throw a ball with some body rotation and maybe a step forward;
- stand on one foot; and
- pedal a tricycle.

You can encourage your preschooler's large motor abilities by:

- providing your child with opportunities to run, jump, and climb at home and through outside activities;
- playing kickball and catch often;
- providing your child with an age-appropriate bike; and
- letting your child bounce on large sofa cushions for developing balance.

WARNING SIGNS

Consult your doctor or a developmental specialist if your five-year-old:

- has difficulty with many of the tasks listed in this section;
- falls frequently;
- has trouble judging space (For example, he has difficulty putting a book back on a shelf or setting a cup down without spilling.);
- avoids gross or fine motor play; and/or
- participates in only one fine motor or gross motor activity (For example, he rides a bike, but refuses to walk on a balance beam or to swing.).

Fine (small) motor skills

At about four years of age, your child should be able to:

- open and close large buttons;
- complete simple puzzles with four or five pieces;
- cut on a line;
- copy simple shapes, such as a circle or square; and
- use a fork or spoon with minimal spills.

■ ■ ■

You can encourage your preschooler's small motor abilities by:

- having your child color, draw, and trace objects;
- letting your child play with clay or dough;
- doing puzzles with your child;
- encouraging your child to use safety scissors;
- helping your child string beads on yarn (Encourage him to pick up beads with index finger and thumb.); and
- asking your child to help you cook (tear up lettuce leaves and cut olives with a table knife).

SELF-HELP SKILLS

Your child's motor skill delays can affect his self-help abilities. Your former preemie may have difficulty washing and drying his hands, getting dressed, or he may take longer to become toilet-trained.

By four to five years of age, your child should be able to:

- use the toilet and be accident-free during the day;
- wash and dry hands;
- fasten large buttons and zip up a coat;
- dress unassisted;
- get a drink or snack on his own; and
- help with simple household chores.

WARNING SIGNS

Consult your doctor or a developmental specialist if your five-year-old:

- is not toilet-trained during the day;
- is frustrated by most self-help tasks;
- seems overly dependent on you or other adults for assistance with self-help tasks;
- is frequently aggressive or destructive;
- frequently withdraws from or avoids social interactions;
- has consistent difficulty acting appropriately and following rules; and/or
- seems to be angry or sad most of the time.

■ ■ ■

You can enhance your preschooler's self-help skills by:

- giving specific positive feedback ("Wow! You've got your shoe on!" will provide better results than "Why can't you get yourself dressed?"); and
- giving your child simple directions ("Please take your book to your room.").

Social Skills

Children born prematurely sometimes need more time to develop their social skills. Delays in developmental areas, including communication and motor abilities, can affect your child's social development.

By five years of age, your child should be able to:

- play and usually share with other children;
- follow simple rules;
- maintain some self-control; and
- understand simple if-then statements related to behavior ("If you throw the truck, then I'll have to put it away.").

You can enhance your preschooler's social skills by:

- providing your child with opportunities to play with other children while you supervise;
- providing limits, simple directions, and guidance during play;
- listening and acknowledging your child's feelings and helping him read others' feelings (For example, take opportunities to discuss how a friend that your child just played with may have felt. Was he sad, happy, or angry? Expressing one's own emotions is an important social skill, and developing empathy is important to getting along with others.); and
- asking your child to make a sad or happy face and discussing what might make him happy or sad.

BEYOND PRESCHOOL: IS YOUR FORMER PREEMIE READY FOR KINDERGARTEN?

Kindergarten readiness has become an important topic for all parents. Educational research shows children who start out well during the early grades continue to do well in later grades. A child's self-esteem from school performance is also critical during these early school years. Those who feel good about school initially, usually feel good about it during the higher grades.

To give your child the best educational start, you may wonder if you should start his kindergarten year by the school district's cut-off age or wait a year. (Some school districts mandate a certain age.) Even though correcting for gestational age is no longer done by medical and educational professionals, you may wonder if you should take into consideration your child's early birth.

Experts say what you should really consider is your child's *developmental readiness.* Consider the preschool abilities mentioned earlier in this chapter and your child's progress. A developmental evaluation can be helpful. If your child is delayed in one or more areas, another preschool year may help him overcome difficulties. If your child is developing within the normal range, he is probably ready to learn and grow in elementary school.

> *My husband and I have gone back and forth about when our twins should begin kindergarten. They make the cut off with their birth date, but wouldn't have if they had been born on time. They have speech delays and are small for their size. It was a difficult decision, but after two years of preschool, we felt they were ready cognitively for kindergarten. I just hope they are tall enough to reach the drinking fountain!*
>
> —SUZANNE, *MOTHER OF 28-WEEKER TWINS* AARON *AND* BENJAMIN

YOUR FORMER PREEMIE'S MEDICAL HISTORY: TO TELL OR NOT TO TELL

WHEN YOUR FORMER preemie begins his formal education, you will probably wonder if you should share his birth history with the school personnel. Certainly you want to provide your child's educators with information that will help them best teach your child, but you also do not want them to label your child "slow" and expect him to lag behind his peers. Fearful of a label, some preemie parents do not share their children's medical history unless a significant delay, behavior, or medical problem needs explaining. Other parents are quick to tell the prematurity story so teachers will work toward strengthening their children's weak areas.

Some educators believe you should share your child's medical history for several reasons. In most cases, teachers can better serve your family knowing of your child's at-risk condition. Second, your child's medical history communicates your family's emotional background. Learning the ordeal your family has endured tells the school a little about where you as a parent are coming from. Finally, research identifies common behavior and learning problems among NICU graduates and, by knowing about your child's past, informed educators can be alert to signs of potential problems. (You may need to educate your child's teachers about prematurity and the increased risk of behavior and learning problems.)

KINDERGARTEN-READINESS GUIDELINES

Each school district has different guidelines for evaluating school readiness. Some have formal screenings to assess a prospective kindergartner's readiness; others simply provide parents with a list of school-readiness skills. (Some school districts mandate that a child start school at a certain cut-off age.) It is important to note that a school-readiness list should serve only as a *guide* for helping you and the school evaluate your child's abilities. It does not mean that your child should go to kindergarten because he has mastered all the skills, or should not go to kindergarten if he has not achieved them.

The following is a common guide used in schools:

BEFORE STARTING KINDERGARTEN, YOUR CHILD SHOULD:

- speak in complete sentences;
- express himself clearly (describe an incident in an understandable way);
- like being read to and/or like looking at books by himself;
- use scissors to cut a straight line;
- sit for fifteen minutes to work on a fun activity;
- understand rhyming words;
- follow simple directions;
- wash and dress with little assistance;
- take turns with others and understand sharing;
- respond correctly to more complex "what," "why," and "when" questions;
- know how to express anger without hitting or biting; and
- play well with other children most of the time.

If your child does not meet one or more of the above criteria, you may want to consult your doctor, a developmental expert, or an educator. Postponing kindergarten because of one or two delayed skills may not be the best decision for your child. School services may actually help your child overcome difficulties, and holding your child back may even hinder his development of other important skills learned in school.

After consulting experts, rely on your instincts. After all, you know your child better than anyone else.

It is your right as a parent not to reveal your child's past to the school personnel. You may want to get to know your child's teacher better before sharing your child's birth history. Waiting a few months into the school year can also let the teacher get to know your child without the preemie label.

Joe's kindergarten year was a disaster. I told the teacher ahead of time that he was born prematurely. She expected him to be developmentally delayed, so she automatically put him in slow groups, spoke down to him, and generally treated us like "you poor dears." If I had to do it over again, I wouldn't have told the school. Fortunately, his first grade teacher didn't label him and he excelled in her class. She still keeps track of "her star student."

—ANGEL, MOTHER OF 28-WEEKER JOE

■

I told the school that my daughter was a preemie. There was a question on the application asking about medical and birth history. I haven't felt that the teacher has treated my daughter any differently. In fact, at a conference the teacher told me how Michelle wasn't quite at age-level for some tasks, but quickly reassured me that Michelle was in the developmental range. She said, "It's tempting to attribute everything to Michelle's prematurity, but it's far more likely that most delays are normal lags in development."

—*KAREN, MOTHER OF 31-WEEKER MICHELLE*

SCHOOL-AGED LEARNING AND BEHAVIORAL PROBLEMS

ALL ASPECTS OF your child's development are interrelated. Progress (or lack of it) in one area can affect the other areas. For instance, if your child has a hearing problem, it can affect his speech and language skills, which in turn can affect his learning abilities and behavior in school.

Children born prematurely are at risk for specific learning disabilities. Some problems may be caused by underlying cognitive issues (like memory) and/or by problems with understanding and using more complex language skills that school requires. For example, a child may have difficulty remembering spoken facts and details, solving more complex problems, forming relationships among concepts and ideas, or making predictions about what will happen next. Keeping in mind that language is the foundation to all learning, be aware that children born prematurely sometimes have difficulty listening, thinking, speaking, reading, writing, spelling, or doing math.

Former preemies are also at risk for behavior disorders, which can affect school performance. These include impulsiveness, hyperactivity, low frustration tolerance, and poor emotional control.

Because your school-aged preemie is at greater risk for learning and behavioral problems, you should keep a close eye on his performance. Discuss any behavior or learning concerns with your child's teacher or doctor. An evaluation by a developmental or behavioral specialist may be needed.

HE'S OFF TO SCHOOL! WHY DO YOU FEEL SO SAD?

YOUR "BABY" IS finally in school and you have a little quiet time for yourself. Along with your relief and pride, you may feel sad, even a little frightened.

Most parents feel a sense of loss and sadness when their child's growing independence becomes more obvious. For you, a parent of a once medically fragile baby, this sorrow may be stronger. Memories of past difficulties can come flooding back as you fill out your child's medical history or drop off your child's special medications.

Fear is also a common emotion when school starts. As your child's education begins, you may wonder if new preemie-related issues will surface. It is also a little frightening to entrust your once fragile child to the school personnel.

You can ease your concerns by becoming involved in your child's classroom and by getting to know his educators. The more confidence you have in the school, the better you will feel. You may even start enjoying that time alone.

CHAPTER FIFTEEN

Your Child with Special Needs

HAVING A CHILD start school is a major transition for any parent, but it can be especially difficult for a parent of a child with special needs. You worry about the quality of school services and how well educators will understand your child's needs. You wonder how your former preemie will be accepted by his teachers and the other students.

Becoming an informed and active parent will help you feel better about the early school years. Learning about the special education process, which can seem overwhelming, is your first step. This chapter should answer many of your initial questions.

We just got the news that Brittany will need to start special education in the fall and my feelings of guilt have come back to haunt me. I wonder if this would have happened if she had been full-term. I was prepared as I knew statistically it was likely to happen, but it still hurts.

—*KATY, MOTHER OF 28-WEEKER BRITTANY*

■

One of the wonderful aspects of the special education program was the responsibility it lifted from my shoulders. I had previously taken care of Tim's education at home, and the various teachers and therapists came to us for most of the activities. Juggling the various schedules of all the teachers, therapists, and doctors was a nightmare. Keeping up with the work they assigned us was impossible. I just wanted some time to be a mom.

—*MARY, MOTHER OF 26-WEEKER TIM*

Is my former preemie eligible for special education?

According to Federal law, if your former preemie is determined to be eligible, he is entitled to a free appropriate public education (commonly referred to as FAPE), including supports and services, and starting at age three. Under the guidelines of the Individuals with Disabilities Education Act (IDEA), each state, and often each school district, sets its own criteria for eligibility.

Since eligibility requirements vary from state to state and school district to school district, it is important to familiarize yourself with special education information provided by your state and local agencies. To find out about your area's programs, call your neighborhood elementary school and ask to speak to the principal or the school counselor. You can also contact the National Information Center for Children and Youth with Disabilities at (800) 695-0285, and ask for the resource sheet listing special education contacts for your state.

What are my child's educational needs?

When your child is evaluated for eligibility, his educational needs will also be assessed by a multidisciplinary team. In addition to you, this team may include: a special education teacher; a psychologist; an early intervention specialist; a school social worker; a speech-language pathologist; an occupational therapist; and a physical therapist. Information, such as doctors' reports, your child's medical history, developmental tests, and observations from you, should also be used in the assessment.

Many different types of assessment tools are used in the evaluation process. As a parent, you have the right to approve the evaluation tools chosen. For preschoolers, a play-based assessment, involving games, puzzles, pictures, and blocks, is often used. Assessment tools for older children are typically based on the suspected problem area or areas. Schools generally allow for a very wide range of "normal," so if they detect a concern, it is a red flag.

If you want to know more about the assessments chosen for your child, speak to the evaluator or another member of the team prior to the evaluation. Ideally, a meeting will be held to inform you about tests and to obtain consent, but often this is done over the telephone. Following are some questions you may want to ask:

- What assessment tools are you considering for my child and why?
- What do you hope to learn from this assessment, and how will the results be used to help plan my child's education?
- Is the assessment fair to my child? Will his cultural background or disability affect his ability to perform the tasks?
- May I see a sample of the assessment? (This is your right as a parent.)
- How can I help prepare my child for the assessment and evaluation process?
- Who will perform the evaluation, and is he qualified?
- Where will the assessment be given, and at what time? (The evaluation must be given at a time and place convenient for both parents.)

You can prepare your child for the evaluation by making sure he gets a good night's rest and a nutritious meal before the test. Try to remain calm yourself so your child will too. During the assessment, make sure your child knows where you are and that you trust the person administering the assessment.

You can prepare your older child for the evaluation by explaining that it will help his teachers make learning easier for him. You should not use the word "test," as it may frighten your child. Tell your child some activities will be easy and some will be difficult. Encourage him to do his best but not to worry too much. By knowing what to expect, your child should feel less anxious and perform better.

How will my child's educational needs be met?

Once your child is found eligible for special education services and his needs have been determined, an Individualized Education Program (IEP), similar to the Individualized Family Service Plan (IFSP) discussed in chapter 13, must be written. An IEP is a written education plan designed to meet the unique needs of your child. It lists special services your child will receive and also includes:

- your child's present levels of functioning, achievements, performance, and strengths, and his needs in these areas: physical abilities; communication abilities; thinking abilities; social and emotional behavior; developmental or educational growth;
- annual goals with measurable short-term objectives;
- specific special education and related services to be provided to your child, including a description of both the extent to which your child will participate in any regular education program and any special instructional media and materials needed to implement the IEP (According to IDEA, "related services" may include: transportation; physical therapy; social work services; psychological services; speech therapy; occupational therapy; counseling services; extended school year; audiology; recreation; assistive technology; adaptive equipment; therapeutic recreation; and rehabilitation counseling;
- the date your child will begin receiving special education services and the expected length and frequency of services;
- a justification for the type of educational placement that your child will have (According to law, the placement should be in the "least restrictive environment," commonly referred to as LRE.)
- a list of the individuals responsible for implementing the IEP (This will be by professional title, not by actual name); and
- appropriate objective criteria and evaluation procedures and schedules for determining, at least on an annual basis, whether the short-term instructional objectives are being achieved (The parent or school can request a review at any time.)

In addition to you, the team writing your child's IEP may include: your child's special and regular education teachers; the special education administrator or a qualified representative of the local education agency; other individuals who may be helpful to the IEP planning process (such as your child's occupational, physical, or speech therapist); a member of the evaluation team who is knowledgeable about the evaluation results of your child; friends and extended family, if you wish; and any other person who has knowledge or special expertise regarding your child (such as a daycare provider).

> *One of the best aspects of an IEP is the chance to meet with a team of people who bring many experiences to the table. We learn from each other. As each one presents their piece, a clearer picture of Alex and how we can better serve him begins to emerge. Sometimes hearing an observation from a resource person can accomplish more than all the words you can say about your child. Sometimes a pattern will emerge—a fine motor delay or an attention delay—that is having multiple impacts in different settings.*
>
> *We are known for our marathon-length IEPs. I ask a lot of questions, review each goal, and add my own requests. Every year there seems to be one or two issues that require a lot of negotiation.*
>
> *It can be overwhelming. You sit there, alone, as expert after expert explains what is "wrong" with your child. They use a lot of jargon, too. My husband, who is used to attending a number of high-powered meetings each day, was absolutely silent and intimidated during his first IEP meeting.*
>
> *IEPs are exhausting, but when they work, I leave feeling like we have a unified team who will really focus on my child the following year.*
>
> —*Allison, mother of 26-weeker Alex*

PARENT TIPS:

Getting the Most Out of IEP Meetings

Some parents who have participated in the IEP process use words like "intimidating," "frustrating," and "confusing" to describe their experiences. Others find the IEP process "enlightening" and "helpful." Most likely you will feel a little anxious when you face the IEP team. Adding to that stress is the fact you are about to make major decisions regarding your child's future. By knowing what to expect and being prepared, you can make the most of your IEP meetings. Consider the suggestions given below from parents who have been there.

Before the Meeting

- Come prepared with a notebook of information and records on your child. You can even send a copy in advance. Some things you might want to include in the notebook are: your child's evaluations and assessments, school progress reports, medical records (including hospital discharge summary), therapy reports, correspondence with the school or medical professionals, homework samples, and your own report/assessment of your child.

- Meet with your child's teacher and therapists. Get a feel for your child's strengths, weaknesses, and current levels of accomplishments. You can do some of this by telephone.
- Write down your ideas about your child's accomplishments and weaknesses. Try to determine what your goals are before the meeting. Are there any holes that are not being addressed in your child's education? Do you have any unanswered questions?
- Observe your child and see what things he is trying to do. Make those skills foremost in the IEP goals. Also, watch for frustration-causing experiences—these may be areas with which your child needs help.
- Ask for evaluation and assessment results before the meeting so you can prepare. (This is your right as a parent.)
- If given a choice of where to have the meeting, hold it in a comfortable location.
- Before the meeting, think about what your child needs for success in school and what goals you would like your child to work toward in the next year. Also, think about what your family's priorities are. For example, it may be more important to you that your child works more on his fine motor skills, such as handwriting, and less on his gross motor skills in physical education class.
- Call the special education supervisor or school principal before the meeting and ask to be introduced to the team members. Even a short phone call will ease the tension of that first meeting.
- Request a sample IEP form and become familiar with the information that it contains.

During the Meeting

- Provide the team with insights about your child—what he is like at home, after school, and on vacations.
- Discuss your child's strengths as well as his needs. The tests your child took may not represent your child as a whole person.
- Make suggestions in any area of planning.
- If you do not understand something, ask for an explanation.
- Make sure the supports and services the team discusses for your child are based on his individual strengths and abilities, specific difficulties, and/or learning needs—not on his disability. If you do not feel that this is what the team is doing, speak up and redirect the conversation.
- Document what is said at the IEP meeting. Get agreements in writing, as required by law.
- Ask the team what you can do at home to support your child's IEP.

- Ask for intermittent "report cards" on your child's progress and a midyear meeting to review your child's IEP.
- Pay close attention to the goals set for your child's IEP and make sure they are not things he can already do or is near mastering. Also, make sure they are not unrealistic.
- If you become emotionally upset during the IEP meeting, know that most members of an IEP team will understand if you ask for a brief recess.
- You do not have to sign the IEP at the meeting. You may want to take a few days to review it, then sign or request changes.

After the Meeting

- Closely monitor your child's progress and discuss any concerns with an appropriate member of the team.
- Keep the lines of communication open at all times.
- Communicate your child's feelings and concerns to the IEP team.

Where will my child's needs be met?

Your child's IEP team, which includes you, should create the best educational program for your child. If you have several options for your child's schooling, observe the programs and talk with participants—parents, educators, children—to form your own opinion.

YOUR CHILD'S EDUCATIONAL OPTIONS

Preschool Options

Some of your choices for educating your preschooler with special needs are:

- at home (especially if your child is medically fragile);
- in a good daycare center;
- in a regular preschool;
- in a regular preschool with a special needs teacher provided by the county;
- in a regular preschool with support services periodically visiting the school;
- in a special education preschool;
- in a special education preschool for part of the day and in a regular preschool for another part; or
- in Head Start, a government-funded preschool program that incorporates children with special needs (Head Start primarily serves preschoolers who meet certain low-income eligibility requirements, but 10 percent of participants must be children with a diagnosed disability and 10 percent do not have to meet strict income criteria. Contact your local school system to see if your community has a Head Start program.)

When Emily was approaching three years old, I began to see that she was reaching the point where I could no longer provide all that she needed. Her physical limitations from cerebral palsy had prevented her from socializing with other children, and it was difficult to even find a baby-sitter. I realized she needed her world to expand beyond our home and yard, beyond shopping and visiting relatives.

Although she could have continued in her at-home early intervention program for another six months, I signed the form to transition Emily into the next level. I was strongly leaning toward her attending the center-based preschool special education program, but I needed to visit the center first.

After visiting the center, I was shocked. Emily was so far behind the other children receiving these special education services. My Emily was so much like a baby—communicating with only cries and whines, not being able to even sit without assistance. Luckily, I was able to confide in a close friend and, while doing so, I realized that Emily needed the chance to show us what she was capable of doing. Someone pointed out that in the months between our visit and the time Emily would enter the center, most of the children would be transitioned into kindergarten and many new students would enter the program. The makeup of the center would be completely different.

I thought a lot about all that Emily had not had the chance to experience. How could we possibly know what she was capable of if we didn't give her the chance? Should I really let my fear of her "failure" stop me from giving her the chance she deserved? Shouldn't I at least believe in her enough to give her a chance?

Transitioning to preschool also became a chance for me. I had not returned to work since Emily's birth and had spent most of my time caring for her and her brother. Juggling therapy appointments and doctor visits took so much of my time that I thought I might actually enjoy my children more if I were working outside the home. I looked forward to having others care for Emily for part of the day, so I could just be a mom.

Still, I had to find the courage to trust Emily's care to all these other people. I remembered those first nine weeks of Emily's life when I felt that she belonged to the hospital. It sounds silly, but I felt like I was giving her away, and I needed to convince myself that Emily would return every single day.

The first week of preschool, I stayed with Emily. I fell in love with the teacher, speech therapist, and classroom aide. I met Emily's one-on-one aide and felt totally confident with leaving my daughter in her care. I watched the metamorphosis occur as my Emily became a preschooler in front of my eyes. The first week she added two to three words a day to her vocabulary!

Once again, I have found that the only thing I had to fear was the fear itself.

—SANDY, MOTHER OF *30*-WEEKER EMILY

Elementary School Options

When considering elementary school options for your child with special needs, you will find many choices. Some of them are discussed below.

A special education classroom in a regular school

Many preschools and elementary schools have self-contained special education classrooms. Children with special needs may spend all or part of the day learning with a special education teacher in this room. They may go to a regular classroom for some subjects.

Other children with special needs may learn in a regular classroom and go to the special education classroom for part of the day. For example, a child with a learning disability may leave the classroom three days a week for reading instruction. In most cases, children with special needs are included in full-school activities like assemblies.

PARENT TIPS:

Signs of a Good Teacher

Parents suggest you look for these characteristics in a teacher:

- The teacher should be organized and accepting, and rules for the class should be clear.
- The teacher should be willing to go the extra mile to incorporate your child into classroom activities.
- The teacher should communicate with you about what your child does and does not do well.
- The teacher should be enthusiastic about working with your child and enjoy the challenge, rather than viewing your child as an interference in the classroom.

A regular classroom

According to the law and starting at age three, children with disabilities have the right to a free appropriate public education in the school setting that allows the most contact with typical children. Including disabled and non-disabled children in the classroom, often referred to as inclusion, is growing in popularity.

Including children with special needs in the classroom often takes creativity as well as the dedication of educators, support staff, and parents. In an effective inclusion program, a teacher will adapt activities to include all students, even though their individual goals may be different. Modification to classroom curriculum can allow a child with special needs to stay in the classroom with friends and meet goals. During class, an assistant may need to help a child with special needs, or the child may need to leave to receive outside related services, such as speech therapy.

Home schooling

Home schooling is another option for educating your child with special needs. According to some parents, home schooling gives their children a safe place to learn and grow in their own way and at their own pace. Home schooling allows for an individualized educational program, and there is no set curriculum that must be followed. Another benefit is home schooling provides one-on-one instruction.

Guidelines for home schooling vary from state to state. Call your state education department for more information.

A private school

If your child's needs cannot be met in your neighborhood school and the IEP team agrees that your child requires special placement, either public or private, the school district is financially responsible for that placement. However, if your neighborhood school does not agree that your child needs special placement, you must prove the district's inability to meet your child's needs in order to receive financial assistance.

There are private schools across the country that specialize in teaching children with disabilities. For a list of schools, refer to a recent edition of the *Directory for Exceptional Children* at your local library.

SOCIAL SUCCESS IS AS IMPORTANT AS EDUCATIONAL SUCCESS

YOUR CHILD IS not just "a child with special needs," but someone who needs to play, to laugh, to learn, and to make friends. Your child needs to feel that he belongs. Studies show that children with special needs who feel they "belong" in their school and class learn better than those who feel left out.

Try to provide your child with the same opportunities for a happy childhood that other children are given, and involve him in everyday school activities as much as possible. By participating in an educational plan encompassing your child's social, as well as his educational needs, your child can achieve his fullest potential.

EPILOGUE

Coping, Healing, and Finding Meaning

The emotional effects of prematurity can linger long after the physical healing of your baby. Your child's early birth and the months that followed were a traumatic event—one that does not suddenly end upon homecoming. In fact, difficult emotions can (and probably will) surface throughout your life.

Recognizing that it is normal for you to continue having troublesome feelings is the first step toward emotional healing. Next, you must give yourself time to sort through these feelings and find ways of coping. These final pages will help you get started.

COMMON EMOTIONS FOLLOWING A PREMATURE BIRTH

YOUR FEELINGS FOLLOWING your baby's birth and how you cope are unique, but it may help to know that you are not alone. Parents of children born prematurely often experience many similar emotions. Regardless of their baby's gestational age at birth and severity of illness, all preemie parents suffer a loss—the loss of a dream—and must grieve.

When your baby was born early, your expectations for a term pregnancy, a healthy newborn, and a "perfect" family were shattered. Emotional and physical preparation for your new arrival was cut short. In addition, your early parenting experiences were certainly not what you anticipated.

Grieving after a disrupting and overwhelming life experience is a natural response, and there is no time limit for how long you *should* experience feelings of grief or when you should be "over" your loss. Emotions associated with your baby's birth can occur at unexpected moments and can be triggered by many circumstances throughout life.

The following sections discuss feelings of grief that preemie parents most often experience. The brevity of the sections by no means reflects the importance of each issue. Ways of coping, including self-help measures, seeking the support of others, professional therapy, and the use of medications, follow. Your relationships with family members, who are also affected by your baby's preterm birth, are also touched upon.

> *I honestly thought that once I brought my preemie home things would be okay and that life would be better. I was surprised to feel so alone, guilty, and even angry at times. Different feelings would hit me at different times: at night when I should have been sleeping; when I saw fat and happy babies without oxygen; and when I talked with friends who seemed to think that everything was over. My beautiful baby was home, but my emotions weren't "over."*
>
> —RIA, MOTHER OF 30-WEEKER DERRICK

■

> *Every time I think our preemie days are behind us and I am "over" the emotional stress of preeclampsia, HELLP Syndrome, bedrest, an emergency*

EMOTIONAL TRIGGERS

Your emotions may be triggered when you:

- drive by or visit the hospital where your baby was hospitalized;
- hear comments about your child's size or development;
- care for your child when she is ill or hurt;
- look at baby pictures or a video taken in the NICU;
- go through your preemie's old clothes or baby book;
- see or hold a healthy term newborn and reflect on what you missed;
- remember a surgery or a diagnosis on its anniversary date;
- learn your child has a developmental delay or a new medical problem;
- meet another preemie parent or preemie (planned or unexpectedly);
- smell a hospital-like scent, such as disinfectant soap;
- read a newspaper or magazine story or see a television report about prematurity;
- celebrate your child's birthday or Mother's Day;
- recognize the anniversary date of a twin or multiple's death;
- attend a NICU reunion;
- celebrate your child's development, such as rolling over or throwing a ball;
- go to a checkup with your obstetrician;
- become pregnant again;
- reflect on your baby's homecoming, even years later;
- take your child to her first day of school; or
- learn your adult former preemie has a medical or pregnancy concern.

C-section, a 25-weeker, and eighty-four days in the NICU, something happens that wrings my heart and yanks it back to the reality of it all.

As I recently watched a baby being baptized, my heart skipped a beat and tears came to my eyes. I am so thankful for my beautiful little girl, but I wonder if I will ever get over the sorrow and grief associated with her premature birth. When I explain what happened to others, I listen to myself and realize I must feel responsible for what she went through, whether I had control over it or not. I know I will continue to grieve for a long time.

—*Tracey, mother of 25-weeker Taylor*

Shock and Denial: "This Can't Be Happening to Me"

Shock—feeling numb or detached—is your mind's way of protecting you from an extremely difficult event. When your baby was first born, shock may have caused denial of your baby's medical condition. You may have walked around in disbelief, feeling somewhat disoriented and unable to understand or comprehend what was happening.

Shock and denial often occur within the first few days following a preterm birth, but can also be triggered by certain events, such as your baby's homecoming, a later surgery, or if a new medical or developmental concern arises. Accepting the event that causes your shock and denial takes time. Permitting yourself to feel and talking about the experience with someone you trust can help.

> *I believe that pain is a necessary component in the process of healing, but numbness can help us through the most difficult times. For me, the problem is overcoming the numbness that I continue to feel fifteen months after my twins were born prematurely at thirty-one weeks. The numbness helped me get through the hospital experience, but now I can't turn it off. It feels like it's seriously prohibiting me from feeling the pure joy I should be feeling.*
>
> —Veronica, mother of 31-weeker twins Madison and Meagan

■

IS IT POST-TRAUMATIC STRESS?

When a person experiences a crisis that is too overwhelming to handle, the mind sometimes "blocks out" all or part of the event. Eventually, pieces of the memory can surface and cause "flashbacks"—memories, emotions, or sensations—of the original trauma. This may cause feelings ranging from numbness to panic.

A delayed emotional reaction to a traumatic event is often referred to as post-traumatic stress disorder (PTSD). Some experts believe parents who experience the crisis of a preterm birth are at risk for PTSD. Having experienced another traumatic event before the birth of a premature baby may predispose you to this disorder.

In addition to flashbacks, you may be experiencing symptoms of post-traumatic stress if you:

- have recurring and disturbing dreams about the birth of your baby or NICU experience;
- feel as if the birth crisis is happening again;
- feel intense distress (both physically and emotionally) when faced with reminders of the premature birth;
- feel detached from others or emotionally "numb";
- are overly protective of your child and easily frightened about your child's safety;
- are frequently irritable and often have outbursts of anger; and/or
- have other symptoms, such as inability to sleep well, difficulty concentrating, and decreased desire for everyday activities.

Many parents experience strong reactions like those above for a few days. However, if the symptoms last for longer than two weeks, you may be suffering post-traumatic stress, and you should seek help from a qualified therapist.

I have tried to describe my "flashbacks" to my husband, but I wasn't able to explain what I am feeling. I don't actually see things, but I feel the intense anguish and emotions that I felt back during our NICU stay.

—ERIN, MOTHER OF 32-WEEKER CONNER

GUILT AND SELF-BLAME: "WHAT IF?"

For a parent of a child born prematurely, one of the hardest emotions to overcome is the feeling of guilt. It is a natural response to blame yourself for your child's early birth or present condition, but it can hinder the healing process. Constantly asking yourself "what if" questions ("What if I had called the doctor sooner?" "What if I had rested more?" "What if I had eaten better?") can unintentionally have adverse affects on your own health and your relationships with others.

Many experiences can trigger your guilt feelings: If your baby struggles to breathe or eat; a diagnosis of a developmental delay; the need for glasses or a hearing aid; when school begins and you worry about your child's ability to learn. You may also feel self-blame for wanting some time apart from your child, or for the attention taken away from your spouse or other children.

Dwelling on "what might have been" requires energy that could be better directed toward your family's and your present needs. Do what you need to do to let go of the past. Learning about the cause of your early delivery may help you understand the medical reasons. Consult your doctor and ask as many questions as needed. Listed in appendices C and D are support groups, national organizations, and related books that may also help. Meeting other parents who have experienced similar circumstances can also lessen your guilt.

I felt guilty throughout my baby's hospitalization. Guilty when I decided that I needed a break from the NICU to go home and work on the nursery. Guilty for "only" being at the hospital for eight hours a day. Guilty that I had a glass of wine before I discovered that I was pregnant. Guilty because my body let my daughter down. Even now I feel guilty because I am looking forward to things being normal with my current pregnancy. I have too much guilt for one person!

Talking with others taught me that things aren't always my fault. I am attempting to close what I consider to be a very unpleasant chapter in my life.

—KAREN, MOTHER OF 28-WEEKER CARLEY

■

Having a premature infant is a chore. My son didn't sleep through the night until he was eighteen months old, and I was so tired from my own lack of sleep that I found myself angry at him. I felt like I was a bad mother and thought everyone else must think so too. My own mother finally pointed out that I was a good mother and only human for wishing that I had some time to myself.

—MARY, MOTHER OF 32-WEEKER DAVID

■

I feel a lot of guilt because I want to go back to work. The last year has revolved completely around Mara, and I feel fortunate that I can stay home with her. However, I have been out of the workforce for a year now, and I am going a bit crazy at home. I feel guilty because my child fought all the odds to make it, and now I am thinking of putting her in daycare so I can go back to work and feel some normalcy.

—KARYN, MOTHER OF 23-WEEKER MARA

ANGER: "WHY DID THIS HAPPEN TO ME?"

Anger is a common response to the loss of a "normal" birth, healthy baby, and the later difficulties of parenting a child with special needs. At various times and in different situations, your anger may be directed at a healthcare professional, God, your spouse or partner, a stranger, a parent of a healthy term baby, others who do not understand your crisis, or even yourself or your child. Because of your anger, you may become irritable and easily upset. Be careful that your anger does not adversely affect your relationships. Instead, constructively express your anger. Hit a pillow, exercise, or cry. You may even find it helpful to write a letter to the person with whom you are most angry (even if you do not send it, you may feel some relief).

Do not let anyone tell you that you should not feel angry. Holding anger back can actually cause destructive behavior, such as drinking, drug abuse, or child abuse, and can lead to feelings of depression. Anger allows you to release your emotions and work through your pain.

At first I was angry with God, thinking I didn't deserve to feel so much anguish. Then I directed my anger toward the doctors, nurses, and even strangers (like the one who said to me, "At least you have another child at home."). It seemed my life was out of control and I had no explanations and no one to blame.

—MARIAN, MOTHER OF 25-WEEKER GARY

■

I don't think I recognized my anger until long after Mackenzie came home. I didn't have time to be angry while she was sick; I only felt fear and helplessness then. I felt my anger the first time we took Mackenzie to the emergency room and had to fight with the nurses and doctors to listen to what we had to say. From then on I felt a lot of anger toward the medical professionals who tried to discount my child's needs and my knowledge of her needs.

—*Jim,* FATHER OF *26*-WEEKER *Mackenzie*

Fear, Worry, and Anxiety: "Will My Child and My Life Ever Be Normal?"

You may have thought your feelings of fear would end once your baby was released from the hospital, but they may not. An illness or a surgery can certainly recreate feelings of fear that are similar to the ones you felt in the NICU, but so can developmental delays and concerns about your child's future. You may wonder if you will ever stop feeling afraid.

Because of your child's fragile start, you may always feel uneasy about her health and development, even being oversensitive about the mildest symptoms. Feelings of doubt and concern may be heightened by certain situations, such as a doctor's visit or a developmental evaluation.

You can reduce your anxiety by talking to a qualified person you trust and through education. The more you know, the more in control you will feel. For instance, if you are fearful that your child will stop breathing, learn everything you can about her condition and what to do if she did stop breathing. Are you constantly worried that a cold could threaten your child's life? Then learn about the causes, symptoms, and treatments of respiratory illnesses and practice CPR techniques regularly. If you are concerned about how your former preemie will "turn out," consult your pediatrician or developmental specialist. You may also feel less anxious by talking to other parents of children born prematurely.

When my son needed hernia surgery, fear wrapped its fingers around my heart. I was very afraid that he might die. This fear was different than the fear I felt when he was born. I had spent three months getting to know him, nurturing him, and falling in love with him. I was panicked that he might now die and be taken away from me. It felt as though my heart stopped beating while he was in surgery. It wasn't until he had completely recovered and was safely in my arms that the fear slowly disappeared.

—*Megan,* MOTHER OF *30*-WEEKER *Brett*

■

I don't know how to deal with my fears and emotions. I am constantly wondering if my baby will be "normal." I was lucky that Bryce was able to breathe on his own from birth and had no significant medical problems. Yet, because he was born eleven weeks early, I worry about developmental milestones. Will he roll over on time? Does he hold his fist tight because he has increased muscle tone? Why doesn't he make eye contact with me every time I want him to?

Will the worry ever end? This anxiety about my baby is slowly fatiguing me. I wish I could enjoy Bryce's infancy the way I did with his brothers.

—*Leslie, mother of 29-weeker Bryce*

■

When I watched my son get on the bus for his first day of kindergarten, I couldn't help feeling anxious. I wondered if any learning problems would now show up as a result of his prematurity. I thought the worry had subsided, but it seems it will never end.

—*Karen, mother of 29-weeker Anthony*

Sadness: "Why Am I So Unhappy?"

Feeling sad about something bad that has happened to you or to someone you love is perfectly normal. After all, you have experienced tremendous difficulties. Your sorrow may come and go throughout your life. After homecoming, you may feel sad if your baby continues to need medical equipment or when she experiences discomfort. You may feel unhappy because taking care of your child is so difficult. Reflecting on your child's missed "babyhood," even years later, may also cause feelings of sorrow.

When Andrea turned one we had a huge birthday party celebrating a wonderful event! Although the day was filled with joy, my heart was also filled with sadness. The day seemed to bring back so many feelings from the NICU. I wanted to cry because I was happy and because I was sad for what Andrea and our family had been through.

—*Lori, mother of 27-weeker Andrea*

■

We just went to our first family gathering since James was born. I let others hold James and everyone had such a good time. Everyone except me. I felt like such an outsider. I didn't feel like I belonged to James or that I was his mother. It was a strange and unexpected feeling. I think mostly I was feeling sad and sorry for myself. I just couldn't bring myself to be social.

—*Teresa, mother of 31-weeker James*

■

I knew that I was devastated by Ashley's premature birth. During her 125-day hospital stay, there were days when I thought I wasn't going to make it. Fortunately, I knew my limitations and when I had to talk to someone.

Now that Ashley has been home for three months and the "excitement" of the NICU has completely worn off, I have found myself back in the depths of depression. I have difficulty sleeping and dealing with everyday things like laundry. One load is a major ordeal.

I know I need to speak to someone objective, like a counselor, and maybe even start medication. Experience has shown me that trying to let my depression fix itself doesn't work.

—*GRETCHEN, MOTHER OF 23-WEEKER ASHLEY*

WHEN SADNESS TURNS TO DEPRESSION

If your unhappiness will not go away and you begin feeling "empty," you may be depressed and need professional help. Depression is the body's response to being emotionally drained. It is an illness that affects the entire body, not just the mind. One out of five people will become depressed sometime in their life (most often after a traumatic event or loss).

If you have two or more of the following signs of depression and they last for longer than two weeks, consult your doctor or a qualified therapist. You may need help coping with your sadness if you:

- often have difficulty sleeping (you have trouble falling asleep, you wake up in the middle of the night for long periods, and/or you frequently wake up too early in the morning);
- sleep for long periods of time or need more sleep than usual;
- feel tired after a good night's rest;
- feel guilty, helpless, or hopeless much of the time;
- have a decreased appetite and/or enjoyment of food;
- feel unloved or rejected;
- express negative comments frequently;
- have trouble thinking or concentrating;
- experience a significant weight loss or gain; and/or
- have a decreased interest in your usual activities.

These symptoms may also be signs of postpartum depression (PPD), a serious problem that affects 10 to 15 percent of new mothers. PPD can occur up to a year following childbirth. If you suspect you are suffering from PPD, immediately consult your doctor or a qualified therapist. If left untreated, depression can threaten your (and your baby's) health and safety. Do not feel "weak" if you need help dealing with your depression. Recognizing when help is needed takes strength.

■ ■ ■

Loneliness: "The Roller-coaster Ride Doesn't Stop, It Only Gets Lonelier"

Loneliness is not an emotion generally associated with the grief process, but it is a common feeling among parents of premature infants. Loneliness, often accompanied by sadness, can overcome you and affect your ability to heal emotionally.

When your baby was hospitalized, you may have received support from healthcare professionals, other parents in the NICU, family members, coworkers, and friends. Even if they did not always offer the best help, they still listened to your concerns and feelings. Ideally, a few of these people, as well as some new ones, will offer support after homecoming.

You may still feel as if no one completely understands your feelings, however. Some people will think you should be "over" your experience. You may find yourself avoiding certain people, or feel that some people are avoiding you. If you worked before your baby's birth and are now a stay-at-home parent, you may not have the availability of friends you once had. Furthermore, you probably feel isolated and alone if you need to keep your baby away from germs.

To overcome your loneliness, you must find others who will listen and understand what you are going through. Local, national, or Internet support groups for preemie parents are good choices, but others (friends, family members, a clergy person, or a therapist) can also help.

THE LOSS OF A CHILD

If you have lost a preemie twin or multiple, the feelings of grief discussed in this chapter are intensified. The death of any child is an overwhelming loss, and other people's inability to understand can add to your burden. Friends and family may expect your grief to be lessened because of your surviving child. They may make insensitive remarks, or "forget" that you lost a child and concentrate solely on the surviving one.

Healing is a process that will take time. You may find comfort from those who understand. For support and information, contact the loss support organizations listed under "Grief" in appendix C at the back of this book.

When I brought my son home from the hospital, it felt like such a triumphant event! It seemed things would now be "okay" and we could get on with life. The reality set in when a friend stopped by and never gave me a chance to tell her how I felt. She wanted to hear about my happiness, but not about my fear and other feelings. It seemed that no one, not even my husband, would let me express my feelings.

Zachary got sick a month later and my pediatrician didn't even recognize how scared I was. Why did everyone seem to think everything was okay and normal when it didn't feel that way? I felt so alone.

—*Shelly, mother of 28-weeker Zachary*

■

Even though many new moms who choose to stay at home have to adjust to loneliness, my loneliness sometimes seemed unbearable. Kristen came home in the winter on oxygen and a monitor, and our pediatrician told us to keep her inside. Friends wanted to visit, but I was scared of exposing my baby to germs. My husband traveled frequently, so I was alone much of the time.

It was another mom of a preemie who kept me going. We talked on the phone every day. When our babies were healthy, we visited in each other's homes. I felt she was the only person who really understood what I was experiencing.

—*Denise, mother of 28-weeker Kristen*

COPING WITH YOUR FEELINGS

How you handle your emotional difficulties is critical not only to your health but to your family's health as well. Finding ways to cope, through self-care methods, the support of others, professional help, and/or the use of antidepressants, can make you a better person and parent.

Self-help

As discussed earlier, parenting a premature infant can cause feelings of extreme tension and anxiety. There are many ways to reduce stress and promote wellness. You need to find the methods that are best suited to your individual needs. The following are ideas from parents and healthcare professionals:

- Try various relaxation techniques (deep breathing, yoga, meditation). Books, videos, and classes can offer instruction. Write down how each method makes you feel, and choose the one that works best for you. Most methods require practice before any long-term effects are seen. Periodically evaluate whether the technique is continuing to work.
- Recognize your limits and develop realistic expectations as to what you can and cannot do. Learn how to say no.
- Write about your feelings and experiences in a journal. Journal writing helps release emotions, opinions, and perceptions (and creates a nice keepsake).
- Release your emotions creatively through paints, clay, needlework, or music.
- Find ways to make yourself laugh and release your nervous energy. Read a funny book or watch a sitcom.
- Learn ways to manage your time effectively. Books, videos, classes, and even other parents can give you helpful information for organizing your daily, weekly, even long-term schedules and routines.

- A hobby, such as gardening or reading, can create a peaceful time and place during the day.
- Treat yourself to a massage. Studies show that massage has many important health benefits: It can reduce your heart rate, lower your blood pressure, and enhance your immune system.
- Ask a friend or neighbor to come over for part of the day so you can get more sleep, sunshine, or a little time alone.
- Avoid being with people who increase your anxiety.
- Find an exercise program that fits into your life.

Taking care of yourself will increase your ability to stay healthy, enjoy life, and contribute productively to society. Most importantly, it will give your preemie what she needs more than anything—you.

Finding Support from Others

Studies show that parents of preterm children who reach out for help are better able to cope with their crises. However, it is important that support comes from those who can truly help. That person (or persons) could be your spouse or partner, a family member, a friend, a neighbor, a clergy member, a healthcare professional, or another parent of a preemie (individually or as part of a support group). When accepting help from others, make sure they:

- listen with their heart and respond with honesty and thought;
- recognize your feelings and do not tell you how you "should" feel;
- try to understand the true crisis of the preemie experience;
- do not have their own agenda (For example, they do not try to redirect your anger at something they are angry about); and
- understand the kind of support you need (a listening ear, physical help, or advice).

Seeking Therapy

There may come a time when you wonder if you need help from a trained therapist. Simply wanting to sort out your feelings is an appropriate reason to seek one. A therapist can also help if you experience any strong feelings that make you feel uncomfortable or unsure of yourself.

The following are some things to consider when seeking therapy:

- Therapists work in private-office practices, hospital settings, community mental health centers, social service agencies, schools, and in workplaces.
- Therapy does not have to be expensive. Less-expensive therapy is sometimes supported by taxes or private donations through social service agencies or community

WHO ARE THERAPISTS?

When searching for a therapist, it is important to find one who can best serve your individual needs. Listed below are some professionals who may be qualified to help you.

A psychologist. A psychologist has a doctoral degree in psychology. Some have advanced training in therapy. A psychologist cannot prescribe medication, but typically works in conjunction with a psychiatrist should medication be needed.

A psychiatrist. A physician with extensive training in psychological disorders is a psychiatrist. Psychiatrists diagnose any physical causes that are contributing to emotional problems and evaluate the need for medication. They can see patients regularly to manage medication and give emotional and psychological support, or on a consulting basis in conjunction with your doctor and/or therapist.

A social worker. A social worker has a master's degree. Therapy with a social worker generally involves talking and working through feelings and problems. A social worker cannot prescribe medication.

A family counselor. A counselor who has a master's degree and specializes in family issues can help with everyday adjustments to problems in life. Family counselors are unable to prescribe medication.

A pastoral counselor. A clergy member trained and certified by the American Association for Pastoral Counseling focuses on both psychological and spiritual concerns. A pastoral counselor may be found through local churches, synagogues, or other religious institutions.

A nurse practitioner. A nurse with a master's degree may specialize in the diagnosis and treatment of emotional problems. A nurse practitioner may or may not be able to prescribe medication.

mental health centers. Some insurance companies (and sometimes Medicaid) will cover part of the cost. For information on therapy that is partially or completely paid for by public support, look under "Mental Health" in the phone book.

- Therapy can be done one-on-one, in a group, or with your family. Some therapists emphasize thoughts and feelings; others focus on behaviors; and some even use unusual forms of therapy, such as hypnosis. Talk with several prospective therapists on the phone and choose the therapist who feels right to you.
- If you have a preference regarding the gender of your therapist, choose a female or male therapist accordingly.
- Look for a therapist who is warm, sincere, and understanding. You should trust your therapist and feel comfortable about sharing your thoughts and feelings.
- If you feel it is important to find someone who has firsthand experience as a preemie parent, then choose one accordingly. However, any good therapist should be able to help.
- The wrong therapist can actually cause more harm than good. If you have any doubts about your current therapist or feel uncomfortable, seek another therapist.

■ ■ ■

THE USE OF ANTIDEPRESSANTS

Under normal life circumstances, the brain releases chemicals that keep the mind and body "in balance." An extremely stressful event, such as a preterm birth, can disrupt this balance. Your body may compensate by releasing more or fewer chemicals. Over time (months, weeks, or even days), you may lose some or much of your ability to cope, causing symptoms of depression.

Antidepressants can help treat the chemical imbalances associated with depression if you are unable to do so by other measures (such as changing your sleep pattern or diet, adding an exercise program, or receiving therapy). Antidepressants cannot "cure" your depression but can give you the ability to cope more effectively and the energy to help resolve your issues.

HOW OTHERS ARE AFFECTED BY A PRETERM BIRTH

IN YOUR OWN grief, it may be difficult for you to see that those close to you are also coping with your child's premature birth and its effects. Fathers, mothers, grandparents, and siblings all have different ways of handling and expressing their emotions. Learning about these differences can help your relationships with your loved ones.

HUSBANDS, WIVES, AND PARTNERS

The birth of a premature infant can have both a positive and a negative impact on the relationship between the mother and father. Some couples grow closer from their efforts to cope with the trauma; others pull apart. Remember, the arrival of any new baby causes some conflict within a marriage or partnership, so it is only natural that the crisis of a preterm baby may cause some extra strain.

Some parents who survived the prematurity crisis say it made their relationship stronger. Learning how to respect each others' feelings and supporting one another through a difficult journey often brings couples closer. To continue this positive effect, you and your partner need to continue to maintain open communication and respect for each other.

A negative impact occurs for a variety of reasons. The different ways men and women naturally deal with a traumatic event is one cause. Mothers often express their emotions more easily. They frequently have a more realistic view of the crisis, and they are more likely to reach out to others for support.

Fathers are generally more idealistic, trying to remain positive and strong in their efforts to support the mother and child. In an attempt to hold the family together, they often try to "fix" the situation by seeking answers and taking action. Because men are often raised to be self-sufficient, unemotional, and capable caretakers, they may have difficulty seeking help and expressing feelings.

When the mother and father have different ways of handling the prematurity crisis, each may have a hard time supporting the other. If the mother tries to get the father to see things her way, or vice versa, hostility can result.

Another possible negative impact on a relationship is unresolved feelings toward one another. Feelings of blame, anger, and resentment between parents can adversely affect their relationship. Not recognizing how the other person feels or preventing that person from expressing his or her thoughts or emotions can also be detriments.

The key to working through difficulties is healthy communication. If you and your partner do not talk openly and clearly with each other, a wall may be built between you. You both need to try to understand how the other feels and accept any differences. Learning appropriate and effective methods to communicate and cope through books, support groups, or therapy can help.

WARNING SIGNS IN ADULTS

You and your partner may need help coping with the difficulties of a relationship if one (or both) of you continually:

- becomes angry or defensive if the other talks about a sensitive subject;
- criticizes or puts down the other when talking about issues;
- withdraws when the other brings up sensitive topics;
- has difficulty sexually with the other; and/or
- cannot talk about feelings without being afraid of how the other might respond (For example, Mom is afraid to tell Dad how she feels about him going to work every day, or Dad is uncomfortable asking Mom to spend more time with him.)

Your Other Children

Siblings struggle with the emotional crisis of prematurity, too. They may feel angry about the lack of attention, worried about their brother or sister, guilty that they somehow caused the preterm birth, and anxious about parent separations. Even young children can feel as though their lives are out of control.

Your children will need time to adjust. You can help by providing special moments of togetherness and allowing them to express their feelings. About ten to fifteen minutes before bed is a good time to encourage your older children to talk about their feelings. You can also read books about having a sibling born prematurely. A local support group for siblings of children with special needs may also help.

As your children learn to cope, keep in mind that the experience of having a critically ill brother or sister can have later positive effects. If given support, siblings of preemies can become exceptionally caring and compassionate people.

WARNING SIGNS IN CHILDREN

Children often express their emotions through actions, rather than words. Although some temporary reactions are normal, your child may need help coping if she continues to display warning signs. Consult your pediatrician or a therapist if your child continues to:

- take steps backward in her development, such as bedwetting, regressing to thumbsucking, or throwing tantrums;
- withdraw by playing alone more frequently or with an imaginary friend;
- complain about small scratches or bruises more frequently, or seems to have an unusual number of complaints, such as stomachaches or other illnesses;
- display unusual and angry behavior, such as crying, screaming, hitting, biting, or picking on others;
- develop destructive behavior; or
- act like the "perfect child" by doing everything she thinks you want her to do.

Having a sister who is a preemie is hard. She got all the attention, and I barely got any for a long time. We couldn't play rough with her because she was so small. When we finally could run around playing, she would always get her oxygen cord all tangled up. I didn't like watching her suffering while she got her shots, either.

I think it's cool she made it through everything, and she's just a regular kid. I kinda like her being small cuz she's cute that way. Everybody likes my sister. I like the way she laughs.

—*Frankie, ten-year-old brother of 26-weeker Mackenzie*

Grandparents

Your parents feel not only emotional pain for their premature grandchild, but also anguish for you. They may not know how to handle their emotions, and might not always do and say the things you feel are helpful. Do not forget that they are grieving too, and may need to find their own sources of support and perhaps professional help.

To help your relationship with your parents, try to be understanding (although this may not always be easy). For example, if your parents are taking over too much of the housework or older children's care, it may be because they feel helpless and unsure of what they should do.

On the other hand, your parents may withdraw and seem less supportive if they do not understand or are frightened by the medical issues surrounding their grandchild. To help your parents become more comfortable with and better understand their grandchild's concerns, encourage them to talk to healthcare professionals, attend support group meetings, and read this book.

Your parents may also not offer help because they do not know what you need from them, or they are respecting your privacy. Consider how your family typically handles stressful situations. As with all relationships, communication is essential. Try to be honest with your parents about your feelings and needs. Let them know what you need from them and what you find intrusive. Remember, it is okay to be angry at your parents, but it is critical to express that anger constructively. Family therapy may be necessary.

FINDING MEANING FROM THE PREEMIE EXPERIENCE

ALTHOUGH THE REALITY of the preemie experience may sometimes be difficult to bear, you must never give up hope. In time, you will find meaning from your heartache and courage.

Many parents of preterm children give meaning to their difficult experience by helping others. They start support groups, write for preemie-related publications (a few even write books!), and offer peer support to parents in the NICU. Some even go back to school to become NICU nurses or counselors.

It does not matter when or how you find meaning from the preemie experience—but it is important that you remain hopeful. Throughout the difficult times, never stop believing in your child, your family, and yourself.

Emergencies: Choking and CPR

The following information is a brief review of choking and resuscitation procedures. If you have not taken a cardiopulmonary resuscitation (CPR) class, sign up for one today. To find a class, look under "First Aid Instruction" in the index of your phone book or consult your pediatrician. The best time to learn life-saving procedures is before an emergency.

CHOKING—UNDER AGE 1

If your child is coughing and remains pink, let her try to cough out the object on her own. Choking on liquids is rarely harmful, and your child should be able to clear the fluid by herself.

If your child cannot breathe and is turning blue:

CALL FOR HELP. Have someone call 9-1-1 immediately if your child is choking on a solid object.

POSITION YOUR INFANT. Sit down. Place your infant facedown on your forearm with your hand stabilizing her head and neck. Keep the head lower than the rest of the body.

GIVE 4 BACK BLOWS between the shoulder blades. Use the heel of your hand. *Never shake your infant.*

TURN YOUR INFANT OVER if she still cannot breathe. Lay her on her back on a firm surface and deliver four rapid chest thrusts over the middle of the breastbone, using only two fingers.

CHECK THE MOUTH for foreign objects or food if your infant is still not breathing. Do not attempt to pull out the object unless you can see it clearly and it is easy to sweep out with a finger.

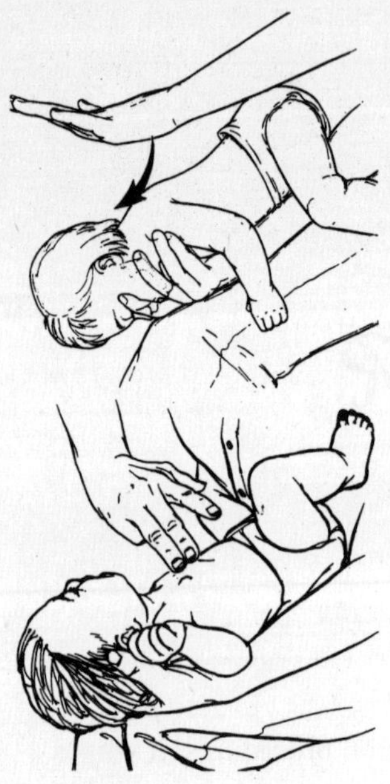

An infant receiving back blows and chest thrusts

BEGIN MOUTH-TO-MOUTH BREATHING. Give two breaths through the mouth or mouth and nose. See CPR guidelines on page 297. If she still is not breathing, repeat all of the above steps.

CHOKING—OVER AGE 1

If your child is coughing and remains pink, let him try to cough out the object on his own. Choking on liquids is rarely harmful, and your child should be able to clear fluid by himself.

If your child cannot breathe and is turning blue:

CALL FOR HELP. Have someone call 9-1-1 immediately if your child is choking on a solid object.

POSITION YOUR CHILD. Stand behind your child. Put your arms around him so that they are just below the lower ribs. Make a fist with your right hand and grab that fist with your left hand.

BEGIN ABDOMINAL THRUSTS. Give a sudden inward and upward jerk of your hands. You want to try to dislodge the object from the windpipe by giving 6 to 10 abdominal thrusts in quick succession. A small child can be placed on his back on the floor. Kneel at his feet and place a fist on the abdomen above the navel but below the ribs. Place the other hand on top of the fist and give 6 to 10 inward and upward abdominal thrusts. Try to do this gently if your child is small.

CHECK THE MOUTH for foreign objects or food if your child is still not breathing. Do not attempt to pull out the object unless you can see it clearly and it is easy to sweep out with a finger.

The Heimlich maneuver on older child

If your child does not start breathing:

BEGIN MOUTH-TO-MOUTH BREATHING. Give two breaths through the mouth or mouth and nose. See the CPR guidelines on page 297. If he is still not breathing, repeat all of the above steps.

■ ■ ■

CARDIOPULMONARY RESUSCITATION (CPR)

In a rare instance your child may require CPR to help her breathe and to provide assistance in pumping the blood through the body. When you took the CPR course, you learned the "ABCs of CPR," a helpful way to remember the order in which your child should be resuscitated. Here is a refresher:

> Anything smaller than this in diameter can choke your child:
>
> ______________
>
> 1.25 inches
>
> Make sure you keep small foods and objects out of reach.

Airway.	Positioning the head and neck so that the air flows easily into the lungs.
Breathing.	You may have to breathe for your child if she is unable to do so. *Never shake your child.*
Circulation.	Chest compressions may be necessary to pump blood to the body.

CALL FOR HELP. Have someone dial 9-1-1.

EVALUATE your child's condition. Shout or gently shake your child to see if she will awaken. Put your ear next to her nose and listen for breathing. Look at the chest to see if it rises with each breath.

If your child is not breathing:

POSITION your child. Lay her on her back on a firm surface. If you think she could have injured her neck, support her head to keep the neck from twisting as you roll her over.

TILT THE HEAD BACK so that her nose is "in the air." Check the mouth to make sure your child has not choked on anything. See choking procedures on page 295 or 296.

BEGIN MOUTH-TO-MOUTH BREATHING. For a child under one, place your mouth over her mouth and nose. Breathe once every 3 seconds (20 breaths per minute). For a child over one, pinch the nose and place your mouth over her mouth. Breathe once every 4 seconds (15 breaths per minute). In each case, start with two breaths and blow enough air into the mouth to make the chest rise. Remove your mouth so the air can escape.

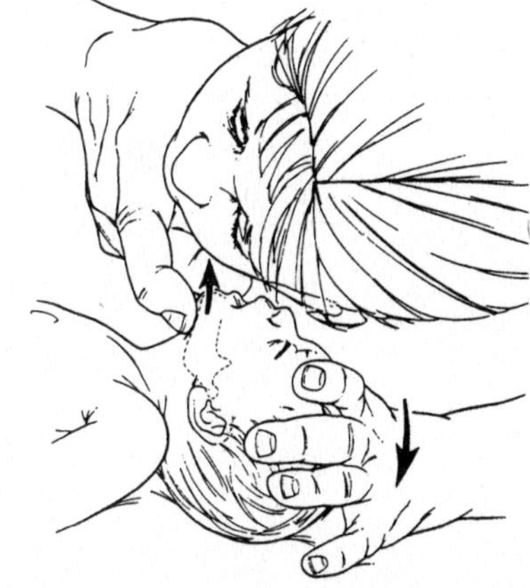

Opening the airway with a head tilt. Tilt the head back so that the child's nose is in the air.

FEEL FOR A PULSE. For an infant under one, place your hand on the baby's arm with your fingers touching the inside of the arm just above the elbow. For a child over one, place your fingers under the ear and

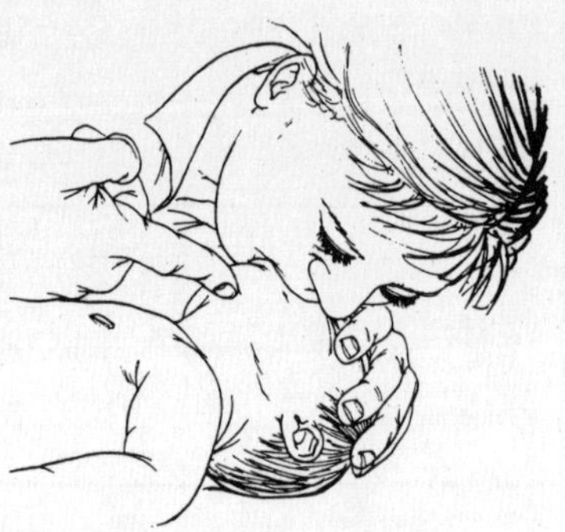

Mouth-to-mouth breathing for an infant. Place your mouth over the infant's nose and mouth. Breathe once every three seconds.

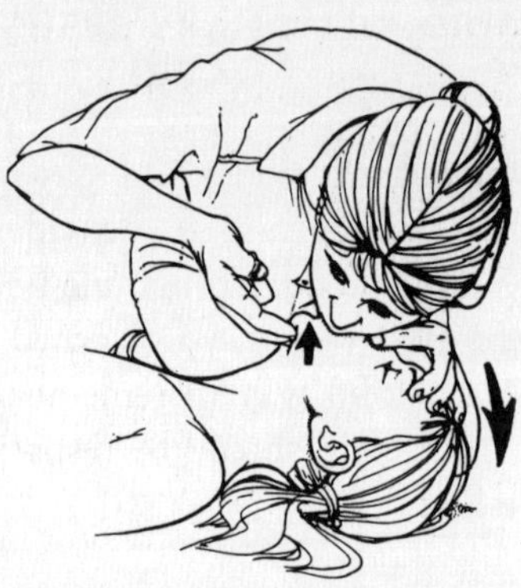

Mouth-to-mouth breathing for a child. Pinch the nose and place your mouth over the child's mouth. Breathe once every four seconds.

just below the jawbone (beside the windpipe). You should be able to feel a pulse if the heart is beating properly.

BEGIN CHEST COMPRESSIONS IF THERE IS NO PULSE. For an infant under one, place three fingers on the breastbone with your index finger at the height of the nipples. The area for compression is where your middle and ring fingers are. Compress at a depth of one-half to one inch at a rate of 100 compressions per minute. Give your child one breath for every five compressions.

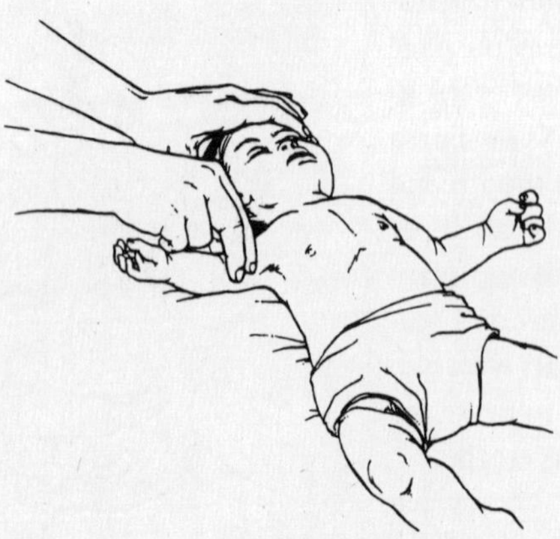

Feeling for a pulse in a child under one. Place your hand on the upper arm with your fingers touching the inside of the arm just above the elbow.

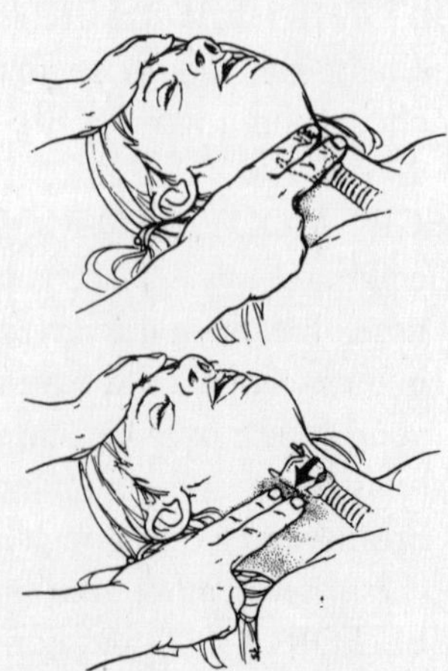

Checking for a pulse in a child over one. Place your fingers under the ear and just below the jawbone (beside the windpipe).

For children over one year, place the heel of one hand over the lower third of the breastbone. Make sure your hand is overlying the breastbone entirely and not pushing on the upper abdomen, which could damage the liver or spleen. Compress at a depth of one to one and one-half inches at 80 compressions per minute. Give your child one breath for every five compressions.

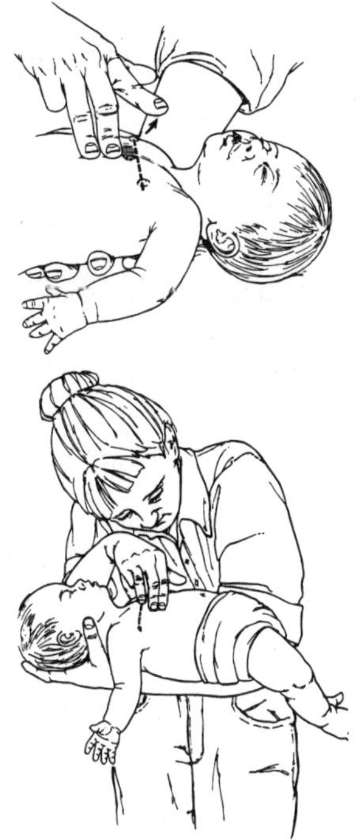

Giving chest compressions to a child under one. Place three fingers on the breastbone with your index finger at the height of the nipples. Press ½ to 1 inch with your middle and ring fingers 100 times per minute.

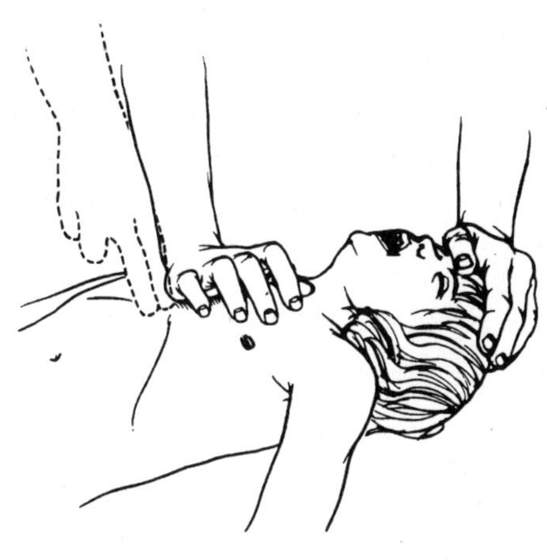

Giving chest compressions to a child over one. Place the heel of your hand over the lower third of the breastbone, pressing 1 to 1½ inches 80 times per minute.

Continue giving breaths and/or chest compressions until paramedics arrive.

For additional CPR instruction for a child with a tracheostomy, see box on page 51.

Conversion Tables

Fahrenheit (F) to Centigrade (C) Conversion

°F	°C	°F	°C
97.0	36.1	101.6	38.7
97.2	36.2	101.8	38.8
97.4	36.3	102.0	38.9
97.6	36.4	102.2	39.0
97.8	36.6	102.4	39.1
98.0	36.7	102.6	39.2
98.2	36.8	102.8	39.3
98.4	36.9	103.0	39.4
98.6	37.0	103.2	39.6
98.8	37.1	103.4	39.7
99.0	37.2	103.6	39.8
99.2	37.3	103.8	39.9
99.4	37.4	104.0	40.0
99.6	37.6	104.2	40.1

(continued)

Fahrenheit (F) to Centigrade (C) Conversion (cont.)

°F	°C	°F	°C
99.8	37.7	104.4	40.2
100.0	37.8	104.6	40.3
100.2	37.9	104.8	40.4
100.4	38.0	105.0	40.6
100.6	38.1	105.2	40.7
100.8	38.2	105.4	40.8
101.0	38.3	105.6	40.9
101.2	38.4	105.8	41.0
101.4	38.6	106.0	41.1

Volume Conversion

1 cubic centimeter (cc)	=	1 milliliter (ml)	=	20 drops		
5 cc	=	5 ml	=	1 teaspoon		
15 cc	=	15 ml	=	1 tablespoon	=	1/2 ounce
30 cc	=	30 ml	=	1 ounce		

APPENDIX C

Family Resources

Many parents of children born prematurely have found the following organizations, hot lines, and periodicals helpful. For additional reading, see appendix D. If you know of a resource that should be added to this list, write to: Amy E. Tracy and Dianne I. Maroney, c/o Berkley Publishing, 375 Hudson Street, Fifth Floor, New York, NY 10014.

Asthma and Lung Disorders

The American Academy of Allergy, Asthma and Immunology
611 East Wells Street
Milwaukee, WI 53202
Physician referral and information line:
(800) 822-2762
www.aaaai.org

American Lung Association
1740 Broadway
New York, NY 10019
(800) 586-4872
www.lungusa.org

Allergy and Asthma Network Mothers of Asthmatics, Inc.
2751 Prosperity Avenue, Suite 150
Fairfax, VA 22031-4397
(800) 878-4403
www.aanma.org

The National Jewish Medical and Research Center
1400 Jackson Street
Denver, CO 80206
(800) 222-Lung (222-5864)
www.njc.org

Breast-feeding

Ameda-Egnell Corporation
765 Industrial Drive
Cary, IL 60013
(800) 323-8750

Medela, Inc. and Breastfeeding National Network
P.O. Box 660
4610 Prime Parkway
McHenry, IL 60050
(800) 435-8316
www.medela.com

International Lactation Consultant Association
4101 Lake Boone Trail
Raleigh, NC 27607
(919) 787-5181
www.ilca.org

La Leche League International
1400 North Meacham Road
Schaumburg, IL 60173-4048
(800) LA-LECHE
www.lalecheleague.org

Lact-Aid International Inc.
P.O. Box 1066
Athens, TN 37371-1066
(423) 744-9090
www.lact-aid.com

HealthONE Lactation Program
4500 East Ninth Avenue, Suite 320 South
Denver, CO 80220
(303) 320-7081

Books

La Leche League International. 1997. *The Womanly Art of Breastfeeding.*

March of Dimes Birth Defects Foundation. 1997. *Breastfeeding the Infant with Special Needs.*

Cesarean Birth

Cesareans/Support Education and Concern
22 Forest Road
Framingham, MA 01701
(508) 877-8266

Childcare

National Child Care Association
1016 Rosser Street
Conyers, GA 30012
(800) 543-7161
www.nccanet.org

Circumcision

National Organization of Circumcision Information Resource Centers
P.O. Box 2512
San Anselmo, CA 94979-2512
(415) 488-9883
www.nocirc.org

Clothing and Preemie Products

Children's Medical Ventures, Inc.: (800) 377-3449
www.childmed.com

La Petite Baby: (404) 475-3247
www.no-odor.com/preemie

The Preemie Purple Heart
www.purple-hearts.com

The Preemie Store and More: (800) 676-8469
www.preemie.com

Premiewear: (800) 992-8469
www.premiewear.com

TLC Clothing Company: (800) 755-4TLC (755-4852)

Diapers

Commonwealth Preemie Pampers: (800) 543-4932

Huggies: (800) 447-9423, ext. 44

Developmental Disabilities

The Council for Exceptional Children
1920 Association Drive
Reston, VA 22091-1589
(703) 620-3660
www.cec.sped.org

Mothers United for Moral Support
150 Custer Court
Green Bay, WI 54301
(920) 336-5333
www.waisman.wisc.edu/~rowley/MUMS/home.html

Delivery of Chronic Care (Project DOCC):
(516) 365-0959
e-mail: projdocc@aol.com

National Association for Developmental Disabilities Council
1234 Massachusetts Avenue NW, Suite 103
Washington, DC 20005
(202) 347-1234
www.igc.apc.org/NADDC

National Information Center for Children and Youth with Disabilities
P.O. Box 1492
Washington, DC 20013-1492
(800) 695-0285
www.nichcy.org

National Parent Network on Disabilities
1130 Seventeenth Street NW, Suite 400
Washington, DC 20036
(202) 463-2299
www.npnd.org

National Parent to Parent Support and Information System
P.O. Box 907
Blue Ridge, GA 30513
(800) 651-1151
www.nppsis.org

Magazines

Exceptional Parent
1170 Commonwealth Avenue, Third Floor
Boston, MA 02134
(800) 247-8080

Digestive Disorders

National Digestive Diseases Information Clearinghouse
2 Information Way
Bethesda, MD 20892-3570
(301) 654-3810
www.chid.nih.gov

Pediatric/Adolescent Gastroesophageal Reflux Association
P.O. Box 1153
Germantown, MD 20875-1153
(301) 601-9541
www.reflux.org

Early Education

ERIC Clearinghouse on Elementary and Early Childhood Education
51 Gerty Drive
Champaign, IL 61820-7469
(800) 583-4135
www.ericeece.org

National Association for the Education of Young Children
1509 Sixteenth Street NW
Washington, DC 20036
(800) 424-2460
www.naeyc.org

Feeding and Nutrition

Family Health Line: (800) 688-7777

Financial

Social Security Hotline: (800) 772-1213

Medicaid: (800) 555-1212 for your state's toll-free Medicaid number.
www.hcfa.gov/

Books

Rosenfeld L.R. 1994. *Your Child and Health Care: A "Dollar and Sense" Guide for Families with Special Needs.* Baltimore, Md.: Paul H. Brookes Publishing Co.

Formula

Mead Johnson (Enfamil products): (800) 222-9123

Ross Nutrition (Similac products): (800) 367-6852

Grief

A Place to Remember
1885 University Avenue, Suite 110
St. Paul, MN 55104
(800) 631-0973
www.APlaceToRemember.com

Aiding Mothers and Fathers Experiencing Neonatal Death
1559 Ville Rosa Lane
Hazelwood, MO 63042
(314) 291-0892
e-mail: amend;caprimary.net

Center for Loss in Multiple Birth
P.O. Box 1064
Palmer, AK 99645
(907) 746-6123

Centering Corporation
1531 North Saddle Creek Road
Omaha, NE 68104
(402) 553-1200

National Sudden Infant Death Syndrome Foundation
Two Metro Plaza, Suite 205
8240 Professional Place
Landover, MD 20785
(301) 459-3388

Pen-Parents International Support Group for Grieving Parents
P.O. Box 8738
Reno, NV 89507-8738
(702) 826-7332

Pregnancy and Infant Loss Center
1421 East Wayzata Boulevard, Suite 70
Wayzata, MN 55391
(612) 473-9372

RTS (formerly Resolve Through Sharing)
1910 South Avenue
La Crosse, WI 54601
(800) 362-9567
www.gundluth.org/bereave

Books

Davis, D. 1996. *Empty Cradle, Broken Heart: Surviving the Death of Your Baby.* Golden, Colo.: Fulcrum Publishing.

Kohn, I., and Moffitt, P.L. 1992. *A Silent Sorrow: Pregnancy Loss.* New York: Dell Publishing.

Zimmerman, S. 1996. *Grief Dancers: A Journey into the Depths of the Soul.* Golden, Colo.: Nemo Press.

Healthcare Advocacy

Family Voices Patient Advocacy
P.O. Box 769
Algodone, NM 87001
(888) 835-5669
www.family.voices.org

Patient Advocacy Coalition
850 East Harvard Avenue, Suite 465
Denver, CO 80210
(303) 744-7667

Healthcare Products and Services

Apria Healthcare
3560 Hyland Avenue
Costa Mesa, CA 92626
(800) APRIA88 (277-4288)

Ballard Medical Products
12050 Lone Peak Parkway
Draper, UT 84120
(800) 528-5591
www.bmed.com

Pediatric Services of America
3159 Campus Drive
Norcross, Georgia 30071
(800) 950-1580
www.psakids.com

Hearing-Speech-Language Impaired

American Society for Deaf Children
1820 Tribute Road, Suite A
Sacramento, CA 95815
(800) 942-2732
www.deafchildren.org

American Speech-Language-Hearing Association
10801 Rockville Pike
Rockville, MD 20852
(800) 638-8255
www.asha.org

The National Information Clearinghouse for Children Who Are Deaf-Blind
345 North Monmouth Avenue
Monmouth, OR 97361
(800) 438-9376
www.tr.wou.edu/dblink

National Institute on Deafness and Other Communication Disorders Information Clearinghouse
P.O. Box 3777
Washington, DC 20057
(800) 241-1044
www.nih.gov.nidcd

High-risk Pregnancy

National Healthy Mothers, Healthy Babies Coalition
121 North Washington Street, Suite 300
Alexandria, VA 22314
(703) 836-6610
www.hmhb.org

March of Dimes Birth Defects Foundation
1275 Mamaroneck Avenue
White Plains, NY 10019
(888) 663-4637
www.modimes.org

National Perinatal Association
3500 East Fletcher Avenue, Suite 209
Tampa, FL 33613-4712
(813) 971-1008
www.nationalperinatal.org

Sidelines National Support Network
P.O. Box 1808
Laguna Beach, CA 92652
(949) 497-2265
www.sidelines.org

Books

Luke, B. 1995. *Every Pregnant Woman's Guide to Preventing Premature Birth*. New York: Random House.

Hospitalization

Books for children

Rogers, F. 1997. *Going to the Hospital*. New York: Putnam's Sons.

Scarry, R. 1995. *A Big Operation (The Busy World of Richard Scarry)*. Edgartown, Mass.: S&S Children's.

Infant Massage

International Association of Infant Massage
1720 Willow Creek Circle, Suite 516
Eugene, OR 97402
(800) 248-5432

Books

Walker, P. 1995. *Baby Massage*. New York: St. Martin's Press.

Sinclair, M. 1992. *Massage for Healthier Children*. Oakland, Calif.: Wingbow Press.

Video

Loving Touch Infant Massage (video, chart, and audiotape)
Dr. Ruth Rice
Cradle Care
2909 Florence Street
Berkeley, CA 94705
(510) 704-1966

Kangaroo Care

Video

Kangaroo Care Video
Dr. Ruth Rice
Cradle Care
2909 Florence Street
Berkeley, CA 94705
(510) 704-1966

Laproscopic Surgery

Society of American Gastrointestinal Endoscopic Surgeons
2716 Ocean Park Boulevard, Suite 3000
Santa Monica, CA 90405
(310) 314-2404
www.sages.org

Learning Disabilities

Learning Disabilities Association of America
4156 Library Road
Pittsburgh, PA 15234-1349
(412) 341-1515
www.ldanatl.org

National Center for Learning Disabilities
381 Park Avenue South, Suite 1401
New York, NY 10016
(212) 545-7510
www.ncld.org

Mental Health

American Psychological Association
750 First Street NE
Washington, DC 20002
(202) 336-5500
www.apa.org

Federation of Families for Children's Mental Health
1021 Prince Street
Alexandria, VA 22314-2971
(703) 684-7710
www.ffcmh.org

Neurological Disorders

American Academy for Cerebral Palsy and Developmental Medicine
6300 North River Road, Suite 727
Rosemont, IL 60018-4226
(847) 698-1635
www.aacpdm.org

The Arc (formerly the Association for Retarded Citizens)
500 East Border Street, Suite 300
Arlington, TX 76010
(817) 261-6003
www.thearc.org

Autism Society of America
7910 Woodmont Avenue, Suite 650
Bethesda, MD 20814-3015
(800) 328-8476
www.autism~society.org

Epilepsy Foundation of America
4351 Garden City Drive
Landover, MD 20785-2267
(800) 332-1000
www.efa.org

Hydrocephalus Association
870 Market Street, Suite 955
San Francisco, CA 94102
(415) 732-7040
www.neurosurgery.mgh.harvard.edu/ha

United Cerebral Palsy Association
1660 L Street NW, Suite 700
Washington, DC 20036
(800) 872-5827
www.ucpa.org

Pediatricians

For a referral to a pediatrician in your area, send the name of the area where you live and a self-addressed stamped envelope to:
Pediatrician Referral Source
P.O. Box 927
Elk Grove Village, IL 60009-0927

Premature Infants

The Alexis Foundation
P.O. Box 1126
Birmingham, MI 48012-1126
pages.prodigy.net/thealexisfoundation/THEALEXIS1.html

American Association of Premature Infants
P.O. Box 46371
Cincinnati, OH 45206
(513) 956-4331
www.aapi-online.org

Association for the Care of Children's Health
19 Mantua Road
Mount Royal, NY 08061
(609) 224-1742
www.acch.org

Newborns in Need, Inc.
6078 Lundy Road
Houston, MO 65483-2225
(417) 967-2589
www.newbornsinneed.org

Partners in Intensive Care
P.O. Box 41043
Bethesda, MD 20824
(301) 681-2708

Internet

There are many Internet support groups and resources for parents of preemies. These are some favorites:

Early Edition Internet Newsletter
home.vicnet.net.au/~earlyed/welcome.html

Coming Home Advice
home.earthlink.net/~gbangs/advice.html

For Parents of Preemies, Answers to Commonly Asked Questions
www2.medsch.wisc.edu/childrenshosp/parents_of_preemies/index.html

Parents Place
www.parentsplace.com (search under "premature infants")

Preemie-l Mailing List Homepage
home.vicnet.net.au/~garyh/preemie.htm

Preemie Resources
members.aol.com/MarAim/Preemie.htm

Premature Baby and Child Resources
www.comeunity.com/premature/preemiepgs.html

T-Bone's Survival Tips for New Preemie Parents
members.aol.com/Kbone91/tbone.html

Tommy's CyberNursery Preemie Web
www.flash.net/~cyberkid

Books

Barsuhn, R. 1996. *Growing Sophia: The Story of a Premature Birth.* St. Paul, Minn.: deRuyter-Nelson Publications, Inc.

DePree, M. 1996. *Dear Zoe.* New York: HarperCollins.

Mehren, E. 1991. *Born Too Soon.* New York: Bantam Doubleday Dell Publishing Group.

Newsletters and magazines

Neonatal and Pediatric ICU Parenting Magazine
c/o Campbell, Merrill and Associates
176 Brush Creek Road
Irwin, PA 15642

The Preemie Parent Connection
c/o PaperWorks
2668 State Highway 812
DeKalb Junction, NY 13630

Respite Care

Access to Respite Care Help
800 Eastowne Drive, Suite 105
Chapel Hill, NC 27514
(800) 473-1727
www.chtop.com/archbroc.html

Siblings

Books

Collins, P. 1990. *Waiting for Baby Joe.* Morton Grove, Ill.: Albert Whitman & Company.

Hawkins-Walsh, E. 1985. *Katie's Premature Brother.* The Centering Corporation, Omaha, Nebr. 68103

Lafferty, L., and Flood, B. 1995. *Born Early: A Premature Baby's Story for Children.* Grand Junction, Colo.: Songbird Publishing.

Murphy-Melas, E. 1996. *Watching Bradley Grow: A Story about Premature Birth.* Marietta, Ga.: Longstreet Press.

Resta, B. 1995. *Believe in Katie Lynn.* Nashville, Tenn.: Eggman Publishing.

Twins and Multiples

Mothers of Super Twins
P.O. Box 951
Brentwood, NY 11717-0627
(516) 434-MOST (434-6678)
www.mostonline.org

National Organization of Mothers of Twins Clubs, Inc.
P.O. Box 23188
Albuquerque, NM 87192-1188
(800) 243-2276
www.nomotc.org

Triplet Connection
P.O. Box 99571
Stockton, CA 95209
(209)474-0885
www.inreach.com/triplets

Twin Services
P.O. Box 10066
Berkeley, CA 94709
(510) 524-0863
www.parentsplace.com.readroom.twins

Magazine

Twins Magazine: (800) 821-5533

Internet

Support Group for Parents of Multiples with Special Needs
www.onelist.com/subscribe.cgi.specpar

Vision Loss

American Academy of Ophthalmology
P.O. Box 7424
San Francisco, CA 94120-7224
(415) 561-8500
www.eyenet.org

American Action Fund for Blind Children and Adults
1800 Johnson Street
Baltimore, MD 21230
(410) 659-9315
www.actionfund.org

American Council of the Blind
1155 Fifteenth Street NW, Suite 720
Washington, DC 20005
(800) 424-8666
www.acb.org

Blind Babies Foundation
1200 Gough Street
San Francisco, CA 94109
(415) 771-5464
www.bbf.org

Blind Children's Center
4120 Marathon Street
Los Angeles, CA 90029
(800) 222-3566
www.blindcntr.org

National Association for Parents of the Visually Impaired
P.O. Box 317
Watertown, MA 02272
(800) 562-6265
www.spedex.com/napvi

National Association for the Visually Handicapped
22 West Twenty-first Street, Sixth Floor
New York, NY 10010
(212) 889-3141
www.navh.org

Prevent Blindness in Premature Babies
P.O. Box 44792
Madison, WI 53744-4792
(608) 845-6500
www.rdcbraille.com/pbpb.html

Internet

Children's Vision Care
www.children-special-needs.org

ROP Support Group
www.konnections.com/eyedoc/ropsupp.html

References

WORKS CONSULTED

Ahmann, E. 1966. *Home Care for the High-Risk Infant.* (2nd ed.) Gaithersburg, Md.: Aspen Publishers.

Ballard, R.A. 1988. *Pediatric Care of the ICN Graduate.* Philadelphia: W. B. Saunders Company.

Bernbaum, J.C., and Hoffman-Williamson, M. 1991. *Primary Care of the Preterm Infant.* St. Louis, Mo.: Mosby-Year Book.

Betz, C.L., et al. 1994. *Family-Centered Nursing Care of Children.* (2nd ed.) Philadelphia: W. B. Saunders Company.

Brazy, J.E. 1996. *For Parents of Preemies: Answers to Commonly Asked Questions.* University of Wisconsin and the Center for Perinatal Care at Meriter Hospital.

Harrison, H. 1983. *The Premature Baby Book.* New York: St. Martin's Press.

Merenstein, G.B., and Gardner, S.L. 1998. *Handbook of Neonatal Intensive Care.* (4th ed.) St. Louis, Mo.: Mosby-Year Book.

Zaichkin, J. 1996. *Newborn Intensive Care: What Every Parent Needs to Know.* Petaluma, Calif.: NICU Ink.

CHAPTER REFERENCES

CHAPTER 1

American Academy of Pediatrics and Safe Ride News Publication. What every premature baby needs to know . . . before riding in the car. *Safe Ride News*, Summer 1990.

American Academy of Pediatrics Policy Statement. 1996. Safe transportation of premature and low birth weight infants. *Pediatrics*, 97(5):758–760.

Block, C., et al. 1989. Home care for high-risk infants the first year. *Caring*, 8(9): 11–17.

Brazelton, T.B. 1981. *On Becoming a Family*. New York: Delacorte Press/Seymour Lawrence.

Browne, J., et al. 1996. *Family Infant Relationship Support Training Manual*. Available from: The Children's Hospital Family and Infant Interaction Program, Denver, Colo.

Consolvo, C.A. 1987. Siblings in the NICU. *Neonatal Network*, 5:7–11.

Freidman, S., et al. 1989. Preterm infant care after hospital. *Pediatrics in Review*, 10(7):195–99.

Hanson, M.J. 1993. *Playing with Your Baby*. Available from: PRO-ED, 8700 Shoal Creek Blvd., Austin, TX 78758.

Hatcher, D., and Lehman, K. 1985. *Baby Talk for Parents Who Are Getting to Know Their Special Baby*. Available from: The Centering Corporation, 1531 North Saddle Creek Road, Omaha, NE 68104.

Hussey-Gardner, B. 1988. *Understanding My Signals*. Available from: VORT Corporation, P.O. Box 60132, Palo Alto, CA 94306.

Maroney, D.I. 1995. Realities of a premature infant's first year: Helping parents cope. *Journal of Perinatology*, 15(5):418–22.

McKinn, E.M. 1993. The difficult first week at home with a premature infant. *Public Health Nursing*, 10(2):89–96.

Meck., N.E., et al. 1993. *NICU Individualized Transitional Planner*. Available from: University of Kansas Medical Center.

VandenBerg, K.A. 1993. *Reading Your Baby's Cues and State*. Available from: PRO-ED, 8700 Shoal Creek Blvd., Austin, TX 78758.

———. 1993. *Suggestions for Supporting Development in the First Six Months*. Available from: PRO-ED, 8700 Shoal Creek Blvd., Austin, TX 78758.

Chapter 2

American Academy of Pediatrics Task Force on Infant Positioning and SIDS. 1992. Positioning and SIDS. *Pediatrics*, 89(6):1120–26.

Feiten, D.J., and Bauer, A.T. 1994. *Owner's Manual*. Available from: Greenwood Pediatrics PC, 6065 South Quebec Street, #100, Englewood, CO 80111.

Redshaw, M. 1985. *Born Too Early: Special Care for Your Preterm Baby*. New Zealand: Oxford University Press.

Ross Laboratories. 1989. *Caring for Your Premature Baby; Ross General Information Series*. Available from Ross Products Division, 625 Cleveland Avenue, Columbus, OH 43215-1724.

Chapter 3

Affonso, D., et al. 1992. Reconciliation and healing through skin-to-skin contact provided in an American tertiary level intensive care nursery. *Neonatal Network*, 12(3):25–32.

Anderson, G.C. 1989. Skin to skin: Kangaroo care in western Europe. *American Journal of Nursing*, May: 662–66.

Brazelton, T.B., and Cramer, B.G. 1990. *The Earliest Relationship*. Reading, Mass.: Addison-Wesley Publishing Company.

Craig, G.J. 1996. *Human Development*. Englewood Cliffs, N.J.: Prentice-Hall.

Field, T. 1997. Infant massage. *Massage and Bodywork*, Winter: 20–26.

Gaensbauer, T.J., and Harmon, R.J. 1982. Attachment behavior in abused/neglected and premature infants. In Emde, R.N., and Harmon, R.J. *The Development of Attachment and Affiliative Systems*. New York: Plenum.

Harmon, R.J., and Culp, A.M. 1981. The effects of premature birth on family functioning and infant development. In Berlin, I. (ed.) *Children and Our Future*. Albuquerque, N.M.: University of New Mexico Press.

Isabella, R.A., and Belsky, J. 1991. Interactional synchrony and the origins of infant-mother attachment: A replication study. *Child Development*, 62:373–84.

Jenkins, R.L., and Swatosh Tock, M.K. 1986. Helping parents bond to their premature infant. *Journal of Maternal Child Nursing*, 11:32–34.

Karen, R. 1998. *Becoming Attached*. New York: Warner Books.

Kitzinger, S. 1994. *The Year After Childbirth*. New York: Charles Scribner's Sons.

Klaus, M.H., et al. 1995. *Bonding: Building the Foundations of Secure Attachment and Independence*. Reading, Mass.: Addison-Wesley Publishing Company.

Ludington-Hoe, S.M., and Golant, S.K. 1993. *Kangaroo Care: The Best You Can Do to Help Your Preterm Infant*. New York: Bantam Books.

Macey, T.J., et al. 1987. Impact of premature birth on the development of the infant in the family. *Journal of Consulting and Clinical Psychology*, 55(6): 846–52.

McClure, V.S. 1997. Why massage your baby? *Massage and Bodywork*, Winter: 106–10.

Novotny, P.P. 1988. *The Joy of Twins*. New York: Crown Publishers.

Sears, W., and Sears, M. 1996. *Parenting the Fussy Baby and High-Need Child*. New York: Little, Brown and Co.

Taubenheim, N.M. 1981. Paternal-infant bonding in the first-time father. *Journal of Obstetric, Gynecological, and Neonatal Nursing*, July/August: 261–64.

Thomasgard, M., and Metz, W.P. 1995. The Vulnerable Child Syndrome revisited. *Developmental and Behavioral Pediatrics*, 16(1):47–53.

Infantile Apnea and Home Monitoring
gopher.nih.gov:70/00/clin/cdcs/individual/58.apnea

The Gentle Truth about Bonding

www.pathfinder.com/ParentTime/Growing/gentlet.html

Chapter 4

Apria Health Care. 1996. *Home infant monitoring patient instructions*. (#RES-20006). Available from: Apria Healthcare Respiratory Services, 3560 Hyland Avenue, Costa Mesa, CA 92626.

Doull, I.J.M., et al. 1997. Tracheobronchomalacia in preterm infants with chronic lung disease. *Archives of Diseases in Childhood*, 76:F203–5.

Groothuis, J.R., and Rosenberg, A.A. 1987. Home oxygen promotes weight gain in infants with bronchopulmonary dysplasia. *American Journal of Disabled Child*, 141(9):992–95.

Knecht, L.D. 1991. Home apnea monitoring mothers' mood states, family functioning, and support systems. *Public Health Nursing*, 8(3):154–60.

Storgion, S.A. 1996. Care of the technology-dependent child. *Pediatric Annals*, 25(12):677–83.

Infantile Apnea and Home Monitoring
gopher.nih.gov:70/00/clin/cdcs/individual/58.apnea

What Is a Tracheostomy?
members.aol.com/trachtube/what.htm

CHAPTER 5

Brugman, S.M., and Larsen, G.L. 1995. Asthma in infants and small children. *Clinics in Chest Medicine*, 16(4):637–56.

Furman, L., et al. 1996. Hospitalization as a measure of morbidity among very low birthweight infants with chronic lung disease. *Journal of Pediatrics*, 128(4):447–52.

Goldson, E. 1990. Bronchopulmonary dysplasia. *Pediatric Annals*, 19(1): 13–18.

Northway, W.H. 1992. Bronchopulmonary dysplasia: Twenty-five years later. *Pediatrics*, 89(5):969–72.

Northway, W.H., et al. 1990. Late pulmonary sequelae of bronchopulmonary dysplasia. *New England Journal of Medicine*, 323(26):1793–98.

Understanding Asthma. 1992. Available from: National Jewish Center for Immunology and Respiratory Medicine, 1400 Jackson Street, Denver, CO 80206.

University of Arizona Department of Pediatrics, Division of Neonatology. 1980. *Parent Handbook on BPD*. Available from: University of Arizona Health Sciences Center, Department of Pediatrics, Division of Neonatology, Tucson, Ariz.

Von Mutius, E. 1996. Progression of allergy and asthma through childhood to adolescence. *Thorax*, 51 (Suppl 1):S3–6.

Childhood Asthma
www.aaaai.org/patpub/resource/publicat/tips/tip20/html

Childhood Infection (Bronchiolitis)
kidshealth.org/parent/common/bronchiolitis.html

Childhood Infections (Influenza)
kidshealth.org/parent/common/flu.html

Childhood Infections (Pneumonia)
kidshealth.org/parent/healthy/pneumonia.html

Childhood Infections (Respiratory Syncytial Virus)
kidshealth.org/parent/common/rsv.html

Tell Me about Bronchopulmonary Dysplasia
www.cheo.on.ca/bpd/BPDtell.html

When Children Meet Hospitals: Tips for Successful Introduction
funrsc.fairfield.bdu/~jfleitas/honesty.html

What Is an Allergy? What Is Asthma?
www.mdnet.de/asthma/single/whatis.html

CHAPTER 6

Anderson, L.T., et al. 1989. Behavioral characteristics and early temperament of premature infants with intracranial hemorrhage. *Early Human Development*, 18(4):273–83.

Batshaw, M.L. 1997. *Children with Disabilities*. (4th ed.) Baltimore, Md.: Paul H. Brookes Publishing.

Eastwood, S. 1986. *About Hydrocephalus: A Book for Parents*. Available from: The Hydrocephalus Association, 870 Market Street, Suite 955, San Francisco, CA 94102.

Fawer, C.L., et al. 1987. Periventricular leukomalacia and neurodevelopmental outcome in preterm infants. *Archives of the Diseases of Childhood*, 62(1):30–36.

Fazzi, E., et al. 1992. Neurodevelopmental outcome in very-low-birth-weight infants with or without periventricular hemorrhage and/or leukomalacia. *Acta Paediatrica*, 81(10):808–11.

Fujimoto, S., et al. 1994. Cerebral palsy of cystic periventricular leukomalacia in low-birth-weight infants. *Acta Paediatrica*, 83(4):397–401.

Jackson, P.L. 1997. *Information sheet for primary care needs of children with hydrocephalus*. Available from: The Hydrocephalus Association, 870 Market Street, Suite 995, San Francisco, CA 94102.

Lanzi, G., et al. 1990. Early predictors of neurodevelopmental outcome at 12–36 months in very low-birthweight infants. *Brain and Development*, 12(5):482–87.

Miller, F., and Bachrach, S. 1995. *Cerebral Palsy: A Complete Guide for Caregiving*. Baltimore, Md.: The Johns Hopkins University Press.

Monset-Couchard, M. et al. 1996. Mid- and long-term outcome of 89 premature infants weighing less than 1000 grams at birth, all appropriate for gestational age. *Biology of the Neonate*, 70(60):328–38.

Selzer, S.C., et al. 1992. Long-term neuropsychological outcome of high risk infants with intracranial hemorrhage. *Journal of Pediatric Psychology*, 17(4):407–22.

Szymonowicz, W., et al. 1986. Neurodevelopmental outcome of periventricular hemorrhage and leukomalacia in infants 1250 grams or less at birth. *Early Human Development*, 14(1):1–7.

Wildrick, D. 1997. Intraventricular hemorrhage and long-term outcome in premature infants. *Journal of Neuroscience Nursing*, 29(5):281–89.

Wilkinson, I., et al. 1996. Neurological outcome of severe cystic periventricular leukomalacia. *Journal of Paediatric and Children's Health*, 32(5):445–49.

Williams, M.L., et al. 1987. Neurodevelopmental outcome of preschool children born preterm with and without intracranial hemorrhage. *Development Medicine and Child Neurology*, 29(2):243–49.

CSMC NICU Teaching Files: IVH/PVL Management and Prophylaxis
www.csmc.edu/neonatology/syllabus/ivh.management.html

Hydrocephalus
cpmcnet.columbia.edu:80/dept/nsg/PNS.Hydrocephalus.html

Hydrocephalus Fact Sheet
neurosurgery.mgh.harvard.edu.ha.fact-sht.html

Periventricular Leukomalacia
user.aol.com/cynthia679/pvl.html

Seizures
healthanswers.com/database/ami/converted/003200.html

Chapter 7

Bergman, I., et al. 1985. Cause of hearing loss in the high-risk premature infant. *Journal of Pediatrics*, 106(1):95–101.

Dobson, V., et al. 1996. Color vision measured with pseudoisochromatic plates at five-and-a-half years in children from the CRYO-ROP study. *Investigative Ophthalmology and Visual Science*, 37:2467–74.

Ittyerah, M., and Sharma, R. 1997. The performance of hearing-impaired children on handedness and perceptual motor tasks. *Genetic Social and General Psychology Monograph*, 123(3):285–302.

Kim, J.Y., et al. 1992. Myopia in premature infants at the age of six months. *Korean Journal of Ophthalmology*, 6:44–49.

Leslie, G.I., et al. 1995. Risk factors for sensorineural hearing loss in extremely premature infants. *Journal of Paediatrics and Children's Health*, 31(4):312–16.

Lue, C.L., et al. 1995. The course of myopia in children with mild retinopathy of prematurity. *Vision Research*, 35:1329–35.

Luoma, L., et al. 1998. Neuropsychological analysis of the visuomotor problems in children born preterm at ≤ 32 weeks of gestation: a 5-year prospective follow-up. *Development Medicine and Child Neurology*, 40(1):21–30.

Meadow-Orlans, K.P., et al. 1997. Support services for parents and their children who are deaf or hard of hearing. A national survey. *American Annals of the Deaf*, 142(4):278–88.

Michael, A.J., et al. 1991. Management of late-onset angle-closure glaucoma associated with retinopathy of prematurity. *Ophthalmology*, 98:1093–98.

Page, J.M., et al. 1993. Ocular sequelae in premature infants. *Pediatrics*, 92:787–90.

Pollard, Z.F. 1984. Lensectomy for secondary angle-closure glaucoma in advanced cicatricial retrolental fibroplasia. *Ophthalmology*, 91:395–98.

Rigo, T.G., and Trahan, H.P. 1993. Communication disorders in infants and toddlers. In Billeaud, F.P. (ed.) *The Infant/Toddler Hearing Evaluation: What the Audiologist Can Tell Us* (pp. 115–145). Newton, Mass.: Andover Medical Publishers.

Schwartz, S. 1996. *Choices in Deafness*. Bethesda, Md.: Woodbine House.

Snir, M., et al. 1988. Visual acuity, strabismus, and amblyopia in premature babies with and without retinopathy of prematurity. *Annals of Ophthalmology*, 20:256–58.

Stoffman, P. 1995. *The Family Guide to Preventing and Treating 100 Infectious Illnesses*. New York: John Wiley and Sons.

CSMC NICU Teaching Files: Eye Exams and ROP
www.neonatology.org/syllabus/eye.exam.html

Iowa Health Book. Is My Baby's Hearing Normal?
www.vh.org/Patients/IHB/Oto/AAO/ChildHearingLoss.html

Iowa Health Book. Middle Ear Infections: Information for Parents and Patients
www.vh.org/Patients/IHB/Peds/Infectious/Otitis/OtitisMedia2.html

Retinopathy of Prematurity
www.konnections.com/eyedoc/ropstart.html

Screening Examination of Premature Infants for Retinopathy of Prematurity
med-aapos.bu.edu/AAPOS/ropscreen.html

Chapter 8

Angelos, G.M., et al. 1989. Oral complications associated with neonatal oral tracheal intubation: a critical review. *Pediatric Dentistry*, 11:133–40.

Ash, S.P., et al. 1987. An investigation of the features of the pre-term infant palate and the effect of prolonged orotracheal intubation with and without protective appliances. *British Journal of Orthodontics*, November: 253–61.

Berube, M.C., et al. 1994. Home care of the infant with gastroesophageal reflux and respiratory disease. *Journal of Pediatric Health Care*, 8(4):173–80.

Lucas, A., et al. 1990. Early diet of preterm infants and development of allergic or atopic disease: randomised prospective study. *British Medical Journal*, 300:837–40.

Merrett, M.L., et al. 1988. Infant feeding and allergy: 12-month prospective study of 500 babies born to allergic families. *Annals of Allergies*, 61 (Part II):13–19.

Provisional Committee on Quality Improvement, Subcommittee on Acute Gastroenteritis. 1996. Practice parameter: the management of acute gastroenteritis in young children. *Pediatrics*, 97(3):424–35.

Rothenberg, S.S., et al. 1997. Laparoscopic fundoplication to enhance pulmonary function in children with severe reactive airway disease and gastroesophageal reflux disease. *Surgical Endoscopy*, 11:1–3.

Seow, W.K. 1984. Developmental defects in the primary dentition of low birth-weight infants: adverse effects of laryngoscopy and prolonged endotracheal intubation. *Pediatric Dentistry*, 6(1):28–31.

Sterling, C.E., et al. 1993. Home management related to medical treatment for childhood gastroesophageal reflux. *Pediatric Nursing*, 19(2):167–73.

Viscardi, R.M., et al. 1994. Delayed primary tooth eruption in premature infants: relationship to neonatal factors. *Pediatric Dentistry*, 16(1):23–28.

Children's Hospital of Iowa Virtual Hospital: Vomiting and Diarrhea
www.vh.org/Patients/IHB/FamilyPractice/AFP/April1995/VOMDirea.html

Dr. Reddy's Pediatric Office on the Web: Constipation
www.drreddy.com/nostool/html

Dr. Reddy's Pediatric Office on the Web: Gastroenteritis
www.drreddy.com/gastro.html#diarrhea

Group Health Cooperative: Diarrhea
www.ghc.org/health_info/self/children/diarrhea.html

Guidelines for Dealing with Constipation in a Toddler
www.parentsplace.com/cgi-bm/objects/nutrition

Chapter 9

Browne, J., et al. 1998. *Guidelines for Providing Positive Oral Experiences*. Available from: The Center for Family and Infant Interaction, Denver, Colo.

Freil, J.K., et al. 1993. Improved growth of very low birthweight infants. *Nutrition Research*, 13:611–20.

Gardner, S.L., and Hagedorn, M.I. 1991. Physiologic sequelae of prematurity: the nurse practitioner's role. Part VI. Feeding difficulties and growth failure. *Pediatric Health Care*, 5:306–14.

Lucas, A., et al. 1991. Randomised trial of nutrition for preterm infants after discharge. *Archives of Disease in Childhood*, 62:324–27.

Shaker, C.S. 1997. Behavioral state activity during nipple feedings for preterm infants. *Neonatal Network*, 16(7):43–47.

Stoppard, M. 1995. *Complete Baby and Child Care*. London: Dorling Kindersley.

VandenBerg, K.A. 1990. Nippling management of the sick neonate in the NICU: the disorganized feeder. *Neonatal Network*, 9(1):9–16.

Will My Baby "Catch Up"? Growth and Prematurity
www.comeunity.com/premature/child/growth/catchup.html

Chapter 10

American Academy of Pediatrics. 1997. Breast-feeding and the use of human milk. *Pediatrics*, 100(6):1035–39.

Biancuzzo, M. 1994. Breast-feeding preterm twins: a case report. *Birth*, 21(21):96–100.

Danner, S.C., and Cerutti, E.R. 1993. *Nursing Your Premature Baby*. Available from: Childbirth Graphics, P.O. Box 21207, Waco, TX 76702-1207.

HealthONE Lactation Program. 1990. *The Storage and Handling of Breast Milk for non-hospitalized Infants*. Available from: The Lactation Program, 1719 E. Nineteenth Avenue, Denver, CO 80218.

Kavanaugh, K., et al. 1995. Getting enough: mother's concerns about breastfeeding a preterm infant after discharge. *Journal of Obstetrics, Gynecology, and Neonatal Nursing*, 24(1):23–32.

Lemons, P.K., and Lemons, J.A. 1996. Transition to breast/bottle feedings: the premature infant. *Journal of the American College of Nutrition*, 15(2):126–35.

Meier, P.P. 1997. *Breast-feeding your premature baby*. Available from: Ross Products Division, 625 Cleveland Avenue, Columbus, OH 43215-1724.

Meier, P.P., et al. 1994. A new scale for in-home test-weighing for mothers of preterm and high risk infants. *Journal of Human Lactation*, 10(3):163–68.

Meier, P.P., and Mangurten, H.H. 1993. Breast-feeding the pre-term infant. In Riordan, J., and Auerbach, K. (eds.) *Breast-feeding and Human Lactation*. Boston: Jones and Bartlett Publishing.

Sattered, E. 1986. *Child of Mine: Feeding with Love and Good Sense*. Menlo Park, Calif.: Bull Publishing.

Sears, W., and Sears, M. 1991. *Keys to Breastfeeding*. New York: Barron's.

Walker, M. 1994. *Breastfeeding Your Premature or Special Care Baby: A Practical Guide for Nursing the Tiny Baby*. Available from: Lactation Associates, 254 Conant Road, Easton, MA 02193.

Chapter 11

Bell, K. 1997. Feeding your preemie. *Preemie Parent Connection*, DeKalb, N.Y. 2(6):1–2.

Creskoff, N. 1998. Investigating feeding problems. *Newsletter of the Children's Hospital for Physical Medicine and Rehabilitation*, Denver, Colo. 1(2):1–3.

Friel, J.K., et al. 1993. Improved growth of very low birthweight infants. *Nutrition Research*, 13:611–20.

Philadelphia Child Guidance Center. 1993. *Your Child's Emotional Health*. New York: Macmillan Publishing.

Trollope, J. 1988. *Your Baby: Healthy Eating*. Des Moines, Iowa: Better Homes and Gardens Books.

Wolf, L.S., and Glass, R.P. 1992. *Feeding and Swallowing Disorders in Infancy: Assessment and Management*. Tucson, Ariz.: Therapy Skill Builders.

Chapter 12

American Speech-Language-Hearing Association. *Prematurity and Speech-Language Skills*. Available from: Consumer Affairs Division, American Speech-Language-Hearing Association, 10801 Rockville Pike, Rockville, MD 20852.

———. *How Does Your Child Talk?* Available from: American Speech-Language-Hearing Association, 10801 Rockville Pike, Rockville, MD 20852.

Ayres, A.J. 1989. *Sensory Integration and the Child*. Los Angeles: WPS.

Billeaud, J.F. 1993. *Communication Disorders in Infants and Toddlers*. Newton, Mass.: Andover Medical Publishers.

Bly, L. 1983. *The Components of Normal Movement During the First Year of Life and Abnormal Motor Development*. Monograph, Neuro-Developmental Treatment Association, University of North Carolina, Chapel Hill, N.C.

Duncan, N., et al. 1996. Language abilities in five- through seven-year-olds in children born at or under 28 weeks gestational age. *Journal of Medical Speech-Language Pathology*, 4(2):71–79.

Frankenburg, K. 1988. *Denver Development al Activities*. Available from: Ross Products Division, 625 Cleveland Avenue, Columbus, OH 43215-1724.

Goldberg, S.R., and DiVitto, B. 1983. *Born Too Soon: Preterm Birth and Early Development*. San Francisco: Freeman.

Hack, M., et al. Long-term developmental outcomes of low birth weight infants. In *The Future of Children*, 5(1), Spring 1995. Center for the Future of Children: The David and Lucile Packard Foundation.

———. Hanson, M.J., and Vandenberg, K.A. 1993. *Homecoming for Babies after the Intensive Care Nursery: A Guide for Parents in Supporting Their Baby's Early Development*. Available from: PRO-ED, 8700 Shoal Creek Blvd., Austin, TX 78758.

Hanson, M.J., and Vandenberg, K.A. 1993. *Homecoming for Babies after the Neonatal Intensive Care Nursery: A Guide for Professionals in Supporting Families and Their Infants' Early Development*. Available from: PRO-ED, 8700 Shoal Creek Blvd., Austin, TX 78758.

Holmes, D.L., et al. 1984. *The Development of Infants Born at Risk*. Mahwah, N.J.: Lawrence Erlbaum Associates.

Katz, K.S., et al. 1989. *Chronically Ill and At-Risk Infants: Family Centered Intervention from Hospital to Home*. Palo Alto, Calif.: Vort Corporation

MacArthur, B., and Dezoete, A. 1992. *Early Beginnings: Development in Children Born Preterm*. New Zealand: Oxford University Press.

Martin, K.L. 1997. *Does My Child Have a Speech Problem?* Chicago: Chicago Review Press.

Menyuk, P. 1995. *Early Language Development in Full-term and Preterm Infants*. Mahwah, N.J.: Lawrence Erlbaum Associates.

A Parent's Guide to Understanding Sensory Integration. 1991. Available from: SII, 1402 Cravens Avenue, Torrance, CA 90501-2701.

Rosenblith, J.W. 1992. *In the Beginning: Development from Conception to Age*. Newbury Park, Calif.: Sage Publications.

Chapter 13

Early Intervention for Infants and Toddlers: A Team Effort (Digest #461). Available from: The Educational Resources Information Center (ERIC), 1920 Association Drive, Reston, VA 22041 37:2467-2474.

Early Childhood Connections for Infants, Toddlers, and Families: Getting Ready for Your IFSP Meeting. Available from: Peak Parent Center, 6055 Lehman Drive, Suite 101, Colorado Springs, CO 80918.

Frazier, J., and Brecht, M.L. *Parent-Child Interaction Program: Descriptive Material for a Speech-Language Treatment Program Based on Use of Facilitative Techniques by Parents*. Available from: The Department of Audiology and Speech Pathology, The Children's Hospital, 1056 E. Nineteenth Avenue, Denver, CO 80218.

Heincke, C.M. 1993. Factors affecting the efficacy of early family intervention. In *At-Risk Infants: Interventions, Families and Research* (pp. 91–99). Baltimore, Md.: Paul H. Brookes Publishing.

Peterson, N.L. 1987. *Early Intervention for Handicapped and At-Risk Children: An Introduction to Early Childhood Special Education*. Denver: Love Publishing.

Rosin, P., et al. 1996. *Partnerships in Family-Centered Care: A Guide to Collaborative Early Intervention*. Baltimore, Md.: Paul H. Brookes Publishing.

Sandall, S.R. 1993. Developmental intervention for the medically fragile infant at home. In Krajicek (ed.), *The Medically Fragile Infant*. Austin, Tex.: PRO-ED.

Smith, B.J. *Does Early Intervention Help?* (Digest #455). Available from: The Educational Resources Information Center (ERIC), 1920 Association Drive, Reston, VA 22091.

Stephens, L., and Tauber, S. 1996. Early intervention. In Case-Smith, J., et al. *Occupational Therapy for Children* (pp. 648–69). St. Louis, Mo.: Mosby-Year Book.

Chapter 14

Brenner, B. 1990. *The Preschool Handbook: Making the Most of Your Child's Education*. New York: Pantheon Books.

Fishel, E. 1993. Starting kindergarten. *Parents*, 68:165–69.

Getz, M. 1990. Off to school they go: the NICU graduate in school. *Parent Care News Brief*, 5(2).

Halsey, C.L., et al. 1996. Extremely low-birth-weight children and their peers: a comparison of school-age outcomes. *Archives of Pediatric and Adolescent Medicine*, 150(8):790–94.

Israeloff, R. 1995. Is your child ready to start kindergarten? *Parents*, 70:99–104.

Speech and Language Milestone Chart. 1995. Available from: Learning Disabilities Association of America, 4156 Library Road, Pittsburgh, PA 15234.

Chapter 15

The Benefits of an Inclusive Education: Making It Work. 1997. Available from: The National Association for the Education of Young Children, 1509 Sixteenth Street NW, Washington, DC 20036.

Cantor, R.F., and Cantor, J.A. 1995. *Parents' Guide to Special Needs Schooling: Early Intervention Years*. Westport, Conn.: Auburn House.

Free Appropriate Public Education for Students with Handicaps. Available from: U.S. Department of Education, Office for Civil Rights, Washington, DC 20202-1328.

Hensley, S.C. 1995. *Home Schooling Children with Special Needs*. Gresham, Ore.: Noble Publishing Associates.

Individualized Education Programs (Digest #LG2). 1994. Available from: The Educational Resources Information Center (ERIC), 1920 Association Drive, Reston, VA 22091.

A Parent's Guide to Accessing Programs for Infants, Toddlers, and Preschoolers with Disabilities. 1994. Available from: The National Information Center for Children and Youth with Disabilities, P.O. Box 1492, Washington, DC 20013-1492.

Parker-Martin, P. 1997. *Evaluating a District-Wide Preschool to Kindergarten Transition Process for Young Children with Special Needs.* (Doctoral dissertation, University of Phoenix).

Pinkerton, D. 1991. *Preparing Children with Disabilities for School* (Digest #E503). Available from: The Educational Resources Information Center (ERIC), 1920 Association Drive, Reston, VA 22091.

Questions and Answers about the IDEA (Digest #ND21). 1993. Available from: The Educational Resources Information Center, 1920 Association Drive, Reston, VA 22091.

Questions Often Asked about Special Education Services. (Digest #LG1). 1994. Available from: The Educational Resources Information Center (ERIC), 1920 Association Drive, Reston, VA 22091.

The Rights of Individuals with Handicaps under Federal Law. Available from: U.S. Department of Education, Office of Civil Rights, Washington, DC 20202-1328.

Epilogue

Afflect, G., et al. 1991. *Infants in Crisis: How Parents Cope with Newborn Intensive Care and Its Aftermath.* New York: Springer-Verlag.

Affleck, G., and Tennen, H. 1991. The effect of newborn intensive care on parents' psychological well-being. *Children's Health Care,* 20(1):6–14.

Beck, C.T. 1998. A checklist to identify women at risk for developing postpartum depression. *Journal of Obstetrics, Gynecological, and Neonatal Nursing,* 27(1):39–45.

Blackburn, S., and Lowen, L. 1986. Impact of an infant's premature birth on the grandparents and parents. *Journal of Obstetrics, Gynecological, and Neonatal Nursing,* March/April: 173–78.

Claflin, C.J. 1993. Assessment of the impact of the very low birth weight infants on families. In *At-Risk Infants: Interventions, Families, and Research* (pp. 57–77). Baltimore, Md.: Paul H. Brookes Publishing.

Cronin, C.M.G., et al. 1995. The impact of very-low-birthweight infants on the family is long lasting. *Archives of Pediatric and Adolescent Medicine,* 149:151–58.

Cupoli, J.M., et al. 1984. The shapes of grief. *Journal of Perinatology,* 5(2):123–26.

DeMier, R.L., et al. 1996. Perinatal stressors as predictors of symptoms of posttraumatic stress in mothers of infants at high risk. *Journal of Perinatology,* 16:276–80.

Fraley, A.M. 1990. Chronic sorrow: a parental response. *Journal of Pediatric Nursing,* 5(4):268–73.

Hughes, M.A., et al. 1994. How parents cope with the experience of neonatal intensive care. *Children's Health Care,* 23(1):1–14.

Hynan, M.T. 1988. Helping siblings cope with a high-risk illness. *Intensive Caring Unlimited,* 6(2):1–2.

———. 1997. Grandparents in the NBICU. *Parent to Parent Update,* Fall: 4–5.

Maroney, D.I. 1994. Helping parents survive the emotional roller coaster ride in the newborn intensive care unit. *Journal of Perinatology,* 14(2):131–33.

McFayden, A. 1994. *Special Care Babies and Their Relationships*. New York: Routledge.

Seaward, B.L. 1997. *Managing Stress: Principles and Strategies for Health and Wellbeing*. (2nd ed.) Sudbury, Mass.: Jones and Bartlett Publishers.

Tarbert, K.C. 1985. The impact of a high-risk infant on the family. *Neonatal Network*, February: 20–23.

Theut, S.K., et al. 1990. Resolution of parental bereavement after a perinatal loss. *Journal of the American Academy of Child and Adolescent Psychiatry*, 29(4):521–25.

Weil, A. 1995. *Health and Healing*. New York: Houghton Mifflin.

Weiten, W. 1997. *Psychology Themes and Variations*. (3rd ed.) Belmont, Calif.: Brooks/Cole Publishing.

Wilson, A.L. et al. 1982. The death of a newborn twin: an analysis of parental bereavement. *Pediatrics*, 70(4):587–91.

Wood, A.F., et al. 1997. The downward spiral of postpartum depression. *Maternal Child Nursing*, 22:308–17.

Worthington, R.C. 1989. The chronically ill child and recurring grief. *The Journal of Family Practice*, 29(4):397–400.

Dealings: Why Is This So Hard?
home.vicnet.net.au/~earlyed/nov/dealings.html

Depression, Postpartum Depression and Finding Help
members.aol.com/Kbone91/depression.html

Guilt: Dealing with the Emotions of Having a Preemie
home.vicnet.net.au/~earlyed/sept/guilt.html

Helping Parents Cope with a High-Risk Birth: Terror, Grief, Impotence and Anger
www.uwm.edu/people/hynan/minnaep.html

Posttraumatic Stress
healthmind.com/ptsd.html

Posttraumatic Stress Disorder
www.mentalhealth.com/dis1/p21-an06.html

What Every Parent Needs to Know: Feelings and Emotion
members.aol.com/Kbone91/emotions.html

Note: To conserve space, *et al.* was used for three or more authors.

Glossary

Acute: An illness with a sudden onset and a short course.

Advocacy: Taking action, physically and verbally, for your child's best interests.

Airway: The route air follows from the mouth or nose to the lungs.

Alveoli: 1) The small sacs in the lungs where oxygen and carbon dioxide are exchanged (oxygen is moved from the lungs into the blood); 2) The milk-producing glands in the breast.

Anesthesia: Medication that eliminates or reduces pain, or temporarily produces a change in the level of consciousness for surgical procedures.

Anesthesiologist: A medical doctor who administers anesthesia.

Antibiotics: Drugs that kill bacteria.

Antibodies: Protein substances in the blood that fight infections.

Apnea: A pause in breathing that lasts for twenty seconds or longer.

Apnea monitor: *See cardiorespiratory monitor.*

Areola: The dark area around the nipple of the breast.

Artery: Blood vessels carrying oxygenated blood leading away from the heart.

Aspiration: Breathing a substance other than air into the lungs (such as formula or stomach contents).

At-risk infant: A baby who is at risk of developing a specific problem and who can benefit from intervention.

Audiologist: A medical professional who diagnoses and treats hearing problems.

Axillary temperature: A temperature taken under the armpit.

Bacteria: Microorganisms that can cause infections.

Baseline weight: A first weight measurement that serves as a reference point for monitoring weight gain over time.

Bilirubin: A substance released into the body when red blood cells are broken down; an excess can cause a yellowing of the skin.

Blood pressure: The pressure the blood exerts against the walls of the blood vessels. The pressure causes the blood to flow through the arteries and veins.

BRADYCARDIA: A slower-than-normal heart rate.

BRAIN BLEED: *See intraventricular hemorrhage.*

BRONCHOPULMONARY DYSPLASIA (BPD): A chronic lung disease typically caused by long-term ventilation and high levels of oxygen for 28 days or more.

CANNULA: A small tube with prongs that delivers oxygen into the baby's nose.

CARDIOLOGIST: A medical doctor who diagnoses and treats problems with the heart.

CARDIOPULMONARY RESUSCITATION (CPR): A method of reviving a baby or child whose breathing and/or heart rate has stopped or slowed abnormally.

CARDIORESPIRATORY MONITOR: Equipment used to measure a baby's heart and breathing rate.

CENTRAL NERVOUS SYSTEM (CNS): The brain and spinal cord.

CEREBRAL PALSY: A chronic, nonprogressive condition in which posture or movement is atypical because of damage to or a malformation in the brain.

CHEST PHYSIOTHERAPY (CPT): A technique of vibrating a child's chest and loosening secretions in the lungs to improve breathing.

CHRONIC: A prolonged illness.

CONGENITAL: A problem existing before or at birth.

CONTINUOUS POSITIVE AIRWAY PRESSURE (CPAP): Air or supplemental oxygen mechanically pushed into a baby's lungs to keep the air sacs open after each breath.

CORRECTED AGE (ADJUSTED AGE): The age your baby would be if born on his or her due date.

DEHYDRATION: The significant loss of fluids from the body.

DESATURATION: When the oxygen level drops below the desired level (most doctors say 95 percent saturation).

DISCHARGE SUMMARY: A brief report written by a physician summarizing a baby's medical problems in the NICU.

EARLY INTERVENTION: In-home or community-based services, which are private or government-funded, for children with developmental delays.

EDEMA: The excess of fluid in the body tissues that often causes visible swelling.

ELECTROLYTES: Chemicals in the blood that include sodium, potassium, chloride, and bicarbonate.

ENDOTRACHEAL TUBE (ET TUBE): A small plastic tube inserted into the trachea (windpipe), allowing air and/or oxygen to pass to the lungs, bypassing the nose.

ESOPHAGITIS: Areas of the esophagus that are reddened, swollen, and irritated.

ESOPHAGUS (FOOD PIPE): The tube that moves food from the mouth to the stomach.

FEEDING PUMP: A small device that mechanically pumps formula into an attached feeding tube.

FEEDING TUBE (GAVAGE TUBE): A narrow, pliable tube inserted into a baby's mouth or nose and leading to the stomach. *Also see gastrostomy tube/button.*

FLEXED: Joints that are bent.

FORTIFIER: A commercially prepared substance added to breastmilk that provides additional calories and nutrients.

FULL-TERM: Born between thirty-seven and forty-two weeks gestation.

FUNGUS: A microorganism (such as Candida) that causes infection.

GASTROENTEROLOGIST: A medical doctor that specializes in the treatment of the stomach and intestines.

GASTROESOPHAGEAL REFLUX (GER, OR REFLUX): The backward flow of the stomach contents into the esophagus (food pipe).

GASTROINTESTINAL (GI) TRACT: The esophagus, stomach, and intestines.

GASTROSTOMY TUBE/BUTTON (G-TUBE): A feeding tube or button inserted directly into the stomach through the abdomen.

GAVAGE TUBE: *See feeding tube.*

GESTATIONAL AGE: The number of weeks between the first day of the last menstrual period and the date of birth.

HOME MONITOR: *See cardiorespiratory monitor.*

HYALINE MEMBRANE DISEASE: *See Respiratory Distress Syndrome.*

HYDROCEPHALUS: The excessive accumulation of fluid in the ventricles (chambers) of the brain.

HYPOXIA: The lack of oxygen in the body.

INFLAMMATION: A tissue response showing swelling, redness, and pain in a specific area.

INTRAUTERINE GROWTH RETARDATION: The growth of a fetus is slowed or stopped while still in the womb.

INTRAVENOUS (IV): A needle inserted into a vein that allows the administration of fluids, nutrition, and/or medications.

INTRAVENTRICULAR HEMORRHAGE (IVH): Bleeding into the brain ventricles (and possibly the surrounding tissue).

INTUBATION: An endotracheal tube is inserted via the mouth or nose into the trachea to assist with breathing.

LARYNGOMALACIA: The larynx is abnormally soft or "floppy" and collapses during breathing.

LARYNX: The upper part of the trachea (the windpipe), which contains the vocal cords.

LET-DOWN REFLEX: Hormone release that causes a mother's breastmilk to go into the holding reservoirs behind the nipples.

MALNUTRITION: Inadequate nourishment.

MICROORGANISM: An organism that is not visible without a microscope.

MOTOR SKILLS: A child's abilities involving movement of muscles and coordination; large motor skills include crawling and walking; fine motor skills include using utensils and writing.

MUCUS: Fluids in the nose or airway that are normal unless produced in excess and interfere with air flow.

MULTIDISCIPLINARY TEAM: A group of healthcare professionals with diverse specialties (medical, social, educational, developmental, etc.) who work together to develop a well-organized approach to the total management of the child.

NASAL CANNULA: *See cannula.*

NASO-GASTRIC TUBE (NG TUBE): A plastic tube passed through the nose into the stomach; used for giving nutrients or medications or for withdrawing the stomach's contents.

NEBULIZATION EQUIPMENT: A device that administers an inhaled medication to a baby or child.

NEONATOLOGIST: A physician who specializes in the medical care and development of premature infants and sick newborns.

NEUROLOGIST: A medical doctor who specializes in the nervous system and its disorders.

NORMAL SALINE: A liquid that contains 0.9 percent sodium (salt).

NUTRIENTS: The proteins, fats, vitamins, minerals, and carbohydrates that a child needs for proper growth.

OCCUPATIONAL THERAPIST: A healthcare professional who specializes in helping a child with the developmental tasks requiring the use of the arms, hands, mouth, and tongue.

OPHTHALMOLOGIST: A medical doctor who treats the eyes.

Oral-motor development: The development of the muscles in the mouth used for speech and eating.

Overstimulation: When a child with an immature nervous system becomes stressed (looking away, hyperalert expression, crying) because of too much activity for his brain to process.

Oxygen: A colorless, odorless gas that is essential for life. Increasing oxygen can aid a baby who has difficulty breathing; room air is 21 percent oxygen.

Oxygen saturation: The amount of oxygen the blood is carrying.

Oxygen therapy: Any method of delivering supplemental oxygen to a baby.

Pale: The skin lacks pink color, looking whitish or gray.

Pediatrician: A medical doctor specially trained to diagnose and treat children and adolescents.

Percussion and postural drainage (PP&D): *See chest physiotherapy.*

Periodic breathing: Breathing that is interrupted by ten- to twenty-second pauses.

Periventricular leukomalacia (PVL): Damaged brain tissue surrounding the ventricles that may result in brain cysts.

Physical therapist: A healthcare professional who specializes in helping a child learn better ways to coordinate movements and balance.

Posture: The positioning of the structure of the body.

Premature baby: Used to describe a baby born at/or less than 35 weeks gestation.

Prone: Lying on the stomach.

Pulmonologist: A medical doctor specializing in the structure and function of the lungs; diagnoses and treats breathing problems.

Pulse oximeter (pulse ox): A noninvasive device that monitors the oxygen saturation of a baby's blood.

Rectal temperature: The body temperature taken by inserting a thermometer into the rectum (anus).

Red blood cells: The cells in the blood that carry oxygen.

Referral: A recommendation to a particular healthcare provider.

Reflux: *See gastroesophageal reflux.*

Respirations: Breaths.

Respiratory: Associated with breathing.

Respiratory Distress Syndrome (RDS): A breathing disorder of premature infants caused by the lack of surfactant in the alveoli of the lungs.

Respiratory syncytial virus (RSV): A virus that commonly causes infections of the upper and lower respiratory tract in premature infants.

Respiratory therapist: A healthcare professional who is trained in the use of respiratory equipment.

Respite care: When a qualified caregiver assumes responsibility for a child, allowing parents time to rest and rejuvenate.

Retinopathy of prematurity (ROP): A retinal eye disease found in infants born prematurely.

Retracting: When the chest wall draws in excessively with each breath; a common symptom of respiratory distress in infants.

Rooming-in: Staying overnight with your infant in a hospital room to practice caring for your baby.

Secretions: *See mucus.*

Sibling: A brother or sister.

Side effect: A secondary effect of a medication or therapy; usually undesirable.

State: Level of awareness (deep sleep, light sleep, drowsy, quiet alert, active alert, and crying).

SUCTION: The removal of mucus from the nose and mouth.

SUPINE: Lying on the back.

SURFACTANT: The substance formed in the lungs that helps keep the small air sacs (alveoli) from collapsing.

SWADDLING: Securely wrapping a baby in a light blanket to calm him.

TACHYCARDIA: A faster-than-normal heart rate.

TRACHEA: The windpipe.

TRACHEOMALACIA: The trachea is abnormally soft or "floppy" and collapses during breathing.

TRACHEOSTOMY TUBE (TRACH): A flexible tube that is surgically inserted into the trachea to help an infant breathe.

VEIN: A blood vessel leading toward the heart and carrying oxygenated blood.

VENTRICLES: Small chambers; the two lower chambers of the heart; the central chambers in the brain.

VIRUS: A tiny organism that lives in the body and that can multiply and cause an infection.

VULNERABLE CHILD SYNDROME: A parent perceiving his or her infant or child as more vulnerable to illness or injury than the "typical" child.

VISUAL: Having to do with sight.

WHEEZING: The whistling sound made during breathing, caused by obstructions in the small airways (bronchioles) of the respiratory tract.

X RAY: An electromagnetic wave that produces an image of internal body parts.

Photo and Illustrations Permissions

Illustrations pages 6–7: by Dusty Christian. From Joy Browne, Ph.D., Ann Marie Macleod, M.S., P.T., and Suzanne Smith-Sharp, B.S., Manual for the "Family Infant Relationship Supporting Training" program. Supported by the Maternal and Child Health Bureau MCJ-089407, the Children's Hospital Association, Center for Family and Infant Interaction, Denver, Colo.

Illustrations pages 11, 12: Adapted text and illustrations used with permission of the American Academy of Pediatrics. From Policy Statement (1996): Safe transportation of premature and low birth weight infants, *Pediatrics,* Vol. 97, No. 5, May 1996. Copyright © 1996 by American Academy of Pediatrics.

Illustrations pages 39, 80: Compliments of Apria Healthcare.

Photo page 43: Courtesy of quadruplets Alex, Emily, and Kyle, in loving memory of sister Katie.

Illustrations pages 44, 45, 74, 96, 102, 122, 133, 205: by Mary Jo Broer.

Photos pages 49, 104: Courtesy of parents Cynthia and Richard Bissell.

Illustrations pages 101, 110: Compliments of the Hydrocephalus Association.

Photo page 81: Courtesy of Dr. Susan Brugman.

Photo page 124: Courtesy of mother Suzanne Smith-Sharp.

Illustration page 179: Used with permission from Ross Products Division, Abbott Laboratories Inc., Columbus, OH 43216. From *Guide for the Breastfeeding Mother*, © 1996 Ross Products Division, Abbott Laboratories Inc.

Illustration page 180: Used with permission from Ross Products Division, Abbott Laboratories Inc., Columbus, OH 43215. From *Breastfeeding Your Premature Baby*, © 1997 Ross Products Division, Abbott Laboratories Inc.

Illustrations page 183: Reprinted with permission from *Handbook of Neonatal Intensive Care,* 4th ed., G. B. Merenstein and S. L. Gardner, 1998. St. Louis, Mo.: Mosby-Year Book, Inc. pp. 344–45.

Illustrations page 184: Used with permission from Ross Products Division, Abbott Laboratories Inc., Columbus, OH 43216. From *Professional Guide to Breastfeeding Premature Infants*, copyright © 1997 by Ross Products Division, Abbott Laboratories Inc.

Illustrations page 185: Reprinted with permission from *Handbook for Neonatal Intensive Care*, 4th ed., G.B. Merenstein and S.L. Gardner, 1998. St. Louis, MO: Mosby-Year Book, Inc., p. 346.

Photo page 204: Courtesy of mother Dianne I. Maroney.

Illustrations pages 219–220 (hypertonic infant illustrations) reprinted with permission from Judy C. Bernbaum, M.D., and Marsha Hoffman-Williamson, Ph.D., *Primary Care of the Preterm Infant*, 1991, St. Louis, Mo.: Mosby-Year Book, Inc. pp. 218, 224, 226, 228.

Illustrations page 220 (*right* and *bottom*): by Shane Walsh.

Illustrations in appendix A: Used with permission from *The Journal of the American Medical Association*, 1997, Vol. 268, p. 2254, copyright © 1992 by The American Medical Association.

Index